CONDÉ NAST

Also by

SUSAN RONALD

A Dangerous Woman:
American Beauty, Noted Philanthropist, Nazi Collaborator—
The Life of Florence Gould

Hitler's Art Thief:
Hildebrand Gurlitt, the Nazis, and the Looting of Europe's Treasures

Shakespeare's Daughter (fiction)

Heretic Queen:
Queen Elizabeth I and the Wars of Religion

The Pirate Queen:
Queen Elizabeth I, Her Pirate Adventurers, and the Dawn of Empire

The Sancy Blood Diamond:
Power, Greed, and the Cursed History of One of
the World's Most Coveted Gems

France:
The Crossroads of Europe

CONDÉ NAST

THE MAN AND HIS EMPIRE

SUSAN RONALD

ST. MARTIN'S PRESS ❧ NEW YORK

First published in the United States by St. Martin's Press, an imprint of
St. Martin's Publishing Group

www.stmartins.com

Designed by Steven Seighman

Library of Congress Cataloging-in-Publication Data

Names: Ronald, Susan, author.
Title: Condé Nast: the man and his empire—a biography / Susan Ronald.
Description: First edition. | New York: St. Martin's Press, 2019. | Includes
   bibliographical references and index.
Identifiers: LCCN 2019016758 | ISBN 9781250180025 (hardcover) |
   ISBN 9781250180049 (ebook)
Subjects: LCSH: Nast, Condé, 1873–1942. | Publishers and publishing—
   United States—Biography.
Classification: LCC Z473.N28 R66 2019 | DDC 070.5092 [B]—dc23
LC record available at https://lccn.loc.gov/2019016758

Our books may be purchased in bulk for promotional, educational, or
business use. Please contact your local bookseller or the Macmillan Corporate
and Premium Sales Department at 1-800-221-7945, extension 5442, or by email
at MacmillanSpecialMarkets@macmillan.com.

First Edition: September 2019

10 9 8 7 6 5 4 3 2 1

In memory of
Stephen F. Bashford—
one of the really good guys.
Gone too soon.

CONTENTS

PART IV: Saving the Empire

PART V: With the Eye of an Eagle

NOTE ON SPELLING AND EXPRESSIONS

As Condé Nast ran a truly international business, some correspondence—particularly with his British counterparts—appears in British English in the book. For example, I have used the British edition of *Always in Vogue* by Edna Woolman Chase as a primary source book, so all quotations from it will be spelled in British English. I have not changed any British spelling, punctuation, or expressions into American English but have provided a "translation" by way of a footnote only if I believed one was required. Similarly, there are a number of spelling errors and abbreviations in some letters, which I have not corrected other than to add letters or words [in brackets] or as a footnote for ease of understanding. Letters by Michel de Brunhoff are written in English and have the Frenchman's grammatical errors intact. To handle this any other way, in my opinion, would detract from the flow of the letters with a ubiquitous use of [*sic*], while adding nothing to the context and, for many, possibly diminishing their enjoyment of those I've included. I also refer to what we call World War I as the Great War, in the parlance of the day, until its sequel—World War II—made it possible to add a number this most devastating of conflicts. Many of the French expressions used have been incorporated into English, but for those that haven't, I provide a translation on the same page. The various dances mentioned in the book are called by their proper names, but to find out how they can be told apart, or indeed how to dance them, you will need to consult old films available online.

PROLOGUE
The Ringmaster—1919

C ondé Nast might have wondered why a publisher should feel like the ringmaster of a circus that would put Ringling Brothers and Barnum & Bailey's to shame. True, he aimed to create the "most excellent and stunning greatest show,"[1] albeit in the publishing world. Did that mean he was expected to tame and shackle his employees to prevent them from behaving like wild animals? He would have been discomfited by the image racing through his mind. He was a quiet, reflective sort of chap, never garrulous or given to outbursts of bad temper.

Though middle aged, the forty-six-year-old Nast was still deemed handsome, with his even features, slim physique, and perfect posture. Some thought he was a bit bankerish with his wire-rimmed pince-nez, slightly receding hairline, and immaculately tailored three-piece suits. He was noted for his measured, gentlemanly manner, his numeracy, and his careful management style. Those who didn't know him well thought he was standoffish. Others were floored by his incredible eye for detail. Above all, Condé was painfully shy and always mindful of his coveted place in New York high society. But a ringmaster? Never. . . .

Of course he wanted the best in every field—illustrators, photographers, designers, writers, editors, layout people, and even advertisers. How else could he craft the best publications? Why, even his dear friend and editor in chief at *Vanity Fair*, Frank Crowninshield—everyone's favorite raconteur—was guilty of high jinks, not to mention of poaching top talent from Condé's cash cow, the highly successful *Vogue*.

As far back as the spring of 1915, Edna Woolman Chase, Condé's editor in chief at *Vogue*, complained that Frank had his eye on "a small dark-haired pixie, treacle-sweet of tongue but vinegar-witted" who was working on captions and special features. One of her first pieces was about houses, Condé recalled, and was cleverly titled "Interior Desecration." It made a fair few avant-garde interior designers turn away in shame. This woman was courageous, too. She even dared to become a lab rat for her feature article "Life on a Permanent Wave"—when perms were still hazardous and took an entire day hooked up to heated electric rods after the hair was soaked in a reagent (usually cow urine and water or caustic soda) to show results.[2] The pixie's name was Dorothy Rothschild. Within the year she became Dorothy Parker.

Condé had to smile at the memory. Of course Dorothy was too witty to remain the writer of special features and punchy one-liners like "From these foundations of the autumn wardrobe, one may learn that brevity is the soul of lingerie." At times she borrowed from nursery rhymes, as when she hoped to tweak the noses of *Vogue* readers: "There was a little girl who had a little curl, right in the middle of her forehead. When she was good she was very very good, and when she was bad she wore this divine nightdress of rose-colored mousseline de soie, trimmed with frothy Valenciennes lace."[3] The suggestion that *Vogue* readers might actually have sex was anathema to the Palm Beach and Newport sets, and the offending quip was deleted at the proof stage.

Although *Vanity Fair*'s editor, Frank Crowninshield (called "Crownie" by his staff and close friends), was the quintessential Edwardian gentleman, he was the first to truly admire Dorothy's way with words. So he duly poached the quiet, little, seemingly unassuming lass from *Vogue*. What else could he do? He adored her humor, and in 1915, together with George Shepard Chappell, the three of them wrote *High Society: Advice as to Social Campaign-*

*ing and Hints on the Management of Dowagers, Dinners, Debu-
tantes, Dances and the Thousand and One Diversions of Persons of
Quality.* Their entertaining jests were illustrated by the pen-and-
ink drawings of Anne Harriet Fish, the internationally famous artist for *The Tatler* and *Vanity Fair* in London.* Born in Bristol,
England, "Fish," as she was known to every witty household, was
adored on both sides of the Atlantic. Still, she wasn't the problem
in managing his circus, Condé ruminated.

On her own perhaps Dorothy hadn't been at fault? Then Condé
thought back to his private assistant, Albert Lee, and his daily, almost religious, tracking of the Allied forces in the Great War on a
huge map of France taped to the office wall. Lee painstakingly set
the battle lines, as reported daily in *The New York Times*, in colored pins back and forth across no-man's-land. (Just how he charted
the infinitesimal movements by the yard, meter, or foot is anyone's
guess.) Being an inveterate biter of the hand that tossed her tasty
morsels to write about, Dorothy taunted the poor man by dashing
into *Vogue*'s offices early in the morning and devotedly rearrang-
ing Lee's weary armies. While Lee eventually suspected that German spies had invaded *Vogue*, Frank pounced like any decent
predator, and enticed Dorothy to soar under his wing, proclaiming, "Her perceptions were so sure, her judgment so unerring, that
she always seemed to hit the centre of the mark."[4]

The fact was that Frank, too, adored practical jokes. An arch-
player of many pranks, he had rather notoriously—and repeatedly—
tied black thread to the legs of chairs in the guest bedrooms of
country mansions where he was staying, then slipped the end of
the thread out the bedroom door. When its occupant prepared for
bed, the chairs would suddenly move, causing its mystified resident to either swear off alcohol or believe that the house was
haunted.[5]

It should have come as no surprise to Condé that Frank encouraged Dorothy's antics. Life at *Vanity Fair* was more akin to a kin-
dergarten than editorial offices—except of course for the crap

---

* This *Vanity Fair* was the political satirical magazine published in London.

games. Why, Frank even proudly called his private office "a combined club, vocal studio, crap game, dance-hall, sleeping lounge and snack bar." Its very informality bred the utter chaos on which the magazine mysteriously thrived.[6] Crowninshield introduced America to modern art and artists like Pablo Picasso and Henri Matisse, as well as modern women writers like Colette and Dorothy Parker. A New York club man par excellence, Frank was one of the founders of the Coffee House, an antidote to the stuffy—but necessary—Knickerbocker Club.

Despite Frank's inclination to mirth, Condé reflected, the issue was not with his friend, or even with Dorothy. It was that wise-cracking cocktail of a trio he had hired at *Vanity Fair*: Dorothy Parker, Robert Benchley, and that gentle beanpole of a man, Robert Sherwood. What lunacy had possessed him to hire Benchley as his managing editor? Did he *really* believe Benchley might feel some responsibility to write those "serious" articles at *Vanity Fair* as originally promised? Condé had been fooled by Benchley's Boy Scout appearance and good manners, his sandy—if thinning—hair, pale-blue eyes, serviceable off-the-rack suits from Rogers Peet, and, naturally, his sensible galoshes. Benchley didn't swear, smoke, or drink back then, either. He was married and lived in Westchester County with his wife and young son. As for Sherwood, nicknamed "Sherry," Condé should have known that anyone that tall—six feet seven[*] in his stockinged feet—*and* who wore his straw hat at such a jaunty angle would be trouble.

Can you hear Condé's sigh across the past century? Well, Benchley's pledged "serious" articles that got him the job in the first place turned out to depict the funereal world of the undertaker. And why should Benchley's hobby for the gruesome, if practical, netherworld have been taken up quite so enthusiastically by Dorothy? It added insult to injury that Condé Nast Publications paid for Benchley's subscriptions to their macabre reading—*Casket*

---

[*] 2.04 meters.

and *Sunnyside* magazines. *Sunnyside* had, according to Dorothy, a joke column called—steel yourself now—"From Grave to Gay" that particularly tickled her fancy. "I cut out a picture from one of them, in color," Dorothy recalled, "of how and where to inject embalming fluid, and hung it over my desk until Mr. Crowninshield asked me if I could possibly take it down. Mr. Crowninshield was a lovely man, but puzzled."[7] *Puzzled?* Actually, Frank recalled that there was a ghastly parade of color photos of cadavers in various states of preparedness for the grave, and ordered Dorothy to take them down. Perhaps she could replace them with prints by the artist Marie Laurencin instead?

Bluntly put, both Condé and Frank thought the trio's daily imbroglios and prolonged lunch hours at Childs Restaurant had become too routine and must stop. Dorothy herself would write later that they were behaving "extremely badly."[8] So the long-suffering Condé asked his vice president, Francis Lewis Wurzburg, to strictly enforce the company's code of punctuality. Everyone, without exception for rank or talent, must comply. The tenderhearted, loyal Wurzburg obliged, sending around a memo that all employees were to be at their desks at nine o'clock sharp. That meant at their desks. Not chatting in the corridors. Not loitering in the cloakrooms. Cards, the size of normal playing cards, were duly printed and handed out to would-be offenders, demanding that they state their reasons for their tardiness.

Benchley was the first to fall foul. Arriving eleven and a half minutes late, he found the card neatly placed on his desk. Applying himself to the task with vigor, Benchley rolled up his sleeves and began writing his sorrowful tale of the missing eleven and a half minutes. Wasn't the office deafened by the roar of the Hippodrome's* elephants as they broke loose shortly before nine that morning? "A clutch, a gaggle, a veritable herd of elephants came trumpeting from the Hippodrome, shouldering their way through

---

* The Hippodrome, at the time the world's largest theater, was located diagonally across from the *Vogue* and *Vanity Fair* offices, then located at 19 West Forty-fourth Street, at the corner of Sixth Avenue ("Avenue of the Americas" to tourists).

Forty-fourth Street" and rampaging across Sixth Avenue. "Frantic guards came rushing after them, pressing all passing civilians into a posse to help in the round-up." It was worse than herding cats at a crossroads, Benchley plowed on. "The first thing I knew I had been swept up to West Seventy-second Street," Benchley wrote. "Some of the animals had been trapped; others were still at large." Just imagine the pandemonium, Benchley exclaimed in ever-smaller letters curling around the edges of the card. Down they went to West End Avenue and the Hudson River docks, where the elephants tried to "board the boats of the Fall River Line" before they were finally herded back "to the Hippodrome, thereby averting a major marine disaster" but unfortunately causing him to be eleven minutes late for work.[9]

If Condé blamed himself for their shenanigans, he was selling himself short. He was a pioneer, a visionary, a prospector who had found gold in promoting the "New Woman." Since the 1890s the New Woman had adorned the pages of novels in Europe and North America as sports loving, defiant, intelligent, an original modern vision of feminism, equal to any man working in offices, factories, and workshops. It was she who demanded social and political reform, and the right to vote.

Condé was the first to bring European style, culture, and the modern arts to America with each issue of his publications, widening the country's horizons from its parochial perspectives. He had broken the glass ceiling by promoting Edna Woolman Chase—a woman of no experience—from a gofer to top management (something many employers still fail to do today). Soon enough he would be credited with creating café society; throwing the most awesome parties; finding young, untested talent from the international arena who would change the way we think; and becoming one of the foremost Americans influencing the export of the country's can-do attitude, know-how, products, fashion, and style to the world. He wrote the first paycheck ever for the British playwright Noël Coward. Aldous Huxley, Compton Mackenzie, and P. G. "Plum" Wodehouse were on his staff. He was the first to publish Edna St. Vincent Millay (writing as Nancy Boyd), Donald Ogden Stewart, Robert Benchley, Dorothy Parker, e. e. cummings, and many more in any magazine. Condé was also a high-tech pioneer—promoting cutting-edge technologies in photography and printing, making his publications a byword for all that was modern.

So what did it matter that he had left Benchley in charge of *Vanity Fair*, assisted by Dorothy and Sherwood, while he and Frank swanned off to Europe for two months? So what if Edna was also journeying to England and beyond for *Vogue* at the same time? Worrying was part of his job, and he couldn't help but fret as their ship the *Aquitania* sailed for Europe. It made him uncomfortable to leave the circus animals in charge of his greatest gift to fun-loving, hard-thinking New Yorkers, *Vanity Fair*. But, the Great War was over, and court must be paid to all those in France and Britain who had suffered so cruelly. A delay in their plans was frankly impossible. Besides, truthfully, what real damage could the trio do in a mere sixty days, or two editions of *Vanity Fair*? Condé wasn't an unreasonable man, and even if the battle lines had been drawn, for now he must let them win the skirmish.

PART I

HOW TO MAKE A MILLIONAIRE

———◄○■○►———

The only way to do great work is to love what you do.
—Condé Nast (and later, Steve Jobs)

※

1. LIVING DOWN MR. DISAPPOINT

Keep away from people who try to belittle your ambitions.
—MARK TWAIN

C ondé Nast's life began rather inauspiciously, despite his glowing horoscope. For those who came into the world on March 26, 1873, it proclaimed: "The Sun was in the sign of Aries when you were born, giving you a very active and energetic nature and a great desire for rulership."[1] Naturally the prediction hadn't taken into account his paternal grandfather's German Methodist ministry and dour outlook on life, or his father's belief that only suckers had to work hard to earn their fortune.

Grandfather Wilhelm Nast was known as the "patriarch of German Methodism" in the United States. He was also the owner and editor of the highly influential Cincinnati-based German-language paper called *Der evangelische Apologete* which he founded in 1837.* Born in Stuttgart in 1807 and orphaned at seventeen, Wilhelm arrived in the United States in 1828 after completing his university education at Tübingen, Germany.[2]

He was a deeply religious man who, as a Lutheran from a litany of Swabian clergymen, suffered a prolonged crisis of con-

---

* From its inception the *Christian Apologist* was the foremost German Methodist publication, eagerly awaited by its subscribers each week. By the 1880s, however, subscribers complained that there were few if any "entertainment" articles and began to abandon the strictly religious paper for others in either German or English.

science. His first job in New York was as a teacher. Unfulfilled, Wilhelm remained a tortured spirit and began traveling in search of an answer to his dilemma. He made it as far as Ohio, where he taught at Kenyon College. There he took a Methodist class, officially converting to Methodism in 1835. That same year the Ohio Methodist Conference made him a missionary to the German population of Cincinnati—a booming city of some 38,000 souls. More than 20 percent of its population was of German origin, and it was Wilhelm's job to convert as many of them as possible to Methodism. While he was a man of few words off the pulpit, preaching the faith as "born again" brought new meaning to Wilhelm's life and the lives of those he served. Yet, despite Wilhelm's finding his mission, his depressive nature and periodic crises of conscience remained with him until his dying day in May 1899.[3]

In his late twenties Wilhelm believed it was time to fulfill his earthly function and marry. Eventually he set his eyes, if not his heart, on twenty-year-old Margaret Eliza McDowell, who was eight years his junior and also a convert to Methodism. On June 21, 1836, Wilhelm proposed marriage, addressing a letter to his "Dear Sister." He rather loquaciously wrote that "after long hours of prayer over the matter" it was his conclusion that he "would be much more happy and useful" if she would agree to be his partner for "life's uneven journey." As if that weren't off-putting enough, Wilhelm concluded that he would need to seek permission from the elders in his ministry to marry her, as he would be traveling the Ohio circuit on behalf of German Methodism after they wed. He also begged Eliza to "ask the Lord for direction" before giving her reply.

Evidently Eliza was happy to accept his formal proposal, and the couple married on August 1, 1836. They set up house in Cincinnati, where she taught at the Worthington Seminary, despite the fact that she had little formal education herself. Initially Wilhelm would visit his young wife only once every six weeks.[4] Within the first year of their marriage, Wilhelm also found the energy to set up the *Apologete*. At long last he was doing what he wanted: writing about his religion, converting lost souls, and preaching to unseen masses who longed to hear his message of salvation. In short order Wilhelm became Ohio's most highly respected, Bible-thumping speaker and defender of the Methodist "evangelical truth." Later he became president of Wallace College, a German Methodist affiliate of Baldwin University in Berea, near Cleveland. As time passed, Eliza noticed a change in him, writing to her sister that Wilhelm's "gloominess is wearing off."[5]

Or maybe Eliza was just less aware of his grim nature as their family grew. Their first son, Ernst, born in July 1838, died young of cholera. The second child, William Frederick—Condé Nast's father—was born on June 14, 1840. He was followed by a sister, Josephine Pulte, in 1842, and another boy, Albert Julius, in 1846. The baby, Franzeska Wilhelmina, known as Fanny, completed the family in 1848. Fanny was thought to be most like her mother, with lustrous dark hair and a liking for all those beautiful adornments of life—like silver buckles and brightly colored hair ribbons—so frowned upon by the austere German Methodist community.[6]

Condé's father, William Frederick, was Eliza's favorite. In fact William was quite the handsome charmer and dreamer. At sixteen he worked in a local bank, but he saw no future in banking. Wilhelm had already sensed that his eldest son was not safe in Methodism when he learned that his son regularly attended the theater. To Wilhelm's mind the theater was "the moral enervation of the age" and "the most direct road to the grossest vices."[7] When William moved to New York in 1859, he wrote home that he was unhappy because he knew so few people there. Wilhelm admonished his son, writing that he hadn't succeeded because he had "suffered too many friends" in Ohio.[8] Perhaps William could devote more of his time to the ministry, his father wondered frequently. While that proved an abomination to Condé's father, he did return to Cincinnati two years later, again job hopping in the hope of finding some treasure trove to milk.

Though William was one of the reception committee for President-elect Abraham Lincoln as he passed through Cincinnati

on the way to his inauguration, the honor did not get him the rec-
ognition he felt was his due. Surely the new president could reward him, as the son of the publisher of the *Apologete*, with a
consulship? In William's eyes such a position would not fail to lead
to a fast buck. Naïvely, William thought Lincoln had specifically
singled out the German American community to thank. Its unswerving support in the northwestern states, supporting his abo-
litionist "Free State" platform, would surely make William a shoo-in
for promotion.

So Condé's grandfather pulled out all the stops, introducing
William to his Kentuckian friend, Green Adams, an auditor at the
Department of the Treasury. Hard on the heels of this introduction, Wilhelm wrote to the new secretary of state, William H.
Seward. While no one knows for certain which, if any, of these
contacts was successful on William's behalf, the young man was
nonetheless appointed American consul in Stuttgart, the city of
his father's birth.[9]

Such an auspicious appointment for any young man of twenty-
one might have turned his head. In William's case his head spun
around and around. Eliza accompanied her son to Stuttgart with
the other children, and breathlessly wrote home to her husband
that William had Parisian tailors make him three suits, since German craftsmen were so very inferior. You can almost see her eyes
gleam with excitement as she wrote, "One of them was a court suit,
hat, and sword." Eliza was certain that this time her charming,
handsome son would succeed. He attended the opera, worked ever
so hard to break into diplomatic circles, and spoke such a beautiful French with the Württemberg nobility—how could he fail?
Wilhelm wrote to his son with considerable disdain: "I am tor-
mented with the fear that it [the consulship] will be your ruin . . .
with your notions of life." Of course Wilhelm thought that European nobility was filled with "empty-headed, hollow-hearted
courtiers" and warned his son to steer well clear of every last one
of them.[10]

Aside from one recorded incident in March 1862 when William
hired a private detective to root out a Confederate agent buying

arms and courting sympathy for the seceding American states, it seems his consular duties bored him rigid. He had a generous salary of one thousand dollars annually,* but it hardly measured up to William's personal worldview of his new station in life. "I have been introduced to the family of the King. Princes, Ministers and Chamberlains have called upon me," William bragged in a letter to his mother.[11]

Extravagant presents, far beyond his means, like a silver cigar case and jewelry and gloves were sent to his family. Soon enough troubling rumors wafted back to Washington. Citizens complained that they had left money with Consul Nast in Stuttgart to send to relatives in America, but the transfers were never made. That forced Wilhelm to become personally involved in his son's affairs: He felt he had to make good on at least one payment until William could afford to reimburse him. Then came the allegations of gambling and charging extortionate and illegal fees for his services. These were published in papers in Germany and in the United States. When the scandal hit the *Cincinnati Volksblatt*, the local German-language newspaper, the Nast family was publicly humiliated.

Of course William denied all charges, claiming he was the victim of blackmailers. But his father knew better; the scales had fallen from his eyes years earlier. Wilhelm feared an English-language public humiliation would follow with a congressional investigation and begged his son to return home. For once William did not argue, departing for the United States abruptly in 1864. At the end of the day there was no congressional investigation, no charge of malfeasance or corruption. The only people who suffered were William's German creditors, who pursued the former consul for many years to come.[12] Despite more get-rich-quick schemes involving railroad speculation, selling unwanted land to European immigrants for a 20 percent commission, and later buying up swampland in Florida, William's great fortune continued to elude him.

---

* The rough equivalent of $23,800 in 2017 values may not seem generous, but he would have had few personal expenses while consul.

Yet William, for all his adolescent, pie-eyed belief that hard work
was beneath him, somehow made the sound decision to marry
well. While it was the ultimate blow to his father, William's choice
of bride, Esther Ariadne Benoist—a devout Roman Catholic—was
inspired. If Jane Austen had advised him, her pearls might have
run to a variation on the opening line of *Pride and Prejudice*: "It
is a truth universally acknowledged, that a single man [not] in pos-
session of a good fortune must be in want of a [wealthy] wife."
Such was the case in 1868 with William.

Not only did Esther possess a reputed three-hundred-thousand-
dollar fortune, but she came from a fine, cultured French family.
Among her ancestors were Guillaume Benoist, in the fifteenth
century, a chamberlain to King Louis XI, who was known as "the
Cunning" and "the Universal Spider" for his web of spies and de-
ceit spun throughout the courts of Europe. Another was Antoine
Benoist, court painter to Louis XIV. Esther's great-great-
grandfather, the Chevalier Antoine Gabriel François Benoist,[*]
sailed originally to Canada in 1735 and served as an aide to General Montcalm in the battles against the British during the French
and Indian War. Her grandfather, François Marie Benoist, was
born in Canada in 1764. As an adult he worked the Indian fur
trade along the Missouri River, becoming active in St. Louis cultural life after the Louisiana Purchase by the United States in
1803. François Benoist married Marie Catherine Sanguinette, who
was the daughter of one of St. Louis's foremost physicians, Dr. Auguste Condé, who was also a surgeon to the French army. Esther's
father, Louis A. Benoist, helped found the St. Louis Philharmonic
Society in 1859 and opened the first private bank in St. Louis, with
branches in New Orleans (Benoist & Hackney, later Benoist &
Shaw) and San Francisco.[13] Quite possibly William may have felt
that Esther was the closest he would come to marrying royalty.

William knew that Louis Benoist was extremely wealthy. He

---

[*] He later became the Chevalier de St. Louis and returned to France to die.

had seen the splendid Benoist home, Oakland House, built in 1853 near St. Louis. What William forgot was that Louis was also the father of numerous progeny.* Married three times, first to Eliza Barton, then to Esther Hackney of Virginia—who bore six children before her death, the fourth of whom was Condé's mother—and finally to Sarah E. Wilson, who gave birth to a further nine children, Louis had fifteen little mouths to feed and keep in splendor.[14] Although William's motives were shockingly clear, Esther must have had a thirst for adventure somewhere in her nature to buck her staunch Catholic upbringing and marry the handsome "Protestant" rapscallion. Either that, or she mistakenly believed that the love of a good woman could change her man.

The proposed marriage was a terrible misfortune to the bridegroom's parents, who believed their grandchildren would become priests or nuns. Nonetheless Wilhelm tried to keep an open mind. While visiting Esther, he wrote to his younger son, Albert, that she had lovely red hair, was "beautiful . . . in bearing mind and heart," and truly, deeply in love with William.[15] What he did not know was that Esther was also strong willed.

Wilhelm and Eliza were in an awkward position when the wedding invitation arrived. He did not want the Catholic community of St. Louis to think that he sanctioned the marriage, but neither did he want to hurt or disappoint the happy couple. He turned to his son Albert for advice, setting forth his fears.[16] In the end Eliza remained at home, and Wilhelm attended the ceremony. The officiating priest was sensitive to the dilemma the groom's father faced, making every concession possible, including not wearing his ceremonial robes and avoiding any "ecclesiastical feature or blessing."[17] The wedding feast was enjoyed by all, and Wilhelm was delighted with his decision.

Soon after the wedding the young couple moved to New York, where William was set up (presumably by Louis Benoist) as a stock-

* Today Oakland House is owned and maintained by the Affton Historical Society, which began restoration of the historic property in the early 1970s. It is open to the public and is most frequently used as a wedding venue.

broker. All four of their children were born there: Louis in October 1868, Esther Ethel in May 1870, Condé Montrose on March 26, 1873, and Estelle Josephine in January 1875. Sadly, not even the love of a good woman could tamp down William's idle dreams of wealth. A friend wrote to his father that William was "like Archimedes, who had a lever powerful enough to move the world—but could not get a fulcrum."[18] When Condé was three years old, William skedaddled back to Europe, claiming it was only there that he could make his millions. Each year there would be packages for the children, but he seldom wrote to his wife. And each year Esther's fortune dwindled to pay property taxes and daily expenses to feed her family.

Eventually she returned home to St. Louis with her brood. Though she sold the Missouri landholdings inherited on the death of her father, soon enough her three hundred thousand dollars became two hundred thousand. She wrote to her husband, first in London, where he had made the harebrained invention of a machine to dry and bale straw, to come home. He affectionately replied that he would not return to "eat his wife's bread."[19] She tracked him down to Paris, where he had gone to organize a stock company to manufacture paper from baled straw and manure. Again he wrote back that his process would revolutionize newsprint. Imagine. . .

The children attended St. Louis public schools. On weekends they visited their maternal grandfather's home, where Condé and his brother and sisters dreamed of what might have been, while playing with their numerous cousins. It was always a sadness to Condé that he never knew Louis Benoist; his mother's father had died in 1867, six years before he was born.

Meanwhile the Nasts were mortified by William's flagrant abandonment of his family. His parents could not comprehend his callousness. Only his brother, Albert, was not surprised, firmly believing that William would never return. His sister Fanny called him "Mr. Disappoint." And so the years passed, and passed again—that is, until October 1890 when Mr. Disappoint returned at last.

Condé was seventeen. In all his father had been gone for thirteen long years. The return of the prodigal husband was so exceptional that it was reported as far away as Chicago. According to *The Sandusky* (Ohio) *Daily Register*, though the couple had been married for twenty-two years, they had lived together for only nine. "After thirteen years' separation," the article goes on to describe how the couple met again at the home of one of William's relatives in Chicago. They "were reconciled and they will journey hand in hand henceforth down the highway of life. . . . Owing to the social prominence of the people, the affair has created [a] considerable . . . ripple in their home" of St. Louis.[20] It did not go unnoticed by Condé or his other siblings that if their mother had not been left well provided for by her father, they would have starved.

William was a hard act to ignore, and certainly not one to follow. His son Condé had grown up with an overripe sense of right and wrong, a sense of duty, abiding admiration for his mother, and a steely will not to follow in the footsteps of Mr. Disappoint.

2. FANNY'S "EVEN-HANDED" JUSTICE

Life is not fair; get used to it.
—BILL GATES

Condé Nast's aunt Fanny had tremendous common sense. She keenly observed her brothers William and Albert, and her elder sister, Josie. She realized that none of them could take care of their parents in their old age, so it would have to fall to her. Fanny thought that Josie was the prettier daughter and knew she loved the theater, beautiful clothes, and the company of lively friends. So did Fanny, but she kept her desires within the reasonable expectations of a girl growing up in a strictly Methodist household. Josie had less horse sense.

That was reason enough for Wilhelm and Eliza to try to marry Josie off to one of his disciples, Michael J. Cramer, a leading reporter and reviewer of religious books, who referred to Wilhelm as his "spiritual father" and Nast's Race Street Church as his "spiritual birthplace." But Josie would not be pushed into a loveless marriage with a man whose "soft, sickening love letters" made her stomach churn. So Cramer took his affections elsewhere and soon after got engaged to Gen. Ulysses S. Grant's youngest sister instead.[1]

Four years later, in 1867, Josie finally married the man she loved, Dr. William Joseph Andrews. Although not "a renewed man," at least her homeopathic doctor was a Protestant. They moved initially to Muncie, Indiana, where Josie constantly complained of the squalor and the local "hog and hominy diet," as well as her husband's patients' annoying habit of being uncommonly slow in paying their bills. By the time they moved to New Jersey a few years later, Josie's husband had taken to drink and was admitted to a sanatorium.[2] Josie learned forbearance during her years of woe, never once claiming she should have married Cramer, whom President Grant named as American minister to Denmark and later Switzerland. And that was probably down to Fanny.

Fanny saw William's and Josie's folly clearly. She also saw that Albert's Methodist piety would not keep her or her parents in the style to which she would like them all to become accustomed. Fanny appreciated women's fashions and all objects of beauty as much as her sister did. Although stylish things were not befitting the Methodist ideal, they never kept Fanny from being a loyal church member. At thirteen she stopped attending German Sunday school to go to English-speaking services instead. It was the only way for Fanny to integrate with or meet like-minded people. Despite an indifferent academic career at high school, she was the first woman to graduate from Wallace College, an Ohio Methodist College that later merged with the Baldwin Institute.

At the age of twenty-three Fanny was courted by a shy, young man who was also a first-generation-born Methodist. His name was William A. Gamble, the son of James Gamble, the Irish soap maker and one of the two founders of Procter & Gamble in Cincinnati. In 1872 Fanny and William were married near Cleveland. James Gamble settled a small fortune on the happy couple. They lived for many years at the Gamble mansion in Cincinnati, spending their summers at the Gamble properties at Lakeside. William Gamble died in 1897, leaving Fanny a very wealthy woman in her own right, but, sadly, childless. It was a love match, and one that relieved the entire Nast family of their financial worries.* Even Josie benefited.[3]

---

* On Wilhelm Nast's death in 1899, his personal wealth was $25,000, thanks in no small part to the railroad stock given to him in 1882 by William Gamble.

So too did Condé. Actually Fanny was the *only* Nast family member who kept in touch with Esther throughout her long years of privation. When it came time to think about a university education for the Nast boys, Aunt Fanny said that she could help only *one* of them, despite having the ability to pay for both. Obviously, to Esther, it must be the eldest son, Louis, who was a gifted musician. According to family legend, however, when Aunt Fanny came to visit and saw a tidy patch of garden tended at the front of the house alongside a wilderness, and learned that the well-maintained one was Condé's responsibility, she opted for the younger son instead.[4]

But that apocryphal tale omits Fanny's innate ability to read people wisely. Surely she would have known that Condé supported the highly publicized Parnell Defense Fund in 1889. Essentially the fund was one of the first international crowd-funding exercises for a good cause, provoked by an incident that incensed God-fearing, freedom-loving Americans. The outcry began when *The Times* of London openly accused Charles Stewart Parnell, leader of the Irish Parliamentary Party (which demanded Home Rule from Britain), of the May 1882 killings of Lord Frederick Cavendish, chief secretary for Ireland, and Thomas Henry Burke, permanent under secretary of the Irish Office, in Phoenix Park, Dublin. Cavendish had been in the country for only a few hours when he was assassinated. The Irish National Invincibles, a radical breakaway faction of the Irish Republican Brotherhood (itself a precursor to the IRA, or Irish Republican Army) claimed responsibility. Shortly afterward the Invincibles' leader testified against his cohorts, and five men were hanged on his evidence in 1883.

In March and April 1887, *The Times* printed forged letters as "proof" that Parnell had been behind the Phoenix Park murders. An appeal rang out in North America calling for those outraged by the accusations to contribute to Parnell's defense for the forthcoming inquiry to clear his name.

Fanny must have addressed the matter with Condé directly—maybe over a scoop or two of chocolate ice cream, which she knew might tempt him to tell all—as the defense of Parnell hinged, too, on the thorny family issue of Catholicism versus Protestantism. When questioned, the ever-so-sincere Condé stood by his letter to the editor from the Christian Brothers' College. He had made a personal—if perhaps meager—contribution as part of the Christian Brothers' College donation. The college had forwarded its $15.25 in response to the *St. Louis Dispatch* article, which began: "Every Irishman in America has been aroused to extraordinary indignation by the persistent efforts of the London *Times* to blacken the character of Charles Stewart Parnell. For weeks that paper villainously attacked the leader of the Home Rule party to lay all manner of crimes at his door. Forgery was resorted to in a vain attempt to bolster up the lies."[5]

The Christian Brothers' College stated:

> *In the history of journalism in this or any other country there is not on record a more patriotic or philanthropic undertaking than this in which you have engaged.... He [Parnell] is a man who has given himself... and everything that the world holds dear in exchange for the drudgery of political life... the degradation of the felon's cell at the hands of lying and worthless tyrants, and the libeling of that foul and degrading sheet, the London* Times.[6]

Condé believed in fighting for a cause, and, smitten by his forthright manner, his matronly aunt Fanny was inspired to back a young man of principle. In Condé she also saw a young man with a deep drive to succeed, a man of his word. He was not flashy, not tall (around five feet eight[*]), with a fine, straight nose and a soulful, deep, penetrating brown-eyed gaze. By his twenties he would become nearsighted and wear a wire-rimmed pince-nez to correct his vision—and continue to wear it long after it became unfashionable.

Maybe she asked Louis about his feelings about Parnell, too,

---

[*] 1.75 meters.

and his answer was unimpressive. Perhaps there was no need, since Louis reminded her of her brother William. To her, the disarray she saw before her that day in the front garden was emblematic of a troubled mind. When she saw Condé, a fastidious dresser, careful, thoughtful, and caring, with a strong sense of right and wrong, her mind was easily made up. She may have been generous but was not prepared to squander good money on a young man like Louis, who would most likely not stick the course at college or appreciate his good fortune.

And so, in the autumn of 1891, Condé went off to Georgetown University to face a bright future. Louis deserted his family for Paris, where he earned his living as a pianist. Louis never returned to the United States, and unlike their mother and sisters, never accepted any money from his brother, Condé, after he had become a success. Even years later, when Condé visited Paris regularly, Louis refused to see him. Louis would die in Paris, unreconciled with his family, and written out of his mother's will.

But, what of Condé's sisters? Had Fanny ever considered them for a university education? Despite Fanny's own college degree, apparently that was a bridge too far. Or was it? Had Fanny spotted that dash of daring in the Nast daughters, too? They were New Women who had taken to the bicycle as an expression of their freedom. They were certainly that—and more.

Ethel had a bit of her father's reverence for the fabulous. While she wanted to be a nun, as her Methodist grandparents had feared, she failed to find an order she thought would suit her needs—hardly a recommendation for a woman wishing to serve the Lord. So, off she went to Rome in a vain attempt—in more ways than one—to establish her own religious order. Undaunted by setbacks, she traveled widely. She had Wilhelm's natural way with words, becoming a lively High Victorian travel writer in *Catholic World*. "We passed a restless night, haunted by discordant cries and phantoms of murderous Turks," was a line graphically depicting her story "From Jerusalem to Nazareth on Horseback," written in 1900.

Her short story titled "The Buried Casket" was published a year later. Full of gothic horror, it is a tale of family dishonor, melodramatically told, chockablock with a buried treasure of jewels and more than its fair share of things that go bump in the night.[7]

Condé's other sister, Estelle, was also rather exotic, if not downright scandalous. She fell in love with a married man and ran off with him. Their mother, Esther, begged the man's wife to give him a divorce in the hope of saving her daughter's reputation. Amazingly, due in no small part to Esther's strength of character, the wife agreed. What Esther hadn't reckoned with was that her daughter would refuse to marry him. Instead Estelle became a painter, moved to Florida, and much later in life, married the widower of her best friend. Once Condé had sufficient wealth, he had a customized sleeper-bus built for her to tour America when the mood struck. He also enabled her to design and build her own raspberry-pink home in West Palm Beach.[8]

There is no doubt that the good-looking boy, abandoned as a three-year-old by his father, remained marked by his childhood in a kaleidoscope of ways. He had become his mother's "little man," with all the baggage that the name implies, including being a man long before his years allowed. He was shy, meticulous, highly numerate, and driven to succeed. He had a rare aesthetic vision and a love of beauty—and women. Perhaps like his Nast grandfather, somehow, he saw *his* loves being replicated on the printed page, through the illustrator's brush and pen and the best writing imaginable. But nothing pointed to his becoming a multimillionaire with a thirty-room penthouse on New York's Park Avenue, and even Condé would have scoffed at the image of his being the fast and fabulous giver of innovative parties introducing the "smart set" of café society to the Four Hundred of Mrs. Astor's ballroom, much less marrying into Mrs. Astor's crowd. Nor did Aunt Fanny wish it for him. In the beginning all Condé wanted was to make a difference and to support his family, sorely let down by his father.

So was Aunt Fanny's "even-handed" justice a poisoned chalice? Had she forced Condé to accept her gift of a university education that drove a wedge between Condé and his brother, or was the wedge already there? Hadn't the devil-may-care Louis received his own justice in his aunt's eyes? Hadn't he chosen to blame both Aunt Fanny and Condé for his personal shortcomings? And why should Condé have passed up a once-in-a-lifetime opportunity to make the most of his family connections to get ahead? Life can simply be unfair.

Whatever the circumstances of her gift to Condé, Aunt Fanny knew that he was the son who would look after his mother and sisters. She recognized her own dedication to family in him. He was the son who would help right the wrongs done by her brother, and the man who would make the most of the unique chance he'd been given. It was Condé who possessed the wherewithal to smooth over the years of abandonment. He would indulge their every whim whenever he could.

Although no one could have predicted that he would be one of America's stellar magazine publishers of the twentieth century, it is fitting that he became the man who first gave countless women a sense of identity and style at a time when riding a bicycle denoted a dizzying freedom from suffocating chaperones, and women could only dream of "girl power," much less the right to vote. He was a man born with taste, style, and flair, who intrinsically understood what women wanted. The reason was simple: Condé Nast adored women. In expressing that love, he also elevated the United States' tastes and showed the country how to create its own aesthetic, to learn to appreciate what was modern—in dress, architecture, painting, illustration, music, the new art of photography, and so much more. But all that lay in the future.

For now, like his aunt Fanny, the college-age Condé knew what he wanted, and from the moment he packed his trunk to go to Georgetown University, he steered a course to raise his family back to their previous exalted status. Naturally there would be more than one or two bumps on the road, but it would hardly have been a life well-lived if there weren't.

3. IT'S NOT WHAT YOU KNOW . . .

The only source of knowledge is experience.
—ALBERT EINSTEIN

I t's who knows *you* that counts. From the autumn of 1891 when Condé reached Georgetown University in Washington, D.C.,* he made it his business to be well known. Throughout that first, important freshman year, he sensed not only whom he should befriend but also which activities should propel him to the forefront of the student body's collective mind. He decided to make his mark in sports, and the preeminent sport among young men of the upper classes was tennis.

Although he excelled at tennis and played a decent game of squash, he was not remotely what his fellow students could call sporty. That said, Condé took charge of the tennis association and managed the baseball team. By the autumn term of his sophomore year, he was winning coveted tennis titles in both men's singles and doubles. He was a finalist in Washington's District Tennis Tournament in both the men's singles and doubles in October 1892;[1] and in July 1894 he came in second in the Seabright tourney in New Jersey.[2]

---

* Georgetown University, founded in 1789 by John Carroll, is the oldest Catholic and Jesuit teaching institution of higher learning in the United States. Today it is a world-class academic and research institution. While its School of Nursing was established in 1903, it only became fully coeducational in 1969–70.

Condé took up the family interest in editorship and became the first student president of Georgetown's athletic association, the Yard, which organized the university's intercollegiate and intramural sports fixtures. Having a participating student rather than a Jesuit faculty member as its leader made it a dynamic force. Given Condé's hunger to succeed, he played an active role in its transformation.[3] As its president he discovered he was a natural advocate in publicity, scheduling, fund-raising, and controlling the finances for the association.

Condé worked alongside his good college friend, the dashing and wealthy Robert J. Collier, son of the publishing magnate Peter Fenelon Collier. Robert had light-brown hair fashionably parted in the middle and was around six feet in height, but stood as tall as if he owned the world. It was his demeanor, his way with words, his love of aviation, horseback riding, and yachting, rather than his average looks that made him swashbuckling. Collier was a first-generation American and a Catholic, like Condé, but his family came from County Carlow in Ireland.

Publishing was in the Collier family blood too. Fenelon Collier had started out publishing books dedicated to the Roman Catholic market in the United States; however, he made his real fortune in publishing encyclopedias and popular novels through the Collier's Library. With so many points of similarity except money, it is little wonder that Condé and Robert became fast friends. Together they took on the duties of editing the *Georgetown College Journal*, and in their final year, Robert became its editor in chief. The pair also shared a love of music, and Condé was reported in the *College Journal* as playing the flute, "appealing . . . to the most musical audience."[4] When Condé's father, William, died on April 7, 1893, Collier placed the obituary notice in the *College Journal* on behalf of his friend.[5] Chances are that Condé was relieved by his loss.

Graduating in June 1894, Condé had won a distinction in rational philosophy and mathematics and was selected to deliver the bachelor's oration. This scholastic specialism along with his natural abilities as a promoter and editor would become the cornerstones of his future life. Collier read the class poem in a deep, mellifluous voice at the graduation ceremony and won a prize for the most scholarly contributions to the *College Journal*.[6] After graduation the friends parted company. Collier went on to Harvard for a year, then spent another year at Oxford University in England before joining his father's publishing firm. Condé remained at Georgetown for another year to earn a master's degree with a view to going into the law. It was only in June 1895 that Condé returned to St. Louis, hoping to attend George Washington University's law school that fall.

Luck would intervene. After a year at law school, in the summer of 1897, Condé was asked to help out the printers' firm in which the family had invested some two thousand dollars. After a detailed study, Condé developed a plan. He would travel throughout the South and Midwest to sell advertising for the St. Louis Exhibition.* Its numerous booths sold wine, beer, and various delicacies. There were mechanical, agricultural, and floral halls; a Gothic fine arts hall; and a three-story-high wire "gallinarium," or Chicken Palace. Horseracing, with its own grandstand and jockey club, provided popular entertainment. With such glittering prizes for advertisers, and Condé's enthusiasm for his task, the printers were saved.[7] He had demonstrated to his own satisfaction an understanding of the interrelationship between printing, publishing, subscriptions, and advertising.

When Collier visited his friend that same summer, he was impressed by Condé's approach to advertisers. On returning to New York, Collier, hands planted firmly but nonchalantly in his trouser pockets (as he would do when he was determined to get his way), asked his father if Condé could join him at their failing magazine, *Collier's Weekly*. Fenelon Collier thought Condé was an up-

---

* The St. Louis Exhibition held its first fair in 1856, with the support of prominent citizens (Condé's Benoist grandfather participated with the "St. Louis Agricultural and Mechanical Association"). Fairgrounds were purchased an hour's carriage ride to the northwest of the city, and it was an immediate success as the largest county fair in America.

standing and clever young man and agreed. Besides, they had
nothing to lose. Correspondence between Collier and Condé ensued. Laying on the charm, Collier said he couldn't promise him
much, only twelve dollars a week, but how would that take care of
Condé's family? he asked disingenuously.[8] He knew he had dangled an irresistible carrot at Condé.

What risks would Condé run by accepting Collier's offer? He was
no impetuous youth, given to whims or fancies like his father.
Condé studied *Collier's* history. Founded in 1888 by Peter Fenelon
Collier, *Collier's Weekly* was born out of *Collier's Once a Week: An
Illustrated Weekly Newspaper*. Its success rested comfortably on the
popular book sets by fashionable authors sold on the installment
plan. *Collier's Once a Week* sold for seven cents and proclaimed
that it was a "magazine of fiction, fact, sensation, wit, humor,
news."[9] It attracted big-name writers of the day like H. Rider Hag-
gard. There was a "Woman's World" column; the de rigueur social column, called "Social Silhouettes"; a theater lowdown; and a
humor feature. Under the editorship of a young journalist, Nugent
Robinson, *Once a Week* grew to a circulation of 250,000, making
it one of the top-selling American weeklies of its day.[10] When Robinson left *Collier's* in 1892, a succession of newspaper editors (notably from *The New York Herald* and *The New York World*) made
Once a Week a slightly breezier version of *Harper's Weekly*.[11]

In 1895, when Robert Collier returned from Europe to take
things in hand, one of the first things he did was to change the
name to *Collier's Weekly: An Illustrated Journal*. The earlier version was a mass-market publication, sold inexpensively, and cru-
saded for social reform. Its investigative journalism was highly
respected and aimed at the middle classes. Its annual advertising
revenue was around five thousand dollars.[12] While Collier appreciated the earlier successes of the magazine, he also knew its popularity was a by-product of the Collier's Library. So it came as no
surprise that circulation declined in the early-to-mid-nineties. Society was changing rapidly, and readers were eager for news, pub-

lic affairs, and society columns as well as understanding the new photographic arts. Soon his weekly would become a leader in the new halftone news picture. But Collier did not step into his role a fully formed editor in chief, and Condé knew it. In Collier's own words, "I had just come from Harvard with the idea that popular journalism needed a little true literary flavor. I showed my judgment of the public taste by ordering a serial story by Henry James [*The Turn of the Screw*]. The illustrations were by John La Farge, and I have never yet discovered what either the story or the pictures were about."[13]

What Collier needed was a young man with a vision similar to his own. A man who shared his love of music and had a deep sense of business ethics, even if that man wasn't particularly an early aviation enthusiast like Collier.* He needed a man he could trust—a man who could sniff out the advertisers for his new-look magazine. Condé had proved himself after graduation in saving the family's investment through an innovative approach to advertising, and Collier trusted him unreservedly. He knew Condé would understand the need to back his vision of *Collier's Weekly* as a magazine that sought to appeal to the college-educated man, without excluding women.†

Collier had won the debating medal at Georgetown. His ability to persuade was impressive, and he knew it. So it came as no surprise when, in what may seem an act of blatant rebellion straight out of William Nast's bag of tricks, Condé accepted his friend's offer. Not only had Condé enjoyed the experience of selling advertising for a "quality" publication and saving an investment for the family that summer, but he also recognized that the law,

---

* Collier was also a good friend of the aviation pioneer Orville Wright, a director of the Wright Company, and president of the Aero Club of America. In 1911 Collier bought the Model B Wright airplane and loaned it to the U.S. Army. It was the first airplane to fly reconnaissance over the border with Mexico along the Rio Grande.
† All but a handful of institutions of higher education did in the United States in the 1890s. In 1803 Bradford Academy of higher education in Massachusetts admitted women. In 1831 Mississippi College became the first higher education institution to grant a degree to two women, Alice Robinson and Catherine Hall.

frankly, was not for him. Besides, Collier had two things Nast lacked: tremendous popularity as a result of his "gift of the gab," and a pedigree that was as valued in Newport, Rhode Island, society as it was in New York's. With barely more than the clothes on his back, Condé joined Collier in Manhattan. He was twenty-four years old, reserved, but had already acquired his persona of elegance. Condé knew that New York afforded untold opportunities for a man on the make—and he was confident that alongside Collier the risk of failure was minimal.

Condé was well aware that selling advertising for a failing national magazine was a daunting project. From 1885 to 1905—that double decade of phenomenal change—Europe and North America underwent unprecedented transformations and challenges industrially, financially, politically, socially, and culturally. European empires were challenged; American cities grew beyond all reckoning. The American West and South progressed and even outstripped growth in the powerhouse North. Revolutionary inventions—including labor-saving devices, improvements in communication, enhanced entertainment, and modern modes of transport—gave birth to new industries. Europeans, Asians, and South Americans who saw little hope in the countries of their birth immigrated to the United States and Canada—*plus ça change*—giving rise to what was seen by many as an "immigration crisis." Radical ideas shaped new political movements that transformed the social order. Shifting religious beliefs spurred by revolutions in education added to the most dramatic change of all to society: the emancipation of women.

Magazines were seen as the popular informers and interpreters of this ever-changing contemporary world. Collier wanted his journal to be the best: improving illustration, hiring the best authors for short stories (it was the heyday of that literary form, after all), and writing about things that mattered to his readers.[14] To achieve that goal Collier raised the price of the journal to ten cents. It was Condé's job to attract national advertisers whose products would be sold with integrity and no false promises. In an age before national legislation regarding truth in advertising, it became their unique selling point.

Granted, advertising the newfangled typewriter like the Caligraph or the Remington might be desirable, but surely it would be better for Condé to aim to get the account of the eight-dollar Smith-Premier Hammond?[15] It would be trickier to assess if the "W. L. Douglas $3 Shoe for Gentlemen" was of sufficient quality, or if Mrs. Pinkham's portrait advertising "Vegetable Compound for Female Complaints" could live up to Collier's exacting requirements. And what about Royal Baking Powder's "Absolutely Pure" slogan? Was it better than Dr. Price's Cream Baking Powder or its other competitors? And what about Durkee's Salad Dressing being "Unequalled for Excellence," or Armour's Extract of Beef claiming to produce "That Feeling of Contentment"?[16] While *Collier's Weekly* was not responsible for the advertisements placed, Condé knew that readers would nonetheless associate Collier's with any advertisers making false claims.

So Condé, with his methodical approach, analyzed what other good general or "class" publications did. "Class" in this sense did not mean stylish or sophisticated, but rather publications that aimed at a well-defined socioeconomic group. In Condé's own words a class publication was "nothing more or less than a publication that looks for its circulation *only* from those having in common a certain characteristic marked enough to group them into a class. . . . The publisher, the editor, the advertising manager and the circulation man must conspire not only to get *all* their readers from one particular class to which the magazine is dedicated, *but rigorously to exclude all others* [emphasis in original]."[17]

To Condé's mind, the question remained: Did *Collier's Weekly* seek to be a general magazine or a class publication?

4. THE ADMAN BEFORE *MAD MEN*

Sometimes we don't get to choose where our talents lie.
—DON DRAPER, *MAD MEN*

S o Condé reviewed the back copies of *Collier's Once a Week* and the previous year's advertisements in *Collier's Weekly*. He saw a thin, dull fortnightly that was more about current events than good fiction. What little advertising it had was a matter of widespread and general concern. Advertisements were placed at the back of the book, sold by the fraction of a column inch. What *Collier's* needed to consider, in Condé's opinion, was if it wanted to appeal to a specific market, and if so, which one.

Collier had made huge investments in *Collier's Weekly* since taking over, employing top illustrators and writers, and using the state-of-the-art technology of "color." When all was said and done, fiction was a broad market, and that troubled Condé. Advertisers in such a journal would be showing off their goods to a wide range of readers, making their ads more miss than hit. Collier saw the merit of Condé's analysis to aim for a discrete market, but with a raft of satisfied advertisers who made the magazine almost wash its face, any change made Collier uneasy. Soap, three-dollar men's shoes, bicycles, and all manner of medicinal "cure-alls" were the backbone of the company's profits. Still, if advertising Procter & Gamble's Ivory Soap—"99 $44/100$ % pure" and "It floats"—made Collier sleep better, it certainly wouldn't hurt Aunt Fanny Gamble's pocket either.[1] Besides, the magazine did a wonderful job advertising the popular novels in Collier's Library, which was still the company's bread and butter.

What Collier hadn't realized was that Condé had hit on a gold-plated genius reason to create a class publication. Circulation numbers stood at a paltry 19,159. For advertisers who wanted to get their products known nationally, it held little appeal. Condé's experience in approaching modern-day industries about promoting their products backed up his research, too. *Collier's Weekly* could successfully advertise novels—even novels to take on holiday—but selling the aspirational vacation itself, or how to make one's travel plans, was missing. Condé knew when he said, "I have so many hundred thousand readers, among them there must be a great number rich enough to buy your car," it would be a point scorer for the executive placing his ads in *Automobile and Motor Age*.[2] He was aware, too, that the majority of general readers couldn't afford to purchase pianos, private education, jewelry from Tiffany & Co., or the $250 Victor-Victrola, much less the recordings to play on it.[3]

So the bulk of *Collier's* advertising concentrated on affordable soaps (Pear's, Fairy, and Ivory); home remedies (such as Dent's Toothache Gum, Beeman's Dental Gum, the Philo Burt corset for spinal deformities, Parker's Ginger Tonic for the avoidance of appendicitis brought on by constipation); corsets and hosiery (for instance the all-over Oneita rubber suit or Thomson's Glove Fitting Corsets and President Suspenders); household goods (like the Enterprise Food Chopper or the Electric Works' "Electronic Wonders at Little Cost") and foodstuffs (Ralston breakfast foods, Grape-Nuts). Occasionally a piano or two would crop up, but these were the exception.[4]

Despite his skepticism Collier agreed that Condé could make important changes to the national advertising sales campaign for *Collier's*. Condé was the first adman in the United States to introduce a systematic division of the country into territories for the sale of advertising space, with key divisional offices located within each region. Nonetheless he remained wedded to the idea of a class publication, and persuaded Collier to create "class" special issues, like the automotive and yachting specials. Over time Collier agreed to theme his fortnightly magazine as Condé suggested. So, for example, the October 5, 1901, edition concentrated on the sea, with an update on the thrilling America's Cup race, a report on Rear Adm. Winfield Scott Schley's court of inquiry,* and a short story called "The Pirate's Daughter."[5]

Not only did Condé influence the creation of special numbers, but he also gave advice regarding *Collier's* look and feel. Circulation soared. Condé was aware that few believed unaudited circulation figures, so he arranged for these to be independently assessed. The numbers didn't lie. Maxfield Parrish, one of the more popular magazine illustrators, became a regular contributor. Frederic Remington contributed Western action illustrations. Collier was thrilled. He spent lavishly on stories and articles by some of the top writers of the day like Frank Norris, Rudyard Kipling, O. Henry, Booth Tarkington, Jack London, Winston Churchill, Edith Wharton, P. G. Wodehouse, and Arthur Conan Doyle among others.[6]

But the real "snatch" was Charles Dana Gibson in 1903. Condé urged Collier to woo the fabulously popular Gibson, dubbed "the darling of the nineties," who was deemed the near-exclusive property of *Life*.† With Condé firmly at his side, Collier persuaded Gibson to join him. Collier signed up Gibson, with his customary largesse, for one hundred two-page drawings to appear over four years. The cost? A staggering one hundred thousand dollars, or

---

* Schley got off lightly. The court of inquiry, convened at his own behest to quash charges of cowardice made in a book, found on December 13, 1901, that he had disobeyed the Navy Department's orders of May 25, 1898, and that he had not set out for the Battle of Santiago de Cuba with due dispatch. Since so much time had elapsed between the act and the court's findings, and the war was over, there was no punishment.

† *Life* was later reincarnated as a pictorial magazine by Time Inc. at the urging of Clare Boothe Luce, wife of its publisher Henry Robinson Luce, and former employee of Condé Nast's. At this time, it was primarily a humor magazine. Gibson's contract had already been shared for a time with *Harper's Magazine*, and after he drew for *Harper's Weekly*.

double Gibson's usual fee.[7] The following year Gibson was rewarded with his own special issue.

Condé had a good story to tell advertisers, but he told it in an
engaging and self-effacing way. "I am the Advertising Manager of
Collier's," so his pitch began:

> ... *I don't expect you to give me any business. Most manufac-
> turers don't believe in weeklies; and it has only taken three
> months' canvassing to prove to my perfect satisfaction that the
> few who do won't use* Collier's. *However, I accept the situation,
> I don't want to argue with you. I merely want your residence ad-
> dress: We want to send* Collier's *to you regularly. Certain
> things are going to happen; things that you have neither the
> time nor inclination to enquire into.*[8]

Advertisers lapped up the soft sell, and circulation soared again.
When it hit the three hundred thousand watershed, Collier decided to take a step back and hired Harvard Law School graduate
Norman Hapgood as his editor in 1902. Hapgood was thirty-four
and had a reputation for being a scholar, journalist, and connoisseur of the arts. The change was heralded publicly as Collier's rec-
ognition that Hapgood would bring his magazine the same
prestige already enjoyed by *Harper's Weekly* for its influence in public affairs.[9] In fact, the reason was more prosaic: Robert Collier
was getting married.

Of course Condé was invited to the celebrations. That July the
wedding took place at the home of the bride's father, James J. Van
Alen, in Newport, Rhode Island, where only family and intimate
friends attended. The bride, Miss Sara Stewart Van Alen, daughter
of James Van Alen and Emily Astor, had recently converted to Roman Catholicism. To win Miss Van Alen's hand, Collier needed
the "approval" of the leader of high society's Four Hundred,
Mrs. Caroline Schermerhorn Astor, who was also the bride's grandmother. "Since that hour," the newspaper reported, "his final success has been assured . . . he is popular with the younger [society]
set in Newport and New York." The article also took a sideswipe

at Robert's father, Peter Fenelon Collier, "as a keen cross-country rider" who had "galloped himself into the 400,"[10] referring to his purchase of the best hunters in County Meath, Ireland, and his donation of trophies for most of the horse shows he entered and— oh, by the way—won. It also mentioned that "on the arrival of Count Castellane in the United States, it is alleged that he [Fenelon Collier] befriended the count in a substantial manner when the latter was laying siege to the heart and the fortunes of Anna Gould."[11] Anna, who was unkindly described as having facial warts, a clubfoot, and the face of a captured chimpanzee, was the youngest daughter of the robber baron Jay Gould, also known as the Vampire of Wall Street.[12]

In truth Fenelon Collier financed the bankrupt Count Boni de Castellane's quest to secure Anna Gould's heart and fortune, since he had neither to call his own. But with Fenelon Collier's money and the count's aristocratic good looks, Anna persuaded her family that it was true love. Fortunately, the Four Hundred were happy to turn a blind eye to Fenelon Collier's actions, since Anna's father had ensured that his family would not be fully accepted in high society.[13]

Such high society would have dazzled—perhaps even daunted—a man of less fortitude and determination than Condé. Rather than be impressed, however, he used his exposure to Collier's friends and in-laws as a learning experience, for he too had ambitions to become one of the Four Hundred.

5. BATTLING THE FAKIRS, SWINDLERS, AND MANUFACTURERS OF BAD WHISKEYS

The truth gets buried under an avalanche
of money and advertising.
—BARACK OBAMA

Those early years of Condé's initiation into publishing were awash with charlatans, mountebanks, and scandalmongers who held the truth in disdain. In the world of popular news no one was more powerful or had more contempt for the facts than the newspaper magnate William Randolph Hearst. No one could touch Hearst's ability to create the sensational from the ordinary in an ocean of publicity, not even his idol, the great Joseph Pulitzer. Having inherited enormous wealth from his father's silver mines and other investments, Hearst used his money to build a newspaper empire to rival Pulitzer's own.

When Hearst's *New York Journal* began to threaten Pulitzer's circulation at *The New York World* in 1895, the aging publisher finally took note of the new boy. But it was too late. Many of Pulitzer's editors, writers, and illustrators had already been poached by the "Hearst Summons." By 1897 it had become an institution in American journalism, where the "summoned"—like the *World's* Arthur Brisbane—knew they would be unable to resist the temptations that "the Chief" Hearst offered, both financially and in terms of power.[1] Brisbane became Hearst's friend and the backbone of his journalism empire. Not bad for a "one-time socialist who had drifted pleasantly into the profit system . . . in some respects a vest-pocket Hearst—a personal enigma, a workhorse, a madman for circulation, a liberal who had grown conservative, an investor."[2] Lesser men—and women—came under Hearst's seemingly magnetic influence and hadn't the willpower to escape. Once Hearst had begun his lifetime practice of poaching his competitors' ablest staff, there was no stopping his attempts to crush his opposition. So when it came to telling the truth, Hearst became one of Robert Collier's greatest adversaries.

In looking back over his career, and his association with James H. Hare, one of the great early news photographers, Robert Collier explained that when "Jimmy Hare blew in," his life changed course abruptly. Hearst was brewing the biggest fake news story yet of his career: inventing the beginning of the Spanish-American War. Understandably Collier dispatched Jimmy Hare to Cuba to see what was really happening. "Sending Hare to Havana that morning involved me in more troubles and wars and libel suits than any one act in my life," he lamented. "It turned me from the quiet paths of a literary career into [an] association with war correspondents, politicians, muckrakers, and advertising men."[3]

Hearst was undeniably behind many of the libel suits and troubles. When stripped of his press credentials, Hearst seemed shy, modest, indecisive, and a courteous gentle giant of a man (he was nearly six feet three)[*] with a timid disposition. With his press hat on, he was a brazen "Caesar, Charlemagne, and Napoleon." Unlike Condé, Hearst's shyness and persona were a sham, save for his high-pitched girly voice. His father once said, "There's only one thing that's sure about my boy Bill. I've been watching him and notice that when he wants cake, he wants cake, and he wants it now."[4] Hearst was nothing short of a megalomaniac who delighted in catching people out, playing practical jokes on unsuspecting employees, inventing news, and admiring his own "greatness."[5] He had whipped up an orgy of articles condemning the Spanish occupation of Cuba, and applauded the island's rebels. The Pulitzer *World* correspondent, Sylvester Scovel, had been jailed by the Spaniards, and Pulitzer was mounting a campaign to free him. En-

---

[*] 1.91 meters.

vious of their free publicity, Hearst sent Frederic Remington as his war correspondent/illustrator to beef up the story.

But once in Havana, Remington cabled that he was bored: "Everything is quiet. There is no trouble here. There will be no war. I wish to return.—Remington." Like a Napoleon, Hearst responded: "Please remain. You furnish the pictures and I'll furnish the war.—W. R. Hearst."[6] And so he did. When the American battle cruiser *Maine* blew up in Havana Harbor,[*] Hearst engaged in the most ruthless, truthless campaign in news history, claiming that the Spaniards had blown up the American ship. He financed "fact-finding" missions to Havana attended by a carefully selected group of congressmen and senators happy to have an all-expenses-paid holiday. He put words into Vice President Theodore Roosevelt's mouth, "cheering" his newspapers of "great influence and circulation" and ignoring "suggestions of various kinds that . . . cannot be described as patriotic or loyal to the flag of this country."[7] Even Roosevelt's denial in the *New York Post* that any such statement had been made to Hearst's *Journal* was ignored. The enraged vice president said: "The alleged interview with me . . . is an invention from beginning to end. It is difficult to understand the kind of infamy that resorts to such methods."[8]

In contrast to Hearst's "yellow journalism," *Collier's* was widely admired for its news reporting, "as The National Weekly by the thorough way in which it covered our war with Spain." The chief *Collier's* correspondent, twenty-five-year-old Frederick Palmer, was experienced, writing about his second war. Jimmy Hare's photographs told the story clearly in pictures.

To Condé's and Robert Collier's consternation, the truth seemed to be a commodity in diminishing supply in newsprint. Hearst and others who bent it to their will, meanwhile, grew in popularity. That said, there were other publishers, too, who worried about their reputations, like Cyrus Curtis, owner of the *Ladies' Home*

---

[*] Contrary to the war fever excited by Hearst's publications, the USS *Maine* more than likely blew up as the result of an onboard munitions explosion.

Journal, and Arthur B. Turnure, owner of *Vogue*, which first appeared in December 1892. Of the two, Turnure had the most to lose by any association with the Hearst news and magazine empire, since his 250 stockholders were members of the *Social Register*, and included the wives of Stuyvesant Fish, Cornelius Vanderbilt, and D. Percy Morgan. Turnure himself was from a wealthy family, as was his art director at *Vogue*, Harry McVickar, whose great-grandfather was the wealthy merchant and prominent New Yorker Stephen Whitney. McVickar was also a member of the Four Hundred.[9]

The *Ladies' Home Journal* began life as the "Woman and the Home" section of Curtis's magazine, *Tribune and the Farmer*. Initially edited by Mrs. Curtis, who had no such grand connections, the magazine grew to more than four hundred thousand subscribers by the autumn of 1887, selling advertising space at the rate of two dollars an agate line.[*] By 1893 subscriptions had increased to seven hundred thousand. Its back-page advertisement sold for four thousand dollars.[10] Four years earlier Curtis believed he had assured his magazine's future by hiring Edward William Bok.

Bok, who was seven years old when his parents immigrated to the United States from the Netherlands, was known to have a streak of reforming, idealistic zeal. While he had done a great deal to improve the *Ladies' Home Journal*, he was not above making a gaffe or two—like commissioning Kipling's poem "The Female of the Species," containing the line "The female of the species is more deadly than the male."[11]

One of Condé's greatest character traits was that he did not suffer from the "not-invented-here-syndrome." He learned from all his subordinates and competitors—both good and bad—and devised over time an ethos that served him well throughout his career.

---

[*] Since 1870, the agate line has been used as the unit of space measuring one column wide and one-fourteenth inch deep in classified advertising.

Probably no one incident demonstrates this better than the *Ladies' Home Journal's* battle against "the Nostrum of Evil."

Collier's had earned its distinctive reputation with its reporting on the Spanish-American War and its series on immigrant labor problems in 1903, when articles attacking noxious medicines first appeared in *Ladies' Home Journal*. Later that same year *Collier's* editor Hapgood wrote a humorous editorial poking fun at William Jennings Bryan's magazine, *The Commoner*, which had been "hammering monopolies" and giving large advertising space to a product called "Liquozone"—a remedy claiming to cure more than "forty diseases from cancer to dandruff."[12] At Condé's urging, Hapgood barged into the hottest crusade in the world of advertising. Patent medicines that made false claims were dangerous, perhaps deadly, and if the magazines continued to accept their advertising, in Condé's opinion, they were guilty by association.

"Even the highest-grade magazines were filled with the most unreliable patent-medicine advertising," Edward Bok wrote. "The business pages fairly reeked with them. It was the acceptable business in the offices of all magazines, high and low."[13] That is, until Cyrus Curtis decided that the pages of his magazine should be free of them, issuing a direct order to the advertising department that "no advertisements of proprietary medicines of any kind would be accepted for publication." The finance director bewailed the decision and tried to get Bok to prevail on Curtis to change his mind. When Bok approached Curtis, the latter just looked back at him blankly. Despite putting his publication in serious financial difficulty for the next several months, Curtis stuck to his guns.

Condé, on behalf of Robert Collier, took up the cudgels next. So began the series of articles by Samuel Hopkins Adams, who had previously been connected with *McClure's Magazine*. They ran in *Collier's* from 1904, titled "Fraud—Articles on the Nostrum of Evil and Quacks." The first series concentrated on specific remedy types and their dangers: "Peruna and Bracers," "Liquozone," "The Subtle Poisons," "Preying on the Incurables,"

and "The Fundamental Fakes." In its introduction *Collier's* asserted its exposure of:

> *patent-medicine methods, and the harm done to the public by*
> *this industry, founded mainly on fraud and poison. Results of*
> *the publicity given to these methods can already be seen in the*
> *steps recently taken by the National Government, some State*
> *Governments and of a few of the more reputable newspapers.*
> *The object of the series is to make the situation so familiar and*
> *thoroughly understood that there will be a speedy end to the*
> *worst aspects of the evil.*[14]

First among the offenders was Pond's Extract, with its claims
to cure meningitis. Peruna exploited fears over the outbreak of yellow fever in New Orleans, and "acetanilid will undoubtedly relieve headaches of certain kinds; but acetanilid, as the basis for
headache powders, is prone to remove the cause of symptoms per-
manently by putting a complete stop to heart action."[15] The article
then attacked the so-called testimonials given by satisfied patients:
"The man who dies in spite of the patent-medicine—or perhaps
because of it—doesn't bear witness for what it did to him."[16] Bona
fide testimonials from purchasers of the various medicines ran frequently in the form of advertising, but no one knew if the writer
was already dead of his or her uncured illness.

The second series in *Collier's* concentrated on all the quack
practitioners: "For every ill there is a 'sure-cure,'" *Collier's* reminded
its readers. "The more deadly the disease the more blatantly certain is the quack that he alone can save you, and in extreme cases,
where he has failed to get there earlier, he may even raise you from
your coffin and restore you to your astonished and admiring
friends. Such things have happened—in the advertising columns
of newspapers."[17]

Next *Collier's* lashed out at newspapers that were so kind, con-
siderate, and careful of their advertisers as to publish the "homi-
cides" that would be injurious to the advertiser's own health. A
Chicago newspaper was accused of "compelling its political editor

to tout for fake [e]ndorsements of a nostrum." How did *Collier's* know? An insider told the weekly that only two Chicago papers were free from the practice.[18]

Robert Collier was thrilled with the results. In 1905 Condé was promoted to business manager at *Collier's*, earning not far from a mammoth forty thousand dollars a year.* By October 1906, *Collier's* "The Great American Fraud" unmasked most advertising scams related to patent medicines and forced Congress into passing a reform that evolved into the Food and Drug Act.

That same month *Collier's* lost the advertising of the Postum Cereal Company, of Grape-Nuts fame. Condé had approved the campaign in the magazine protesting against the untruthful allegations that the cereal could prevent appendicitis, and a good deal more besides. Charles W. Post rebutted the claim by asserting in national newspapers—some of which were certainly owned by William Randolph Hearst—that it was merely "sour grapes" that made *Collier's* attack the company's products. Sour grapes? Why yes, old CW replied, for Post refused to advertise in their weekly magazine.

What CW hadn't counted on was that Robert Collier would sue Postum Cereal Company for its clear allegations of blackmail against *Collier's*. Five years later, in January 1911, long after Condé had moved on to new pastures, *Collier's* was awarded fifty thousand dollars in damages. Though the verdict was set aside on appeal due to a legal technicality, Robert Collier was happy, nonetheless. The original verdict was vindication enough.[19]

The campaign to promote the nation's welfare was also waged against the likes of the sleazy society magazine *Town Topics*, and Hearst's newspapers. *Town Topics*, a voyeuristic tabloid that often viciously bit the high-society hands that fed its columns, was the

---

* In general purchasing power terms it equates to approximately $1.15 million in 2018; however, given the much broader middle class today, it "felt" like $15–26 million. (Source: measuringworth.com.)

first to be tackled. On October 20, 1904, it published a rather scandalous paragraph about Alice, the eldest child of Theodore Roosevelt, accusing her of "wearing costly lingerie [and] indulging in fancy dances" and "indulging freely in stimulants. . . . Flying all around Newport without a chaperone was another thing . . . but if the young woman knew some of the tales that are told at the clubs in Newport she would be more careful in the future about what she does and how she does it."[20]

In reply *Collier's* editor Hapgood wrote an editorial calling *Town Topics* "the most degraded paper of any prominence in the United States" and a "sewer sheet." Before it went into print, Robert Collier personally added a last paragraph. He asserted that the editor of *Town Topics* had a social standing "somewhat worse than that of an ordinary forger, horse-thief, or second-story man."

But was it libelous, Condé asked? Col. William d'Alton Mann, *Town Topics'* editor, had already garnered a reputation for extorting "loans" or "cash payments"—euphemisms for blackmail—for *not* printing some of the more colorful profiles in his social column. Robert Collier, as a gallant young society man, was well aware of the practice, and sought to bring it out into the open.[21] Colonel Mann somehow persuaded the Manhattan District Attorney's Office to place the matter before a grand jury for adjudication, and Hapgood was indicted on charges of criminal libel. *Collier's* lawyers dug up enough on Colonel Mann's dubious practices to cause the jury to sympathize with the written statement, and Hapgood was acquitted. The crusading reporter Mark Sullivan wrote later that:

The Town Topics *suit did for* Collier's *what Collier most desired and needed. The first-page stories and heavy headlines with which the daily papers reported the trial, the parade of names of the best-known figures in New York yielding to intimidation or occasionally resisting it, as the* New York Sun *said, "with courage, celerity, and artistic thoroughness"—all combined to give* Collier's *esteem, éclat, kudos. It became, and for years re-*

mained, the most influential periodical in the country, in many respects the most distinguished America has ever had.[22]

While Sullivan's praise exaggerates *Collier's* significance a hundred years on, there is no doubt that Condé learned scores of valuable lessons about running a national publication while at *Collier's*. By 1907 Condé was the United States' highest-paid executive, but he'd decided that it was time for him to put his own ideas to the test. Rob Collier couldn't believe his ears when Condé told him. "You know perfectly well, Condé," he said, "no one else is going to pay you that much money. You're not worth it." Condé amiably agreed. He wasn't going to go out and get another job. "I'm going out to see if I can't make more than that," he replied.[23]

6. A NATURAL TALENT TO SNIFF OUT LIFE'S PATTERN

His talent was as natural as the pattern that was made by the dust on a butterfly's wings.
—ERNEST HEMINGWAY ON SCOTT FITZGERALD, *A MOVEABLE FEAST*

Condé believed in himself, despite his fatherless childhood. For that he had his mother, Esther, to thank. She instilled in him a work ethic and a sense of responsibility that might have overwhelmed someone else. But it was Condé himself who made the most of the tools at his disposal: his quiet way; sense of dignity; rational, mathematical mind; simple good looks; urbane manner; and the desire to understand what women wanted. He had become a man of great determination and a natural talent in the publishing field. Most of all, he recognized excellence, trends—societal patterns—and how to capitalize on where society was heading. He had also begun to notice that women were generally interested in him—personally.

Long before he quit his lucrative job at *Collier's*, Condé had invested in another business, the Home Pattern Company. While not a publishing house per se, it provided him with a foothold in the industry he had earmarked for growth in the decades to come: fashion publishing. Granted, it didn't take a genius to see that the role of women was changing rapidly. While Condé attended Georgetown, he couldn't help noticing the New Woman: smoking, bicycling, defiant, full of original ideas including the right to gender equality in everything. As an avid reader of his research material—magazines—he would have had to be utterly unaware of his surroundings not to notice this phenomenon.

In the 1890s in both Britain and the United States, more than a hundred novels were published about the New Woman. This was the golden age of the short story. Magazines fizzed with tales either eulogizing or satirizing her. Newspapers debated the whys and wherefores of this New Woman, passing judgment on her demands for social, cultural, and political reform. On the London stage, the character Colonel Cazenove in Sidney Grundy's hit show, *The New Woman* of 1894, remarked, "Everything is New nowadays." That same year William Barry noted in the *Quarterly Review*, with more than a hint of self-satisfaction, that "The New Woman will not continue long in the land. . . . Like other fashions, she is destined to excite notice, to be admired, criticized, and forgotten."[1] Condé regarded such old-fashioned ideas with disdain.

The novelist Henry James remarked in *The American Scene* that the American New Woman was streaks ahead of her British counterpart since her social life was "constituted absolutely by women." At home this modern Amazonian would "not be threatened or waylaid" since "the woman produced by a woman-made society alone has obviously quite a new story . . . grown in the air in which a hundred of the 'European' complications and dangers didn't exist."[2] Others asserted that "the American woman is regarded by many people as the highest development of modern feminism . . . as we see her on this side of the Ocean [she] is an exotic of the 'orchidaceous type.'" The *North American Review* noted in 1897 in an article titled "Petticoat Government" that the New Woman was "flourishing throughout the length and breadth of this huge continent."[3] Amid such admiration for the American New Woman, it came as no surprise to Sherlock Holmes fans that *the* woman for him—and, by the way, the only person to outwit the consulting detective—was the American Irene Adler, in *Scandal in Bohemia*.

In New York City alone, the 1890s saw some 250,000 women as

the main breadwinners—excluding all those in domestic service. Three hospitals in Philadelphia were exclusively run by women. "It was not possible for women to remain the colourless, dependent creatures of the past," Lady Jeune wrote in *The Modern Marriage Market* (1897). "And as they have become emancipated they have more or less chosen their own careers, and thousands of women are now living proofs of the advantages of a change that has given them an aim in life which they can pursue successfully."[4]

Karl Marx's daughter Eleanor argued in *The Woman Question* that the position of their sex—"new" or not—relied entirely on economics. Letters to newspapers on both sides of the Atlantic and in Japan stated that economic inequality was the deciding factor in the failure of marriage. Henrik Ibsen's *A Doll's House*, first performed in 1879, became a hit with this as its central theme. Indeed, most distressing of all to New York's elite was the fact that social prominence no longer relied on lineage but rather on the millions on deposit in the bank. Society's mirror was revolving at a pace that made any venture based on women's fashion both exciting and risky.

So Condé studied scores of fashion magazines from France, Britain, and North America and knew that these rapid social and cultural changes had an impact on fashion. Labor-saving devices such as Isaac Merritt Singer's even-stitching sewing machine (1850) were widely advertised. French-style department stores opened in New York, Philadelphia, and Chicago, temptingly displaying their items for sale. They brought European fashions to middle-class women in America, albeit at a price. Manufacturers marketed their vacuum cleaners and electric washing machines in 1900, suggesting to middle-class women that such appliances would give them more time to make their own clothes. Condé's Home Pattern Company was on hand to promise these same women that they too could afford high fashion, and emulate the style and flair of the Parisian couturiers.

Condé knew that the department store also had an impact on fashion. London preceded the trend in both France and America by more than fifty years with the arrival of Harding, Howell & Co. on Pall Mall. Both European capitals outshone New York, especially in fashion designers, stylists, and boutiques for "mesdames." In France fashion became the centerpiece of its luxury textile markets, promoting lace from Calais, silk from Lyon, vegetable dyes from warmer provinces, and wooden hoops for ladies' skirts from the country's abundant pine forests.[5] Professional dressmakers remained a must for the wealthy, but discerning women of slender means had the skills to sew, and yearned to make copies of the latest haute couture fashions. But where were the patterns they craved? Condé observed that fashion was, in and of itself, a separate art form comprised of many parts. This simple realization revolutionized the way American women, in particular, would begin to see and clothe themselves.

Condé's vision was pioneering. Ever cautious, he set his sights on what may seem mundane to many today: fashionable women's dressmaking patterns. It was the first step toward his becoming a successful fashion publisher without the failures that brought down so many who had gone before. Yet it was a risky enterprise for anyone who did not believe in his power to change an entire national market. Back then, pattern books were given gratis to customers who bought fabrics from the shops. If Condé could make a success of the pattern business that touched so many advertisers and so many women who aspired to haute couture, then surely he would be easing his way into high-end fashion publishing through the back door with a ready audience and established relationships with advertisers. At least that was the plan. That said, the key to his success would be to attract the kind of women who attended New York's Patriarch Ball. Even eighteen-year-old, bright-eyed, petite Edna Woolman Chase, the future editor in chief of *Vogue*, looked upon the Patriarch Ball with more than a tad of envy. Edna knew she would never be asked to go, since she had neither the pedigree nor the money in the bank.

Long before Black Friday meant an orgy of pre-holiday shopping, New Yorkers of the Gilded Age christened the day following Thanksgiving

as the eagerly awaited arrival of the ball season, which would last
until Lent in March or April of the following year. In 1892, of all
the balls, none was more prestigious than the Patriarch Ball given
by the Society of Patriarchs. The society's founder, the Georgia-
born Ward McAllister, was, like Robert J. Collier, an arriviste—or
"bouncer"—as many of New York's aristocracy referred to those
who hailed from "new money." McAllister and his father were min-
ing lawyers in California during the Gold Rush of 1849. Still, he
rightly earned his place as a "patriarch" through his mother, Lou-
isa Charlotte Cutler, an heiress with a family connection to William Backhouse Astor, Sr.[6] Indeed, Edith Wharton's observation
that "old connections, gentle breeding, perfection in all the requi-
site accomplishments of a gentleman . . . and an unstained private reputation," so dear to New York's aristocracy, had become
McAllister's creed.[7]

The Patriarch Ball of 1892, organized by twenty-five "representative men of worth, respectability, and responsibility"—with the
support of Mrs. Astor, naturally—were charged with distributing
invitations personally to people of wealth, thereby uniting "old
money" and "new money" into the same privileged community.
Specifically it was intended to determine who among the nouveau
riche should be accepted into "society."[8] There were other balls
during the season, with the most exclusive being the Assembly
Balls. These began in 1882 and were usually held at the Waldorf
or Delmonico's, their participants determined solely by a committee of fifty women, each giving out nine personal invitations.[*]

Names that ring loudly as integral to American high society
today, such as Morgan, Carnegie, and Vanderbilt, were not auto-
matically included as invitees to the Patriarch and Assembly Balls,[†]
making for some thrilling competition and extravagant one-

---

* Assembly Ball events were held annually from 1882, and eventually replaced the
Patriarch Ball. Its original committee comprised the high society ladies Mrs. John
Jacob Astor, Mrs. August Belmont, Mrs. Paran Stevens, and Mrs. Hamilton Fish.
† In the 1880s they were still thought of as having emerged among those "carpetbag-
gers" made newly rich by the Civil War and the Industrial Revolution.

upmanship when they attended. In 1883, just one year after the first Assembly Ball, Mrs. William K. Vanderbilt put on a lavish costume ball for twelve hundred outrageously attired society guests at her 660 Fifth Avenue home. The fancy-dress ball cost some $250,000—or $6 million of anybody's money today—with champagne outlays soaring to $65,000 and flower arrangements to $11,000.[9] While Mrs. Astor's ballroom may have been limited to four hundred guests, Mrs. Vanderbilt's was quite evidently far grander. Perhaps Mrs. Astor took comfort from *Town Topics'* scandalous remark in 1877: "Where were the Vanderbilts socially, even 5 years ago?"[10]

In fact the myth of the Four Hundred in society was dictated by McAllister, not Caroline Schermerhorn Astor. The stout, pudgy McAllister, noted for his outsize handlebar mustache, called Mrs. Astor "Mystic Rose," after Dante's Mystic Rose in Paradise around whom all heavenly figures revolved, and it was he who spilled the beans about the Four Hundred. "There are only about four hundred people in fashionable New York Society," McAllister boasted on March 24, 1888, to a reporter from Horace Greeley's *New-York Tribune.* "If you go outside that number you strike people who are either not at ease in a ballroom or make other people not at ease . . . who have not the poise, the aptitude for polite conversation, the polished and deferential manner, the infinite capacity of good humor and ability to entertain or be entertained that society demands."[11] And so the Four Hundred were born.

There were more than four hundred names on the *Social Register,*[*] that official arbiter and who's who of all names "in" society. Condé's name was, to him alone, conspicuous by its absence. Of course, to succeed as a top-class fashion publisher that would

---

[*] The *Social Register* was first published in the 1887 by society publisher Louis Keller. It was a product of Gilded Age excess, published biannually. Its first edition included mostly families from early settlers. The only Jew and person from new money included was the publisher Joseph Pulitzer. Keller also owned *Town Topics* before selling it to the scandalous William d'Alton Mann. Malcolm Forbes bought the *Social Register* in 1976.

need to change. Like McAllister's father, he would need to marry an heiress to fast-track his nameplate into society's bible. At the age of twenty-nine, in 1902, while he was still acting as business manager at *Collier's*, Condé's resolve to marry well was rewarded.

Collier had introduced Jeanne Clarisse Coudert to Condé at a riding weekend in New Jersey a few years earlier. She was a tall, slender unconventional beauty whose aura of chic and wealth made up for her receding chin and bulging eyes. It was Collier's social prominence, horsemanship, and personal affiliation with Condé that first attracted Clarisse. That Nast was one of the highest-paid executives in America, touching the salary of the president of the United States, gave her faith that he was not after her money. And she had bags of it. But that was Clarisse from the start—selling Condé short.

Granted, the Couderts were "old" money. They had immigrated to the United States in 1823, at the urging of none other than Gen. Gilbert du Motier, marquis de Lafayette, the French aristocrat and friend of George Washington. The first Coudert—a Bonapartist who was obliged to flee a defeated France—settled in New York. In 1853, his three sons, Frederic, Charles, and Louis, founded one of the leading international law firms in America: Coudert Brothers.* Clarisse, the youngest of six daughters and one son of Charles and Marie (née Guion) Coudert, was born in 1878. Charles developed respiratory problems in the early 1890s and died on Bastille Day, July 14, 1897, at his Middletown, New Jersey home. He was sixty-three.[12] When the terms of the will were made public, the bulk of his estate was left to his wife, Marie, naming Charles's brother and senior partner in Coudert Brothers, Frederic, as his executor. Almost immediately there were rumors of a second will. Those with wagging tongues whispered that Marie was "mentally

---

* Coudert Brothers LLP was a leading international law firm for more than a century. Among its clients were the governments of Russia, France, and Great Britain as well as others, notably that of Venezuela. In the 1980s it represented Muhammad Ali, Air France, and Coca-Cola, among others. Coudert Brothers was dissolved in 2006 when it failed to reach a merger agreement with the firm of Baker & McKenzie.

unstable," that the family had never accepted her, and the Couderts had clubbed together to persecute and conspire against her.[13]

Around ten days later the "second will" turned up, again naming Frederic as executor. But this time, Marie was only mentioned as "having been provided for" during Charles's lifetime. Marie was left nothing, while the entire estate valued at some $150,000 went straight to the seven children of the marriage.

As Clarisse was the only child living at home full-time, the situation must have been dreadful for both the nineteen-year-old and her mother. But worse was to come. By mid-November Clarisse was cited in *The New York Times* as the child who brought legal action against her mother to preserve her father's wishes, as per the second will. She demanded that her uncle Frederic remain executor of the estate: "Mrs. Coudert objected to the appointment of her brother-in-law on the ground[s] that he had denied that his brother was the owner of real estate owned in Middletown New Jersey and part owner of the property of the firm Coudert Brothers, in which her husband had been a partner," the *Times* asserted. Marie Coudert claimed that this made him prejudiced: "Mr. Coudert denied that he had taken any such position as was attributed to him by his sister-in-law."[14]

That Clarisse was still a minor lends some credence to her mother's position. But Marie was battling against the odds. In her submission to the courts Marie claimed that her late husband had had undue pressure put on him. Further, he could not have been of sound mind to write her out of his will. That the second will had been written four months before Charles's death indicated to her that her husband had also succumbed at long last to the family pressure against her. Marie's lawyer, John Townshend, also implied that Charles had transferred his ownership of shares and the Fifth Avenue offices to his brothers for one dollar in consideration, and that Frederic and Louis were trying to hide the true worth of their dead brother's estate.[15]

Months of haggling and bitter negotiation ensued. What must have hurt almost as much as being written out of her husband's will was that Clarisse had allowed her name to be used by Frederic

Coudert to fight on against her mother. The bitter nature of Marie's lawsuit against her husband's estate, when Frederic was reputed to be one of the sharpest minds in family law in America, meant that an out-of-court settlement was bound to be reached. Its terms were never made public, and on January 5, 1898, the judge ordered the second will to go to probate.[16] It should have stood as a stark warning to Condé of things to come. Evidently Clarisse had strong opinions. She intended to be heard—and hang the consequences.

Still, this was only the first of the Coudert family feuds regarding wills. When Clarisse's sister, Grace Coudert, died at Versailles on June 5, 1909, she left her estate to her brother-in-law, the duc de Choiseuil, who was the husband of the eldest Coudert sister, Claire. Clarisse and her sister, Aimée, married to the American consul accredited to Java, Frederic Brenning, contested that will, too, claiming it was wrong of Grace to leave family heirlooms "outside the family." Surely Grace had been under the influence of the duc de Choiseuil, since she was residing at the Choiseuil family home during her last illness, *n'est-ce pas?*[17]

Condé and Clarisse were married on August 19, 1902, at St. Patrick's Cathedral in New York City. Even on their honeymoon Condé realized that the strong bonds of French ancestry and Catholicism would not be enough to make Clarisse a good helpmate. Condé thought he loved her, and as a romantic, he hoped love would conquer any problem. Naturally he found her attractive, even though she was not a classical beauty. True, she was elegant, possessing tremendous grace, and she had an instinctive flair with clothes. Her dark-brown wavy hair was pinned up in the fashion of the day to frame her face. Some thought her overlarge brown eyes beautiful and her gaze forthright and penetrating. Her detractors, like Edna Woolman Chase, thought that they resembled a dead fish's. Like Condé she had a fine straight nose, if perhaps slightly long. Her upper lip was thin, her lower lip full, often giving the impression that she was pouting. She had white, slightly buck teeth and a conspicuous overbite. Although dissecting her individual features it makes for a rather unattractive description, Clarisse certainly had a presence. Everyone said she made a striking impression on first sight. Combined with her strong personality, she was a force to be reckoned with. And yet, despite her age—she was twenty-four and the last of the sisters to marry—Clarisse was undeniably spoiled and immature. Condé, nearly six years her senior and a lean, dashing man of experience, making a large noise in business, was prone to indulge her whims with a tendency to paternalism.

Clarisse, in return, worked her social contacts to ensure that Condé's name—alongside those of his mother and sister Estelle—appeared in the *Social Register*. Only then could Clarisse breathe an audible sigh of relief, for she wouldn't have it said that she'd married beneath her. But Condé's bride could not be prevailed upon to include Condé's brother, Louis, and his sister Ethel.[18] What Condé had not yet realized was that Clarisse would never let him forget that his swift entrée into society was entirely due to her. Clarisse never learned that Condé *earned* his place there and would forever change that same society's complexion through his pioneering publications.

Eleven months after the wedding their son, Charles Coudert Nast, was born. Their daughter, Natica (pronounced "Nat-EE-ka"), followed in 1905. Hidden within Natica's name hangs an amusing tale. As the family gathered at the baptismal font for Natica's christening, the priest dipped his fingers in the holy water and looked over at the family group. "And what is this beautiful little baby girl to be baptized?" he asked. Clarisse, in a "quick clear and emphatic" voice replied, "Natica." The priest lowered his hand. "It is not an acceptable name. It is not a saint's name." Clarisse's eyes flashed. "Nonsense." It came from the Native American for "Mary," she advised, ordering, "You may proceed." The priest bowed and stepped away from the font. "Perhaps one of the godmothers would kindly like to offer her name for this occasion," he suggested as he retired to his office to allow the family some moments to discuss the matter. Clarisse was incandescent, but somehow was persuaded that "this time she was not going to get her way, at least not right now." One of the godmothers, an aunt named Margarite, more than likely suggested that her name might suit the priest. And so the ceremony resumed and was completed.

Undeterred by the turbulent priest, however, Clarisse made a dash for the priest's office and altered the baptismal certificate before the ink had dried. She "tinkered with it until she was satisfied" and returned to the rest of the family with a smile. More than twenty years later, when Natica was vacationing in Havana, Cuba, she heard her name called out by a group of little girls. It was the first time she'd heard of anyone else with her name. So she asked some Cuban friends if they had heard her first name used locally, and they all agreed they had. "Natica" was a diminutive of *Natividad*—Mary, Our Lady of the Nativity. Clarisse was right after all.[19]

After Natica's birth Clarisse became restless, believing that life held more than the role of wife and mother. Rightly or not, she believed that she could be a great soprano and reminded Condé that prior to their marriage she had achieved some success. What's more, she'd been taking voice lessons for several years. So in 1906 Clarisse decided she should go to Paris for advanced coaching. And why not? Her sisters Claire and Daisy* lived there quite happily.

Around the same time, Condé was disturbed to learn from the family doctor that Clarisse suffered from the same "phantom" instability that had haunted her own mother. And so a "nurse," Cora Jane Richards, whom the children called "Dicky," was engaged to accompany them. While Clarisse dallied among her sisters' artistic friends in Gay Paree, Dicky became the children's surrogate mother. In New York, Condé quit his lucrative job, and began life anew at the Home Pattern Company.

---

* Daisy (her real name was Léonie) had married Franck Glaenzer, who was a wealthy Parisian. She often sang at the salons on the right bank of Paris, enchanting the French composers Fauré and Debussy at the salon of Winnaretta Singer, princesse de Polignac. The other sisters were Aimée, who married Frederic Brenning after the death of her first husband, McKenzie Semple; and Constance, who married William R. Garrison. Constance's marriage ended in divorce, and soon after she moved to Paris to join Daisy and Claire.

7. HOW TO BUILD A NEW WOMAN'S RAILROAD

*Appearances are deceptive—and Fifth Avenue
is so imperfectly lighted.*
—*THE HOUSE OF MIRTH*, EDITH WHARTON

They say that behind every great man is a woman rolling her eyes. Thankfully Condé had no such opprobrium placed on his aspirations, once Clarisse had swanned off to Paris to become a great soprano. If Clarisse had counted on her sisters to support her efforts, then she was a poor judge of their nature. Claire, duchesse de Choiseuil, was happy to introduce Clarisse to the atelier of the aging sculptor, Auguste Rodin, with clear instructions that Rodin was her very own private property. Of course the most exciting modern artists, musicians, and writers wafted through the sculptor's studio.[1]

While Claire was asked to sing in salons—as any duchess with a voice pleasing enough to the ear was prone to be—the competition to gain entry to the homes of the *salonnières* on either bank of the river Seine was fierce. Back then the uncrowned queen of the Left Bank was the American playwright, novelist, and poet Natalie Clifford Barney. Her "Fridays," as her salons were called, positively dripped with panache and flair, exuding their influence on a carefully stage-managed setting. For some sixty years Barney held sway over the literati of France, Britain, and America from her home at 20, rue Jacob. Some of Barney's favorites when Clarisse attended her Fridays included Sinclair Lewis, Gertrude Stein, T. S. Eliot, Isadora Duncan, and Rodin's secretary, the

Bohemian-Austrian poet and novelist Rainer Maria Rilke. The
Right Bank boasted the musical salon of Winnaretta Singer, princesse de Polignac (and daughter of Isaac Merritt Singer), who
gave the first big break to Claude Debussy, Maurice Ravel, Frederick Delius, Serge Diaghilev, and Igor Stravinsky, among others.[2]
Theirs were just two of the many salons run by American women
of great wealth, where Clarisse longed to perform.[3]

While Clarisse passed a happy year in the heady, sensual, glamorous world of luxury and excess in a Paris seemingly without
boundaries, Condé bet on himself and his investment in the Home
Pattern Company in New York. The company was incorporated on
September 23, 1904, with a working capital of five hundred thousand dollars. Condé's money men were Horace S. Gould, E. E.
McWhiney, and John R. Turner, who were also the first directors.[4] Condé's own injection of expertise and capital came later, in
1905. While Condé was a visionary publisher in every way, he
would only have his first start-up publishing title in 1939 with the
creation of *Glamour*. From the outset he determined that his talents lay in improving existing publications. He firmly believed,
too, in his business axiom, "Spend More Make More." It was Condé's "maddening sense of detail" and easy elegance that would
soon make him a household name.

Yet it was an unexpected incident that forced Condé's departure
from *Collier's* in 1907. The offices of the Home Pattern Company
stood just opposite William Green's printing plant on West Forty-
fourth Street. Condé's manager, Theron McCampbell, looked out
casually and saw flames licking at the windows of the print shop,
and swiftly ordered his staff to leave the building in an orderly
fashion. Fearing that the inferno would ruin the company's original patterns if the printing plant walls gave way in the heat, Mc-
Campbell arranged for the most valuable patterns to be thrown
out a back window. Racing into the street, he collected them and
brought them to safety. Then he organized a volunteer fire brigade
until the New York City Fire Department arrived on the scene.[5]

Apparently no one inside the building saw or smelled the blaze until McCampbell alerted its chief engineer. That was at 6:15 P.M., but it was already too late. Three of the upper floors of the four-story building were completely engulfed by flames before the fire department, which sounded four alarms and called two large tug boats adapted to hose the conflagration with river water, was able to bring it under control some three hours later.

Even though McCampbell was congratulated for his quick thinking, Green's printing plant was mostly destroyed. They had been the printers for a number of journals, including *The Smart Set, Town Topics, Ellis Mail Order Papers, Wine and Spirit Gazette*, and *Ladies' Home Journal Patterns*. At the time the *Ladies' Home Journal* had its offices in the same building. Since Condé had negotiated the franchise to "own label" the Home Pattern Company's products to *Ladies' Home Journal Patterns*, the fire was devastating to both companies. McCampbell told *The New York Times* that Green's printing plant had experienced two other fires at a previous location, but that building's sprinkler system had put those out quickly. McCampbell told the newspaper, too, that the printers were within two weeks of installing the same system at their current premises.[6]

Condé's help was needed to replace their printer, preferably one with better precautions than Green's. Condé was torn between leaving *Collier's* and helping McCampbell out of a tight spot. To boot, within weeks of the fire, the family's nurse, Dicky, wrote that she had had quite enough of Paris. It was no place for the children, or indeed herself. Of course Condé wanted his children to return to New York with Dicky, even if that meant leaving the restless Clarisse to her bohemian pleasures. Rather than look on the return of the children as a distraction, Condé was thrilled to have Dicky care for the children in the family home, while he set about making his fortune.

Yet fire was not the only threat facing the Home Pattern Company. While Condé had successfully transformed the fortunes of the original business by creating regional franchises for "own labeling" and securing a national "brand" advertised as *Ladies' Home*

Journal Patterns, the market was underdeveloped. Home-dressmaking patterns were still seen as free gifts in dry goods and department stores throughout America. The idea that advertisers—who held the financial success of any journal in their hands—might actually pay for advertising with these dressmaking patterns was simply ludicrous.

Condé's vision changed all that. He *agreed* with the advertisers, stating that the individual patterns, even patterns in catalogs, were indeed loss leaders. That said, he maintained that the *fashion news* contained in the dressmaking sheets demanded—even commanded—women's attention. Condé had realized that women, not men, did most of the buying in shops, and that they responded well to his patterns. Within three years of his taking over the Home Pattern Company, he had built up its advertising revenue from a paltry nineteen hundred dollars to four hundred thousand annually.[7]

In changing the preconceptions of advertisers, Condé was aware that he also ran the risk that they might place their money with the competition. In 1907 daily newspapers had begun to advertise free patterns as a means of increasing circulation. The result was devastating to the dry goods stores. So devastating that shops in Boston sent a petition to the city's newspapers: "The advertising of patterns in the daily newspapers tends to conflict with the interests of the dry goods interest. . . . These [pattern] departments are maintained as a means of attracting customers to the stores, and liberal expenditures are made, considering the sales, by the distribution of what is termed fashion sheets."

Theron McCampbell added: "The newspaper patterns are as a rule put out by irresponsible manufacturers. Naturally, the publishers of newspapers are not in a position to judge the relative merits of patterns, and if they innocently flood the market with poor patterns they will be doing a great injustice to the original pattern business as conducted by the merchants of the country, who have invested millions of dollars in it."[8]

The newspapers soon saw the light, or rather the implied threat from dry goods and departments stores. But Condé's company had other, more serious competition, too. There was the well-established Butterick Patterns—which he had ousted at *Ladies' Home Journal* with his patterns and advertising campaign. There was also a bespoke pattern business in the fashion and society magazine *Vogue.* To gain ground against this more threatening competition, Condé instituted a regionalized national sales force that would target large stores and buyers as well as advertisers. As its pattern books came out, there would be demonstrators who would make the rounds of their region to show how to get the most out of a Home Pattern. Still, Condé's true brilliance related to something no other pattern maker had done before: the creation of sizes.

Neither Butterick nor Arthur Turnure's *Vogue* thought size mattered. In fact *Vogue*'s pattern business was the most prosaic of all Condé's competitors. According to Edna Woolman Chase, one day a woman named Rosa Payne strolled into *Vogue*'s offices suggesting they print a pattern she'd made. Its editor, Josephine Redding— an unstylish wearer of sensible shoes and large hats—thought it might be a good idea and agreed. All the reader had to do was snip a coupon from the magazine, mail it with fifty cents to *Vogue*, and "in due course" the reader received the pattern "hand-cut by Mrs. Payne on her dining-room table. . . . The problem of pattern sizes was simple. There was one, and it was a thirty-six."[9]

Of course once Home Pattern devised sizes, others followed suit. Nonetheless most copycats graded their patterns upward or downward from the standard size thirty-six. Only Home Pattern individually drafted its sizes after careful study of the proportions. Each size became its own master pattern.[10] Again, it was a winning formula. Condé's "maddening sense of detail" had made the company's, and his, first fortune.

Still, though he knew that Home Pattern was a small canvas for his talents, in 1908 he became distracted again by Clarisse's return from Paris. She hadn't come back to the family town house cloaked in triumph with a string of professional singing engagements tucked neatly under her stylish belt. Jealous and disappointed, Clarisse demanded that Dicky leave, to Condé's and the children's horror. Although Clarisse was their mother, she was not

maternal. The children adored Dicky, and so did Condé. Nonetheless, Clarisse squeezed into her rightful place, and Dicky was
only allowed back in the family home to care for the children when
they were sick. Condé quietly maintained contact with her outside
the house. After all, Dicky was the children's rock, and he would
always remember and support her.

Amid this personal chaos, professionally Condé had also been eye-
ing the creation of Arthur Baldwin Turnure, *Vogue*. Just how long
he had been following the society magazine's fortunes is anyone's
guess, but Condé's eye for detail coupled with his ambition meant
he was most likely struck by *Vogue* from its first issue—and how
he could improve it.

Turnure was a talented developer of businesses. He, too, studied law, only he obtained his degree, entered the law firm of Van-
derpoel, Green & Cummings, and was admitted to the bar. But the
law held little fascination for Turnure, and he began a paper called
Art Age, followed by *Art Exchange*. He then sold the paper and became art director at Harper & Brothers. There Turnure was responsible for the first richly illustrated edition of *Ben Hur*.[11]

Turnure was simply mad about beautiful books, and was one
of the nine founding members of the Grolier Club, established
in March 1884.* Like Robert Hoe, the printing press manufacturer and bibliophile who invited the eight other founding members to his home to create the Grolier Club, Turnure's great
passion was "to foster the study, collecting, and appreciation of
books and works on paper, their art, history, production, and
commerce."[12]

The Grolier Club, so *The New York Times* declared, "ought to
have . . . a great influence on the art of book-making. . . . Its
professed object is the literary study and promotion of fine book

---

* The club was named after Jean Grolier de Servières, duc d'Aguisy (1489–1565), who
was secretary to the court of Louis XII of France. He was a great bibliophile and
patron of the Aldine Press of Venice, noted for its rich bookbinding.

production. . . . There are now 20 members. Among these are representatives of Harper & Brothers, D. Appelton & Co., Scribner's Sons, Dodd Mead & Co., Houghton Mifflin & Co., and various artists, authors, printers and bibliophiles."[13]

A graduate of Princeton, class of '76, Turnure and his friend Harry McVickar were sons of New York's high society, and they counted many of the Four Hundred among their friends. Turnure told McVickar he wanted to quit his job at Harper & Brothers sometime during 1891, and invited McVickar to join him in a publication dedicated to society and New York City's culture, as its art director. McVickar helped Turnure to secure 250 godparents for their new journal. Among the more famous were Cornelius Vanderbilt, Charles Oelrichs, Peter Cooper Hewitt, Percy R. Pyne, and Mrs. William D. Sloan.[14] But it was its first editor, Josephine Redding—she of the sensible shoes and big hats—who came up with the name of their new enterprise. One day she was thumbing through the *Century Dictionary* (one hopes not in alphabetical order) when she happened upon the definition of the word "vogue":

Mode or fashion prevalent at any particular time; popular reception, repute, generally used as the phrase "in vogue": as, a particular style of dress was then "in vogue"; such opinions are now "in vogue."[15]

In truth Josephine was an extraordinary choice as *Vogue's* first editor. She heartily disapproved of the fashions of the day, and she was not herself remotely stylish. For her, "Women today are all covered with humps. Big, humpy sleeves, humps on their hips, humps on their behinds; it's nonsense."[16] Where all chic women strived to pour their figures into life-threatening shapes with the aid of corsets, Josephine remained quite undefined in her square ways. Indeed, she was behind the novel—and at the time bizarre—idea of showing creations for "stout" women. It was an exercise the novice publication did not repeat, so shocked were the readers to see women who were utterly unlike anything "in vogue." Still, Josephine insisted that the McVickar illustrations merely denoted maturity, since a "lady" could never grow fat.[17]

The inaugural issue of *Vogue* carried a declaration by Turnure, published just above his signature: "The definite object [of this enterprise] is the establishment of a dignified, authentic journal of society, fashion and the ceremonial side of life, that is to be, for the present, mainly pictorial. . . ." No other weekly published at a cost of ten cents—or an annual subscription price of four dollars—could boast such a claim. Nor indeed would one want to repeat any of its several pages of "jokes," such as the one under a half-tone drawing of two young women in animated conversation:

PENELOPE: I'm in awful luck.
PERDITA: What's the matter?
PENELOPE: Engaged, and I have still eight new dresses of which I will never have a chance to try the effect.[18]

Initially *Vogue* had few photographs other than those of society men and women out and about town and country, pouncing on whatever game, recreation, or sport was in season. It was heavily illustrated with drawings of the latest dresses; but generally these had no captions or any mention of the designers. Features concentrated on interior design, reported by society's best-known lesbian, Bessie Marbury[*]; men and sports, written anonymously in

---

* Elisabeth Marbury (1856–1933) was a literary and theatrical agent, whose office at the Empire Theater in New York was the hub of theatrical life. She and her companions Elsie de Wolfe (1859–1950) and Anne Morgan (1871-1952), youngest daughter of J. P. Morgan, bought Villa Trianon at Versailles. Villa Trianon is an early-nineteenth-century house in the town of Versailles, at 57 boulevard St-Antoine. It is being restored by its current owner. The property abuts the park of Château de Versailles, but it has nothing to do with either the Petit Trianon or the Grand Trianon, though the house's proximity to the château surely caused an earlier owner to name it "Villa Trianon." (Source: email from Mitch Owens, who wrote an article on "Elsie de Wolfe's Iconic Bath at Villa Trianon," *Architectural Digest* March 6, 2018.) Miss Marbury's good friend Elizabeth Arden bought her Maine farm, "Maine Chance," and turned it into a luxury spa.

the feature titled "As Seen by Him"; special features such as "Seen in the Shops," "Smart Fashions for Limited Incomes," "On Her Dressing-Table," "The Well-dressed Man," and "Playhouse Gossip"; and only the best society events, *Vogue* patterns, and well-intentioned advice to the wealthy, like, "One should always be kind to [servants] . . . I always make it a point to be scrupulously civil to inferiors."[19]

Over time, any society event worth mentioning, particularly in London and New York, received as many column inches as the magazine could afford. Whenever there was a society wedding to report, *Vogue* was there. In its first three years the most notable of *the* society weddings were of Britain's future prime minister H. H. Asquith to Miss Margot Tennant, and the American heiress Consuelo Vanderbilt to the ninth duke of Marlborough, Charles Spencer-Churchill.[20]

Of course *Vogue* was oblivious to the fact that, as Consuelo wrote later, "I spent the morning of my wedding day in tears and alone. . . . A footman had been posted at the door of my apartment . . . ," indicating that she was expected to bolt if she possibly could.[21] It did, however, report on her lovely lace lingerie, white silk stockings and shoes, and her wedding dress, with its high collar, long tight sleeves to the elbows, and tiers of Brussels lace cascading over white satin. *Vogue* was agog with the description of the court train, "embroidered with seed pearls and silver," and how it was designed to fall from the new duchess's shoulders in billowing glory. Finally, there was a description of her tulle veil and wreath of orange blossoms.[22]

Condé saw that the magazine was ripe for acquisition. It was in financial trouble. McVickar had drifted away from Turnure, but not before a litany of arguments concerning *Vogue* was overheard by the staff. Josephine, whose single-mindedness in fashion and devotion to making pets the main point of interest, never really had the plot to lose. Turnure knew that *Vogue* positively yowled, meowed, and chirped, and told the dear lady that her services were no longer required. However, he severed the connection with Josephine without having a viable replacement. So in time-honored fashion, Turnure called upon family, his sister, the pretty and sunny-dispositioned Marie Harrison, to be *Vogue*'s next editor. Still, *Vogue*'s owner was not heartless toward his former employee. He remained in contact with Josephine through their mutual interest in the Reform of the American Society for the Protection of Cruelty to Animals (RASPCA), a charity of which he was the practical organizer, until his premature death from pneumonia on April 13, 1906.[23]

Condé agreed that *Vogue* delivered on the comings and goings of the idle rich—where was the "in" place to play golf? Or who was aboard John Jacob Astor's yacht *Nourmahal* after the America's Cup races? Better still, *Vogue* let its readers know who had not been invited. It also pronounced on what was chic in the cut and color of a man's morning coat, not to mention which ladies' styles would "declare oneself out of the mode." But for some while Condé could tell that Turnure's initial promising thrust had weakened—in the main, because he could not attract enough advertisers. It was fine trying to sell advertising to society, but Turnure was unable to break into the luxury brands like the manufacturers of pianos and automobiles, which should have been represented in his magazine. The reason was simple enough: *Vogue* did not appeal to a moneyed, aspirational readership.

On the other hand, Condé was confident that he could attract the female reader and advertisers after his success at Home Pattern. And it was on that basic premise that he wanted to buy *Vogue*. That meant ignoring the book of wisdom from William Randolph Hearst and Joseph Pulitzer, who believed magazines could only be viable by building circulation. Instead Condé took a leaf from Fred Munsey's book, owner of the thriving *Munsey's Magazine*. His theory was that the best way to increase circulation was to produce the magazine for much less than it costs you to make—and have advertising create the profit. In this Turnure's *Vogue* had signally failed.

Long before his last illness, Turnure had lost his oomph. He hadn't even noted that *Vogue* took advertisements for a new publication called *The Smart Set*, a "Magazine of Cleverness." He should have realized that *The Smart Set* was a threat to his title. If not, then what about the advertisements promoting *Cosmopolitan* and *Harper's Bazar* that *Vogue* featured?* Where *Vogue* still cost ten cents a copy and clung pointedly to its anonymous articles, *The Smart Set* hit its readers for twenty-five cents. But the reader got so much more by way of laughs and knowledge from its "unparalleled list of contributors, including from both hemispheres [intended to mean Europe and North America] the brightest men and women of the literary and social world."[24]

Turnure's sudden death, aged forty-nine in 1906, was a serious blow to *Vogue*. While he had never quite had his eye on the ball, he was the only one who looked to the title's bottom line. On his death his sister Marie Harrison and her young assistant, Edna Woolman Chase, were left to soldier on alone, rudderless. Marie's credentials as editor in chief were more than sketchy, and her business acumen nil. Worst of all, she had no idea whatsoever that she had stooped to advertising her competition to stay afloat.

On the plus side, *Vogue* had been published consecutively for fourteen years and had a certain charm for the cultivated and socially minded. Its small circulation of fourteen thousand generated stagnant advertising revenues of one hundred thousand dollars annually. Still, compared to the entire U.S. magazine market's increase of 50 percent in ad money in the same fourteen years—thanks to the vast increase in mass manufacturing—*Vogue* was behind the financial curve.[25] The magazine's relatively poor performance did, however, make its purchase more affordable. By uplifting *Vogue's* patterns with his specially designed multisize ones, Condé saw in his personal crystal ball that he could neatly double *Vogue's* income.

His vision was to make the magazine *the* journal for fashion

---

* *Harper's Bazar* only acquired its third *a* at the end of 1929. It got most of its fashion material from the Berlin magazine *Der Bazar*.

internationally. *Vogue* would be the first of his magazines to unite the art of dressmaking to other arts that were more highly regarded. Uniting fashion to the other arts was, for him, creating a "new railroad for the New Woman." He likened *Vogue*, and later all his publications, to "a tray of 2,000,000 needles where only 150,000 contained magnetic gold tips." To his mind, *Vogue* would become the magnet to those gold tips.[26] Condé was embarking on a journey of discovery that would take his *Vogue*, and the New Woman who appreciated his sense of purpose, to another level. *Vogue* was always his beginning, not his final destination, and he intended to take his readership on the most joyous ride of their lives.

And so, with a willing seller and an emotional buyer in Condé—always the best ingredients in good dealmaking—hands were shaken, preference shares opted for by the family, papers signed, and the trade was done between the widow Turnure, Mrs. Harrison, and Condé Nast. Without further fanfare, in the June 24, 1909, issue of *Vogue*, the masthead read:

> The Vogue Company, Condé Nast, President
> M. L. Harrison, Vice-President
> Theron McCampbell, Treasurer
> W. O. Harrison, Secretary[27]

While Condé did not necessarily rate Marie as an editor, he valued her role for the sake of continuity. As is customary in most buyouts, having bought her stake in the company, he signed a separate contract with Marie to remain as *Vogue*'s editor. The addition of the ever-vigilant Theron McCampbell as *Vogue*'s new treasurer signaled that Condé valued his people and their loyalty. McCampbell had demonstrated his constancy since 1905, and now Condé showed his own steadfastness and dedication to Marie and all that went before at *Vogue*. Edna would remain Marie's assistant, too. For several months, Condé changed nothing. He observed and learned. His staff couldn't understand what his motives were. In fact they felt invisible to their new owner. Nothing could have been further from the facts.

Indeed, "The arrival of a new boss not unnaturally filled us with trepidation, especially as the reputation that preceded him was hardly reassuring," Edna wrote fifty years later. "He was reported to be extremely shrewd and very adroit at concealing his feelings and motives. Furthermore, it was said that he had a Machiavellian way of questioning . . . so that they [his staff] might find themselves led into betraying weaknesses or ignorance that could create a most unfavourable impression."[28]

Edna couldn't know that Condé's genius was in not tinkering with the title until he was ready to launch his own new chapter in *Vogue*'s story. Equally, she hadn't realized that his keen eye had already seen something special in her approach to business. After a mere twelve years in New York, Condé was in a position to launch his brilliant concept of the class magazine.

PART II

THE MAN WHO MADE VOGUE, VANITY FAIR, HOUSE & GARDEN, AND SO MUCH MORE...

—————◄■►—————

One Civilized Reader is worth a thousand boneheads.
—THE SMART SET, OCTOBER 1914

※

8. THE GENIE BEAN COUNTER AND HIS CLASS PUBLICATION

He had a passion as cold and burning as dry ice,
the perusal of figures.
—EDNA WOOLMAN CHASE, *ALWAYS IN VOGUE*

At *Collier's* they called him Figure Jim. At Home Pattern Company, he was their "Figure Man," perhaps with a smidgen of double entendre. In truth, his passion was numbers. "He lusted after mathematics," a younger Edna, with thick brown curly hair, recalled. "Endless pages of figures and tabulated statements and comparative statistics covered his desk."[1] *Vogue's* treasurer, Theron McCampbell, had seen it all before at the Home Pattern Company, and admired Condé's grasp of the business world. McCampbell was also powerfully aware that the bookkeeping department had never experienced Condé's level of numeracy. It was an important gift that enabled Condé to read the tea leaves of the business accurately, testing the changes agreed with his editors at every turn. In fact, Condé was akin to a genie: granting the wishes of his editors based on the title's financial performance.

But Condé was so much more. He also had style. He knew where to eat—Delmonico's. To shop: It was hats at Dunlap and Knox. Boots were to be had at Slater's, and haberdashery at Budd's. Ready-to-wear suits—heaven forfend!—were purchased at Brooks Brothers, if absolutely required. Now Condé was in charge of telling his civilized readership—an elite class, if not high society—what to wear, how to act, and where they should be *seen* or *not seen*. He never doubted that he was up to the task.

First he had to make *Vogue* look and feel as if it were what it pretended to be—a magazine of high society *and* those aspiring to break into it. For that he would need to change *Vogue* from a weekly to a semimonthly publication, so he could maintain standards and become profitable. To widen the allure of *Vogue* he felt that the magazine needed to be more beautiful. Over time, glossy pages with a high rag content were ordered. The best artists, photographers, and writers were hired—best, that is, not in reputation but in style.

Clarisse, who had so far contributed little to her husband's business endeavors, turned her hand to redecorating *Vogue*'s offices. She showed Condé photos a fabulous Luxembourgian photographer called Edward Steichen had taken of her in Paris years earlier. Condé had to agree that Steichen's photographs were exceptional. None of the stilted, deer dodging a runaway horse and carriage there. A correspondence was entered into, but nothing came of it.

For reasons that have been lost to time, Clarisse disappeared for the first six months of her husband's new venture. Edna later criticized Clarisse's style, writing that her slash of red lipstick was "used more freely than was customary among women of her social standing at that time." She also felt Edna's cold breath on her neck as she was "turning the pages [of *Vogue*] with her immaculately white-gloved hands."[2] To this day, why Clarisse was not interested in *Vogue*, other than to change the interior decor of its offices, remains a mystery.

In New York, November 1909 was a testing time as demands for better working conditions and pay in the garment industry reached a crescendo. Mrs. Oliver Belmont,* an active suffragette and board member of the Equal Franchise Society,[3] responded handsomely to the garment workers' November call. When a young Jewish clothing worker, Clara Lemlich, strode to the front of a strike meet-

---

* Better known today as the former Mrs. Cornelius Vanderbilt and mother of Consuelo, duchess of Marlborough.

ing called by the International Ladies' Garment Workers' Union (ILGWU), everyone listened. On that November day some thirty thousand garment workers—mainly immigrant Italians and Jews—responded to Lemlich's strike call.

Already known as an ardent non-English-speaking orator among the Russian and Polish Jews of the Lower East Side, Lemlich called for a general strike. Previously she had organized workers against the notorious speedups and fines imposed on garment-factory workers. The speedups did nothing to improve the conditions or increase the hourly wages of the workers, Lemlich passionately reminded her audience. They served only to exhaust the workforce and benefit the booming mass market for department stores and mail-order houses.[4] Lemlich subscribed to Karl Marx's theories, learned at the Rand School, an institution for workers established by the American Socialist Party. The factory owners couldn't let them succeed. Rough tactics were used to keep many of their African American coworkers at their benches, putting them in the invidious position of being damned if they did or didn't join in.[5]

Mrs. Belmont agreed with Lemlich and thought their treatment disgraceful. She was their society activist heroine. She organized a meeting for them at the Hippodrome. Between seven and eight thousand people gathered to listen to the reasons for the walkout, but not before the strikers, who were without funds and were repeatedly beaten and arrested on the picket lines, called on the Women's Trade Union for help. Mrs. Belmont ensured that her friends and acquaintances joined the picket line to protect them. That December she formed a committee of illustrious New York women, which included Anne Morgan and Elisabeth Marbury, to bring the garment workers' cause to public attention in a meeting at the Colony Club. Elsie de Wolfe and Mrs. Philip Lydig* passed

---

* Born Ella Anderson de Wolfe (1865–1950), "Elsie" had made her own fortune in New York and was initially an actress before becoming widely credited with inventing the profession of interior decoration. Her 1913 book, *The House in Good Taste*, was the culmination of her ten years as a decorator and influence staging plays for

the hat in support of the workers afterward, collecting a staggering thirteen hundred dollars. Their actions—fueled by the *Evening Journal*'s nose for yellow journalism—brought this unprecedented uprising of immigrant women "out of obscurity into the public consciousness."[6]

For his part, Condé *knew* that this was what being a New Woman was really about: classlessness, independent-mindedness, caring for one another, exercising their civil rights, educating themselves in the rhetoric of the day, or simply being socially responsible. While a "Protocol of Peace" was eventually signed, the rumbling of labor problems persisted, and would have long-term repercussions on the development of the American fashion industry.

With peace restored for the present, Condé turned his attention to promoting himself. During that first full summer of 1910 after the acquisition of *Vogue*, the Nasts rented a home at Newport, Rhode Island—favored playground of millionaires—or in the words of *Vogue*, "the summer society capital of this country." There Condé's numerate mind could count the luxury carmakers, note the piano manufacturers, sail on the latest yachts. Most significantly, he learned to become one of them. He worked at learning to play a good golf game. He renewed his tennis skills from college. He joined the right clubs: The Racquet & Tennis Club, Riding Club, and Piping Rock. While his name appeared in the *Social Register* from the time of his marriage to Clarisse in 1902, to his mind he had yet to become a person of social refinement and prominence in his own right—an absolute necessity to a man who would credibly predict what was "in" or "out."[7] With his eagle eye taking in fashions—especially what the household staff and chauffeurs were wearing—a determination to succeed, and the ability to learn quickly, Condé soon became "that charming young pub-

---

the theater. She became Condé's favorite interior decorator. Mrs. Philip Lydig was better known as Mrs. Rita de Acosta Lydig, "the most picturesque woman in America."

lisher" so admired among Newport society. His handsome children and society wife did the rest.

Still, his first intervention in *Vogue* seemed to "big himself up" in his suspicious staff's eyes. "To his great satisfaction," Edna recalled in a voice tinged with vinegar, "he succeeded in persuading Mrs. Hermann Oelrichs and Mrs. Roekler to let their motor-cars be photographed for *Vogue* with chauffeurs and footmen standing by." Edna missed the point of his deep satisfaction when she went on to say, "The Ladies themselves did not appear, but it was considered a coup to have such distinguished vehicles complete with attendants."[8]

Edna should have seen that Mrs. Oelrichs's car and chauffeur were captioned as Mrs. Roekler's and vice versa. The blame, however, was firmly placed at the door of the printers. After Edna's assistant took the flack, Edna finally screwed up her courage and apologized to Condé. He listened and gently said, "My dear,"—a boss was allowed to address female staff in those terms back then— "don't let it worry you. These things happen. You know what women are. Those two aren't speaking at the moment, so they'll be mad, but they'll get over it. Don't give it another thought."[9] He already knew the Newport set well.

Edna missed, too, Condé's motives for the shoot in the first place. He already understood that a picture is worth a thousand words, and that the photographs were used to bring in the advertisers of luxury cars. Of course Edna's reasoning was sound, too. If the women had posed, Condé would have approached the ladies' couturiers, jewelers, and any other potential advertiser wishing to be affiliated with Newport's cream of society.

Edna learned quickly that Condé had a clear vision of the future, as any trendsetter must. It far outstripped her own. While he already had the reputation of an urbane, socially irreproachable—at times unapproachable—man, he was not considered warm or humorous. That was due to his restraint and shyness. The social polish he had acquired often made him appear formidable to the uninitiated. Nothing could have been further from the truth. Condé was sane, reasonable, fair, and hardworking. He loathed pretense and humbug. He loved simple pleasures like funfairs, ice cream, Schrafft's ice-cream sodas, and a good solid meal at an inexpensive self-service café, like the Automat. Although his marriage to Clarisse was not a happy one, Condé adored his children and made time for them whenever he could.

That summer of 1910, while Condé commuted between New York City and Newport each week, he had already proved himself to be a loving and caring father. He became, without Dicky and despite Clarisse's excitable nature, the children's bedrock and joke machine. When Coudert asked Condé, as they descended together in an elevator full of Condé's bankers, "Father, make a face like an elephant," what loving father could refuse? Every weekend when he returned to Newport, "he would bring us little gifts and surprises," Natica remembered. He'd "always take back with him 'for the art editor,' my crayon drawings for *Vogue* covers."[10]

What Condé saw in *Vogue* was the ability to create a class publication beyond any yet conceived. Oh sure, there were others like *The Smart Set*—touted as "Caviar for Dilettantes"—and the scurrilous *Town Topics*, which *one* subscribed to only in the name of *one's* servants. Aside from the *Ladies' Home Journal, Collier's*, and perhaps *Munsey's*, most magazine publishers were unaware that advertisements reflected on the publication. Condé, inevitably, believed such a publication would be viewed by its readers as irresponsible and slipshod. It was the lesson learned at *Collier's* in the battle against phony patent medicines. Yet if he could create a class publication where the reader knew precisely what to expect in fashion, editorial, *and* advertisements, then he believed he could change the industry for the better. Not only would the magazine be valued for its articles and fashion, but its advertisements would be equally useful to his readers.

To Condé's mind the real goal was a trusting interdependent relationship between the publication, the reader, and the advertiser. Broad appeal magazines offered far less to the reader and advertiser, for ads had their pages swiftly turned. That was no way for the publisher or his commercial patron to gauge the advertising value: "The manufacturer offering his goods to an audience gathered together by editorial comments of such broad human appeal has not the slightest means of knowing what proportion of them, if any, will be interested in the type and quality of the article he is offering," Condé wrote in 1913.[11] Advertisers in *Vogue* would know that their ads were accepted because they complemented its journalistic integrity and reader interest. Readers would appreciate their goods, since *Vogue*'s readers shared the bond of mutual self-interest. *Vogue*'s readers had the ready cash to buy their luxury goods.

While Condé was clearly not the first person to honor Jefferson's proposition that "all men are created equal," he recognized that "among the 90,000,000 inhabitants of the United States . . . there was a lack of 'equality'—a range of variety of man and womankind that simply staggers the imagination," he wrote. "This vast population divides not only along the lines of wealth, education and refinement, but classifies itself even more strongly along lines of interest."[12] This novel understanding of the divisions within society meant that Condé could increase the circulation of *Vogue* along the lines of interest, without compromising the contract of purity of purpose between the publication, the reader, and the advertiser. It was a simple, brilliant concept.

So it was out with the significance of circulation—other than to judge each issue for the number of returns from the wholesalers or newsstands. In came "manufacturers of pianos and costly motorcars, of jewels and yachts, the purveyors of Mediterranean cruises,"[13] the pricey summer camp for junior, only the best school guide for Mom and Dad, and even which dogs were chic to own. Couturiers were named and interviewed. Fashions from Paris dominated the news for women, as did what the country gentleman should wear when in town parading as the city gent. It was a formula that would catapult *Vogue* into the stratosphere—not in circulation terms—but as the preeminent fashion magazine in the world for more than one hundred years.

———————

Nonetheless the staff were agog when their new publisher inserted in the early February 1910 edition of *Vogue* that: "Beginning with the spring fashion forecast number of February fifteenth *Vogue* will be issued under a plan that will make for a bigger, a better and still more attractive *Vogue*. We will hereafter present the current notes of fashion, society, music, art, books and the drama in two splendid fortnightly numbers, each of them more than twice the size of the present ordinary weekly issue."[14]

Sure enough, the February 15 issue was bigger, bolder, and more beautiful. The newsstand price was fifteen cents, an increase of 50 percent. The annual subscription remained, however, at four dollars. It held sixty-one pages of advertising compared with some forty-seven from the year before, but the quality of the advertiser, too, had changed to manufacturers of luxury goods. Editorially it was fresh, bubbly, and sported the first-ever color-illustrated cover. A new art director, Heyworth Campbell, was hired. Though Campbell had no concept whatsoever of what made for good fashion design (so Edna judged), he had an intuitive flair for the right thing, instinctive good taste, and unerring style.[15]

Condé was building a business to appeal to those who attended the opening of the new Ritz-Carlton Hotel and smart fancy-dress balls. Costumes of famous women attending some of these included interior decorator Elsie de Wolfe as a Dresden shepherdess with a gown of blue taffeta covered in rosebuds, a harem ensemble worn by Mrs. Harry Lehr, Mrs. Hermann Oelrichs's superbly corseted Amneris, and Clarisse's sleekly clad Tosca. Their photographs were featured in the latest editions of *Vogue*.[16]

Inspired by Condé to spread her wings, Edna had a wonderful idea: to commission some of *Vogue*'s artists to design original fancy-dress costumes for publication. They proved very popular and soon enough, won the best and most-original costume prizes at the next fashionable ball. Florenz Ziegfeld saw them and simply had to have them for his "Midnight Frolics" on the New Amsterdam Theatre roof. In one swoop of innovation, Edna had broadened the appeal of *Vogue*. While Condé was initially against the idea—the more conventional use of theatrical designs being to his personal liking—he had to admit that creating a theatrical link for the magazine was genius.[17]

But why was Edna suddenly thrust into the limelight? Simply, Condé and Marie were no longer on speaking terms. Edna had been acting as the go-between for months. Apparently, when the company voted a 20 percent dividend for its ordinary shares, Marie and her sister, the former Mrs. Turnure—now Mrs. Frederick Stimson—cried foul. When Condé had bought *Vogue* both Marie and Mrs. Stimson opted to take *only* preferred shares, even though they had been offered both ordinary and preferred stock. The preferred shares, as is usual, had a fixed coupon attached at a substantially lower percentage than the 20 percent payable for ordinary shares. Condé was adamant. They had opted for preferred shares, with a steady, fixed return. They would receive the percentage coupon allotted to these shares.

So Mrs. Stimson and Marie sued. The case was heard in the New York Supreme Court on December 12, 1913. The plaintiffs argued that the ordinary stock of the company owned by Condé Nast and the advertising manager, Barrett Andrews,[*] should be declared void. Justice Eugene A. Philbin dismissed the case against Condé based solely on Mr. Stimson's, Mrs. Stimson's, and Marie Harrison's testimony. They confirmed that they had been offered ordinary shares at the time of the acquisition of *Vogue* by Condé but had declined these in favor of the fixed coupon attached to the preferred shares. They also testified during their several-days-long cross-examination that *Vogue* had gone from a weakened position in the market to becoming a market leader under Condé's leadership as publisher. While Condé had come to court prepared to give evidence, he never got to tell his side of the story. Justice Philbin dismissed the case as groundless before Condé had a chance to take the witness stand.[18]

---

[*] Andrews would become the advertising director for both *Vogue* and *Vanity Fair* by the end of 1914.

Condé's young lawyer, MacDonald DeWitt, could not have been happier. The contract DeWitt had drawn up for *Vogue*'s purchase from the Turnure family had stood the test of New York's Supreme Court. To boot, DeWitt and Condé became fast friends after their first successful battle, and DeWitt's law firm continued to represent Condé Nast Publications long after Condé's death.[19]

And so, by the end of 1913, Marie Harrison resigned. Edna Woolman Chase stepped into Marie's shoes as *Vogue*'s third editor. She would become a fixture at the helm of *Vogue* for more than fifty years. Often Edna was critical of Condé's new additions to *Vogue*'s staff. Some, hired for their dress sense, or because they danced gracefully, or because they played a smashing good game of bridge, became staffers by Condé's sole wishes. Some came aboard because they were fashionable "debs." By her own admission Edna "put up with them for varying lengths of time" but inevitably pronounced them as not being editorial "world-beaters" to her publisher. Condé, with an almost razor-like riposte worthy of any champion fencer, struck back voicing his own dislike of Edna's pet editors.[20] Each seemed to understand that too much paternalism and goodwill could be stultifying for a publication that was leading the way to the future on Condé's "new railroad" to transport the modern woman through the twentieth century. Despite disagreements, theirs would be a long-lasting relationship kindled by mutual respect and exasperation. As the magazine expanded and the British and French editions of *Vogue*—in 1916 and 1920 respectively—came into being, Edna would become omnipotent as editor in chief of all three.

9. WHAT WOMEN WANT

Romance lurks in strange places, but perhaps nowhere so much as behind shop windows.
—*BRITISH VOGUE*, EARLY JANUARY 1922

Romance. Beauty. Unconfined fashion. Being "smart." Fabulous music. And dances. Lots of dances. These were the "must haves" of the second decade of the twentieth century, and Condé gave them all to his audience, both its wealthier and its more aspirational readers. For those with tighter pocketbooks, there were also columns headed "Smart Fashions for Limited Incomes"; animal lovers had "Concerning Animals" (still warming *Vogue's* first editor's cockles); then "Sale and Exchange," and naturally, "Society."[1]

In response to the increasing unrest in the labor force in America, Condé's March 1911 issue of *Vogue* heralded an important addition to its many editorial departments—"Noblesse Oblige"—dedicated to how society intended to make a difference in the lives of those who were less fortunate. *Vogue* had blossomed into a periodical of more than one hundred pages advertising regularly such labor-saving devices as washing machines, foods such as Campbell's soups, and luxury goods, in addition to shops where one could be tantalized by the latest fashions. In Condé's eyes *Vogue Patterns* catered to the less-well-off cousins of women in fashion, who still belonged to high society.

Condé and *Vogue* were prospering. In March 1913 he took a financial interest in two other magazines: *House & Garden* (with a circulation of 24,000) and *Travel* (circulation 30,000). Together with his old friend Robert Collier, he also bought a monthly periodical called *The Housekeeper*, which had a circulation of 375,000. As was often the case, publishers bought titles solely for their subscription lists. For Condé it was for the subscription list *and* the relationship with its advertisers. *The Housekeeper* was published for the next year by the company of Collier & Nast until they closed it down. How Condé and Collier divided the spoils from the acquisition of *The Housekeeper* was never released. *Travel* never left the starting blocks; after garnering its subscription list, Condé swiftly handed over the magazine to its copublisher, Robert M. McBride.[2]

Now that the lawsuit with the Turnure family was firmly behind him, Condé could concentrate on the future of his young empire. Spring 1913 was a joyous season for the arts in America. In the Midwest there was a full-blown literary renaissance with three new magazines: *Reedy's Mirror* in St. Louis and the Chicago-based *Poetry* and *The Little Review*, which claimed to reveal unknown geniuses in every issue. Then the 1913 Armory Show introduced Americans to European modern art, and the old aristocracy shivered in disgust. Buffalo's sexually shameless heiress Mabel Dodge and the Paris-born son of an old New England family, Frank Crowninshield, were among the organizers.

Mabel Dodge brought her brand of fashion to America, too. Her weekly salon dedicated to bringing down social barriers flourished at her new Fifth Avenue apartment at the northern edge of Greenwich Village. Invitees belonging to the mighty Four Hundred had to listen to the likes of Carl Van Vechten, the first American critic of modern dance, and the anarchist Emma Goldman (imagine those aristocratic eyes popping out of their sockets!). Appearing, too, at Dodge's salon were the fiery Socialist and union leader, Big Bill Haywood; Alfred Stieglitz expounding on photography as "an art" (hear the tongues clicking?); and Isadora Duncan demonstrating the blessings of corsetless, free-form dancing.

Mabel's coorganizer, Francis Welch Crowninshield, called Frank or "Crownie" by his acres of friends, was the *Bookman* editor at the time. He was also the former *Century* editor, and *Munsey's* literary agent in London, a wit, connoisseur of arts and letters, and urbane proponent of gracious living. In his role as press agent for the Armory Show, Frank jumped to the defense of the European artists he loved "to stem the indignation . . . by hinting that there could be no possible harm in aesthetic experiments."[3] Mabel and Frank were determined to bring European culture to America, which in their opinions was in need of some substantial civilizing.[4]

Critics—the only animals who are paid in folding money to bare their fangs—feasted on their prey. Odilon Redon's artwork *Silence* was described by Kenyon Fox as making "insanity pay."[5] Perhaps Fox was right, since one of the founders of the Museum of Modern Art in New York, Lillie P. Bliss, bought it for her collection. It hangs in the museum today. Van Gogh's self-portrait was scoffed at by the *Evening Post* as "rubbish." Pictures by Degas, Picasso, Toulouse-Lautrec, Matisse, and other later household names fared little better. However, Marcel Duchamp's *Nude Descending a Staircase* attracted the greatest opprobrium of all: Nudes were simply unacceptable in polite society.[6] Frank remained adamant that "intelligent Americans everywhere determined to study the phenomenon dispassionately and on its aesthetic merits alone."[7] Despite the critics the Armory Show changed the way Americans thought, and some 250,000 people flocked to see it in both New York and Chicago. Frank was right: Curiosity triumphed over critique.

Taking some eighteen months to put together, the 1913 Armory Show brought European modern and experimental art to America for the first time. Opening on February 17, 1913, at the 69th Regiment Armory on Lexington Avenue and Twenty-sixth Street in Manhattan, it shocked, astounded, and delighted visitors in equal measure. It was a revelation to Americans, introducing them to fauvism, cubism, expressionism, and futurism. Several artists were hanged in effigy when the show came to Chicago.

In Paris, fashion had gone through an historic revival, thanks to its self-anointed king, Paul Poiret. Born into relative poverty in the 1st arrondissement of Paris, Poiret was at heart an *artiste*, with the temperament one would expect from such a being. Capricious and full of artifice, Poiret was nonetheless an inspired dressmaker. When the Parisian couturier Jacques Doucet took him on as an apprentice, both men prospered.[8] Poiret's "Hellenic" toga gowns were the rage of 1909. In 1910 his "Sultan Style" and harem pants stunned the reigning pope, Pius X, into denouncing the couturier's "Joséphine" gown, celebrating one hundred years of France's trendsetting empress. His garments were simple fashions intended to reinvigorate his urban aristocratic clientele. The political message, however, did not translate well across the Atlantic. Still, *Vogue*'s critics dubbed him, "the Prophet of Simplicity," quoting the couturier at length. "It is what a woman leaves off," Poiret asserted, "not what she puts on, that gives her cachet."[9] Condé knew that the more a couturier changed fashion, the more *Vogue* would become its gospel.

Indeed, *Vogue* recognized that all Parisian fashions sold magazines. It published a picture titled *Matinée de Septembre* (better known as *September Morn*) by the French artist Paul Chabas. The French art publishers Braun et Compagnie, led by Philippe Ortiz in New York, had hundreds of prints made of the painting, which won the hotly contested 1912 Medal of Honor in the Paris Spring Salon. Ortiz then sold the painting to a New York client to hang in the chic Hoffman House Bar. The only problem was that Edna had made an elementary licensing error, publishing the art without either Ortiz's or the artist's permission. Litigation was threatened if *Vogue* did not pay one thousand dollars immediately for its mistake.

Of course Condé agreed, expressing his fulsome apologies and admiration for the painting. A few weeks later he invited Ortiz out to lunch. Ortiz went, expecting some sort of a trap. Instead, Condé brought him into his confidence that Condé Nast Publications, Inc., had plans to expand. The company was in deep negotiations to acquire a magazine entitled *Arts and Decoration*. Would Ortiz consent to become its editor? Condé asked. Ortiz said yes. It was the beginning of a seventeen-year relationship.[10]

The incident was proof to Condé that *Vogue* should pay more attention to the arts generally. There seemed to be an increasing crossover between fabric design and fine arts. An article called "Dress Plagiarisms from the Art World" noted that cubism was being absorbed into fashion. Poiret sprinkled his silk with "square-cut confetti" patterns. A new cubist color, dubbed "mandarin," which was really a warm yellow, was the color of that year. Opening her first shop in early 1914, Gabrielle "Coco" Chanel was already making waves. She employed new clothing shapes from "simple draping" to the "broken silhouette" of the cubists. Chanel was the one to watch, Edna predicted. Within the year Chanel was deemed "elegant" by *Vogue*, but her style was "based on elements alien to elegance—comfort, ease, and common sense."[11]

Condé might have felt bewildered by the rapid pace of change affecting sales at one of his core advertisers—corset makers. First Duncan, now Chanel. All those lovely corset advertisers would be in financial difficulty if women suddenly decided to run around without. Edna persuaded Condé that *Vogue* should include articles on the virtues of the lightest of women's attire—lingerie—which would mention those heaviest of garments, corsets. The virtues of Valenciennes and Chantilly lace, point de Venise, and creamy point d'Hollande were extolled for their tasteful placements on corsets and lingerie. Never mind the whalebone. Corsets for all shapes and sizes were advertised. Romance was promised by rainbow silks spun from the sun-kissed fields of Nîmes in the South of France. Corsets were now "garments of romance" that "busy artisans have embroidered ready for the Modern Woman to wear."[12] Where Isadora Duncan was a great advertisement for chiffon scarves, her craze for aesthetic dancing, translating emotion into motion, did little to placate Condé's bread and butter. Sooner or later corset makers would have to evolve with the times.

Besides, corsets restricted movement far too much for the modern generation of men and women. Above all else, they loved to dance—and then dance some more. In *Vogue*'s "According to Him," couples were encouraged to "Take Up the Rugs and Let's Trot." They were diverted with tales of tea tangos or the maxixe—a Brazilian tango that contributed to later samba styles of dance—often featuring the husband-and-wife ballroom dance team, Vernon and Irene Castle. Vernon, born the son of a pub landlord from Norwich in England, and much like Fred Astaire,* became every man's image of the suave, debonair man-about-town. His wife, Irene, born in the northern New York City suburb of New Rochelle, was every woman's dream of grace and style. Together they became an international sensation, performing American dances like the turkey trot and the grizzly bear at the Café de Paris before storming Broadway. Condé befriended them, ensuring proper coverage in *Vogue* of Irene's elegant, flowing gowns, made by the British couturiere Lucile;† their invention of the Castle walk; and their other cutting-edge exploits. When they opened their club and dancing school, Castle House, for tea dances, Mrs. Stuyvesant Fish, Mrs. Anthony J. Drexel, and Mrs. William Rockefeller were sure to attend, and *Vogue* was on the spot to capture them in photographs.[13]

Condé saw that competition and change abounded everywhere. New voices in literary criticism were heard in *The Masses*, *The New Republic*, and elsewhere as writers aimed to teach Americans about all things European. The mighty H. L. Mencken—"the Sage of Baltimore"—and George Jean Nathan, the satirist and literary and drama critic for *The Smart Set*, added their muscle to the task of sweeping out the cobwebs left by all those writers of fustian who had passed before.[14] At long last Freud had been discovered by

---

* Once Fred Astaire came on the scene, Fred's dancing was compared to Vernon's—that is until he became more famous.

† Lucy, Lady Duff-Gordon, opened her first fashion house in 1893 at 24 Burlington Street in London, serving wealthy clientele, including royalty and theatrical stars. Her sister was Elinor Glyn, the screenwriter and romantic novelist.

Americans and was immediately and widely misunderstood. So was the British social reformer Havelock Ellis—physician, writer, and hero of the emancipated—who worked at changing everyone's thinking on sexuality. Everywhere the "intelligentsia" was vibrant with new ideas and passions.[15] This was the brave new world that Condé had to conquer. The problem was that as a class publication, *Vogue* could only reflect this world through its book reviews and commentary on the drama of life through fashion.

As early as 1913 Condé recognized that *Vogue* had its limitations, despite being a commercial success. Grateful to Edna for her tireless contributions, Condé paid off the mortgage on her first home when she and her husband divorced; he then gave her a check for five hundred dollars for a down payment on her new home.[16]

His acquisition of *House & Garden* in 1913 proved a winner too. Richardson "Dick" Wright had recently returned to the United States fresh from a medley of American newspaper postings in Siberia and Manchuria in 1911–12. He had been offered a job as a literary critic for *The New York Times* when Condé asked him to come instead to *House & Garden* as its editor. Condé certainly knew his man. Wright was also the president of the Wine and Food Society and the chairman of the Horticultural Society of New York, having already written more than twenty books on eating, drinking, and country pursuits.[17]

In June 1914 Wright became part of the furniture. He was a maven when it came to household furnishings, too, who could invariably spot the right piece for the right place in any room. That said, however, his first loves were cooking and gardening. And he was a seriously decorated gardener, winning countless horticultural prizes and writing some forty books on the subject. Wright and his wife had no children, but as both he and *House & Garden* blossomed, Wright founded scholarships for boys to private schools and institutions of higher education.[18]

With his new acquisition bedding in nicely, Condé turned his attention to a small magazine called *Dress*—intended to appeal to men—and bought it. Almost immediately he completed his spending spree with the purchase of the name *Vanity Fair* in the United States for three thousand dollars. The magazine had made a rather unsavory reputation for itself as a Broadway scandal sheet. Not the sort of publication that would appeal to Condé's core readers at *Vogue*, who valued society.[19] But Condé knew what he wanted even if it was unclear which road he might take to get there. He decided that the best course of action would be to combine the two titles into a new publication, which he called *Dress and Vanity Fair*. The first issue hit the newsstands in September 1913. It carried the latest in fashion, music, theater, international news, and other topics that simply did not fit into *Vogue*. Condé was its editor, but even he had to admit it lacked pizzazz. Who, though, could make it fizz like the greatest spectacle to hit New York in years—like the Armory Show?

Condé, of course, knew Frank Crowninshield, or rather, could be counted among Frank's miles of influential friends. Frank always lit up a room when he entered it, and no one—anywhere—ever—had a bad word to say about him. Often peering over his half-moon spectacles with his smiling blue eyes, an elfin grin peeking out beneath his neatly trimmed mustache, a practical joker given to performing magic tricks at the most unlikely of times, Crowninshield was everyone's favorite person to while away a languid hour. He was a must-have dinner guest and New York's most engaging raconteur. Even more wildly popular than Robert J. Collier, Frank would become Nast's anchor, best friend, and front man in dealing with the public.

When the first two issues of *Dress and Vanity Fair* were a relative flop, Condé turned to Frank for advice. Only a year older than Condé, Frank was born in Paris and spent his early childhood there.* His father, a respected poet and mural painter, took on the

---

* Frank was also great-uncle to Frederick Bradlee, an actor and author, and his brother, Ben, was editor of *The Washington Post* during the Pentagon Papers and Watergate scandals.

directorship of the American Academy in Rome, exposing Frank, along with his older siblings, Helen and Edward, to the best of European art. He was from a Boston Brahmin family and, like his father, married his love of prose with art throughout his career. Frank was the former editor of several highly regarded magazines, including *Munsey's*, *Metropolitan*, *The Century*, and *The Bookman*. Condé was certain that Frank was his man for *Vanity Fair*.

Frank was a gentleman of Edwardian urbanity, charm, and humor. "There is no magazine that is read by the people you meet at lunches and dinners," he told Condé. "Your magazine should cover the things people talk about—parties, the arts, sports, theater, humor, and so forth."[20] There had been at least three magazines called *Vanity Fair* at different times in the nineteenth century, and Frank knew that overcoming *Vanity Fair*'s lurid reputation as a sort of peekaboo periodical that "had never seen the inside of a club or lady's house" would be a challenge. Still, everyone in society had read Thackeray's *Vanity Fair*, and many would recall that it owed its title to John Bunyan's allegory *The Pilgrim's Progress*, in which "Vanity Fair" was conceived as a fabrication of evil, a fair at which were sold all sorts of preferment, titles, lusts, pleasures, honors—even countries and kingdoms—all for the devilish delight of the purchaser. Since the devil had been banished in modern America, it made sense, nonetheless, to name a magazine as a tribute to all the refined and epicurean pleasures and pastimes of the day.[21] Condé asked Frank if he would be interested in taking over as editor, offering free rein. It was a challenge Frank relished.

From the very first issue of Frank's *Vanity Fair* the limiting words "*Dress and*" were unceremoniously plunged into oblivion. It had something none of the other smart magazines possessed: a slick, modern soul. Slick like the Armory Show. Slick like the Twentieth Century Limited—the train that surprisingly ran on time, to the minute. Modern like forged-steel penknives, pencil erasers that did their jobs, precision-made automobiles (frequently called by their British name, "motorcars"), labor-saving devices that had never been touched by the phrase "built-in obsolescence," and children's toys that lasted beyond Christmas morning, sparing many a parental eardrum. From his first issue in March 1913 Frank saw to it that *Vanity Fair* would deliver on its promise and guiding principles:

> Vanity Fair *has but two major articles in its editorial creed: first to believe in the progress and promise of American life, and, second to chronicle that progress cheerfully, truthfully, and entertainingly....At no time in our history has the wonder and variety of American life been more inspiring, and, probably as a result of this, young men and young women, full of courage, originality, and genius are everywhere to be met with. This is particularly true in the arts....Let us instance one respect in which American life has recently undergone a great change. We allude to its increased devotion to pleasure, to happiness, to dancing, to sport, to the delights of the country, to laughter, and to all forms of cheerfulness....Now* Vanity Fair *means to be as cheerful as anybody. It will print humor, it will look at the stage, at the arts, at the world of letters, at sport, and at the highly vitalized, electric, and diversified life of our day from the frankly cheerful angle of the optimist, or which is much the same thing, from the mock-cheerful angle of the satirist.... For women...we mean to make frequent appeals to their intellects. We dare to believe that they are, in their best moments, creatures of some cerebral activity; we even make bold to believe that it is they who are contributing what is most original, stimulating, and highly magnetized to the literature of our day, and we hereby announce ourselves as determined and bigoted feminists.*[22]

What?

This was *not* a popular view among men of the times. But Frank had already spotted one of the most talented female writers of that generation lurking behind her eyeglasses at *Vogue*: Dorothy Rothschild, soon-to-be Parker. Edna had hired Dorothy as a copywriter for *Vogue*, writing descriptive ditties beneath drawings of lingerie and other dainty fashions. It was little wonder that Frank was able to steal away Edna's "small, dark-haired pixie, treacle-sweet but vinegar witted," since, in Dorothy's words, Edna "reigned over her staff in much the same way as Catherine the Great ruled Russia."[23] While Edna's memoir, *Always in Vogue*, cowritten with her actress daughter, Ilka, portrays *Vogue*'s editor in chief as the most reasonable of women, many agreed that she was an autocrat. She had to be.

On a personal level Edna demanded that female employees appear for work wearing hats, white gloves, and black silk stockings, despite paying them a pittance. For a woman like Dorothy who couldn't housetrain her dog, this was quite a tall order. Of course personal conversation—or worse, idleness—was forbidden, too. Dorothy could not help but mock the often severe, all-work-and-no-play Edna when a nameless *Vogue* editor tried to commit suicide by hurling herself in front of a subway train. How she missed her mark was anyone's guess, Dorothy said. Edna was outraged by Dorothy's response to the drama. But then, Dorothy always ridiculed the accepted norms, be they office paintings, marble tables, silk curtains, uniformed chauffeurs, or attempted suicides. She called *Vogue*'s plush reception area the entrance to a whorehouse. And while she scorned *Vogue*, she lusted after *Vanity Fair*. She dropped scores of her poems onto Frank's desk while pretending to pass by casually, until he finally agreed to publish her "A Musical Comedy Thought." So when Frank later asked Edna if Dorothy could transfer across to *Vanity Fair* in 1916, Edna couldn't push her delinquent charge out the door fast enough.

Dorothy immediately repeated all the scuttlebutt from the ladies' washroom, the one place Frank could not go. "How *could* Mrs. Astor think chinchilla appropriate for mourning?" was just one of the juicy tidbits he was given as an appetizer. Naturally Condé knew about Dorothy and her antics at *Vogue* and thought that if Frank wanted her, so be it. Frank was master of his own domain and had little, if any, interference from his tolerant publisher. "It was always . . . easy for [Frank] to persuade Joseph H. Choate* to write for us," Condé said proudly, "or Irene Castle to

---

* A distant relative, lawyer, and former ambassador to the UK (1899–1905).

pose for photographs, or John Sargent to permit our use of his
sketches, or Aldous Huxley to work on our staff or Joe Louis to
pass an hour or two before the cameras in our studio, or to persuade August Belmont and Harry Payne Whitney to cooperate in
photographing their horses in their stables, or Isadora Duncan to
help in a benefit dance recital."[24] *Vanity Fair* was on the rise, and
with such clever people as Fish as illustrator and Dorothy Parker
and Robert Benchley as writers, Frank had Condé's full confidence.

10. COUTURIERS, CUTTHROATS, AND CONFLICT

Fashion today needs a new master. It has need of a tyrant to castigate it and liberate it from its scruples.
—PAUL POIRET, *THE KING OF FASHION*

The year 1914 heralded a new age of conflict. At *Vogue* muscular battles were fought among department heads, customers, couturiers, and cutthroat, cut-price fashion rip-offs in the United States.

In February 1914 Edna Woolman Chase became managing editor of *Vogue*. She was thirty-seven years old, but with a head of thick prematurely gray hair worn in a high knotted bun at the back of her head. She could easily have passed for forty-seven. Petite, slender, with fine facial features and dark circles under her eyes, Edna was nonetheless forbidding to many on her staff. She herself thought it was her Quaker upbringing and sense of duty that drove her. She soon found that relations between department heads, even at this most paternalistic of companies, could be tedious. Edna's favorite bête noire was Barrett Andrews, *Vogue*'s advertising manager. Andrews, like Condé, held common shares in Condé Nast Publications, Inc., and had done rather well for himself. Edna held to the philosophy that nothing inflates the ego like a sudden windfall, and Andrews was no exception. Not that Andrews was a bad person. Back in 1910 he was walking back to the office when he heard screams coming from the Truck Company 7 building on East Twenty-eighth Street and dashed to help rescue the victims trapped in an elevator that had fallen seven stories.[1]

But it rankled with Edna that Andrews had benefited from Condé's favor in a way she had yet to experience, meaning the ownership of stock and trips to Europe aboard the latest ocean liner,
White Star's mammoth SS *Olympic*. Then, too, Andrews was a
Sphinx Club committeeman, giving him a status far beyond Edna's reach in the advertising world.[*]

What really made her gnash her teeth was Andrews pressing
her to give editorial credits for merchandise—much of it considered unworthy by Edna. Indeed, Andrews wagged a reproving fin-
ger at her, firing the unforgettable reprimand: "Remember, young
lady, it's the advertising department that makes it possible to pay
your salary." Such words would have never crossed Condé's lips,
Edna thought. She flung back at Andrews: "And you remember
that what I make is all you have to sell and if it's not right both
you and I will soon be out of jobs."[2] She would have been within
her rights to remind Andrews, too, that his precious Sphinx Club
was the first supporter of "truth in advertising" and that *he* was
on its vigilance committee.[3]

Independent of Andrews, Edna found some of their advertisers, *Vogue*'s real customers, also insistent on editorials for their
products. One such advertiser prevailed on her limited patience
insisting that his elasticated veil—practical but ugly—merited a
special editorial for its uses to nervous brides. When the meaning
of the word "no" seemed lost on him, Edna tossed her grenade. "If
I were to publish your bad-style veil and someone else's bad-style
shoes or handbags or gloves, we would soon lose that prestige
which you value and you wouldn't want to be in our magazine at
all. . . . I will not show editorially merchandise that I myself do not
think is correct." Then she referred the admonished manufacturer
to Andrews to place his advertisement. He mulled it over, then

---

[*] Founded in 1896 by a group of eight advertising men who called themselves the
Sphinx Club. In 1906 it sponsored the first advertising course at New York University. Later incarnations were called the Ad Club, then the Advertising Men's League,
before it finally adopted the name the Advertising Club of New York in 1915.

shook hands with Edna. He kept on advertising and asked her how *she* would improve his product.[4]

Philippe Ortiz, he of the filched *September Morn* by Paul Chabas, was flitting between New York and Paris for Condé when the acquisition of *Arts and Decoration* fell through. During that time they had assessed together the direction in which the couturier market was heading. Condé believed Ortiz would be the very man to create an exciting association or syndicate of Parisian couturiers, who were always jealous of one another's innovations. With *Vogue* as its creator and protector in the United States, Condé could offer a cooperative approach to conquering their rather large market in North America. Ortiz agreed.

In Paris, Ortiz met with Poiret. He thought the concept of a French fashion syndicate, particularly with regard to the American market, was a wonderful idea—as long as it came from *Vogue*. Poiret knew he had made many enemies on his way up, and doubted anyone would want to follow his lead. The next thing Ortiz knew, Poiret launched into a diatribe against American dressmakers. He had heard about the brazen thefts of Parisian fashions by copycat American manufacturers—you could hardly call them designers, could you? Poiret asked with a Gallic shrug. Then, unexpectedly becoming the voice of *all* French couturiers, Poiret bemoaned that their creations were not recognized, credited, nor paid for in America. These American *pirates* were menaces to the houses of Worth, Rodier, Bianchini, Lanvin, Chanel, Paquin, Redfern, and *bien sûr* Poiret. A French fashion syndicate with *Vogue* as its guardian angel would give them presence, even clout.

What the fashion houses hadn't grasped was that Condé's idea was as much about protecting *Vogue* as serving the needs of the French couturiers. Even though photography or illustration of French fashions was a cornerstone of *Vogue's* visual and editorial policy—American copycats could buy the magazine anonymously from any newsstand with the intent of imitating the styles on display. In sponsoring a French syndicate, Condé made it clear that copies from the great fashion houses would never appear in his magazine. To do so would be to unashamedly cut off his nose to spite his face.

Ortiz decided with Condé that it was also essential to invite the French publisher of the fashion magazine *La Gazette du Bon Ton*, Lucien Vogel (pronounced with a soft *g*), into the scheme. Vogel had trained as an architect but spent his life in publishing. He was a snappy dresser who fancied yellow waistcoats and checked suits, on the premise that it made him look the quintessential British gentleman. Of course his speech was peppered with Gallic "Mais voyons," "C'est extraordinaires," and "rigolos," so no one was fooled. When Edna eventually met Vogel, she compared him to a "dandified frog," with "round, protruding blue eyes and a chin lost in the flaring points of his exceptionally high white collar."[5]

Crucially, Condé and Vogel held each other in mutual high esteem. *La Gazette*, though a small magazine, was produced to the highest standards with hand-colored plates engraved on handmade paper. With the death of the royal family during the French Revolution, fashion as an art form also lost its patrons—that is, until *La Gazette* was born in 1912. Its arrival on the newsstands as a gossipy, entertaining magazine, free from the French penchant for intellectualization, was refreshing. It was precisely what Condé hoped to achieve at *Vogue* in the United States, too. *La Gazette* magically exuded an elitism by its association with culture. It waxed lyrical on the current craze in Paris for all things Russian, like the Ballets Russes, promoted by the remarkable impresario Serge Diaghilev. Until the Ballets Russes splashed onto the Parisian scene in 1909, fashion had been a world "dominated by corsets, lace, feathers, and pastel shades." *La Gazette* reported that Parisians soon found themselves "in a city that overnight had become a seraglio of vivid colors, harem skirts, beads, fringes, and voluptuousness."[6]

Vogel's wife was the vivacious Cosette de Brunhoff. She was the daughter of *Comoedia Illustré* publisher, Maurice de Brunhoff. Her brothers were Michel, an editor, and Jean, creator of the beloved children's book elephant, Babar. Lucien was the son of an illustrator and had worked alongside his talented father-in-law on the production of the Ballets Russes catalogs. Cosette understood magazine editing and art, making her and her husband a perfect team. Her brother Michel, who trained as a comic actor and would have been lost to publishing if only he had been able to remember his lines, was the editor of *Jardin des Modes*.[7] Both Vogel and de Brunhoff viewed fashion as a serious business—not mere eye candy but rather a pleasure "that cannot be judged inferior to the other arts."[8] From a love of fine paper to the best and latest print technology and intelligent layouts, the inaugural editorial in *La Gazette* could have been written by Condé too:

> When fashion becomes an art, a fashion gazette must itself become an arts magazine. Such is La Gazette du Bon Ton.... The revue will itself be a work of art: everything should be a delight to the eye ... nothing has been overlooked, no element will be neglected that is necessary to make the Gazette du Bon Ton *the ultimate revue of art and fashion, a precise chronicle of the elegant life of our day.*[9]

Condé, Vogel, and de Brunhoff were brothers-in-arms sharing the same business ideals. They served as inspirations—at times wet nurses, agony aunts, or agents to their immensely talented writers and illustrators—and they found kindred spirits in one another. Of course Vogel signed on to Condé's brainchild of the syndicate, bringing along with him the Parisian cream of couturiers.

At first glance it might have seemed odd that the British couturiere Lucile, Lady Duff-Gordon, the inventor of the "catwalk" fashion show and a journalist for *Vogue*, did not utter a syllable against the concept. Ordinarily outspoken, she might have shouted that such a cooperation was unjust to British designers. However, though two years had passed since the sinking of the RMS *Titanic* in April 1912, Lucy was disgraced, having been compelled to face a Court of Inquiry in London for her alleged cowardly behavior along with her husband, which Hearst's *New York American* newspaper encapsulated in the headline: DUFF GORDON SCANDAL, COWARDLY BARONET AND HIS WIFE WHO ROWED AWAY FROM THE DROWNING,

SIR COSMO DUFF GORDON SAFE AND SOUND WHILE WOMEN GO
DOWN IN THE TITANIC.[10] Lucy was still hiding out with Elsie de
Wolfe at the Villa Trianon, keeping a low profile.

As sabers rattled in European capitals in June 1914, *Vogue* covered *La Gazette*'s illustrators, dubbed by Edna as the "Beau Brum-
mels of the Brush." They were friends who had studied together
at the École des Beaux-Arts. As *Vogue*'s June 15, 1914, edition made
clear: "It is not so very long ago that for an artist . . . to have stooped
to dabble in a thing so materialistic as the fashions, or to have
mixed the colors of his palette for a scheme of interior decoration,
would have been considered a profanation of his talent. . . . Art
has come down from its heights and decided to carry off with it
the fascinating damsel Fashion to join in its gay revels and even
play for it the Muse."[11]

Indeed, *La Gazette*'s artists "made fashion the art of the day
instead of art being the fashion."[12] Though Condé did not speak
French, he was still a Francophile from birth, an avid follower of
French women's fashions, and had a keen eye for a transatlantic
ally. He personally sanctioned *Vogue*'s article on Vogel's Beau
Brummells.

What's more, Condé's influence inspired Vogel to promote in
his own magazine an edition in which a Beau Brummell would
draw a design of one of its couturier backers—seven of the greatest Parisian fashion houses of the day.* Until then the artists shared
in the magazine's profits, but now that a whiff of American commercialism had crept into *La Gazette*, they revolted. Edna was outraged. "If the great masters of old didn't think it beneath them to
faithfully render the silks and velvets, the ruffs and buttons and
plumes of the sitters," she fulminated, "I can't see why it should
be so irksome to modern-day fashion artists to let a subscriber see
what the dress she may be interested in buying is really like."

Their problem was that they had been asked to design a true

* These were Chéruit, Doeuillet, Doucet, Lanvin, Poiret, Redfern, and Worth.

fashion drawing, not a croquis, or impressionistic sketch. Vogel's idea infringed on the artists' copyrights, they claimed, although copyright at the time was more elastic than a rubber band. Eventually Vogel brought his artists around with the promise of more francs, and that he would also publish original designs by the Beau Brummells. Of course the same couturiers who kicked at the cheap copycat American designs also pinched the fashions the Beau Brummells created.[13] It was the same old story, the artists moaned.

Poiret thundered that he did not so much *copy* or *steal* designs, or indeed expressionist or cubist works, for his fabrics as use them to *energize* his brain "as one embellishes one's house, and to accumulate artistic riches from museums and from all the beauties of nature." It was certainly not theft, Poiret reiterated perhaps too forcefully, so much as an assimilation of current trends in the decorative arts.[14]

Unlike fashion designers in the United States, French couturiers were at the forefront of society, uniting bohemian and artistic communities with *Le Tout-Paris*—or anyone who was someone in Paris. They were feted by high society and *les élégantes*, who would only be seen in their fashions. After Serge Diaghilev's Ballets Russes exploded onto the Parisian stage, his costumier, Léon Bakst, became the first designer to erase the line between theatrical costumes and day wear by offering his theatrical collection to the public in 1912. Perhaps seeking to dethrone Poiret, Bakst worked with Jeanne Paquin to transform his costumes into "street dresses" redolent of the much-loved Ballet Russes production *Schéhérazade*. Each dress was given an evocative name like "Niké" or "Isis," making Paquin and Bakst envied "in the salons and artists' ateliers, in tea houses and theaters, in the halls of grand hotels and transatlantic steamships, and in deluxe train compartments."[15] *Vogue* also promoted Bakst's entry into women's fashion: "With his wonderful eye for color and for line, and his sense of picturesqueness, is it not natural that he should wish to create garments that could be worn by *les élégantes* of the twentieth century?"[16]

Within the year of the first Bakst-Paquin collection, Poiret had set about "assimilating" the latest trends, adding to the mix a sense of connoisseurship, often "orientalizing" or creating neo-classical gowns. His clientele was always wealthy, ranging from the demimondaines to the superstars of the day.

Still, Bakst was not the first person to call on the decorative arts in fashion. It had been the founding principle of Charles Frederick Worth, an Englishman, since he set up his haute couture house in Paris in 1858. Worth transformed individual dressmaking into an artistic extravaganza blending the visual and decorative arts. The velvet-coated, beret-wearing Worth produced only the most exquisite of fashions with hand decorations, embroidery, and handmade lace. He was the first to brand his "works of art" with a label bearing the signature of his atelier on each item of clothing. If you were a woman of significance you traveled to the House of Worth to have your clothing sculpted for you, whether you were from Cucamonga, New York, London, or Timbuktu.[17]

That was until the end of June 1914. When Archduke Franz Ferdinand, heir to the Austro-Hungarian throne, was assassinated in Sarajevo, Europe seemed to hold its collective breath. Few appreciated what the previous twenty years' of industrialization would do to modern warfare. Its great tools and inventions to advance society and unchain human energies would bring the world to the brink of the abyss. In the United States the large corporations that belonged to the men who built America—Vanderbilt, Morgan, Rockefeller, and Carnegie—took advantage of sales wherever they could be found, even in the financing and manufacture of munitions. By the time the guns of early August were fired, Condé knew he would have to shelve his plans for expansion in Europe for the foreseeable future.

Yet life somehow rolled on. The August 15, 1914, edition of *Vogue* featured the *Grande Semaine*—the sailing season's highlights—at Deauville, emphasizing the strong use of color in fashions and gratefully praising the women's release from the hobble skirt, which made the wearers walk like penguins. There was, of course, no mention of war. The issue had been "put to bed" before the archduke's assassination. In Paris that summer Edna's task was to woo the fashion houses, and bring back to America the best they had to offer for the coming season. Instead she locked horns with artists and couturiers over the poor sketches and inferior designs they tried to palm off on the American public. At the end of the day she brought back only seventy-five millinery fashions, and wonderment at the illogical and self-defeating ideals of the couturiers. If she—or Condé, for that matter—had spoken French, she would have known that it was merely the French way of making a point. Why agree when being ornery was so much more fun?

That July, Edna left Paris on the Hamburg America liner SS *Imperator*—the last German ship to sail from Cherbourg. Like Condé, she understood that a war could decimate the French fashion business. It had become a vital industry, providing France with a great deal of foreign exchange and world prestige. Without French designers working, *Vogue*'s pages, too, might dwindle to a thin voice in the fashion world.[18] And yet every able-bodied couturier felt honor-bound to join up. Designers Jean Patou and Paul Poiret were on special duties for the army, not only in creating chic uniforms but also in the relentless search for an "invisible" blue. Their myriad outfits not only failed in their mission—after all, how much blood, guts, and mud does it take to render "unchic" and "unblue" even the most carefully crafted garment?—but their dozens of shades of blue created confusion. "Which one is the correct color blue for the uniforms of the French army?" common soldiers were heard to ask.

While they fiddled with their "blues," inventive designers like Coco Chanel forged ahead. Unable to source exotic feathers or silks that proliferated before the war, Chanel, though still recognized in couture circles only as a milliner, successfully adapted locally available fabrics to her simpler designs of straw hats and felt berets reminiscent of the French countryside of her youth. Wearing Chanel's hats caught on as a symbol of patriotism. The military look became high fashion, with most of Paris's socialites clamoring for a Chanel hat and her own handmade pair of high-heeled military boots. The cosmetics industry flourished, too, as young women began wearing rice powder to remove the shine from their noses. Fashion, always a way of life for Frenchwomen, had become a patriotic and recreational pastime in war.[19] When the reclusive writer Marcel Proust skulked around Paris in the early evenings to check on his investment in the gay brothel on rue de l'Arcade, he too observed the transformation in fashions, writing: "Young women were wearing cylindrical turbans on their heads and straight Egyptian tunics, dark and very 'unwarlike.' . . . Their rings and bracelets were made from fragments of shell casings from the 75s," better known today as brass artillery shells.[20]

Vogue's journalist Anna Van Campen Stewart told Americans tales of zeppelins, darkened theaters and museums, sugar rationing, the closure of Paris's famous tea shops, the planting of vegetables in the capital's formal gardens, and the grazing of sheep on its lawns—mere inconveniences rather than hardships. When the war began Condé was forty-one and too old to fight, but he still wanted to make a personal contribution to help France and Great Britain. The question was how? And how, too, would Edna be able to fill Vogue's pages with fashion news during the conflict?

11. THE SPIRITED MRS. CHASE LANDS HER BIG FISH

You'll never get really smart women interested in this. . . .
They wouldn't dream of it; it has too much to do with trade.
—CONDÉ NAST QUOTED IN *ALWAYS IN VOGUE*

C ut off from France for women's fashions and Great Britain for men's styles, high-end retail and *Vogue* soon felt the impact of the war. Edna's task was finding an original idea. She said later it came to her while "riding on top of a Fifth Avenue bus one early autumn day."[1] While Edna was daring, she does not refer to riding on the roof of the bus. Until 1953, New York City's Fifth Avenue Coach Company ran double-decker buses.

Was it something she saw, like a flash of an advertisement for the silent film *The Magic Cloak of Oz*, starring Mildred Harris? Hollywood was still in its infancy, but its motion pictures were already enthralling the masses. Or was it a billboard for Olive Schultz's New York taxi service from the Women's Political Union on Forty-second Street that got her thinking? Perhaps Edna was counting all the Maxwell Motor Company's automobiles, one of the many advertisers in *Vogue* she needed to keep happy. After all, Maxwell had just begun hiring women for its sales force. Edna was mindful that their promotion came with a push and a shove from the suffragists Crystal Eastman, Mary Beard, and Inez Milholland, who understood that the "fairer sex" made great salespeople. Or just maybe it was the thought of Wilma K. Russey, who had recently shocked New York by deciding to work as a cabdriver, adorned in her leopardskin hat and stole, brown skirt, high tan boots, and long black gloves? Was Edna counting all those similarly clothed women in furs—who were also suffragists—cranking up their motorcars for another demonstration of girl power and control?[2] Or had Edna simply noticed fewer young men going about their business, wondering if they had volunteered for the American Ambulance Corps on Flanders' fields?

Later Edna claimed it was the recollection of doll shows that Arthur Turnure's *Vogue* had given between 1896 and 1898. She dashed off the bus at Fifty-seventh Street and rushed to see Henri Bendel, owner of the luxury department store that had invaded the long-standing residential area of midtown Manhattan. "If *Vogue* organizes an exhibition of original designs, created by the best New York houses and presented on living models . . . ," Edna ventured, "charges admission and devotes the proceeds to a French charity, will you head the list of exhibitors?"[3] Bendel, who had begun to import Chanel's hats only a year before the outbreak of war, immediately agreed.

By the time Edna saw Condé she had worked out a plan for the first-ever charity fashion show in New York. But Condé thought it was a terrible idea, "You'll never get really smart women interested in this," he said. Then, as he paced his office thinking, Edna was unsure whether his demeanor—the habitual small steps the hopelessly nearsighted Nast made, the ever-erect posture, his rigid gait—meant he was giving it further thought. A few moments later she knew where she stood. Her proposal smacked of society women "going into trade," Condé concluded. Besides, what society woman bought *American* fashions, Condé asked? It was one thing getting a luxury department store to agree to exhibit—indeed, any luxury department store in New York should be delighted with the concept. What did Edna expect? "That Mrs. Astor would sponsor her favorite cold cream? That Mrs. Belmont would reveal her preferred cigarette?" On reflection Edna agreed with Condé, but only for the time being.[4]

As a woman, she knew that society was changing rapidly. The world of her youth had vanished. Sooner or later women would get

the right to vote. Women cycled without chaperones, drove automobiles on their own, were mechanics, sales assistants, and even
fashion magazine editors. Gender lines had become blurred, and
the shorter skirts pioneered by Paris fashion houses since 1910
were at the heart of the change. Society had become divided, even
belligerent. Evangelical fire-and-brimstone advocates sought to
wipe out prostitution, gambling, and alcohol, taking the good fight
to the dens of iniquity. But there were few, if any, converts. The
sinners played on. "Boston marriages" among the New Women like
Jane Addams and Vida Scudder mirrored the households of Parisian lesbians. Edna, a recently divorced single mother, also knew
that the distribution of information regarding birth control—
Margaret Sanger's "What Every Girl Should Know," initially
printed in the socialist magazine *The New York Call*—had been
banned in 1913 by the U.S. Post Office under the Comstock Law
of 1873.[5] How could society possibly remain the same?

Even films had tired of the wilting heroine. The 1907 silent
movie *Down with Women* told the story of a man whose life was
saved twice, once by a woman doctor, then by a woman lawyer.
William Randolph Hearst's popular film serials that began in 1914
The Perils of Pauline showed forceful, canny heroines.[6]

If the war continued past Christmas, as many were certain it
must, it would devour the young men of Europe, perhaps even
America. Women would be needed to take on their nations' output. Not just poor immigrant women, but society women, too. British
upper-class women like Vera Brittain were joining the Voluntary Aid
Detachment (VAD) in droves as nurses, initially stationed at home
hospitals. It was not uncommon for some twenty nurses to share a
bathroom in freezing, ill-lit lodgings. Complaints about "tepid
water [that] trickled slowly into the bath" were common.[7]

So, undaunted, the spirited Edna resolved to try her luck. Society hostesses often opened their doors to her as the editor of
Vogue. She argued her point with Condé repeatedly, until he finally relented. If she could get the backing of New York's socialites, then he would agree to her idea.

For a woman born and raised a Quaker, Edna knew how to pick

a fight for a good cause. To succeed she would have to win over
one of New York's triumvirate of the Gilded Age: Mrs. Hermann
Oelrichs, Mrs. Oliver Belmont, or Mrs. Stuyvesant Fish. Theresa
"Tessie" Oelrichs was a woman of little humor, known privately
as "the drill sergeant," who ensured that society's rules were obeyed.
Alva Vanderbilt Belmont, infamous for forcing her daughter, Consuelo, to marry the duke of Marlborough, was hardly a sympathetic
character to Edna either. However, the last of these three, Marion
"Mamie" Fish, was haddock-faced, sharp-witted, and a self-styled
"fun maker." She also believed that the rich should create employment in times of high inflation, to relieve the plight of the poor.
While Mamie was famous for insulting her guests—saying of
Mrs. Theodore Roosevelt, for example, that she reputedly dressed
herself for three hundred dollars a year and looked it—she, at least,
should lend a sympathetic ear.

So Edna telephoned Mamie at her Garrison, New York, home,
and arranged an appointment to meet her.* Taking the milk train
to arrive on time at ten in the morning, Edna was told by Mamie's
secretary that her employer had changed her mind, saying that
"Mrs. Fish did not feel that the subject . . . would be of interest to
her . . . after all." Edna was defeated but not out for the count. As
she stalled for time, trying to think of another way in, and praying
she could prove Condé wrong, the secretary mentioned that her
son was an artist. Aha! thought Edna. *Vogue* publishes drawings,
the secretary prattled on, and wouldn't it be wonderful if *Vogue*
could look at them? How delightful it would be if his drawings
should find favor in her eyes. . . .

Edna's heart rose from the depths of her taupe spats. She said
she *could* look at his drawings but could not, of course, promise
publication. But even if *Vogue* couldn't publish them, she would
be happy to offer advice. Edna sensed her moment: "How interesting it was that she, his mother, should be working in this particular house . . . for . . . the kind of woman who should sponsor

---

* Behind her back Mrs. Fish got as good as she gave. Her Garrison house was irrev-
erently called "the Fisheries" by her socialite friends.

our own American dressmakers in these troubled times."[8] Edna *so* regretted Mrs. Fish's decision. The proverbial carrot dangled for mere seconds before the elated secretary leaped in, offering to help her employer change her mind and scurrying off. When she returned she announced that Mrs. Fish would see Edna in the rose garden in ten minutes. What a little maternal pride won't do for a brace of good causes.

Edna nearly put her foot in it when she claimed to know the great lady had complained to her own dressmaker that American seamstresses could create fashionable styles just as well as the French houses. Mamie fortunately ignored the remark. Mrs. Astor was telephoned at once, and Mamie asked her to join her in this worthy cause "this instant." The canny Mamie nodded at Edna, saying: "She will certainly be a patroness, and so will all the others. Can't afford not to."[9] Mamie was right. A full complement of New York's Gilded Age society signed up, giving birth to the first charity fashion show in the United States.

Condé was magnanimous in defeat. Even Clarisse took time out from her salon singing and interior decoration pastimes to help. Frank enthusiastically joined in, opening up his substantial contacts in the arts. Seven of the best-dressed women on *Vogue's* lists—which included Mrs. William K. Vanderbilt and Mrs. Harry Payne Whitney but *not* Mrs. Stuyvesant Fish,* who had the money but sadly no flair with clothes—were asked to serve on the show's jury.

New York's society women bargained with the Ritz-Carlton to hold the event for the benefit of the Committee of Mercy, which devoted its activities to the widows and orphans of the Allies against Germany. Thanks to the favorable publicity, the organizers were inundated with offers by American fashion houses eager to take part. But soon enough Edna had another problem on her hands: how to say no to *Vogue's* advertisers. Again, New York's

---

* It was whispered behind her back that Mamie could barely read or write.

socialites came to the rescue. They advised her to say that final decisions regarding the gowns to be shown would be made by the Fashion Fête's jury.[10]

Models to show the clothes were the next challenge: All professional models were wedded to their European fashion houses, and most lived in Europe. As advertisements were placed for women of a specific dress size, height, weight, age, and experience, Edna couldn't help noticing that her models came in all shapes and sizes, from all walks of life *except* modeling. Still, they simply would have to make do.

At last, in the ballroom of the Ritz-Carlton on November 4, 1914, New York's high society mingled with its dressmakers and models. Rather than feeling they were promoting trade, the society women who made it happen felt daring, almost revolutionary. Their debutante daughters sold programs, proclaiming that all the American designers were participating to help their brethren in need in France and Britain. The gray velvet curtains parted to reveal Mrs. Ray Dennis, costumed as the *Vogue* Girl, in an exquisite panniered dress, designed to be fuller at the sides by adding several extra layers of fabric. The Metropolitan Opera basso Andrés de Segurola, dressed as an early-nineteenth-century dandy, joined her. Their byplay had him wager that American dressmakers could not create designs comparable to those from France.[11]

AT LAST! AMERICAN FASHIONS HAVE ARRIVED, the *New-York Tribune* declared four days later in its two-page spread. "A New Dignity Now Attends the Phrase New York Dressmaker," so the subtitle read. The *Tribune* was fulsome in its praise:

> *The Fashion Fête was the simplest solution of a dilemma that has been thrust upon us through the war. Few suggestions are now emanating from Paris, and there are not likely to be many more for some time to come.... A group of society women and* Vogue *charged all New York's important establishments to put on their thinking caps and devise new models. The result was several hours of enjoyment for many people, many hours of toil*

*and anguish for the artists who designed the costumes and fi-
nally a large sum of money to enrich the Relief Fund for whose
benefit the Fête was held.... In its main purpose the Fête was
successful, for the most important result is the added dignity
and authority the American dressmaker receives as a consequence.*[12]

While Edna and Condé read the high praise for their extravaganza with pride, William Randolph Hearst, who'd recently acquired *Harper's Bazar,* saw his opportunity to bring Condé down a
notch or three. To Hearst's mind there was only one publisher to
cater to people of taste and breeding, and he was it. He owned six
magazines: *Cosmopolitan, Hearst's International, Motor, Motor
Boating,* and *Harper's Bazar* in the United States, as well as *Nash's
Magazine* in London. For a megalomaniac whose empire stretched
across the nation with his newspapers; the semi-independent news
agency, International News Service; Hollywood productions; vast
acres of ranches, mines, and New York real estate worth millions;
and the fact that the mayor of New York City ate out of his hand—
it felt like treason. Hearing Condé—a man who only owned three
piddling society magazines—praised so highly, like some kind of
hero, made Hearst downright angry.[13]

But Hearst's anger turned to fury when Condé sponsored another fashion show at Newport, Rhode Island, in the gardens of
Rosecliff, Mrs. Hermann Oelrichs's mansion. The evening affair
took place on Rosecliff's floodlit lawn, with the ballerina Lydia
Lopokova—the future wife of the economist John Maynard
Keynes—hidden in the great garden urn, shivering in her chiffon
costume as she awaited her cue. The point was made by the great
society in attendance that *Vogue* was upholding the finest tradi-
tions of smart dress. Advertisers clamored to join *Vogue's* pages.
So Hearst shot first, and let the consequences go to blazes. He
wasn't the sort of man to admit that there might even be any ramifications: Off to Europe by cable went his broadside attacking
Vogue.

Soon after, Philippe Ortiz reported that their charitable efforts on behalf of the Allies against Germany had fallen on deaf
ears. Instead, *Harper's Bazar*'s cry from the battlements shouted
that *Vogue*'s intention was clear: It was to abandon the French
couturiers. The only way to stop *Vogue*'s seditious actions was
to close their doors to the perfidious magazine and concentrate
their efforts on *Bazar*. Hearst would prove their generous paymaster; Hearst had money and influence; Hearst was a great
man.

Condé retaliated with a cool head. Ortiz was sent back to Paris
with a personal message to the recently reopened French fashion
houses. The French *Syndicat* (which Condé had helped form) was
offered a fully sponsored *Vogue* "French Fashion Fête" in New
York, with the same patronesses as the American fashion show.
The doors that had slammed shut in *Vogue*'s face only months
earlier were opened wide again.

Exactly one year later the French Fête took place at the Ritz-
Carlton. Although it was well attended by the rich and the notable, and highly praised for its organization, few French designs
were sold. Only Henri Bendel bought many of the fashions. The
sales were described as abysmal. Fearing such an outcome and
protecting his back, Condé had made a preemptive strike against
Hearst. Months before the fete, Nast created a charitable committee to raise money for the disadvantaged seamstresses of France.
In May 1915 he took the unusual step of writing an appeal to
Vogue's readership: "In accepting . . . the direction of [the Sewing
Girls of Paris Fund] in America, I have been impelled not merely
by that general sympathy the call of distress always awakens, but
rather by the strong conviction that *Vogue*'s readers who, perhaps have worn more French gowns than any group of women
in the world, will, in the coming to the aid of the sewing girls of
Paris, recognize not only a welcome opportunity, but a definite . . .
obligation."[14] *Vogue* was the first contributor with a check for five

thousand dollars payable to Le Sou du Loyer de l'Ouvrière.* When Ortiz was sent back to Paris with a check for one hundred thousand gold francs to give to the head of the workers' association, its representative wept.[15]

So much for Condé's and *Vogue*'s round one with Hearst's *Harper's Bazar*. Round two would surely follow.

---

* "A Cent for the Rent of the Female Worker" (in this case, the seamstress).

12. ENTER STAGE RIGHT FRANK CROWNINSHIELD—AND *BROGUE*

What Marie Antoinette was to eighteenth-century France,
Mary Pickford is to twentieth-century America.
—FRANK CROWNINSHIELD, *VANITY FAIR*

ogue carried the candle of sympathy for a war-torn Europe with features and photographs of Consuelo, duchess of Marlborough (now estranged from the duke), Lady Randolph Churchill, and Mrs. Paris Singer (daughter-in-law of Isaac Merritt Singer, inventor of the sewing machine) as "American Women Who Are First in War." Women from every quarter were joining up to make a difference, and as they did, *Vogue* offered helpful hints on how to get by with less.

American society women living in France mobilized their connections as well as their money. The American salonnière Winnaretta Singer de Polignac[*] worked tirelessly with Nobel Prize winner Marie Curie to create the first X-ray ambulance corps. With Consuelo, duchess of Marlborough, Winnaretta helped fund the 350-bed hospital in Suresnes on the outskirts of Paris (later known as L'hôpital Foch). Winnaretta urged her friends to join her and the pianist-turned-politician Ignacy Paderewski in financing humanitarian supplies to Poland. While the United States was not yet at war, American women strongly supported the Allies against the kaiser both at home and abroad. Though Condé and Vogel remained brothers-in-arms in a figurative sense, the war prevented

---

[*] Sister-in-law of Mrs. Paris Singer.

Condé from developing a closer relationship with *La Gazette du Bon Ton*.

Condé's fledgling publication *Vanity Fair* could easily have foundered on the shells fired during this first horrific mechanized war. Yet he had the foresight to leave the magazine, more or less, to Frank's intuition. That said, Condé did interfere once, early in the magazine's history, hiring Ewart "Red" Newsom to write the "Well-Dressed Man" column, an addition loathed by Frank. "A gentleman *knows* how to dress," Frank said.[1] The column made him feel as if he were some Seventh Avenue ruffian, hawking men's clothing, roaring above the din in Manhattan's garment district. Yet Condé was insistent. The column would attract quality advertisers—and so it remained.

Frank stayed true to his declaration of "cheerfulness" and "celebration" despite the war. *Vanity Fair* confronted how Americans coped with the often terrifying Machine Age, modern art, the emergence of big business, urbanization, the isms of the twentieth century—communism, fascism, futurism, modernism—and the rights of men. Each issue would have at least one feature article on two or more of these topics, couched in such a way as to be "cheerful."

Take Stephen Leacock's December 1915 composition "Are the Rich Happy?" Leacock informed the reader in the second sentence: "I have never known, I have never seen, any rich people. Very often I have thought that I had found them. But it turned out that it was not so. They were not rich at all. . . . They were pushed for money. . . . Pinched, I think is the word they use. . . . The fact that they ride home in a limousine has nothing to do with it."[2] The title's question is answered by an acquaintance of the author's, Sprugg:

I have seen Sprugg put aside his glass... after he had drunk his champagne—with an expression of something like contempt. He says that he remembers a running creek at the back of his father's farm where he used to lie at full length upon the grass and drink his fill. Champagne, he says, never tasted like that....

Wealth, if one has enough of it, becomes a form of social ser-
vice. One regards it as a means of doing good to the world, of
helping to brighten the lives of others, in a word, a solemn
trust.... There are cases among them of genuine, light-hearted
happiness. I have observed that this is especially the case
among those ... who have the good fortune to get ruined.[3]

Years later Condé claimed that Crowninshield's "interest in the
modern French art movement, at first, did us a certain amount of
harm. We were ten years too early in talking about van Gogh,
Gauguin, Matisse, Picasso, etc."[4] At the time Frank was peeved.
To him a "cheerful" smart magazine dedicated to showing the
latest also meant including what could be termed "revolutionary."
He had been promoting new writers and encouraging the most
recent trends in literature, yet no one balked or seemed to notice
that. Perhaps the fault lay with society? He predicted from the
outset that *Vanity Fair* would attract "young men and young
women, full of courage, originality, and genius," because they "are
everywhere."[5]

But that doesn't give credit to Frank's magnetic charm and
clairvoyance. He saw trends that would stick before they had taken
hold. Frank was at the heart of what made *Vanity Fair* simply *the*
magazine for smart people. It was the most reliable and accurate
"social barometer of its time."[6] From the outset, *Vanity Fair*
attracted—and continued to appeal to—the talents of such established writers, jouralists, movie stars, and public figures as Sherwood Anderson, Djuna Barnes, Clarence Darrow, Theodore Dreiser,
T. S. Eliot, Douglas Fairbanks (senior and junior), F. Scott Fitzgerald, Janet Flanner, Ford Madox Ford, Paul Gallico, John Maynard
Keynes, Stephen Leacock, Walter Lippmann, A. A. Milne, Bertrand
Russell, Carl Sandburg, William Saroyan, Gertrude Stein, Dalton
Trumbo, Walter Winchell, P. G. Wodehouse, Thomas Wolfe, and
Alexander Woollcott. That was due to Frank and a decent word
rate.[7]

He was the shining example of a tastemaker, regularly commissioning articles that accurately predicted trends that would leave

• Condé Nast as a little boy. (*Courtesy of private collection*)

• Condé Nast in his late twenties, around 1900, while he worked at *Collier's* weekly. (*Courtesy of the Library of Congress*)

• Condé Nast aboard ship with his indomitable mother, Esther. (*Courtesy of private collection*)

• Photograph of Clarisse Coudert Nast, Condé Nast's first wife, by Adolphe de Meyer, circa 1911. (*Courtesy of private collection*)

• Condé Nast and Frank Crowninshield at the fights. They were good friends with heavyweight champions Joe Louis and Jack Dempsey. (*Courtesy of private collection*)

• Cut-out stand-up photograph of Condé Nast and Frank Crowninshield in their golfing clothes, 1920s. (*Courtesy of private collection*)

• From left to right: writer Dorothy Parker, *Vogue* editor in chief Edna Woolman Chase (seated), Condé Nast, *Vanity Fair* editor in chief Frank Crowninshield, writer Robert Benchley. (*Courtesy of Condé Nast Publications*)

▴ Publisher Condé Nast (*center*) conferring with *French Vogue* editor in chief Michel de Brunhoff (*left*) and I. S. V. Patcevitch. (*Courtesy of Condé Nast Publications*)

▸ Condé Nast's eldest daughter, Natica, dressed in a wedding gown. Photograph by Adolphe de Meyer, 1919. (*Courtesy of the Library of Congress*)

▾ Frank Crowninshield photographed in 1945 with his arms crossed. He had already endured the loss of Condé Nast and his beloved *Vanity Fair*. (*Courtesy of Condé Nast Publications*)

• Newlyweds Condé and Leslie Nast playing backgammon. (*Courtesy of private collection*)

• Condé's daughter, Leslie Nast, as a baby. (*Courtesy of private collection*)

• Condé dancing in his famous ballroom with young Leslie. (*Courtesy of private collection*)

• View of the front of the house, Sands Point, from the front lawn and lily pond. (*Courtesy of private collection*)

• Cecil Beaton with a peacock posing on his arm, head turned slightly away from him. (*Courtesy of Condé Nast Publications*)

• View of the tennis court with the pool below and Long Island Sound from the Sand Points garden. (*Courtesy of private collection*)

Jack Dempsey, heavyweight boxing champion, wearing a dark three-piece suit, white shirt, and patterned tie. Dempsey wrote articles for *Vanity Fair* and both Condé Nast and Frank Crowninshield counted him among their friends. (*Courtesy of Condé Nast Publications*)

• Left to right: Alexander Liberman, Nina LeClerc, Michel DeBrunhof, Edna Woolman Chase, Iva Patcevitch, Thomas Kernan, Despina Messinesi, Peggy Riley (Bernier, Russell), standing at the entrance to *Vogue*'s office, 4 Place du Palais Bourbon, Paris. (*Courtesy of Condé Nast Publications*)

• Left to right: *Vogue* employee Dr. Hoguet; personal assistant to Condé, Mary Campbell; and Condé Nast, featuring war care packages in front of a Condé Nast Publications Inc. train wagon. (*Courtesy of Condé Nast Publications*)

▸ Rex and Leslie Benson, circa 1938. (*Courtesy of The Beaton Collection, Sotheby's*)

▸ Iva Patcevitch, successor to Condé Nast Publications as its president after Condé's death in 1942. (*Courtesy of private collection*)

▸ Opera singer, actress, and Condé Nast's lover, Grace Moore, wearing a fringed vest over a satin evening gown, posing for *Vogue*. (*Courtesy of private collection*)

▸ Portrait of Harrison Williams, Condé's friend and financial adviser, who helped ruin Condé Nast. (*Courtesy of the Library of Congress*)

• Leslie Nast playing piano at the 1040 Park Avenue apartment. (*Courtesy of private collection*)

• Waddill Catchings in 1936 while he was under investigation by the newly formed Securities and Exchange Commission. (*Courtesy of the Library of Congress*)

• Leslie Foster Nast in 1930. (*Courtesy of private collection*)

• Photograph of the famous ballroom at 1040 Park Avenue. (*Courtesy of private collection*)

their mark on society. Writers needn't be "known" for their way with words, as articles by Babe Ruth, Picasso, and Joan Crawford showed. Frank was a great egalitarian, equally comfortable talking to bohemians or waitresses as he was joking with the boxer Joe Louis or Mrs. Astor.

Taking on *Vanity Fair* just months before the outbreak of the Great War was risky. Who knew if the great American public was ready for the groundbreaking ideas Frank had in mind? But Condé believed in him, and that was good enough for Frank. So he took advantage of great Europeans seeking a safe harbor in America, like the 1916 article about "Sarah Bernhardt Here Again," attributing her enduring popularity to her ability to feed lines to her fellow actors. American writers living in Europe, too, made an appearance, like Gertrude Stein's "Have They Attacked Mary. He Giggled," in 1917, as did a portrait of the French-based American actress and theater entrepreneur Maxine Elliott.

Frank introduced the European photographers Baron Adolph de Meyer and Edward Steichen to America, "when their work was branded as wild and absurd"; reminding others later that "they are now the highest-paid photographers in the world."[8] He created the celebrity photograph. *Vanity Fair* was the first to include African Americans as part of its standard repertoire, like the actor-singer Paul Robeson, world heavyweight champion Joe Louis, and the Olympian Jesse Owens. Afterward, other household names would join their ranks.

Frank promoted fresh American and European artists and voices. Corey Ford (writing as John Riddell), Edna St. Vincent Millay (writing as Nancy Boyd), Donald Ogden Stewart, Robert Benchley, Dorothy Parker, P. G. Wodehouse, e. e. cummings, Aldous Huxley, Compton Mackenzie, Thomas Mann, and Robert E. Sherwood, among others, *all* wrote their first magazine articles published in the United States for *Vanity Fair*.

Frank's tastes for nominations to *Vanity Fair*'s "Hall of Fame" were equally eclectic. When the American-born Henry James was nominated, he said it was "because though, through his devotion to the cause of the Allies, he has become a British subject, we shall always insist on calling him 'our Henry James.' Because he has done more to reveal us to ourselves than any other American novelist . . . and finally because the British have welcomed him with open arms and we lose him with regret."[9]

Despite its occasional outrageousness—like Robert Benchley's "The Art of Being a Bohemian" in 1916; or Baron de Meyer's deeply disturbing portrait of the Russian ballet dancer Vaslav Nijinsky, whose madness is etched in high relief by the camera; or Dorothy Rothschild's (Parker's) poem "Any Porch," published in September 1915—*Vanity Fair* was Condé's and Frank's gift to smart people. With Condé's pioneering vision and Frank's dedication and hard work guiding their avant-garde contributors, it would be every thinking person's favorite read. Only twenty months after Frank took over the publication, *Vanity Fair* was the top-rated periodical for advertising linage of all American monthlies with some 403,219 lines, outstripping *Vogue* by some distance.[10]

Frank put the phenomena of all that was modern into words and pictures. The dance craze that has since been said to take off in the 1920s had already touched down in 1915. The emergence of café society, women's suffrage, cabarets, the automobile, Freud's and Einstein's theories, and talking about sex made "mugwumps"* of anyone who couldn't take pleasure in a universe smartly depicted with the lightest of editorial touches. *Vanity Fair* was, quite simply, New York. Hitching high society to the emerging café society that was evolving to replace the stodgy, closed world of the Gilded Age was an art at which both Condé and Frank excelled. Their parties were an effortless blend of the new and the old, a cocktail of the absurd and the sublime. But the parties hid a sound business decision, too. Condé's mind for figures always kept a tally of the most amusing and sociable people from Europe and America. He computed who attended, how long they stayed, how much it

---

* "Mugwump" was originally used for those who remained aloof or independent from politics. It's essentially a fence-sitter, best described by Dave Purchase in the electronic edition of *New Republic* 1997: "I'd say they mugwumped—you know, mug on one side of the fence, wump on the other."

cost per head, and who would be invited to the next party in a few weeks' time.

Frank's tremendous strength was his knack for making friends easily. He loved gags (especially sending telegrams signed by famous people), chess, bridge, and repartee. He was never without a deck of cards for a spot of sleight of hand with friends who, more often than not, popped in on a whim, like Harry Houdini or Charlie Chaplin. "Editorial lunches were brought in consisting of eggs Benedict, kippered herring, chocolate éclairs and *café special*," while it was not uncommon for him to submit expenses from the Automat or Schrafft's. Like Condé and Edna, he would often "go for a quickie" at the Automat opposite the office.[11]

Perhaps it was in one of these more relaxed moments that Condé discussed his "European problem" with his two trusted editors as they spooned their Horn & Hardart's rice puddings. The French market was closed to *Vogue* for the duration. The British market had been satisfactorily penetrated prior to the war, in no small measure due to the efforts of George W. Kettle, the London head of the Dorland Agency, representing Condé Nast Publications for advertising in Europe. Dorland's William Wood spearheaded the plan to sell *Vogue* at the best newsstands in the West End of London. So by 1914 some four thousand imported copies of *Vogue* had grabbed a toehold in the British magazine market.[12]

Edna bristled. She knew where the discussion was heading. The mere thought of further expansion horrified her. She vetoed any growth until such time as *Vanity Fair* had proved itself financially. Frank agreed that expanding during wartime would be folly, yet as a true cosmopolitan who had spent his entire youth in France and Italy, he felt that by turning their backs on Europe, they would be spurning civilization. Condé agreed. It would not be the first or last battle Edna would lose regarding the growth of the business. While he valued both his editors' opinions, neither of them had his vision or business acumen. Nor did they have a burning desire to show Hearst that *Vogue* would remain *the* fashion magazine of preference to society. In truth both editors regarded their magazines as private fiefdoms, but in Edna's estimation, expansion equated a dilution of her power.

The decision to consider a thrust into the British market was made for Condé by the war itself. By mid-1915 only one in three merchant navy convoys made it through the German naval ring of mines and U-boats in the Atlantic.* This meant that importing *Vogue* to Great Britain was not only dangerous but economic suicide. Paper supplies were swiftly rationed on both sides of the ocean, and nonessential shipping was all but banned. Despite a lack of support from Edna, Condé gave Kettle the go-ahead to form a British-based *Vogue* (affectionately referred to in-house as *Brogue*), using the Dorland Agency as its advertising agent. William Wood led the new management team, since he had been responsible for distribution of American *Vogue* in Britain. "Nothing which had made *Vogue* what it is will be deleted," the Dorland Agency promised potential advertisers. "On the contrary, each issue will be supplemented with carefully selected articles dealing with English society, Fashions, Furniture, Interior Decoration, the Garden, Art, Literature, and the Stage." All this exposure to the advertisers' main consumers could be theirs at a reasonable twenty-five pounds for a full black-and-white page, or thirty-five for a full-page advertisement in color.[13] (What British *Vogue* did not include at the outset was the seemingly trifling silver-screen news from an ersatz place then called Hollywoodland.)

Dorland attracted advertising from producers of fashionable clothing, such as Maison Lewis, Aquascutum, Gooch's Ltd., and Spunella, Queen of Silks; the world leader in cosmetics manufacturing, Helena Rubinstein; and London's chic department stores, including Whiteley's, Waring & Gillow, Selfridges & Co., and Peter Robinson's. Wisconsin-born Harry Gordon Selfridge had his start at Marshall Field's department store in Chicago and recognized the quality that Condé's publication would bring to the fashion world of London. Never one to miss an opportunity at self-

---

* This was one of the main reasons for America's eventual entry into the war.

promotion, Selfridge stated in the first issue of British *Vogue* that it was "a beautifully printed journal." From a standing start, the first issue of September 15, 1916 carried twelve full-page, two half-page, and fifty-eight box advertisements.[14]

While Condé was occupied with consolidating *Vogue's* international position, Frank's ultimate concern was with *Vanity Fair*. It should be like a nurse, always taking the pulse of its times, while remaining cheerful through its satire and criticisms of ostentation, while avoiding intrusiveness into private lives but exposing duplicity by public figures, Condé and Frank had agreed. Hearst had served two terms as a congressman in 1902 and 1904 and smarted under the nickname "William Also-Ran-dolph Hearst" for the myriad elections he'd lost. In contrast, Frank's interest in anything political was almost nil. His broader, less personal, yet more poignant canvas was epitomized by ramblings like Dorothy Parker's "The Office: A Hate Song" of May 1919. The opening lines read: "I hate the office; / It cuts in on my social life."[15] Who hasn't been there?

That said, once a reluctant United States entered the Great War in April 1917, articles began to appear by those who fought. American lieutenant E. M. Roberts had volunteered to join the Tenth Canadian Battalion and fought in Britain's Royal Flying Corps— the predecessor of the Royal Air Force—during the war of 1914–18. That Frank commissioned an article for publication in March 1918 titled "Excursions into Hunland" by an American who had joined the Canadian army,* and who had flown for some twenty-two months on sorties over northern France and Germany, was a political statement in itself. John Jay Chapman's "Mr. Wilson's Inelastic Intelligence," published in February 1920, was as political as *Vanity Fair* got in Frank's twenty-two years at its helm.

His most remarkable gift to young, unknown writers, artists, and photographers was giving them a hearing. His softhearted

* Canada had been at war along with Great Britain since 1914.

rejection letters ("Rejection does not necessarily mean a lack of merit . . .") always offered hope. Similarly, firing people was something he found distasteful. Above all Frank loved discovering new talent and bringing it onto his staff: "They have already proved their place as masters when *Vanity Fair* first sponsors them," Frank said. "But the point is that the world at large has never even heard of them, and may normally be expected to disregard them for several more years. It is *Vanity Fair's* function to continue resolutely and often, amid abuse and derision, to bring them to the attention of the world."[16]

Alas for Frank, talent brought mayhem along as its traveling companion.

13. FROM *VANITY FAIR* TO MAYHEM

Nietzsche's stuff was never syndicated. . . . Gloom may be all
very well for a lot of unshaven Russians, but for a good
hustling American, there's nothing like chasing sunbeams.
—DOROTHY PARKER, "THE FIRST HUNDRED PLAYS ARE
THE HARDEST," *VANITY FAIR*, 1919

Only Condé Nast was more surprised than Dorothy Parker
when Frank promoted her to drama critic early in 1918.
It had been mere months since Edna had "turned her over
to my tender care," Frank recalled.[1] She was talented but unproven,
Condé reminded him. Nonetheless Frank was in a pinch. Plum
Wodehouse, *Vanity Fair*'s drama critic, wished to take an indefi-
nite leave of absence to gorge his ego in his own theatrical productions. The alternative to Dorothy would mean that Wodehouse
would be forced to quit, since any drama critic worth his byline
would never take over in such circumstances. And why should
Frank create a ruckus? Wodehouse was going places, he argued.
Along with Guy Bolton, he had cowritten the smash-hit musical
revue *Miss 1917*, with music by Victor Herbert, Jerome Kern, and
others.[*]

How could Crowninshield refuse Wodehouse's request? Who
else on his staff but Dorothy had the ability to review New York
plays? he asked Condé. Since the United States was at war there
was a shortage of talented men available. Condé trusted his editors to explore the outer reaches of the envelope he'd created, and

---

[*] The pit orchestra was conducted by the unknown George Gershwin, who was paid
thirty-five dollars a week, marking the composer's Broadway debut.

having pointed out the negatives, he firmly supported Frank's decision. So Dorothy was given her big break as New York's only female drama critic. For her it was a meaningful distraction from thinking about her husband of seventeen months, Edwin Pond Parker II, serving in the U.S. Army overseas.

As "a tired business woman . . . seeking innocent diversion," Dorothy chose to review five of Broadway's musical comedies.[2] She would never let on that her choices were made to stave off the public's preoccupation with the war and the growing "Spanish flu" pandemic,[*] or that they were selected by Frank. The musical comedies gave her pen, assiduously dipped in satirical curare, free flow to cut deeply into four of the five musicals. A quick death followed. She even suggested for one, "If you don't knit, bring a book."[3] The fifth musical—*Oh, Lady! Lady!*—another Bolton, Wodehouse, and Kern collaboration—received her fulsome praise, and thrived. Naturally there may have been a tad of self-interest in her glowing review. If Wodehouse stayed on Broadway, she'd keep her job. In no time Dorothy's own bravura performances made her a *Vanity Fair* star—and a target for many Broadway producers' high dudgeon.

Dorothy became *Vanity Fair*'s Becky Sharp, and her spicy one-liners were on every New Yorker's lips. But her personal life was hardly scintillating. "It may be that a life of toil has blunted my perception of the humorous," she wrote. The truth was she found her married life a trial. Peace returned a different Eddie to her—a poor reflection of who he once was. Granted, she always claimed that she married him to change her name because she was a "poor" Rothschild. But she *would*, wouldn't she? Heaven forbid anyone should think that the flippant Dorothy was head over heels in love.

Once First Lt. Parker was shipped out to France, things would never be the same. As an ambulance driver, collecting the dead and wounded at night without the benefit of headlights, through

---

[*] The pandemic caused fifty million deaths worldwide, more than those who died in combat or of illness in the Great War. (*Source:* Centers for Disease Control and Prevention.)

the shell-pitted fields and often under bombardment, Eddie often found that his ambulance was nothing more than a hearse by the time he reached the nearest field hospital. Still, Eddie did his duty. He had become the man his fellow soldiers called "Spook," a great ambulance driver under enemy fire, until a shell burst before his eyes one night. When they found Eddie thirty-six hours later, the wounded he was carrying were dead, and he was a ghastly shadow. Only alcohol and morphine kept him glued together after that.[4]

Condé, too, finally admitted defeat on domestic bliss in 1919. Despite the parties, the children, and his business successes, his marriage to Clarisse was over. Never the most stable of women, Clarisse had tried—and singularly failed—to establish herself as a soprano, then an interior designer, then a stage designer, then an adviser on entertaining to Mary Pickford (including Miss Pickford's choice of clothes). As a stylish but aging society woman who saw her husband surrounded by beautiful women at *Vogue*, Clarisse was envious of her husband's success. However, no matter how she tried, she could not find any niche to make her happy. She was bitter that it had been *her* family name that raised Condé to the *Social Register*, and she constantly repeated the old plaint. The facts showed a different perspective. Though the Coudert name facilitated Condé's rapid rise to the *Social Register*, he had taken society by the scruff of its neck, given it a shake, and was already turning it into an unrecognizable and more democratic café society that welcomed people from business and the arts. Clarisse ignored that, wildly plunging herself headlong into her next "business" effort, which despite Condé's help always failed. In 1919 she moved the children (aged sixteen and fourteen) out of the family home at 470 Park Avenue, taking another apartment at 1000 Park Avenue instead. Publicly Condé was seen about town with other women on his arm. Whatever their differences, their religious faith kept them bound as husband and wife.

That's not to say that Condé was a saint. Indeed, his affair with the American opera singer Grace Moore had begun before he and Clarisse lived apart. Grace was born in a village in the Cumberland Hills of Tennessee, but her operatic voice and girl-next-door good looks made her a hit as the Metropolitan Opera's soprano. She was a "bottle lemon blonde" with flirtatious blue eyes and measured a mere five feet four inches in her bare feet.* Like many aspiring actresses and singers, including Barbara Stanwyck and Paulette Goddard, Grace got her first big break as a singer at the Black Cat Club in Greenwich Village before her career at the Met and in movies. One of Condé's later loves, Helen Brown Norden, described Grace as "an animated swizzle stick."[5]

Grace was a woman who reveled in her shapely figure as much as her voice and loved sex with Condé—always on the black silk sheets that she took everywhere with her. (And why not, since the great opera soprano Nellie Melba used to travel with pink ones?) Once, when Condé was staying at Claridge's Hotel in London, he forgot to check in his paramour who was arriving later that evening. While they were enjoying the raptures of their first night together in a while, the hotel manager knocked at the door and begged Condé to ask the lady to leave. In true prima donna style, Grace rounded on him: "I came three thousand miles to be with this man!" she shouted. "Now, you just get out of here and leave us alone!"[6]

By the time Condé began seeing her, her operatic career had been launched and she was widely known as the "Tennessee Nightingale." The first summer after his separation from Clarisse, Condé was cavorting with Grace among Le Tout-Paris, introducing her to all the notable, the great, and the outrageous in Parisian society.[7] A divorce, certainly for Clarisse, would have been a double whammy: It would free Condé to marry again and be a public rejection of her Catholic beliefs. For Condé, divorce would have been the best solution to avoid a scandal for Miss Moore. Although Grace was Condé's first publicly recognized lover, she was far from the last.

Despite the personal pitfalls and devastation caused by the Great War, 1919 was a boom year in America. The armaments in-

---

* 1.65 meters.

dustries in the United States and Great Britain absorbed many of the returning heroes into their businesses. American banks called "Chase" and "First National" were falling over one another to give loans to Germany's new Weimar Republic and cash in on the "peace dividend." The United States was preparing for its first international dominance of the world stage, with President Woodrow Wilson's Fourteen Points imposed on Germany in whatever treaty would emerge at Versailles' Hall of Mirrors. The price the Allies would pay for America's decisive entry into the war was scrapping Europe's old ways of balancing power.

But Wilson was a novice at the old games. He made the mistake of allowing Prime Minister Georges Clemenceau of France to take his place as the permanent chair of the proceedings, then compounded his error by listening to him. Once the voice of British Prime Minister David Lloyd George was added to the noxious European cocktail—siding with Clemenceau to "squeeze them until the pips squeak" and demanding outlandish reparations against Germany[8]—the seeds of World War II were sown.

For Condé the Armistice of November 1918 allowed him to dust off his international dreams. The following year, 1919, would be the new pinnacle for Condé Nast Publications, Inc., and planning began even before the New Year was welcomed in. For Edna that meant traveling to London to bring British *Vogue* into line with the successful class publication ideal, which in-housers called "the Condé Nast formula." She had resolved long before to stop its hybrid appearance as some kind of a *Vogue* incorporating *Vanity Fair*.

For his part, Frank longed for a return to his mother ship of culture, France, and to share his findings with the readers of *Vanity Fair*. Inevitable changes would need to be considered now that men were returning from war, too.[*] Robert Benchley's name was

---

[*] Women over thirty had been granted the right to vote in Great Britain in February 1918. On June 4, 1919, Congress passed the constitutional amendment giving women the right to vote, but this was only ratified on August 18, 1920.

mentioned to Condé as a potential managing editor. Benchley had spent his war writing blurbs for Liberty Bonds and working free-lance for *Vanity Fair* and *Life,* in those days a humor magazine. Dorothy, meanwhile, attended theatrical premieres not suspecting a thing.

The move to hire a managing editor came from the sudden death of Condé's dear friend Rob Collier. He had died of a heart attack the previous November, shortly after returning from France. Condé, Orville Wright, Joseph P. Kennedy (father of the future president), Francis P. Garvan (the government-appointed alien property custodian during the war[*]), and Finley Peter Dunne (the American humorist and editor of the *Chicago Tribune*) were among the pallbearers. It was an eye-opening blow for Condé. If *his* publications were to survive beyond his lifespan, a new generation would need to be brought on board and given some reins to hold on to.

By giving Crowninshield a young managing editor, not only would he be lightening Frank's load but Condé could also enjoy Frank's companionship in that first summer of peace. Frank had only one candidate for the job: Robert Benchley. Condé knew that *Collier's Weekly* was about to be sold, and that Benchley's name was at the top of the list to become editor of *Collier's* magazine. He wasted no time in interviewing Benchley, who agreed that changes were needed at *Vanity Fair.* Benchley told Condé that more serious articles and satire were necessary to raise the tone of the magazine. Condé immediately liked Benchley and hired him for one hundred dollars a week.

Dorothy had a rude shock when she came to work on Monday, May 19, 1919. Benchley was already head-down at his desk, sharing her office. He also had the foresight to buy Dorothy a bowl of roses to sweeten the bitter pill of his appointment. Crowninshield pointedly invited Benchley to have lunch with him at his club, the Coffee House, which still excluded women. On their return

---

[*] During both world wars the United States confiscated "enemy property," which included, among other assets, property, patents, and royalties across every industry.

Dorothy and Benchley exchanged nothing more than a soft smile while he studiously continued the article he had been writing. Then he dashed off to Grand Central for the 5:37 train to Crestwood Station, servicing Tuckahoe, Eastchester, and northern New Rochelle.[9]

Robert Charles Benchley seemed an unlikely boss, much less "best pal" for the playful Dorothy. He was middle-class, small-town New England. He was the former president of the *Harvard Lampoon*. At five feet ten and a half inches, slender, with thinning fair hair and blue eyes, Benchley was the outward antithesis of the diminutive, dark Dorothy. He was sensible where she was self-destructive. He wore long johns and galoshes, while she often forgot her coat. He didn't smoke, drink, or swear, and believed in being faithful to his wife. Though plenty of people found terrible things to say about Dorothy—with some cause—it was universally agreed that Benchley was a man for whom no unpleasant word could be uttered.[10] But the pair had in common humor and an unhappy childhood. When Robert's older brother, Edmund, was killed in the Spanish-American War, aged twenty-one, their mother exclaimed: "Oh, why couldn't it have been Robert?" An eight-year-old boy never recovers from such a statement, even when his mother is repentant.[11]

Until that first day Dorothy had only read Benchley's loony pieces for *Vanity Fair*. She scratched her head, trying to square the physical "Mr. Benchley" with the Benchley of the byline. There was no "leaping of the mind," no "fascinating little skid off the hard road and right up to the edge of the swamp" that so attracted Dorothy.[12] What Benchley thought of her can hardly have been less perplexing. Here was this tiny, polite, soft-spoken nymph with an acidic, witty tongue that enthralled all New York. Though they warily circled around each other like boxers preparing for a punch, their friendship developed from sharing an office to, more often than not, sharing their lunch hours too.

Neither knew that there would be more changes to come. Frank had been scouting around for another man to join the team. What Frank actually thought when the stooped, six-foot seven-inch, rail-thin giant named Robert E. Sherwood appeared in his Canadian Black Watch uniform, complete with kilt, is anyone's guess. Whether through awe or fear, Frank hired Sherwood on the spot for a three-month trial period with the vague title of "drama editor."[13] When Dorothy heard that Sherwood had been shot in both legs and gassed, she was sympathetic, but still wondered aloud how the enemy had managed to miss their target. It is an understatement to say that Sherwood made quite an impression on everyone he met. But at the outset Dorothy and Benchley felt decidedly uneasy with the towering beanpole. Sherwood still had trouble breathing and spoke little as a result. To boot, he was tremendously shy. When he wanted to write a letter or article, he had to sit on the floor with his back to the secretary while he dictated.

If the trio made for an odd threesome in the office, it was nothing compared with their outings on the town. Several days after Sherwood's arrival, Dorothy and Benchley found him lurking outside the office building, waiting for them. Could they please accompany him down Forty-fourth Street, he asked? Sure. Sherwood added the caveat that he had to walk between Dorothy and Benchley. Their puzzled looks forced Sherwood to come clean. "In those days," Dorothy recalled with a whimsical smile, "the Hippodrome, a block from the office, had engaged a troupe of midgets and Mr. Sherwood . . . wouldn't go down the street unless Mr. Benchley walked on one side of him and I on the other, because, with his six feet seven inches, he was afraid the midgets might tease him if he were alone." Sure enough, as they set out the midgets ran squealing up to them shouting, "Hey, Legs!," making well-worn facetious remarks like, "Remember to duck under the Sixth Avenue El," and demanding to know "how the weather was up there."[14] It may have embarrassed Sherwood, but it broke the ice with Benchley and Dorothy, and the trio became inseparable.

And so the mayhem commenced. One of Benchley's early "serious" articles submitted to Frank was titled "The Sex Life of the Newt." Frank cleaned it up by merely changing the title to "The

Social Life of the Newt." It was, in Benchley-speak, a scientific experiment, and therefore serious. He described how the male newt "is flashing his gleamer frantically two blocks away . . . in the stress of his handicap courtship, standing on his fore-feet, gesticulating in amorous fashion with his hind feet in the air . . . [it] might well have been the origin of what is known today in scientific circles as 'the shimmy.'" The use of the word "shimmy" made the article of some considerable relevance to the dance-mad 1919 reader. But when Benchley soured his scientific experiment by "a change in personnel" (a rubber eraser for a female newt), he still allowed the poor male to "gyrate and undulate in a most conscientious manner, still under the impression that he was making a conquest."[15]

It was the appetizer of the feast to come. Benchley's sense of the absurd spread infectiously to Dorothy. While still a schoolboy at Phillips Exeter Academy, Benchley was given the task of writing an essay on a practical subject. What could be more practical than finding out the secrets of the undertaking trade? he thought. And so he sought out the local practitioner, interviewed him, and wrote his essay. It was practical, "dead on target" too, if startling to his English teacher. Renewing his theme in a freshman essay at Harvard, Benchley stuck with his subject, certain that his Harvard professor would hardly know the ins and outs of embalming to sufficiently criticize the paper.[16] Of course he was right.

Regaling Dorothy with his lugubrious antics, he decided that they simply must subscribe to an undertaking magazine or two. After all, what could be funnier than death? With each new issue aimed at funeral directors, Dorothy and Benchley downed tools and thumbed through their copies of Casket and Sunnyside as soon as they arrived. Frank was puzzled as to why Vanity Fair had subscribed to these two publications but daren't air his innermost thoughts to his talented troupe, even when howls of laughter echoed around the office walls. Dorothy had taken to cutting out pictures of cadavers and diagrams of "how and where to inject the embalming fluid." She claimed that only one of the offending drawings hung over her desk. Edna and Frank had different memories.

"I dared suggest that they might prove a little startling to our occasional visitors," Frank recalled later. Dorothy was offended but felt sorry for Frank, whom she thought was lost in a fog of Edwardian manners. She would always remember Frank as "a lovely man, but puzzled . . . we behaved extremely badly."[17]

While no one understood yet the full extent of the social and cultural changes brought on by the Great War, the trio was precocious in showing off their talents for the anarchic over the authoritative. They possessed an infectious liberation to follow their own whims, so prevalent in society in the decade to come. Of course Crowninshield happily shared in some of their antics, writing on the pressing topics of the day like "Hints on Social Climbing"; "The Diary of a Newport Flapper"; "Peace Reigns in the Canine World"; and "What Is Worse Than a House Party?" Hollywood and its silent films were beginning to steal some of the thunder from Europe, and the New York Algonquin Hotel resident, the actor Douglas Fairbanks Sr., was asked by Frank to write on America's modern Neverland.

Frank probably ascribed his trio's behavior to the quick changes happening everywhere. They would soon settle down, he thought. Perhaps Lew Wurzburg, Condé's trusty administrative officer left in charge, could make the *Vanity Fair* three see sense? Whatever the oversight or reason, Condé, Edna, and Frank set sail for Europe on the *Aquitania*—having received a bon-voyage present of the tackiest, biggest horseshoe flower wreath Dorothy, Benchley, and Sherwood could buy. On their way back to the office, it was agreed that their hours should be adjusted as suited their needs. Benchley felt rotten that Sherwood's salary was so mean, but he hadn't the authority to raise it, despite being left in charge of *Vanity Fair*. So Benchley did the next best thing: He purchased several articles from Sherwood. The first was bought for seventy-five dollars, more money than well-known contributors were paid. When the editor of the men's fashion column left on vacation— with an unfinished column—Sherwood was assigned to complete it. He predicted that the "best-dressed men would soon be wearing waistcoats trimmed with cut jade and peg-topped trousers."[18]

The *Vanity Fair* gang was just getting started when another literary troika hit town with a bang. It was inevitable they would all meet up. What was less inevitable were the consequences.

It was Dorothy who received the invitation to welcome Alexander Woollcott, the *New York Times* drama critic, back from the war. She was one of the thirty-five guests to the party since she was the drama critic for *Vanity Fair*. However, the hosts, John Peter Toohey and Murdock Pemberton,[*] had neglected to include Benchley and Sherwood.[19] Her attendance sans Benchley and Sherwood was as unthinkable as her making an appearance without her clothes on. So she simply invited them to come along with her, ignoring the hosts' "oversight."

Woollcott was hardly a combatant. Grossly overweight, he resembled an overfed human owl with eyes like raisins that sank behind his spectacles into his jowls. His biting repartee was an acquired taste, and his friends were greeted with the pat one-liner, "Hello, repulsive." Where Dorothy's wit was understated and never bitchy, Woollcott's one-liners were, according to the humorist James Thurber, "Old Vitriol and Violets."

While the lunch party at the Algonquin Hotel was in Woollcott's honor, two others formed the returning hero's triumvirate: Capt. Franklin Pierce Adams and his bag carrier (literally), Pvt. Harold Ross. Adams was the *New-York Tribune*'s journalist "F.P.A.," whose witty column, "The Conning Tower," had long ago earned Dorothy's awed reverence. Harold Ross had bamboozled his way onto the editorial team of the American Expeditionary Force's publication, *Stars and Stripes*. When Ross first met Woollcott, the insults flew. Ross asked where Woollcott had worked as a civilian.

---

[*] Toohey was a publicist but was credited by Harold Ross as having come up with the title of his magazine, *The New Yorker*, at a Round Table lunch. Pemberton was *The New Yorker*'s first art critic.

The human owl replied, "*The New York Times*—drama critic."
Ross threw his head back in laughter, and Woollcott added without missing a beat, "You remind me a great deal of my grandfather's coachman." How that turned into a long and ultimately
perverse friendship mystified most of their friends.[20]

Where the *Vanity Fair* gang solidified their friendship in the
best of circumstances, Woollcott, Adams, and Ross had forged
theirs in the crucible of war. The *Stars and Stripes* began as an
efficient vehicle for disseminating army directives and as a propaganda tool. Under the inspired guidance of Woollcott, Adams, and
Ross it became the enlisted man's chronicler of history and a mood
changer. Ross proposed that the American Expeditionary Force do-
nate money to "adopt" French war orphans through a Red Cross–
administered fund. Within nine months, more than two million
francs were raised in support of 3,500 French children. Even General Pershing "adopted" two French children.[21]

Just as Dorothy, Benchley, and Sherwood hung out in New York,
the *Stars and Stripes* troika—along with irregulars like Ring Lardner and Heywood Broun—hung out on Saturday nights at a Parisian bistro called Nini's, in Montmartre. One Saturday Woollcott
turned up with the clerk of the YMCA's motion picture bureau,
Jane Grant. Despite Grant's initial impression of Ross—that he
"was a misshapen question mark . . . the homeliest man I'd ever
met"[22]—they married once they returned to New York.

Dorothy sat silently throughout most of the lunch party. Had anyone realized she was the author of the piece about the cowardice
of "the numerous heroes who nobly accepted commissions in those
branches of the service where the fountain pen is mightier than
the sword?"[23] Fortunately she had used a pseudonym. She was uncomfortable sitting next to the very men she had criticized. She
was also jaundiced, particularly when Woollcott spewed about
"when I was in the theatre of war" until finally a friend shut him
up by saying, "If you ever were in the theater of war, it was in the

last-row seat nearest the exit."[24] As she, Benchley, and Sherwood walked back to the office afterward, none of them saw any good reason why they should not have a regular get-together with the *Stars and Stripes* three. Ever. But from this odd beginning, the famous Algonquin Round Table was born.

14. BACK TO THE BUSINESS OF "FRIED FISH AND STEWED EELS"

Put your best apples on top, in the shop window.
—LETTER FROM CONDÉ NAST TO ALL EDITORS IN 1941,
QUOTING ALFRED HARMSWORTH, LORD NORTHCLIFFE

Contrary to Edna's fear that Condé was taking risks, he was seizing a great opportunity by expanding into Europe. As with everything planned by Condé, the move was calculated and mathematically proved to ensure success. British *Vogue* was no whim foisted on him by the Dorland Agency or others. Neither was it a response to Hearst's success in acquiring *Nash's Magazine* in England a few years earlier. Condé knew that to be a market leader in fashion, *Vogue* must cement its relationship with British purveyors of menswear, sporting gear, fashionable furniture, and those little vanity items so appreciated by the men and women of the American *Social Register*.

British *Vogue*, while still leaching red ink, was Condé's trusted spearhead into European fashion. Besides, expansion into Britain was something of an emotional return to the mother ship. Not only would he back British *Vogue*'s market position, but he also planned to augment it by creating a new British *House & Garden*. He saw this title as an elegant publication appealing to owners of stately homes and mansions. Since the war, many estates could no longer afford acres of gardeners and miles of household staff. Condé had nearly doubled the American *House & Garden* circulation since he had taken it over in 1914 and saw no reason why a British version shouldn't succeed along the same lines.[1]

So Condé made a study of the British and French magazine markets, just as he had followed the careers of the latest generation of British press barons—especially Alfred Harmsworth (Lord Northcliffe since 1905) and his younger brother Harold (Lord Rothermere since 1914). In fact Condé admired Northcliffe more than any other publisher, envying his iron grip on his publications as well as his marketing flair. And yet Condé's own strengths most resembled the younger Rothermere's, as both men were masters of all things financial. Above all else Condé knew the Harmsworth brothers were innovators from whom he could learn a great deal.

In 1889 the brothers were struggling to finance payments for their first magazine, *Answers to Correspondents*. They couldn't rival other titles like *Pearson's Weekly* or the market leader, *Tit-Bits*, for the quality of their readers' competitions. So they came up with another notion that captured the nation's imagination. That October the brothers asked their readers to guess what the gold reserves held at the Bank of England would be on December 4—a patriotic move during the Second Boer War.* There were more than seven hundred thousand entries—for a magazine normally selling fewer than one hundred thousand copies each month. Each entry needed to be witnessed by five people who were not related or living at the same address as the entrant. At a stroke Alfred Harmsworth made his publication available to millions. The Christmas issue of *Answers* sold more than two hundred thousand copies, and the brothers were on their way.[2] By the time Condé visited them in 1919, their publishing business was one of the largest conglomerates in the British Empire.[3] The brothers' publishing operations were worth a staggering £10.3 million,[4] or about $2.38 billion in today's values.

While Condé did not share the Harmsworth brothers' values of circulation, advertising, and paper quality, there was much to

---

* This was fought from October 1899 to May 1902 between the United Kingdom and the South African Republic of Transvaal and the Orange Free State over the British Empire's influence in South Africa.

commend their strategies for growth. They believed in vertical in-
tegration, owning paper sources and mills in Canada and England.
By controlling their paper and pulp sources, as well as manufacturing their own inks, the Harmsworths knew the precise costs of
their magazines and newspapers and could keep a steady eye on
profits. In fact the profitability of their thirty-eight periodicals depended, in Harold Harmsworth's own prosaic words, on the business of "fried fish and stewed eels," as in "sticking to their knitting"
or simple down-to-earth meals they knew they could cook to perfection. Their Associated Newspapers, which comprised print media from glossies to newsprint, including the *Daily Mail* and *Daily
Mirror* (at the time a women's newspaper), had varying requirements in paper, quality, and illustration. The "glossies," potential
competition for British *Vogue* and *House & Garden*, were held and
financed in a separate company, Amalgamated Press. Condé made
it his business to visit their Imperial Paper Mills based in Graves-
end, Kent, to better understand firsthand how their vertical inte-
gration worked. He was mightily impressed.

The Harmsworths' publishing operations in women's magazines
alone represented some 75 percent of the total women's market.
Their Amalgamated Press published *Woman's World*, and the top
magazine for dressmaking patterns, *Home Chat*—both of which
were of primary interest to Condé. The Harmsworths owned other
women's magazines too: the highly successful *Woman's Weekly*,
Fashions for All, *Home Fashions*, *Children's Dress*, *Mab's Fashions*,
and the *Best Way* series. Condé befriended the brothers. They
alone could keep his troublesome rival, William Randolph Hearst,
in check in Britain.

But for all Condé's studying of the British market, he hadn't as
yet produced a profit. He saw that William Wood's position as his
title's publisher and manager was diluted by divided loyalties between the Dorland Agency and British *Vogue*. George W. Kettle
doubled up too, heading Dorland and acting as Condé's advertis-

ing manager.* A further complication existed: Wood and Kettle were often at loggerheads, giving rise to the office joke that there was "too much Wood under the Kettle."[5]

Edna preferred to think that British *Vogue*'s problems were due to its editor, Elspeth Champcommunal. Nicknamed "Champco" by Virginia Woolf, Elspeth was a fashion designer first and foremost, not a magazine editor. While she happily adopted the Condé Nast formula inherent to his class magazine, and included well-received articles on health, beauty, society, and sport, Elspeth was highly influenced by her Bloomsbury Set friends. She was a British-born Francophile, discreetly lesbian, and had been living in Paris among bohemian friends like Man Ray, Pablo Picasso, and Francis Picabia until Condé hired her from House of Worth in 1916 for his new British title. It was Elspeth who first introduced *Vogue* to the highbrow Bloomsbury Set. Comprising writers, intellectuals, philosophers, and artists, its most famous members were the novelist Virginia and her political theorist husband, Leonard; the acclaimed fiction writer and academic E. M. Forster; the postimpressionist painter Duncan Grant; the economist John Maynard Keynes; the art critic and postimpressionist painter Roger Fry; the art critic Clive Bell and his painter wife, Vanessa (Virginia Woolf's elder sister); and the biographer Lytton Strachey.

What Condé had not appreciated was Elspeth's closeness to the literary elite, both in Paris and London, and how Bloomsbury† in particular was more modern in its outlook on fashion, sex, and acceptance of modern art than much of high society in Britain. The effect was a slide in sales. Condé hoped that by their visit they

---

* It wasn't until much later that the practice of individual advertising companies acting as in-house advertising managers fell into disrepute.

† The Bloomsburies, named after the London district where several members lived, denied being an official group. Their avant-garde work rejected bourgeois attitudes and greatly influenced literature, aesthetics, feminism, economics, pacifism, and views on sexuality. In 1917 Leonard and Virginia Woolf founded Hogarth Press and began hand-printing books. Until 1946 they published 527 titles, including the first UK edition of T. S. Eliot's *The Waste Land* in 1923.

could gently recalibrate his British editor's tastes. It was not the moment to replace Elspeth, particularly as he had other, more pressing affairs to settle. Besides, Edna was far better at handling editorial issues at British *Vogue* than he.

Sailing to Europe that glorious summer of 1919, Condé also knew that for his company to become a world leader in fashion magazines, a French *Vogue* must follow the British title. That said, Condé needed to create a better legal framework with the Vogels in Paris—one where the couple's other titles would not become a matter of divided loyalties. Although Condé had bought a controlling interest in Lucien and Cosette Vogel's *La Gazette du Bon Ton* in the early days of the Great War and published it in the United States as *La Gazette du Bon Genre* (there was already a *Bon Ton*), Condé's motivation was intended as kindness first and a sound business decision second. He wanted above all to assure the Vogels' financial security during the war years, without a thought to making a profit. Naturally, too, he was also investing in the Vogels as his trusted people in Paris for the long term. Acquiring a stake in their titles was, he knew, an emotional investment, given the uncertainty and bloodshed of the war. Nonetheless Condé was convinced that along with their loyal and talented coterie of artists, one day the Vogels would contribute their exceptional spirit and cachet to American and British *Vogue*.[6]

Condé always emphasized the importance of every magazine cover and, maddening though it seemed to Edna on more than one occasion, he was frequently involved in the final decisions for each issue. As he negotiated with the Vogels to become his leading lights at a future French *Vogue* that summer, Condé's vision of acquiring some of the best artistic talent on both sides of the Atlantic seemed close to fruition.[7] The family had significant interests in *Jardin des Modes* too, and the Vogels were also editors of the fashion supplement for the famous society magazine *L'Illustration des Modes*. While they hammered out an agreement for the first editions of French *Vogue*, Condé also had to settle the thorny issues of paper and machinery. The war years meant that France's technical equipment had fallen behind in terms of innovation. So, Condé turned to William Wood in London to resolve the printing issues. Messageries Hachette resolved the distribution problems by agreeing to deliver the magazine in France, despite viewing French *Vogue* as competition to their own publications.

While Condé negotiated for a French *Vogue*, Edna was excited to join in the spectacle that Paul Poiret dubbed "L'Oasis." It took place in Poiret's own home garden—and Edna was a regular guest. Until that summer Parisian high society had fled the capital for cooler climes. Poiret wanted to change their habits and drum up business into the bargain. Edna made sure that this "most amusing, the most beautiful place in Paris [Poiret's garden]," catering to "the demi-monde, the men of letters, the old youth, journalism and the boulevard," would be hailed a triumph in American *Vogue*.[8] Several times a week Poiret gave themed evening parties, like "Nouveaux Riches" or "Moonlight" or "The Circus," conjuring up appropriate costumes for his patrons to wear. If mesdames didn't have the right clothes, they could always go to Poiret's salon for a suitable design.

Poiret was recalling the opulence of the seventeenth and eighteenth centuries, the high life of French kings. *Vogue* called his L'Oasis costumes "an orgy" aimed at putting the great aristocratic fetes organized for Louis XIV to shame for their "abundance, fantasy, and splendid fabrics." Poiret saw himself as more than just a mere couturier, but rather a director—an *animateur*—who could successfully bring the pannier style worn by fashionable women in the eighteenth century to modern, jazz-loving Paris. With Condé's blessing, Edna asked the Spanish artist Eduardo Benito to illustrate Poiret's triumph for *Vogue*.[9] How far Condé had helped her travel. . . .

When Condé sailed home from Le Havre in August 1919 with Frank at his side, he left behind several technical issues to iron out both in London and Paris. He could not have been happy with

his British *Vogue* losses. Similarly, he was troubled by the Vogels'
continued divided loyalties. While Edna remained in Paris to view
the first postwar fall collections, at least Condé could take comfort in *Vogue*'s and *Vanity Fair*'s preeminent positions in the United
States.

15. HOW TO KEEP A PARK BENCH WARM

Shall we their fond pageant see?
Lord, what fools these mortals be!
—PUCK TO OBERON, *A MIDSUMMER NIGHT'S DREAM* (3.2.114–15)

Vanity Fair's three mischievous editors welcomed Frank home that August with mixed feelings. Of course they adored their urbane and witty editor in chief. On the other hand, they had been terrifically delinquent in his absence. They were late with copy, late in the morning, late back from lunch, and late in recognizing that they would be—at best—promptly scolded for misbehaving. They probably never thought that, at worst, Condé would fire them. But if there was one thing to make Condé humorless, it was casualness about company rules on his editorial staff. Benchley, Parker, and Sherwood were blinded to his perspective by the sheer fun of working together.

When Crowninshield walked through the door, his office was unrecognizable, festooned with crepe-paper streamers, assorted rummage-sale parade paraphernalia, and a tacky WELCOME HOME sign. No such frivolity greeted Condé at *Vogue*. In catching up on the daily office details together, Frank and Condé discussed the *Vanity Fair* editors and the ripping good time they'd had at Condé's expense, with precious little attention paid to work. When Dorothy came in late again the next morning, only exceeded in tardiness by Benchley, Crowninshield began to simmer on a low flame. Naturally Dorothy had no excuse. Benchley's breezy entry was due, so he said, to his having to drive his wife to the hospital.

She had gone into labor. When Benchley didn't return to the office in the afternoon, Frank said nothing, but the flame was turned up a notch. Of course the next day, congratulations were heartily given all round for the birth of Benchley's second son, but again work was off the agenda. And so it went, on and on.[1]

Condé was at a loss as to how Frank might tame *Vanity Fair*'s rambunctious whelps without denting their wit and talents. Given that Condé was continually underwriting losses at the magazine, he was compelled to tell Frank that he feared where their antics might lead. Imagine if their high jinks spread to the profitable *Vogue* and *House & Garden*—then where would they all be? Something, he told Crowninshield, had to be done. For the boss of a top company dependent on artistic talents, it was extremely frustrating. For Frank it was a situation he tried desperately to ignore. It was a problem with only one solution.

Parker, Benchley, and Sherwood felt the cold wind of disapproval, which they parried with gripes about their paychecks. They grumbled so loudly about their so-called slave wages that someone reported their boisterous bellyaching directly to Condé. On October 14, 1919, the indefatigable Wurzburg was asked to write a memo headed "Forbidding Discussion Among Employees of Salary Received." Benchley replied in writing with his own memo "Concerning the Forbidding of Discussion Among Employees." Outraged, he spoke for them all: "We especially call your attention to the wording of the last paragraph, regarding the 'instant' discharge of employees violating the new regulation, and would eagerly inquire if *our* obligations under the contracts we have been asked to sign are as elastic as those the management are here construed as being."[2] Later that same day the trio strolled through the offices, casually swinging protest signs from their necks on which their salaries were clearly written in their fight against what they saw as "the spirit of petty regulation."[3]

There was no further "discussion"—nor were there any more memos or visual protests on the topic. Evidently their signed contracts had no such interdiction, and freedom of speech was a federally guaranteed right. That said, Benchley should have brought his flock back into line with some semblance of corporate responsibility. Frank felt that his "amazing whelps" had utterly lost respect for him. He despaired. His philosophy that it was "safest to deal with such felines when they are still cubs, to snare them, in traps, before their teeth have sharpened and their claws grown long" had failed.[4] The problem was that the cubs were full-grown and looking for a feast of fun.

Throughout that autumn Frank tried to put a crimp in the trio's style. He complained about Dorothy's tardiness—and lateness with her copy. She grumbled to Benchley and Sherwood that Frank had no right to expect anything more from her. A full day at the office, capped off with late evenings at the theater, was de trop.

Besides, she not only filled her drama column's content but also wrote added theater pieces under the pseudonym "Helen Wells," *and* contributed verse, *and* wrote captions for Fish's drawings, *and* helped with editing and proofreading, *and* actually *read* unsolicited manuscripts.[5] In fact, she mumbled, the last function in her litany was part of Albert Lee's job. Lee merely stuck a rejection slip to the unread manuscripts before returning them to their hapless writers. But she *read* them and discovered Edmund "Bunny" Wilson, she said. And what thanks did she get from Frank or Condé? Complaints. Well, in Dorothy's opinion, they were taking advantage of her, and the Nast organization should feel "more appreciative" of her efforts, she grumbled to Crowninshield. In her opinion they also owed her a raise.[6] It hardly takes a great deal of imagination to picture Frank suppressing raised eyebrows at her chutzpah, or to wonder how he was able to utter his understated reply. He would discuss the matter with Condé after the beginning of the new year, he calmly said. Dorothy was oblivious that she'd hammered another nail into her corporate coffin.

There was also no mistaking that Benchley and Sherwood had dodged bullets fired at them, but they paid little heed to the spent shells strewn about their feet. During Crowninshield's summer absence, Benchley took steps to increase Sherwood's earnings by purchasing a piece of "juvenilia better suited to a college humor magazine than the country's most sophisticated monthly" for the outrageously inflated price of seventy-five dollars, Frank moaned urbanely afterward. Then there was Sherwood's scandalous treatment of the column "What the Well-Dressed Man Will Wear." It had not gone unnoticed that Sherwood had written that waistcoats would be trimmed with cut jade, shoes would again be cloth-topped, and peg-topped trousers would be à la mode.[7]

Worse revelations were to come. An actors' strike darkened Broadway that August and gave Dorothy the opportunity to flex her fearsome pen with articles like the one called "The New Plays—If Any," featuring a drawing of "George M. Cohan, Strike-breaker." Benchley chipped in with a pictorial "What They Did During the Strike," poking fun at his former employer, the producer William M. Brady, for treading the boards in a lead role rather than allowing the strike to darken his theater.[8]

When Benchley had met Condé for his job interview in 1918, Frank warned him that the publisher believed *Vanity Fair* needed to adopt "a somewhat less frivolous outlook." Benchley had secured the job as managing editor by waxing lyrical on that very topic.[9] Yet he steadfastly ignored his publisher's wishes.

Frank, in his desire to please Condé, had hoped Benchley would act like a shepherd in charge of his flock. Then again, "Crownin-shield would allow any entertaining writer to say practically anything in *Vanity Fair*, so long as it was in evening clothes," Benchley said.[10] In mocking the organization's formal business demands, the "amazing young whelps" hadn't recognized the difficult, and seemingly schizophrenic, demands their antics put on their editor in chief.

They were out of step with their employer and singularly failed to see that they were about to stumble. They disdained Condé's efforts to corporately reel them in. So it was up to Frank. He asked them very gently—and in his usual gentlemanly fashion—to please refrain from exhausting Condé's patience. They responded by blowing off steam at the Algonquin Hotel as part of the famous Round Table.

In the fall of 1919, Georges, the headwaiter of the Algonquin, had moved "the Round Tablers" to greater comfort in the center of the Rose Room—near the front door for all to see. Frank Case, the manager and later owner of the hotel, knew that despite *Vanity Fair*'s editors eating their fill of eggs, the cheapest entrée on the menu, they were good for business, especially when they were joined by their Round Table rivals. Case had even assigned them their own waiter, Luigi, who lovingly placed free olives, popovers, and celery to whet their wit.[11] Any memories of never, ever sitting at the same table again with the war veterans of the Round Table were banished from the trio's thoughts. In fact Dorothy often entertained them with tales of her veteran husband, Eddie.

Discharged from the Thirty-Third Ambulance Company that summer, Eddie was always invited to join in the Round Table get-togethers. But all Eddie did was smile his handsome smile and keep his mouth buckled tight. By October, Eddie ceased to join the fun in body—but Dorothy kept him alive in spirit. She told stories about Eddie that endowed him with a hapless humorous style, beset by slapstick misfortune. Eddie, always Dorothy's unsuspecting victim, would fall down a manhole while reading *The Wall Street Journal* on the way to work. He would break his arm while sharpening pencils. "Some awful things happened to Eddie all in the same day," Donald Ogden Stewart recalled. "He got run over, or something—I forget what it was—but four or five absolutely terrible things happened to Eddie all in that same day, and Dottie was terribly sympathetic, but you screamed with laughter because it was such a line of continual misfortunes."

One day, Dorothy told the Round Tablers, she and Eddie arrived early for a funeral—so early, in fact, that they were the only people at the crematorium—that is, aside from the body. While they peered down at the corpse of their friend, Eddie fiddled with the knobs of the conveyor belt beneath the coffin. The casket began to move, the door to the fires that would consume it opened, and *poof!* Dorothy sighed and shook her head. Eddie ran out before anyone saw what he'd done.[12]

Undeniably no one believed that so many calamities could befall the poor guy. But what none of the Round Tablers knew was that while Dorothy was cracking her Eddie stories, she could no longer deny that Eddie was addicted to morphine. When the "Eddie Catastrophes" stopped that November, few of her friends realized that their marriage was over.

By Christmas the *Vanity Fair* trio were pillorying Condé for his "bookkeeper's mentality." More than likely prompted by Dorothy, they wondered aloud maliciously at the Round Table if Crowninshield was being used by Condé to procure women for him. Benchley's personal disgust at "libertines and social climbers made him label the Nast organization as the ultimate 'white sepulcher,'" while Sherwood told the Round Tablers that employees were "treated like serfs and paid that way, too."

None of them blamed Crowninshield for the deterioration in the atmosphere at *Vanity Fair*, nor did they look to their own irrepressible, irresponsible, irreverent, and increasingly defamatory behavior as a cause for the prevailing iciness at work. Then Frank called Dorothy into his office for a private chat the day before Christmas. He told her he was unhappy with the quality of the magazine, and her contribution in particular. His usual gentle manner was submerged beneath a barrage of complaints that Dorothy believed came directly from Condé. It was so out of character for Frank to haul anyone over the coals, much less for such trivial complaints, she told them. "*Vanity Fair* was a magazine of no opinion," she lamented.[13] She had been hired for her outspokenness and was admired by Crowninshield and all of New York for her wit. How could Frank dress her down for having such outlandish opinions when he was the very man who first appreciated them?

In this bitter, desolate mood over Christmas, with her marriage in tatters, too, Dorothy decided that her opinions mattered, and she would continue to voice them through her drama critic's column. That January, in her "The First Hundred Plays Are the Hardest or A Strenuous Effort to Keep Up with the Oncoming Dramas," Dorothy wrote that "new plays crashed down upon a helpless populace, not by twos and threes, but by dozens and scores. . . . if there were only four openings scheduled for a night, the critic felt that his evening was practically free."[14] She heaped scorn on four plays: *Déclassée, The Girl in the Limousine, The Son-Daughter*, and *Caesar's Wife*.

For *Déclassée*, her pen lashed out at "the persons of three unlisted actors, who in their fortunately brief roles of acrobats whom the capricious Lady Helen befriends, bring things perilously near to burlesque." The British actor Vernon Steele, miscast as an American youth by "an all-wise management," left Dorothy feeling that, among other listed faux pas, "Such touches of realism as this must make Mr. Belasco clutch feverishly at his clerical collar."

Unusually Dorothy dubbed *The Girl in the Limousine* "undeniably very funny, owing to the infallible John Cumberland. I should think Mr. Cumberland would loathe the very sight of a bed, out of office hours." Why? Simply because the play sported "the most densely populated bed in town. . . . Someone is either in or under it, or both, during the entire evening."[15]

The Son-Daughter, a play written by George Scarborough and David Belasco, appearing at the Belasco Theatre, drew Dorothy's real venom. Having panned a play in the previous season titled *East Is West*, Dorothy effectively accused Scarborough and Belasco of plagiarizing that most ghastly of plays: "Last season, in the exuberance of youth, I used to think that no play along the same lines could possibly be worse: that was before the dying year brought *The Son-Daughter*."

Her final black mark was reserved for W. Somerset Maugham's play *Caesar's Wife*, starring Florenz Ziegfeld's wife, Billie Burke. "There are few flashes of Mr. Maugham's brilliance in the dialogue, and the evening seems a long and uneventful one. Miss Burke . . . is at her best in her more serious moments; in her desire to convey the girlishness of the character, she plays her lighter scenes rather as if she were giving an impersonation of Eva Tanguay."*16

On January 8 Sherwood was called into Crowninshield's office. In what Sherwood described as the editor's "exquisite pussyfooting" way, he was informed he would not receive a raise. He was also told that a Mrs. Strauss, currently Natica Nast's music teacher, would be replacing him shortly as editor. Sherwood would need to find a job elsewhere.[17] In retrospect, given that Sherwood's phenomenal talents were amply proved after he left Condé Nast Publications, it was doubly galling for a gifted man on the rise.

That Friday before leaving work, Crowninshield had a "quiet word" with Benchley, telling him that Condé's patience had run out. Dorothy Parker would have to go as *Vanity Fair*'s drama critic. Benchley, of course, strenuously objected and demanded to know why. Later, Dorothy spread the word that Condé's decision was based on Florenz Ziegfeld's irate objections to her column panning Billie Burke's performance in *Caesar's Wife*. Certainly, Ziegfeld was angry, and had threatened to pull all his advertising. But this sort of threat had never worked before with Condé and would have been his first kowtowing to advertisers.

The truth was more straightforward. David Belasco threatened a lawsuit for libel. Dorothy's intimation that his play *The Son-Daughter* was plagiarized by Belasco from an earlier play called *East Is West* could not be allowed to stand unchallenged.[18] A libel suit was quite a different tale from an angry advertiser, and Dorothy simply had to go. All Benchley could do was warn her that she was about to get the chop, then sit back nervously to await the result.

That Sunday, January 11, Crowninshield asked Dorothy to tea at the Plaza Hotel. Before Dorothy arrived (remember, she was al-

* Tanguay was a Quebecoise singer who billed herself as "the girl who made Vaudeville famous."

ways late), he asked the headwaiter to "brighten up the table with roses."[19] She finally bundled in, and Frank began his monologue, leaning forward so no one else could hear. Unfortunately for her, Plum Wodehouse said he wanted to return from his leave of absence, and, in accordance with Wodehouse's contract, that was his right. Sorry, Dorothy. Naturally he was sure they could work out a fair market rate for any "little things from home" that Dorothy might write. He made light of the complaints from Florenz Ziegfeld, David Belasco, and Charles Dillingham*—the three kings of Broadway productions.[20] But Frank told her too that he had apologized personally to Billie Burke. His hopes that delivering his message in a public place would temper Dorothy's reaction were dashed. She told Frank that she would vacate her desk within two weeks, and that he could rest assured any articles she might write would appear anywhere *except* for *Vanity Fair*, before blaming Condé for all her woes.[21] She telephoned Benchley that evening with her side of the story.

On Monday Benchley tendered his resignation. Sherwood had received his notice four days earlier, so following his troupe sooner than planned was simple. Frank hadn't wanted to lose Benchley, steadfastly believing that his managing editor had been led over the precipice by Dorothy and Sherwood. So he asked Benchley to think it over for a few days. That evening the trio dined at the Algonquin with some of the Round Tablers, including the spiteful Woollcott, revealing all. The next day Woollcott's headline to his column in the *Times* read: VANITY FAIR EDITORS OUT—ROBERT BENCHLEY FOLLOWS MRS. PARKER—CRITICISM UNDER FIRE. While not mentioning the return of P. G. Wodehouse to *Vanity Fair*, Woollcott's article claimed that "Mrs. Parker's reception of this news was complicated by the fact that she was well aware of a recent simultaneous fire of complaint on the part of offended subjects of her criticism."[22]

Woollcott misrepresented the facts. And Benchley knew it. He

---

* Since Dillingham was also Grace Moore's theatrical agent, Condé's current romantic interest may have felt unnecessarily threatened by Dorothy's jibes.

had no alternative than to resign. In an apologetic and sincere letter to Crowninshield (on three small office memo sheets) he wrote:

> I do not want you to think that the story in this morning's
> "Times" was inspired by either Mrs. Parker or myself. It came
> as a result of the conversation which took place at dinner last
> night at a table at which were present eight people, including
> Alexander Woollcott.... The subject of the conversation was,
> quite naturally, the recent events in the office, but as Woollcott
> is in no way connected with the news end of his paper, we
> did not give the possibility of its being converted into a news
> story a moment's consideration.... I was extremely sorry to
> see it, and as a matter of fact, I have told reporters from the
> "World" and "Tribune" who came up for stories on what they
> heard was a "walk-out" that there was absolutely nothing in
> it.... My own work is not, in itself, attractive enough to hold
> me in this office with both Mrs. Parker and Mr. Sherwood
> gone from it.[23]

While the trio served out their notice period, they took to wearing red chevrons—symbol of those who had been honorably discharged from the American army. On their last day together
Benchley hung a sign in the lobby of the office building that read
"Contributions for Miss Billie Burke." Even Benchley had bought
into Dorothy's misguided version of the saga in the end. And why
not? Crowninshield had omitted to tell either Benchley or Dorothy about the threatened litigation.

In the aftermath of their departure from *Vanity Fair*, Dorothy
and Benchley set up shop in a tiny office with the comical shingle
hung on the door: "Eureka Nut and Bolt Company." There they
intended to write the play they had been discussing several months
earlier. They even had a cable address: PARKBENCH.[24] But as at *Vanity Fair*, no work was done. Since Benchley had a family to feed,
Dorothy was soon left on her own.

Dorothy would later claim that Condé Nast invited her to go to
Europe with him later that spring when he bumped into her at the

Algonquin waiting for her chums. The remark has the ring of a mix of "Eddie Catastrophes" and a poison dart. She would never be a "corporate" staff writer again. That said, she became a successful screenwriter—spending all her money unwisely. She wrote for Arnold Gingrich's *Esquire* in the 1930s and for many more years, often being paid for no work. She would become the high priestess of wit for all New York, if not the nation. Dorothy never lost her self-destructive streak, always biting the hand that fed or loved her.

Sherwood became an acclaimed screenwriter, Pulitzer Prize–winning playwright of *Idiot's Delight* in 1936 (the first of four Pulitzers), and author of the Pulitzer Prize–winning book *Roosevelt and Hopkins—An Intimate History.* He would go on to become a key speechwriter for President Franklin D. Roosevelt and the chief propagandist for Wild Bill Donovan's OSS forces, the precursor to the CIA.[25]

Benchley, like Parker, became a popular freelancer, working as the theater reviewer for *Life* from April 1920. He was the theater critic for Harold Ross's *The New Yorker*, overlapping with *Life* for four years, where he wrote under the pen name "Guy Fawkes."* He also turned to screenwriting and acting, and won an Academy Award for his 1935 short film *How to Sleep.* The film mocked a Mellon Institute study commissioned by the Simmons Mattress Company. Mellon was furious, but Simmons used stills from the Oscar-winning short to promote their mattresses. The trio's anti-corporate "Condé Past" had apparently been just a warm-up act.

---

* Guy Fawkes (1570–1606) was the putative leader of the Gunpowder Plot to blow up the Houses of Parliament in the reign of James I of England.

PART III

ROARING WITH THE TWENTIES

———◄○■○►———

*The Roaring Twenties were the period of that
great American prosperity which was built
on shaky foundations.*
—J. PAUL GETTY

※

16. "AIN'T WE GOT FUN?"

The rich get rich and the poor get children . . .
—ORIGINAL LYRIC TO THE SONG "AIN'T WE GOT FUN?"

D espite the trio's exit from *Vanity Fair*, Condé Nast had every reason to be proud of his achievements. *Vogue* had already made him a rich man. He, like everyone else, was oblivious to the complications brewing, caused by American banks—Chase, First National, and even investment banks like Goldman Sachs—rushing to finance a defeated Germany with their cheap loans. Few experts suspected what that would mean for America.[1] And if there was one thing Condé believed in, it was his experts. If his investment managers wanted to know about publishing a class magazine, he'd expect them to consult him, just as he took their advice as gospel in the investment business.

As German hyperinflation took hold within the year, the same experts ignored that France's economy, too, was stagnating. While Condé made final preparations for his longed-for French *Vogue*, the French political Left became the popular choice as the country's listless economic conditions deepened into a depression. Communism, rather than socialism, loomed menacingly over French politics and its economy. As these clear warning signs of trouble ahead in Europe went unheeded by so many international pundits; so too did the rise of the political Right in Germany, and the rise of Adolf Hitler in early 1920 as head of propaganda for the new National Socialist German Workers' Party (NSDAP).

Of course Condé read his newspapers. He knew the European economies had become sluggish again after the initial boom of 1919. But he had already waited out the war to put his plan for European expansion into action. Surely, he believed, France was ripe to receive its own *Vogue*, despite any temporary downturn. Like Gus Kahn's wildly popular song "Ain't We Got Fun?" of that summer, where even poverty was treated with a devil-may-care attitude, Condé rightly saw himself squarely among "the rich [who] get rich." Despite Europe's political and economic problems, he would steer *Vogue* to ever greater successes.

At *Vanity Fair* its new managing editor, Edmund "Bunny" Wilson, was grateful to the "amazing whelps" trio. They jokingly called him a scab, while showing him the ropes and introducing him to the gang at the Algonquin.[2] For Condé, Wilson was a talented and serious young man who would bring the fun at *Vanity Fair* back within some sort of corporate boundaries. Condé could hardly know that Wilson would later paint rather unflattering portraits of both him and Frank. Of his editor in chief Wilson wrote: "He was a type of which I have known a few—the born courtier who lacks an appropriate court." Wilson mocked Frank's games, like the "Rape of the Sabine Women," played in the office corridors for all staffers to enjoy.[3] While Frank flirted mercilessly with the secretaries at *Vanity Fair*, and his secretary, Jean Ballot, frequently complained of a bruised bottom, Frank was never seen to be attached to any man or woman romantically. Thanks to Wilson, speculation grew that Crowninshield may have been gay. So Frank let Wilson know that he had "a lady" who visited him in the privacy of his own home once a week. "In spite of his not very attractive habit of seizing you by the arm in a way that seemed calculated to establish some kind of sexual ascendancy," Wilson complained, "I do not believe that he was . . . [a] homosexual." On balance, Wilson believed—like a later *Vanity Fair* and *Vogue* staffer, Allene Talmey—that a better word to describe Frank would be "eunuch."[4]

Wilson was less than charitable about Condé, too: "The glossiest bounder I have ever known, who was incapable of saying good morning without a formally restrained but somehow obnoxious vulgarity."[5] Surely Wilson's friendship with Dorothy, Benchley, and Sherwood had colored his views. It never occurred to Wilson that Condé was shy and conscious that he was no conversationalist. He looked to his alter ego, Frank, to make pleasant and witty remarks. Wilson was responsible, too, for spreading the rumor that the Boston Brahmin–bred Crowninshield had advanced Condé into society. That dubious claim had been the proud property of Clarisse for years. It seems that Wilson, not Condé, hadn't kept abreast of the times. In 1920 a man's name was only as good as his bank balance—and Condé's was swimming in money.

Curiously, Nast was regarded differently by staff at *Vogue* than at *Vanity Fair*. The increasingly imperious Edna was the one they feared, not Condé. Her strict dress code was costly, despite the fact that she paid her hirelings a pittance. When her employees fell short of her high standards, she ordered them to buy clothes that were more fitting to a *Vogue* employee, but never offered to pay.[6] At *Vogue* Condé was known as the boss who kept his door open and remained a man of his word. He was the one who could be relied upon to help in a pinch—always available to anyone, always willing to provide a solution to their problems:[7] "Even at his busiest in the office, he always stopped in the hall to ask some personal, unbusinesslike question that made you feel part of his life, not just part of his organization," an anonymous staffer recalled.[8] Letters abound in which he frets, cares for, congratulates, and commiserates with those who worked with and for him—like his heartfelt condolences to managing editor Betty Penrose at *Glamour* on the death of her mother, finishing, "If I can help in any way please do let me know;" or to Harry Yoxall[*] about the sudden death of Agnes Wright, wife of *House & Garden* editor Dick Wright, in which he says: "You know how devoted they were. . . . Agnes was operated on last Tuesday for what was thought to be a stone in her gall bladder, but they found it was cancer of the liver. She died the following day." In urging Yoxall to cajole Dick Wright into visiting him in London, Condé hoped Yoxall's friendship and

---

[*] The future managing editor of British *Vogue*.

change of scene "would do much to take his mind off his great loss."[9] Today we'd call him a "straight up" kind of guy. Right or wrong, good or bad, the staff always knew precisely where they stood with him, individually and collectively.

Like most paternalistic employers, Condé had an anaphylactic reaction to firing people. It was his company, and anyone who worked for him, to his mind, was part of his family. His task was to keep his magazines on top of the world, to seek out new readerships and ways to grow the business's profitability; not deal with disruptive or lazy staff who wouldn't or couldn't listen to their editors. Giving an employee the sack was worse than divorce. It was tantamount to disowning his own children. And unlike many bosses—then as now—Condé guaranteed losses made at his magazines with his personal fortune.

The 1920s allowed Condé to spread his personal as well as his professional wings. Often seen with delightfully attractive women of an evening out, he became known as quite the man-about-town. He was rich beyond his own imagining, and had a kind face and gentle manner, though he was somewhat mature, turning fifty in March 1923. But above all Condé had acquired that "it factor" of impeccable style and grace. It hadn't hurt either that his reputation as a great lover had made the rounds in New York's café society. He knew there was talk that he was a lothario, though the word "aging" was frequently placed before the noun. In truth Condé was constantly surrounded by beautiful women. Indeed, beautiful women were his business. Freed from the constraints of his unhappy marriage to Clarisse, Condé was never without a gorgeous gal on his arm. What's more, the women loved his attentions. Significantly, he never used his position or power on women, and he understood the meaning of "no."[10]

Though he was enjoying a personal renaissance, what Condé *really* wanted as the twenties erupted onto the social and fashion scenes with its cool flappers, cubist art on fabrics, and bobbed or marcelled (heavily wavy) hair, was to make *Vogue* the international beating heart of that young and smart society. The boom year of 1919 in the United States lasted into the first half of 1920. Even war-torn Europe had a brief commercial renaissance, mostly due to repairing the ravages to its lost workforces, towns, and cities. While millions of American consumers happily bought into the modern era of "motorcars" and "wireless receivers," Europeans read works like Ernst Jünger's war autobiography *Storm of Steel* (1920) or T. S. Eliot's *The Waste Land*, both pondering the dehumanization of the new, horrific mechanical age. Edna spoke out against Americans who "lacked poise in the present" and shared "a slap-happy optimism about the future. . . . People were exposed to money and caught it without any sense of values. . . . . America being a newer country anyway, our *nouveaux riches* tend to be nouveauer too and more articulate about it."[11]

While Americans took—and *take*—great pleasure in vaunting their wealth, the English were hard cases, in Edna's eyes, for claiming a modern form of poverty. "Of course, Mrs. Chase," declared the owner of one stately home, "we can't afford to keep up the garden properly now, as we are so poor."[12] Edna turned up her nose at this all-too-true remark, deeming it "pretense." But owners of stately homes *were* facing shocking changes in their postwar lives. Peace had only made matters worse.

The bad smell at the end of Edna's long, straight nose indicated her distinct lack of understanding of how the civilian and military losses would play out in Europe. The total number of military and civilian deaths and casualties in the Great War is estimated at around 41 million, divided nearly equally as 20 million deaths and 21 million casualties. France lost approximately 25 percent of its soldiers. Britain lost 16 percent of its military, with a higher-than-average proportion among the officer class.[13] The deaths of millions of young men who had died in the Great War "to end all wars" wiped out the great minds of their generation, as well as its ordinary and economically significant sons of the soil and towns.

Yet Edna held to her view, as did many Americans. After all, the United States (unlike Canada) only abandoned neutrality on April 6, 1917. American casualties numbered some 320,000, with

American deaths set at 116,516 men among the 4.7 million U.S. soldiers serving, or two per cent of its military with no civilian casualties.* Condé, too, swept aside the war and its aftermath, emotionally believing that it was time to expand *Vogue* into the spiritual home of haute couture. In Edna's words, "American stock was high in France."[14]

But Condé ignored all this. He had waited long enough. And so, on June 15, 1920, the first issue of French *Vogue*—called *Frog* by insiders—appeared on newsstands. No French editor had been officially appointed, but Cosette Vogel was the only candidate under consideration. What Edna hadn't appreciated was that Condé not only wanted to acquire the services of both Vogels— Cosette and her husband, Lucien, who had edited *La Gazette du Bon Ton* before the Great War—but also planned to take a strategic stake in *Jardin des Modes* and *L'Illustration des Modes*, edited by the Vogel family. And that was with the full knowledge that the current owner, Marcel Baschet, had lost more than a half-million francs in the previous two years alone.

Clearly the Vogels were the catalyst for the acquisitions. Still, Condé and his negotiator, Philippe Ortiz, were hesitant to buy titles that leached investment capital—that is, until Baschet offered *L'Illustration* for free, provided there would be no announcement of the terms of Condé's acquisition, and that he would continue publication and pay the Vogels' contract for at least three months. When Edna was told, she was apoplectic. At the end of the day Condé not only acquired *L'Illustration* but also Baschet's *Jardin des Modes* in 1921, giving Les Éditions Condé Nast three

---

* Canada, as part of the Commonwealth, joined the fight alongside Great Britain. Total Canadian deaths or missing in action are listed as 64,944 Canadian and Newfoundlanders. (Newfoundland was not part of Canada then, and is listed separately.) (Source: *Commonwealth War Graves Commission Annual Report 2008–2009.*) The Spanish flu pandemic of 1918–19 claimed at least another 40 million lives worldwide.

French magazines and the genius of the Vogels as well as Cosette's brother Michel de Brunhoff.

Edna moaned that she had been little consulted during the negotiations. When she found out, she argued violently with Condé. He "now owned three *Vogues* and *Vogue Pattern Book*, *House & Garden*, and *Vanity Fair*. That seemed to me enough."[15] Edna was a gifted editor who had already been working at the company for more than twenty-five years, but she was no entrepreneur. While Condé never complained about Edna's months of haranguing and protests—much less the pitched battles that occurred once Cosette Vogel came to New York to argue her case for the acquisition of *L'Illustration*—he must have sensed that Edna felt threatened. Cosette and her husband lived amid the Parisian fashion scene and knew everyone. Her family were strongly connected to France's artistic and literary communities as well. Cosette was younger, prettier, with a dynamic personality, light red hair, and baby-blue eyes. Who better than Cosette to represent *Vogue*'s enduring claim that fashion represents the drama of daily life? So Edna's objections were overruled. Condé had more than likely made up his mind to acquire *L'Illustration* from the outset and saw Edna's reticence as her being outclassed by the very French, very connected Cosette.

Condé's expansion did not stop there. He had set his heart on developing and operating his own printing enterprise. With the enthusiastic assistance of Lew Wurzburg—he of the offending tardy slips—Condé acquired forty acres of scrubland alongside the Boston Post Road in Greenwich, Connecticut. This would become the site of Condé Nast Press. Edna had once criticized Condé for lacking vision when he refused to back her in buying up plots on Sutton Place in Manhattan. Actually Condé knew it would take millions to speculate in such a venture, and he was right—those millions came from the Morgan and Vanderbilt fortunes, who could better afford the gamble.[16]

The Greenwich plant was Condé's own first "stately home." That it became a state-of-the-art printing business surrounded by beautifully landscaped gardens with rolling green lawns was entirely due to Condé's vision. There was barely a tree or a weed on the entire site when he bought it. The soil was rocky in "the way only New England soil can be," with outcrops everywhere.[17] But with dynamite, determination, and money, Condé changed all that.

Nast always believed in consulting experts for help and advice. At Condé Nast Press, the help and influence of Dick Wright, editor of *House & Garden*, can be felt in the exquisite landscaping: some sixty-five tall American elms were transplanted in the central circle into holes blasted out of the rock; rare varieties of deciduous trees, cedars, copper beech, and rare evergreens were strategically placed on the grounds, surrounded by a wealth of unusual shrubs, hybrid rhododendrons, hemlock hedges, vines, climbing roses, seasonal bulbs, and ground cover.

A timed concealed sprinkler system with underground pipework was installed to ensure that the lawns would remain green, well drained, and watered throughout the growing season. The roadway leading to the central building was edged by a four-foot-high drystone wall, again referring to the property's New England roots. European statuary—including a five-hundred-year-old Florentine baptismal font—was strategically placed to bring in the Old World charm Condé loved.[18]

The magnificent, tranquil surroundings, situated on one of the busiest roads in the Northeast, was enhanced by the most modern high-quality printing establishment in the magazine world. With his purpose-built, excess-capacity plant, Condé foresaw other publications in his rosy future.

17. THE HIGH PRIESTESS MEETS HER FORCES OF NATURE

"Vogue, the Ancient Mariner, Charts the Sea of Fashion"
—*VOGUE*, AUGUST 1, 1925

The advent of Prohibition in 1920 hurt Condé's magazines. The sudden loss of quality advertisers of malt whiskeys and fine champagnes, however, was replaced soon enough by other luxury products. But Prohibition did not stop the flow of liquor at Condé's parties. Overnight, as in all big cities, a thriving black market was born, and Condé was one of its buyers of alcoholic refreshments for his guests. Though he was a virtual teetotaler, he believed that a good host always provided what his friends expected to see, and in his case, that something was better-than-100-proof bootleg gin. Just how he managed to have free-flowing French champagne was due to the inventiveness of his secretaries—Estelle Moore, who had followed him from *Collier's*, and the former physical education teacher Mary Campbell. Condé knew that "Prohibition was a time when there tended to be a *lot* of excitement," as a young fashionable woman who graced the parties and future editor of *Vogue*, Diana Vreeland, wrote. "It was because you weren't allowed to drink that you drank anything you could get your hands on. People would go into the bathroom and drink Listerine! Anything that might have a crrrumb of alcohol."[1] Everyone, that is, except Condé, Frank, and Edna.

In a feat worthy of talented magicians, Condé's secretaries sprang into action to organize the legendary café society parties

at his Park Avenue home. It was they who summoned the caterers, planned the menus, ordered the flowers, hired the musicians,
and somehow found all the liquor (more than likely through some
corrupt network at New York's docks), while tallying the much-
talked-about A, B, and C lists that tracked aristocrats, entertainers, musicians, artists, and important businesspeople. As the
twenties progressed, Edna's quiet Quaker disapproval of Condé's
fabulous, lavish revelries became as clear as the judgmental nose
on her face. While she recognized that wining and dining those
who read—or aspired to read—their magazines was a necessity,
she also believed that Condé, like Jay Gatsby, "dispensed starlight
to casual moths," and was squandering his millions on things that
didn't matter.[2] The parties, which began in earnest around 1922,
after Frank moved into Condé's 470 Park Avenue home, received
only the tip of Edna's scorn. She had to keep her criticisms of
Condé's personal spending and largesse close to her chest. After
all, she had been a beneficiary, too, when he paid off her mortgage
back in 1913.[3]

Of course once Frank and Condé became boon companions,
sharing an apartment, seen at sporting fixtures, the same clubs,
and about town together, malicious tongues wagged—in loud stage
whispers. Edna waved the tittle-tattle aside: The only person Frank
truly loved was his brother, Edward, a rather sad man who was
married to the bottle.[4] Condé knew the world thought they were
gay but didn't care. Plans were already afoot for the pair to move
to an even-larger Park Avenue home at number 1040. Condé had
bought the thirty-room penthouse duplex while it was still in the
blueprint stage, transformed it to his needs, and eagerly awaited
its completion.

Edna's feelings on Prohibition were like most people's: There
was nothing wrong with drinking alcohol, so long as it was not to
excess. Edna, Condé, and Frank never entered into the heated
"wet-dry" confrontations raging across America, dividing politicians, the liberal women's networks, and employers. She was quite
aware that women's groups in particular saw alcohol as the root

cause of violence and poverty, but strongly held the belief that *Vogue* must remain as apolitical as possible in these changing times.[5] None of them knew, as yet, that Prohibition would help rob America of some of its greatest literary minds and free-thinkers like Ernest Hemingway, Sherwood Anderson,[*] John Dos Passos, and F. Scott Fitzgerald for nearly ten years, since they wanted to live in Europe where life was cheap and the sale of alcohol was legal.

Frank and Condé were rare men in understanding how women and their roles had changed since 1913. They knew better than most that the modern independent woman saw herself as light-hearted, unconventional, and blissfully unaware what boundaries society might or should impose on her. For some, the razzmatazz of being a modern woman meant "flirting, kissing, viewing life lightly, saying damn without a blush, playing along the danger line in an immature way—sort of a mental baby vamp." She could get away with anything, so long as it was said or done with wit, a smile, or a wild dance.[6] This was the creed of modern women like Zelda Fitzgerald and Tallulah Bankhead. It was tolerated by Edna, in the spirit of remaining apolitical.

And she was right to think that way. For many it was a topsy-turvy world. Moralists in the 1920s were upset by advertisements. Flappers, that "bobbed-hair mob," and female rebels against tradition were seen as the new mass consumer. Lucky Strike cigarettes showed the contemporary independent woman, enshrined in the image of silent movie star Constance Talmadge lighting up to the slogan "Light a Lucky and you'll never miss sweets that make you fat." The old "New Woman" of 1887 was seen in a Coca-Cola advertisement as a well-dressed, refined lady helped from a rowboat by a gentleman wearing a striped blazer, tie, and straw hat. By

---

[*] Anderson gave the newspaperman Hemingway (then working for the *Toronto Star*) an introduction to Gertrude Stein, thereby launching him into Paris's "lost generation" of writers. (Source: *Hemingway and the Little Magazines: The Paris Years*, Barre, MA: Barre Publishers, 1968, 6–7.)

1923 Coke showed a flapper riding the surf in a bathing suit that revealed more than it hid, all to the slogan "Enjoy Life!" Condé, an avid trendsetter in advertising, knew that the old rules were being rewritten. The only problem was that no woman had as yet received her copy of the bewildering handbook. Condé intended for *Vogue*, through its articles, images, and advertisements, to ease the way for her; and Edna, regardless of her personal convictions, had to agree that this was wise.

Changes in women's interests and their place in society were the key to unlocking Condé's view of the fresh and exciting lives women lived in his magazines.* Reporting on and foreseeing fashion trends were at the heart of his compelling need to capture beauty in all its guises in the pages of *Vogue* for readers at home, work, and play. Hiring debutantes, who did little more than waft through the offices of *Vogue* to chat about the latest gossip and spontaneous fashions as they traveled to the "in" places of Newport, Palm Beach, or Paris and Deauville in France, was a crucial part of his editorial policy that agreed with Edna. It facilitated *Vogue's* ability to impart their world—whether aspirational or real—to the magazine's wider readership. Beautiful women and pleasing them through *Vogue* was their business. Features on the British actress and model Lady Diana Manners; "America's sweetheart," Mary Pickford; the actresses Norma Shearer and Greta Garbo interested *Vogue's* readers. They and women like them became regulars at Condé's café society parties. Charlie Chaplin, Frank's friend, was often seen joking with the Marx Brothers, who, in turn, might "cut a rug" dancing with Mrs. Vanderbilt or Mrs. Astor. In the twenties, the wide cosmopolitan circle of Frank's friends had become Condé's intimates, too.

To be a modern woman meant change, and society was transformed with her. Condé had a natural instinct for these shifting sands. It drove his lifelong practice for hiring staff on a whim. What *did* annoy Edna, as Condé's editor, was that he often did so

---

* In France, suffrage for "all women of voting age" only occurred in 1945.

without the immediate boss's knowledge. She could pigeonhole such enthusiasm as Condé's desire to have a great many attractive society debutantes and interesting women populating *Vogue*'s corridors—so long as they told all their dearest acquaintances that they simply *had* to buy *Vogue*, and also telling *Vogue* what their nearest friends were wearing or doing. One debutante, and future editor in chief of *Vogue*, Diana Vreeland, put her views on Condé's attitude to the modern woman into context: "He believed that all women everywhere should have the opportunity to have the prettiest clothes, the prettiest surroundings, and every known method to make themselves more seductive, knowledgeable, and attractive."[7]

Although Condé and Edna worked as a "dream team," he probably hadn't appreciated that she had an inferiority complex, and that there were women whom she believed were threats to *her* burgeoning *Vogue* empire.[8] She was against Condé's overseas expansion in part because she knew she would have to delegate power—most often in London and Paris and even, at times—*egad!*—in New York. This meant that she needed to have trustworthy, hardworking, always less-experienced young protégées whom she could belittle or damn with faint praise. The more talented her assistant editors, the more Edna took the credit for their discoveries. An editor who saw her in action with her subordinates said later: "She had a sadistic trait in her."[9]

Edna had no idea that she'd met her match in the younger, more vibrant Miss Carmel White. Aged thirty-four to Edna's gray-haired forty-five, Carmel was an auburn-haired, slender, diminutive figure with vivacious blue eyes. Like Edna, she was not a beauty, with her long sloping nose and thin, pouty lips that turned downward when not smiling. Yet her magnificent high cheekbones, wide-set clear gaze, and sheer ebullient energy made her a dazzling personality. She was slightly exotic, too, hailing from an artistic and industrious Irish immigrant family, and had a gift of endearing herself to her listeners with her endless Irishisms. Her mother,

Annie Douglass,* was one of New York's foremost dressmakers, owner of the discreet and glamorous T.M. & J.M. Fox, located at 10 East Fifty-seventh Street in Manhattan.

Annie was as tough as army boots and had clawed her way to success in America—first in Chicago, then New York. A *New York Times* reporter wrote: "People will pass the house and never know that the gowns of the richly dressed women they pass in Fifth Avenue are being made inside." She was a formidable woman who had raised her brood of six children alone after the death of her husband, Peter White, aged only forty-three. Carmel was their third child and only five years old when her father died. She later claimed that the abiding image of her father "laid out like a waxen image" on the living room table was responsible for her insensitive rhinoceros hide.[10] Chances are that Carmel both resembled and rebelled against her indomitable mother. Their relationship certainly stood Carmel in good stead in her dealings with Edna.

Carmel learned her dressmaking from the most menial position upward at her mother's establishment. After a romance that ended because her mother was—shock, horror—"in trade," Carmel saw her future, working for Mama, as a mind-numbing proposition. Her first thought of becoming an editor came in the summer of 1914, when Annie took her daughter to Paris to view the new collections. Returning to New York and life as her mother's dogsbody—sometimes selling, sometimes modeling, sometimes sweeping up after the dressmakers—Carmel thought her dream of writing and editing was over. Granted, T.M. & J.M. Fox participated in Edna's first-ever American fashion show in November 1914, and Edna wore Fox's gown named "Golden Dream" to the event. But that didn't lead to Carmel's important introduction to *Vogue*.

The outbreak of war gave Carmel an excuse to return to France, joining the Red Cross in Paris. Like her favorite brother, Tom, she

---

* Annie White probably married Edward Van Pelt Douglass in 1905, affording her and all her children American citizenship. The marriage was not a success. (Source: Penelope Rowlands, *A Dash of Daring*, New York: Atria Books, 2005, 23–24.)

was a workaholic. Describing her job for the Red Cross, Carmel said: "You stood on your feet for untold hours, doling out food and supplies to millions of troops and refugees, and then valiantly one-stepped them off at night to 'Smiles.' Your life fluctuated between grueling stretches of superhuman work, and brief oases of gaiety on leave in Paris, where every officer treated you as the queen."[11]

After the war Carmel was once more "back in my mother's shop [where] my old inferiority complex took over. Though I had proved my executive ability when I was on my own, under my mother I felt I was nobody."[12] That's when Carmel began to search secretly for work in the fashion world. Harrydele Hallmark, who wrote the entertaining column "What the Well-Dressed Women Are Wearing" under the pseudonym "Anne Rittenhouse" for *The New York Times*, unexpectedly asked Carmel to do her a favor. Hallmark had become ill just before the Paris collections were unveiled. Since she couldn't go, could Carmel please take notes for her? Naturally Hallmark was thrilled with Carmel's observations. So Carmel asked Hallmark for an entrée to *Vogue*.[13]

Annie Douglass's fearsome ways had groomed Carmel for that first meeting with Edna. Carmel must have sailed through the interview, since Edna asked her to meet Condé afterward. With his usual unerring eye for talent and young women of promise, Condé thought Carmel might contribute articles to *Vogue*. If they ran, it would be without a byline, as was the custom of the day for beginning writers, he told her.

But the weeks inched by without any word from *Vogue*, and Carmel began to despair. Then, without warning, in December Condé appeared at T.M. & J.M Fox's Fifty-seventh Street shop, asking for Miss White. He apologized to Carmel, saying that he was about to catch a boat to Europe, and that there was a taxi waiting to take him to the docks, but would she consider working for him at *Vogue*? She said later she must have answered but couldn't recall. Their five-minute conversation ended with Condé smiling and calling out as he dashed to his cab, "Goodbye—so it's settled right now, Miss White!"[14]

Carmel's suit for her first day at work—a mortuary-black

Vionnet outfit of crepe de chine with matching black accessories, including a "Miss Jessica" hat from Bendel's—more suggestive of a recent widow than a fashion editor for *Vogue*—was a disaster. Her "business experience was nil," and her writing, with its "airy insouciance," left a great deal to be desired. "I used to edit her letters," Edna wrote, "and gradually trained her into the more conventional paths of business usage, though I think she found it prosy stuff."[15]

Carmel's appointment as a fashion editor at *Vogue* was extraordinary for a raft of reasons. Most obviously, she was a young woman without previous experience working for any fashion magazine, much less *the* fashion publication. More significantly, in the 1920s most establishments warned against employing minority groups, posting signs outside their doors that "No Irish," "No Jews," and "No Negroes" need apply—even in sophisticated New York City. Catholics were just as bad for some. These were the days of President Warren Gamaliel Harding, who was deeply suspicious of "all those immigrants." He signed into law a quick fix to restrict them, so America's extreme Right could elevate the cause of social purity and the protection of women to a more contemporary and disturbing level. These were the days when the Ku Klux Klan spread its fearsome message beyond the Deep South, and when noisy anarchists, communists, and socialists abounded in American cities.[16] These were the days when the sham trial of anarchists Nicola Sacco, a shoemaker and night watchman, and Bartolomeo Vanzetti, a fishmonger, for the murder of the guard and paymaster of the Slater and Morrill Shoe Company during an armed robbery had become the cause célèbre of writers, artists, and academics. Both Dorothy Parker and Robert Benchley campaigned for their pardon after their conviction in July 1921.* Condé, too, disliked any antediluvian notions that prejudiced freedom in society. He

---

* Sacco and Vanzetti were executed shortly after midnight on August 23, 1927. Reference to Parker and Benchley supporting their appeal can be found in John Keats, *You Might as Well Live: The Life and Times of Dorothy Parker* (New York: Simon & Schuster, 1970), 132.

always hired the most talented men and women from minority gene pools, or new immigrants, and didn't care if they were bisexual, lesbian, or gay either.* What mattered was talent.

In London, 1922 saw Elspeth Champcommunal quietly return to the House of Worth as a designer, understanding at last that she was no editor of magazines. More than likely Elspeth suggested Dorothy Todd, another champion of the Bloomsbury Set, as her successor. Both women inhabited the same highbrow world, and both women were lesbians. Still, Todd was hardly what anyone could call a fashion icon. Her friends described her as "energetic, portly, determined, louche, exasperating, intelligent, raddled,† commercial, 'imperious and enterprising' . . . a short, square, crop-headed, double-breasted, bow-tied lady."[17] So much for friends in highbrow places.

Todd apparently had led a life filled with blank pages clouded by an inky and often muddled past. Her grandson, Olivier Todd, recalled that "she always seemed to be wearing an austere iron-grey suit with a black velvet collar, in her buttonhole she had a fresh carnation, white or crimson, changed every day. She moved about in a trail of eau-de-cologne which she took from a round mauve bottle."[18] While Condé, Frank, and Edna were slaving over *Vogue*'s thirtieth anniversary issue in 1922, Todd, freshly back in London from her "training session" in New York, was busy manipulating Condé's successful American formula into a British *Vogue*

---

* "Transgenderism" and "transsexualism" were unknown terms in the day. The first successful "transgender reassignment therapy" was completed on Dora "R" in 1930 in Germany. The term "transsexualism" was coined in 1923 by Dora R's surgeon, Magnus Hirschfeld, but was translated into English by David Oliver Cauldwell, the pioneering sexologist, only in 1949. Hirschfeld fled Nazi Germany in 1932, and in May 1933 a mob attacked the institute where he and Dora had worked, burning all its records. No further information about Dora has survived, but given what happened at the institute and in Nazi Germany, it is safe to assume that she perished at the hands of the Nazis.

† In this case, meaning "debauched."

for her own ends. She saw the opportunity to take Condé's staple blend of high society, high fashion, and the rich and famous and bend it to her elitist, Bloomsbury-centric will. Essentially she planned to turn British *Vogue* into a British *Vanity Fair*. Todd's skill lay in her ability to foist as much high culture on her readers as they could stomach. She always remained within the letter of Condé's formula restrictions for *Vogue*, while simultaneously ignoring the spirit of his guidelines.

Todd commissioned an article for early January 1924's *Brogue* titled "Contemporary Style in Decoration," featuring the work of Duncan Grant and Vanessa Bell. "Houses, like women, are very well dressed nowadays," or so its readers were instructed.[19] It was the first of Bloomsbury's articles announcing its growing influence on British *Vogue*. It would become an increasingly uneasy relationship. Todd had agreed to terms—ten pounds—with Virginia Woolf for four separate one-thousand-word articles. Woolf sat for British *Vogue*'s photographers and its regular "Hall of Fame" feature. Referring to the magazine's popularity, Woolf wrote in her diary that "very likely this time next year I shall be one of those people who are, so father said, in the little circle of London Society which represents the Apostles* on a larger scale."[20]

Unlike Todd's British *Vogue*, French *Vogue* accentuated the transatlantic links with America as an important part of its cultural agenda. Cosette's French edition ran a feature on "American Painters of Women" in 1920. American *Vogue* responded in 1922 with journalist and editor Mary Fanton Roberts's article "Ultra-Modern French Art in New York," about the artists Marie Laurencin and Irène Lagut.[21] *Vogue*'s Franco-American cooperation not only imported culture to the United States but also represented a high

---

* An intellectual society founded at Cambridge University in 1820 by George Tomlinson. Several members of the Bloomsbury Set were also members of the Apostles, including John Maynard Keynes, Virginia's husband, Leonard Woolf, and the biographer Lytton Strachey.

point of American influence in France. A feature called "America Sends the Spices of Life to Europe" pointed out that military aid after the Great War was merely the most obvious export: The best movies, cocktails, tobacco, dances and their dancers, and especially jazz brought America to life in France.

The artistic avant-garde flourished in French *Vogue*, too, but there it was supported by the haute-monde Parisian salons. Their patronage of Diaghilev's Ballets Russes, the artists Picasso, Matisse, Braque, and Cocteau, and the composers Debussy and Ravel helped many modern movements to flourish. In fact Paris had become the international crucible in which the new writing, music, art, and fashion design were fused into a fresh, contemporary art form. American, British, and Irish writers flocked to the French capital to sip its waters of ingenuity. And *Vogue* aspired to become the avant-garde's shopwindow.

Cubism could be found on fabrics, such as Poiret's silk sprinkled with "square-cut confetti" and in new clothing shapes, from simple draping to the broken silhouette. Cubism had a tremendous influence on dress: If the patterns were to be appreciated, women's clothing needed to be simplified. Volume and scale had to be flattened to show modern artistic compositions printed on fabrics, from the established couturiers like Poiret to the Johnny-come-lately Coco Chanel. As the 1920s took hold of the psyche, Chanel's designs became increasingly popular. She returned time and again to cubist shapes and lines suggestive of America's "vast iron horizons" of skyscrapers and bridges. *Vogue* invested heavily in promoting the modern, as did *Vanity Fair*, and it remained a prominent theme in both magazines' reporting on "great chic" throughout the decade.[22]

In New York, Edna was undoubtedly having considerable difficulty maintaining control of British *Vogue*. Todd's shenanigans were allowed to continue. Edna could be excused, of course, because she was preoccupied with the apparent threat of Cosette Vogel. And then there was Carmel. . . . Granted, too, Edna remarried at the

end of 1921, to the British engineer and inventor Richard Newton.* Condé never blamed Edna for taking her eye off the international side of the business. But when Adolph Gayne de Meyer,
Vogue's main New York photographer, suddenly announced he was
going to work for Hearst's *Harper's Bazar*, Edna was caught un-
awares, and a furious Condé contacted Hearst directly. Swiftly a
"no poaching" policy was agreed—which held for some years to
come.[23]

Not only had *Bazar* more than doubled de Meyer's salary, but
he had been promised a base in Paris rather than New York—
something he had always wanted. Edna had considered de Meyer
one of *Vogue's* all-stars since his elegant society photographs first
appeared in its 1913 pages. But with his defection, as if to mini-
mize the loss, Edna described him as "a dilettante in photography
for some years, but the pages of *Vogue* became the setting that developed and exhibited his talent."[24] In those days photography
was used primarily for society and theatrical portraits, not covers.
So the loss of *Vogue's* mainstay photographer was a blow, but not
quite the knockout Hearst may have intended. The magazine's
covers were always illustrated, as were most of the fashion models
shown. Yet, with de Meyer's sudden departure, *Vogue's* second-tier
photographer, George Hoyningen-Huene, often known simply as
Huene, was given his opportunity to shine. With his dramatic staging of a single person or a group, Huene developed portraits for
Vogue that were natural and could be imagined as having been
snapped in any well-appointed room of a socially acceptable home,
except for the fact that the models were impossibly handsome men
and women.

It hadn't taken Edna long to train Carmel in her *Vogue* ways,
but she still found it difficult to delegate jobs to her. Carmel was
a force of nature: witty, funny, and popular with everyone. Edna
couldn't help noticing that Carmel had become a favored companion of Condé's, too, and that he had grown quite fond of her. Of

---

* She had divorced her first husband, Frank Chase, father of her daughter, Ilka,
sometime in 1913.

course Edna was happily married, so it was not some sort of romantic jealousy eating away at her. She feared that Carmel—always a quick study, always fun—might be singled out to replace her as *Vogue*'s editor. She had been with the company some twenty-seven of its first thirty years and had no intentions of retiring or taking things easier.

Perhaps that was the real push behind Edna's idea to put together the thirtieth-anniversary issue of the magazine. By her own admission, she sequestered herself (against company policy) to put together the edition, concentrating on little else. Condé wrote the introduction, titled "A Salutation from One Mere Man to 150,000 Women":

> *To a shy man the making of a birthday speech is something of an ordeal, but on this occasion, when* Vogue *is celebrating its thirtieth anniversary, the pride and pleasure I have felt in receiving congratulations from friends of* Vogue, *and the sense of incalculable debt that I owe to* Vogue's *readers and advertisers, prompt me to utter a word of thanks—out of a very full heart.... It is our enviable fortune to have an audience of 150,000 women so nimble-witted, so sophisticated, so delicately attuned, that our task is not to write down to you, but to keep up with you!... Making a magazine for you is like perpetually playing to a first-night audience of the most astute and responsive character.*

Condé didn't shy away either from heaping praise on *Vogue*'s editor: "There are few women, I think, whose character and tastes are more essentially feminine; and yet there are few men who bring to the solving of business problems a keener insight, broader vision, or clearer thinking than the woman who has stood so diligently watching over the pages of *Vogue* during the past ten years as its Editor-in-Chief, and before that as its Managing Editor."[25]

Frank was roped in, too, for his "Crowniesque" and urbane "Ten Thousand Nights in a Dinner Coat," which dealt with the gamut of social changes since *Vogue*'s inception in the Gilded Age. Naturally

Frank couldn't resist writing his pièce de resistance, featuring a fictional visit to Sing Sing prison in upstate New York with Edna. There they met a man who had been in solitary confinement for thirty years for "dismembering the body of a lady for whom he had formerly entertained the liveliest feelings of affection." The warden told them about the man's utter loss of human conversation, radio, or theater. He had not "jazzed in a cabaret, consumed a bottle of champagne, cut in at a rubber of bridge, played in a round of golf, smoked a Havana cigar, or eaten a dinner in the companies of ladies."

Frank's reply begged pity for his own tragedy, which:

> has kept me prisoner to a social system more cruel and merciless than any within the ken of a mere murderer . . . for thirty years—simply because I am a bachelor in New York, with a change of dress-coats and some little private means—I have known no solitude whatever: I have been forced to eat only the richest food; I have tossed upon strange beds in the country houses of a thousand and one distracted hostesses; I have suffered intolerable and nightly agonies at the theatre; I have battled with French pastry, Greek waiters, Nubian bands, Welsh rarebits, Argentine tangos, and English noblemen at God knows how many cabarets. Willingly would I change my lot with your prisoner's.[26]

The thirtieth-anniversary issue was a huge success, and Edna regained some confidence by virtue of the accolades she received. All that was modern was chic and *Vogue*. Its readers were pictured at the prow of a smart ship as it was launched into an uncertain future.

18. ALL THOSE FLAMING "BRIGHT YOUNG THINGS"

Mr. Condé Nast almost persuades that style is an American invention . . . once in a while convention and novelty make a highly useful team.

—NEW-YORK TRIBUNE EDITORIAL, JANUARY 1926

Condé loved Paris. So too did Frank and Edna. Still, it was Condé, not Frank or Edna, who was suddenly on the wrong end of the gate to the Quat'z'Arts Ball in Paris in the early 1920s. This terrific charity event had a specific requirement that revelers *had* to appear in costume. According to *Vogue's* coverage, it made for rather keen competition among the women attending—many of whom had their couturiers design their often-outrageous attire.[1] Those whose dress failed to get into the spirit of the moment were swiftly shown the door. Others, who only half-heartedly joined in the fun, had a black mark painted on their back. Condé's problem was that he was unwilling to discard his proper evening attire of white tie and tails to don a costume like the others. As he tried to join Grace Moore's party at the Pompeiian-themed ball, he was refused entry. According to Moore: "Condé, correctly arrayed in white tie and tails, was being turned away from the door by the police, who warned him that no one so respectable could survive the bedlam within."[2]

It was a faux pas Frank would not have made, and one that Condé most likely did not regret. Parisians gave charity balls at least once a week in the spring, so there would always be another one. Boisterous balls, even for charity, were an integral part of his world. They were all part of the necessity of being seen. At home

Condé threw at least two large parties a month—often to congrat-
ulate someone for something. Afterward they were reported with
predictable regularity in the New York gossip columns. Most guests
claimed their rightful place in either *Vogue* or *Vanity Fair*. Those
who didn't found that their homes appeared in *House & Garden*.

Prohibition only added to his guests' excitement. The invitees
had to give a password before they could even ascend in the elevator. Revelers found their champagne chilling in a bathtub, but rye,
scotch, gin, rum, vermouth, brandy, and sherry were readily available, too. Menus and invited guests received the same careful
scrutiny, ensuring that just the right cocktail of people attended
the correct party. Such opulence, such care to every detail, reflected Condé's perfectionism. As his larger parties warmed up,
when Condé was satisfied that the scene was perfectly set, he could
often be found in a peaceful corner of his library reading or playing a quiet game of bridge with other like-minded friends.[3] It would
be his parties—and not the bright, shining stars of the day—that
people would recall later.

But it was the flaming "Bright Young Things" who led the world.
Condé believed it was his duty to bring their beauty and allure to
his readers' attention. One of the more outrageous and enduring
of them was that French enfant terrible Jean Cocteau, who was
first published in *Vanity Fair* in October 1922. In his "The Public
and the Artist" he declared: "The opposition of the masses to the
elite has always stimulated individual genius. This is the case in
France. Modern Germany is dying of approbation, carefulness,
faithful application and scholastic vulgarization of aristocratic
culture."[4]

Cocteau aimed this philosophy at a select crowd. The successful "little" bar Le Boeuf sur le Toit was a reflection of this idea,
and nowhere did Le Boeuf get better coverage than on the pages
of *Vogue*. Located on the rue Boissy d'Anglas, in the chic neigh-
borhood near French *Vogue*'s offices, Le Boeuf turned the traditional salon dynamic on its head. Instead of a quiet meeting place
in the homes of patrons where artists and intellectuals jockeyed
for position, here was an open, wildly animated social scene. Le

Tout-Paris were drawn there by the magnetic force of its artistic elite. Opening in January 1922, the bar soon enticed fashionable women away from Poiret's nostalgic L'Oasis, becoming one of Paris's most exclusive nightspots. It was a real-life reincarnation of Cocteau's "Nothing Doing Bar," cloned from the subtitle of the Darius Milhaud–Cocteau ballet *Le Boeuf sur le toit*. Cocteau and Les Six, the revered Montparnasse composers, haunted it, as did the cream of France's wealthy and intelligentsia.[5]

In June 1923 French *Vogue* reported on Le Boeuf in "The Elegant Nightlife of Paris."[6] The writer, Jean LaPorte, considered the "magic" of Le Boeuf as the premier nightspot "where one lived from midnight to six in the morning." It was "seductive," notably absent of film stars, and filled with the capital's "most interesting . . . clientele of young writers, musicians, and painters . . . an open circle that gathers not because of snobbism, but because of shared taste."[7]

The article illustrated a black saxophone player in the crowded bar. "Vence* [*sic*], a demon on the saxophone . . . [and] a black chanteuse with a voice like a locomotive's whistle, singing 'Do it Again' in an unforgettable manner" was just one reminder to *Vogue*'s readers that Le Boeuf's jazz was "always first-rate." Back then it was exciting, French *Vogue* gushed, to see a man in a finely tailored suit sitting next to "a young painter from Montparnasse in a velvet sweater with a floppy tie" and women in evening gowns listening to the music.[8] American *Vogue* also covered Le Boeuf, calling it, with its American jazz, "one of those tiny Paris haunts that within four narrow walls confine two worlds." Erik Satie and Les Six, who composed music that was a mélange of American jazz, French popular music, embellished with their classical conservatory musical training, were at the heart of Le Boeuf's special mix. French intellectualism, shaken with American music and

---

* Vance Lowry, the great saxophonist and banjo player who had made his name with Dan Kildare in London in 1916 in the Ciro Club Coon Orchestra. The novelist Raymond Radiguet described him as "charming and cheerful . . . with a delicious American accent."

cocktails, made the club the transatlantic expression of modernism. *Vogue* sprinkled the Franco-American connection with its own brand of fairy dust: "There are the young bloods at the bar who act as if they owned the place. If they deign to speak to someone sitting at the tables in the outer wilderness, they do it with condescension. . . . The bar is hung with photographs by Man Ray of some of these celebrities. Dear, fat Doucet delights us at the piano, and the little tables are crowded with a public as remarkable in its own way as the young intellectuals at the bar."[9]

That was the key to Le Boeuf's enduring appeal. Where else but Paris could you see a top couturier tickling the ivories with an august audience of musicians, artists, and patrons looking on? That was, and is, style. Or as Honoré de Balzac put it nearly a hundred years earlier: "The person who does not visit Paris often will never be completely elegant."[10] Basically Le Boeuf had style, that je ne sais quoi which oozed success.

Fashion in Paris nonetheless remained *Vogue*'s main priority. The title's new fashion editor, the Chicagoan Main Bocher, had had a burning desire to become an opera singer. Sadly, he hadn't the lungs to become a great tenor, so eventually he honed his skills as an illustrator. However, his real strength was an unerring sense of fashion and style. As French *Vogue*'s fashion editor, his writing about the Paris mode was lively, informative, and precise. Yet Edna thought Main was easily influenced by couturiers, which she deemed unseemly. Then, too, in her estimation his salary expectations were more than grandiose.[11] In 1929 Main was finally booted out by Condé, whose patience had been sorely tried, for the sin of lacking "calm, orderly, administrative capacity . . . as much a born characteristic as pitch deafness," in his scathing memo dated July 5, 1929.[12] Certainly the death of Condé's revered mother, Esther, on July 1 did not put him in an accommodating mood either. Untouched by Condé's words, Main sailed on, oblivious to the storm, thereafter combining his first and second names, and—*voilà!*—the couturier Mainbocher was born. Eight years later he became known as the man who designed the wedding dress and trousseau of Wallis Warfield Simpson for her marriage to the Duke of Windsor. Of course, there were no hard feelings, and *Vogue* duly promoted his collections.

But all that lay in the future. In 1923, Misia, the Russian-born wife of the painter José Maria Sert, ruled the heart of Parisian bohemian society.* Misia was also the inseparable friend of Coco Chanel. She boosted Chanel's rise to the dizzy heights as czarina of the Paris fashion world, with her low-waisted, brief-skirted, and "infinitely graceless chemise frock."[13] But Chanel's real genius began with the use of simple fabrics like jersey,† felt berets, and straw hats, reminiscent of Chanel's childhood in the French countryside. So, when Chanel hit upon this nostalgic note, it caught on. Essentially Chanel was a milliner, and wearing a Chanel hat during wartime became a show of patriotism. Through her long affair with "Bendor," Hugh Grosvenor, duke of Westminster, she became accepted among the British upper crust just as she had with the Parisian beau monde who wintered on the Riviera. Chanel elbowed aside Poiret, just as he had given Jeanne Paquin the push. But when Chanel disembarked from Bendor's yacht, *Flying Cloud*, "brown as a cabin boy," she shattered the last of the Victorian taboos and introduced her longest-lasting fashion—the suntan.

With Chanel's ascendancy, other designers became ever more demanding of space in *Vogue*. Jean Patou, for one, considered Chanel his greatest rival. *Jardin des Modes* editor Michel de Brunhoff begged Edna never—*ever*—to put Chanel and Patou models on facing pages of the magazine. Irate at such kowtowing to couturiers, Edna wrote Patou a scathing letter telling him a few home truths. Her main point was that despite *Vogue's* giving him more

---

* The Serts were married in 1920 and finally divorced in 1927 after a tumultuous marriage that involved them both in a ménage à trois.

† Lillie Langtry, British actress and mistress of King Edward VII, had popularized the use of jersey in the late nineteenth century; the fabric was named after her Channel Island birthplace.

column inches than any other magazine, he had signally failed ever
to write one word of appreciation. If he continued this nonsense,
Edna warned, she would ban him from the pages of *Vogue*.[14]

Shortly afterward, when *Vogue*'s advertising manager, Laurence
Schneider,* came to sell space to Patou, he told Condé and Edna
that he met the couturier in his entirely white private office, which
was guarded by a white Russian wolfhound. The impeccable Patou, seated behind his white desk, had placed a pearl-handled re-
volver on top. While Patou was often as excitable as a Frenchman
in an English farce, the couturier placed his advertising order amid
a sea of calm.[15] Edna's letter had woven its magic.

When Patou came to New York a few months later, he seized
on the notion uttered by one of his clients that French and American women were built differently. The ubiquitous Philippe Ortiz
recommended that *Vogue* help the couturier find the "right" American models so Patou could make more of a splash in the U.S.
market. Dutifully, in November 1924, *Vogue* placed a classified advertisement in the New York press: "A Paris *couturier* desires to
secure three ideal types of beautiful young American women who
seriously desire careers as mannequins in our Paris *atelier*. Must
be smart, slender, with well-shaped feet and ankles and refined
manner. Sail within three weeks. Attractive salary proposition."

Some five hundred hopefuls responded, and Patou asked for
judges to help whittle down the selection to six, instead of three,
models. Condé Nast, Edward Steichen, Elsie de Wolfe, Jean Patou, and Edna Chase became the jury. A successful applicant,
Lillian Farley, also an experienced *Vogue* model, said: "Anyone
watching Monsieur Patou would have concluded that ankles
were the most important asset of a mannequin. Feet and ankles
passing the test, he deigned to look at the hips. . . . None were
wanted."[16]

---

* Barrett Andrews served as a lieutenant colonel during the Great War. He later left
Condé Nast Publications to work for another publishing company in Boston, Massachusetts.

Edna had said long before: "Fashion can be bought. Style one must possess." And Condé always recognized it. Carmel's style drew him to her. She was "keen as mustard," Condé wrote to Edna in a memo soon after she joined the staff. He saw that Carmel had "it"—a way of thinking and being in which dressing well was only the beginning. Condé wanted to cultivate Carmel, to make her into a top editor. "What he liked in girls was something much hotter than I was," Carmel said, "so there was no hint of romance in our relationship." What he wanted was to "mold his new fashion editor into a figure of fashion."[17]

Condé went to Carmel's home, still shared with her mother and siblings, to coach her in the finer details of magazine layout. Carmel was invited for weekends at Newport with Condé, where they were the guests of many of the enclave's "aristocrats"—like Mrs. Cornelius Vanderbilt II at her seventy-room Italianate palazzo, the Breakers. Together they went to the hunting lodges of the same super-rich New York families in the Adirondacks. When not traveling with Condé, Carmel was frequently a guest at Condé's and Frank's legendary dinner parties, where her companion might be anyone from a "presentable gigolo" to Fred Astaire.

As Frank was living with Condé, Carmel also saw a great deal of him. Frank was a great favorite with the White family's maid, Bridget Keogh, who would imitate him arriving at their apartment "jauntily . . . in his frock coat, hands behind his back, eyes peering over his spectacles, twinkling with the joie de vivre he always brought with him." Sometimes Frank would take Carmel to a restaurant in a Greenwich Village hotel where French expats gathered for a "nostalgic reminder of Paris." Another favorite was the Coffee House—which finally accepted women. There he introduced her to a young man—and sometime escort—Charles Hanson Towne, then editor of *Harper's Bazar*.[18] By 1923 Carmel was hiring her own assistants and supervising fashion shoots with the new chief photographer for Condé Nast Publications, Edward

Steichen, introduced all those years before by Clarisse. Steichen could not abide having the redoubtable Edna at his shoots. And so, the fiery, youthful, auburn-haired Carmel was well on her way to overtaking her boss.

Steichen—sometimes referred to as "the Colonel" since he was in charge of all aerial photography for the U.S. Army under Gen. Billy Mitchell,* for which he was awarded the Légion d'Honneur by France—was quite a catch. When Frank published pictures of photographers in a 1923 *Vanity Fair* and bemoaned the loss of Steichen, "the greatest of living portrait photographers," to painting, Steichen immediately wrote to thank him for the accolade but assured Frank that he had burned all his canvases and was back behind the camera.

Born in Luxembourg and raised in Milwaukee, Steichen first made his big splash in photography at the age of twenty in the Photographic Salon of Philadelphia of 1899. His work was commended to the German photographer Alfred Stieglitz a year later, and when the pair met in Paris, they hatched a plan to make photography *the* new art form in America. Stieglitz opened the famous gallery 291 on Fifth Avenue while Steichen, still living in France, provided Stieglitz with modern French art by his artist friends.[†] The relationship with Rodin was particularly close, with the sculptor calling Steichen "my son."[19] Stieglitz's 291 gallery was innovative, showing photography as an art form alongside the work of modern painters and sculptors. What made it even more extraordinary was the fact that the Museum of Modern Art was then only a distant glint in its cofounders' eyes. It was Frank who emphasized to Condé that Steichen was *the* man to replace de Meyer, predicting that photography would soon overtake illustration in all their magazines. Terms were swiftly agreed to with Condé and

---

* William Lendrum Mitchell (1879–1936) is widely regarded as the father of the U.S. Air Force.
† Primarily Brancusi, Cézanne, Matisse, Rodin, and Picasso.

Frank informally over lunch. Their association would last fifteen years until Steichen's retirement.

Condé never had a contract with Steichen, stipulating only that the photographer could work for anyone in the world except Hearst or any of his publications. The movie mogul Sam Goldwyn of MGM would have scoffed at Condé's naïveté, since Goldwyn was allegedly the first who said that a verbal contract isn't worth the paper it's written on. But when Steichen agreed to photograph a fiction article for *Cosmopolitan*, and he subsequently learned that the magazine was owned by Hearst, Steichen cancelled the job. Evidently the Sam Goldwyns of the world didn't know men like Steichen, or indeed Condé.[20]

Another bright young thing who lit up *Vogue* back then was Johnnie McMullin. He was one of those California social animals who cultivated "everybody who was anyone" and was most at home in the upmarket worlds of Park Avenue, Mayfair, the Faubourg Saint-Honoré, Deauville, Palm Beach, or the French Riviera. He would be seen only in the chicest of restaurants, smartest of shops, and the most "in" of nightclubs. McMullin was "small and slight in stature, flawlessly dressed, more a 'manikin' than a man," Edna wrote, "with bright brown eyes, a nose somewhat aquiline, pointed at the end, a sharp tongue, and a fund of human understanding. He was a tremendously entertaining companion and a hard worker." He was also decidedly "mauve" in his tastes—artistic and sublimely gay.

McMullin became a good friend of the interior decorator Elsie de Wolfe while she worked on Condé's new apartment at 1040 Park Avenue. Condé adored McMullin and knew he had a childhood passion for beautiful cars. So Condé asked him to write something. McMullin's first article for *Vogue* was a carefree piece called "Her Motor Car as Seen by Him." He was a smash hit with readers, writing on social events, cars, and men's fashions for both *Vogue* and *Vanity Fair*. He gave international fame to Stroeva, the gypsy singer at Chez Fischer in Paris, and to the Club Alabam's entertainers in New York. Mah-jongg players throughout America tittered at his descriptions of European nightlife, the most sophisticated resorts, and of course the latest haute couture from Chanel. An expert flitter among "in" places, McMullin was always the first on the scene to report the latest fad. Once in London he exclaimed to his confused secretary: "Cancel all my appointments; I have just heard of a white dress waistcoat with *one* button in a shop in Jermyn Street. I must fly!" Much later, when McMullin received a letter from his friend Adele Astaire (at the time Lady Charles Cavendish), addressed to him as "Dear Piddle Pants," his then secretary could take no more and quit.

Condé's business thrived in the fall of 1923. It was also the season of his beautiful daughter's debutante ball. Normally no self-respecting deb from New York's Four Hundred would be seen without her mother at her elbow, any more than she would think of attending her debut ball in a swimsuit. That's what made the invitation to Natica's party so perplexing. It read: "Mr. Condé Nast requests the pleasure of _____'s company at a dance to be given for his daughter, Miss Natica Nast, on Tuesday, 4 December 1923 at half past ten in the evening at the Ritz-Carlton Hotel."[21] The invitation itself sent New York society into a loud buzz worthy of any bee swarm: Why wasn't Clarisse included?

As the evening wore on, speculation grew, whispers rose: Would Clarisse or would she not appear? Condé clearly greeted *his* blue-book guests to *his* daughter's debut. There could have been several reasons for the apparent blunder. Some believed that Condé may have been trying unsuccessfully to get Clarisse to agree to a divorce, and perhaps things had become acrimonious between them. In their exchange of letters, Condé took extreme care and displayed patience with Clarisse's demands and nervous disposition, so that hardly seems possible. More than likely Clarisse had her own reasons. Perhaps she was already seeing her younger stockbroker beau, J. Victor Onativia III, and may have insisted on his involvement. When Condé refused, she may have gone into a sulk. Or Clarisse may have been excluded because she wanted to dominate the proceedings without consulting Natica or Condé. In any event, like Cinderella, Natica vanished at the stroke of midnight, leaving everyone to wonder if it might be a pumpkin coach rather than a New York taxi that drove her back to her mother's 1000 Park Avenue home.[22]

As the guests hummed with speculation during the all-night dinner dance, Condé remained the ultimate host, ignoring his daughter's absence and keeping up appearances. When the breakfast of scrambled eggs, buckwheat cakes, and sausages was served after daybreak, Natica returned, refreshed and sparkling as ever. She "solved" the riddle by telling "fourteen pairs of ears" at her handpicked table: "Mother was invited to the party; but couldn't come, was slightly ill. She just couldn't make it. In the circumstances, I felt that she should share in the beauty and fun of it all. And the only way I could think of to bring that about was to vanish, jump into a taxi, ride out to her own apartment, and tell her all about it. Forgive my disappearing. I just HAD to—!"[23] Of course that didn't explain why her mother's name hadn't appeared on the invitation. Poor Natica.

In 1924 Condé, too, was awarded the Légion d'Honneur, and life seemed bright. Clarisse was seeing more and more of Victor Onativia, and Condé could begin to hope that she might be willing to grant him a divorce. McMullin informed New York in *Vogue* and *Vanity Fair* that the kings and queens of the new social season were the cool, beautiful actress Lady Diana Manners, her fellow British musical comedy actresses Gertrude Lawrence and Beatrice Lillie, the composer George Gershwin, and the Austrian theater and film director-producer Max Reinhardt.

In London there was considerable upheaval at British *Vogue*'s offices. Circulation was down, and red ink flowed freely. After a rap on the knuckles to adhere to guidelines, Todd was still tinkering with Condé's formula. All *Vogue* titles always opened with a review and contents page, followed by society news and photographs, then fashions, and finally articles of interest on the arts, cooking, golf, or travel, with a "thought-provoking" editorial. When Todd abolished British *Vogue*'s "lingerie number" and gave only lip service to the magazine's regular features—"Seen in the Shops," "Smart Fashions for Limited Incomes," and the hostess and beauty articles—a seismic shift was felt across the Atlantic.[24]

It all began when the Bloomsbury Set went "whoring after Todd," as Virginia Woolf wrote in a letter to her friend, the poet, novelist, and garden designer, Vita Sackville-West. "And what's the objection to whoring after Todd? Better whore, I think than honestly and timidly and coolly and respectably copulate with the Times Lit[erary] Sup[plement]." Woolf knew that her entire set and others were guilty of the same crime.* When the early October 1925 edition of British *Vogue* published its editorial, the truth stared back starkly at its readers:

> *London, welcoming returning wanderers, presents a varied spectacle for our amusement.... Few people know what brains are confined within a radius of a hundred yards or so. All the Stracheys, Maynard Keynes and Lopokova, Adrian Stephen, Clive Bell and Raymond Mortimer, whom we know so well, round the corner the house of the Hogarth Press, where sits, most satisfying to me of all writers, Virginia Woolf, and not far away her sister, Vanessa Bell, and the best of contemporary painters, Duncan Grant.*[25]

On his annual trip to London in June 1924, Condé was flabbergasted to see the changes at British *Vogue*. Albert Lee—the same business manager who had moved armies about on his large map during the Great War—had failed to carry out "any of the reconstruction that Condé . . . had planned," supported by *Vogue*'s promotion manager in New York, Harry W. Yoxall, more than a

---

* Others who "whored after Todd" were Aldous Huxley, Clive Bell, Raymond Mortimer, Roger Fry, Ottoline Morrell, David Garnett, Edith Sitwell, Bertrand Russell, and Virginia Woolf's own husband, Leonard.

year earlier. Yoxall wrote in his diary that Condé "was a peculiar person when he gets abroad" and that "more British blood was needed at C.N.'s Publ. G.B.H.Q.—someone with a native comprehension of British psychology to ferret out the true situation with regard to circulation, and, in general, to see what can be done in bringing the magazine more into the current of contemporary British needs."[26] No wonder readership was falling off. Condé had been guilty of the classic American business mistake in Great Britain, based on the misguided principle that the same language— nearly—is spoken, and so business could be run in the same way. Native English speakers often forget that language is also a function of culture.

So Condé installed himself in London for the summer and asked his daughter, Natica, to join him for six weeks to act as his hostess for the events he would attend and plan—including presenting Natica at court. Following so soon after the debacle of her debutante party in New York, Natica knew her mother would "pick her point of attack skillfully." Of course it was a "wonderful idea," Clarisse enthused, "but Natica must arrive with a suitable and exquisite wardrobe for entertaining" at such auspicious levels. Everything imaginable—including costly jewelry—was freshly bought by Clarisse with Natica in tow, and the bills sent to Condé's New York office. On their arrival in London, Condé explained that they were entertaining that very evening, and that he would love to help her pick out the correct outfit. Leading her father to her multitude of trunks and cases containing the new wardrobe, Natica held up a gown she hoped might do. Condé made a pained face and asked to see all the other outfits. They were *so American*. "Good God," Condé said calmly in a bewildered voice. "What was your mother thinking? There is nothing here that is suitable. We must finish our lunch quickly and go to get you something decent for tonight. Then tomorrow I'll have Mrs. Brownford come in and we'll figure more outfits out for the rest of your stay."[27]

While Natica and her father enjoyed their time together, Condé awaited the arrival of Harry Yoxall from New York. He had cabled Yoxall and "asked" him to move back to England with his family, to please "come over and take charge" of the ailing magazine. British *Vogue* would be run henceforth by a troika: Yoxall as business manager, Laurence Schneider (also originally from New York) as advertising manager, and Dorothy Todd as editor.[28]

Yoxall, a British subject and former Balliol College Oxford man, had originally applied to replace Robert Benchley or Robert Sherwood at *Vanity Fair* in New York in 1920, but was hired instead in the promotion department. Like Condé, Yoxall had a love for the scent of printer's ink and called it his "preferred perfume." Though he found designers, illustrators, and photographers "infinitely entertaining," Yoxall was the first to admit that they were equally exasperating, and he found much of their work ephemeral.[29] Of course the telegram was an "ask" from Condé, but Yoxall knew that it was a command not to be ignored.

19. LET THE GOOD TIMES ROLL

Now you've got to sit on top of the world and hold on.
Take everything it brings and love it.
—CONDÉ NAST TO GRACE MOORE

Elsie de Wolfe's chef d'oeuvre at 1040 Park Avenue had its unveiling on Sunday, January 18, 1925, shortly after Condé moved in. With her flair for all things French, and Condé's easy persona as the popular publisher of *Vogue*, *Vanity Fair*, *House & Garden*, and *Jardin des Modes*, no New York apartment could have been decorated more fashionably or opulently. The thirty-room duplex penthouse, situated in the building designed by the sought-after firm of architects Delano & Aldrich, had been modified to Condé's requirements at the blueprint stage. Originally the design included three apartments per floor, with the penthouse designed merely as servants' quarters, in keeping with the needs of the times. During the course of 1924 Condé had the team rework the space to include ten entertaining rooms on the roof, with suites of domestics' rooms and sleeping quarters adjoining the rooftop paradise by the insertion of a new staircase. In the days before air-conditioning Condé had to trust to crosstown breezes to keep his guests cool in the summer and pray they wouldn't complain about the humidity. The conservatory, or solarium, was added sometime between 1926 and 1928.[1]

Elsie's spiritual home was in Versailles at the Villa Trianon. Lately she had invested in and decorated many of the new brownstones on the old Avenue A—renamed "Sutton Place"—and referred to in stage whispers as "the Amazon Enclave" or "Lesbian Commune." She decided that what Condé needed was French style—to reflect both his heritage and the elegance of his magazines. The Louis XV furniture was upholstered in a pale sage-green damask. Regency needlepoint sofas were de rigueur too. Chinese screens and wallpaper were a natural must to complement the French decor; silver tea paper* adorned the ceilings; gilt-framed mirrors and eighteenth-century art were strategically placed along its walls. Long organdy curtains embellished the windows, while Savonnerie rugs graced the French-made parquet floors. (Of course the parquet was especially laid by French workmen brought over for the job.) But the pièce de résistance was the eighteenth-century Ch'ien-lung wallpaper that once hung at the baronial stately home Beaudesert in England.† The wallpaper was offset by the salmon moiré silk curtains that hung in the ballroom, fondly remembered to this day by Condé's younger daughter, Leslie.[2]

Once the conservatory was enclosed, guests were able to sit at tables and admire the view, or wave to playwright and theater director Moss Hart in the Park Avenue apartment opposite.[3] Elsie made Condé's new home the epitome of timeless style—his showpiece to use for the good of his publications. It was also the perfect stage setting for Steichen and his fellow photographers, who often used the apartment as a backdrop for photo shoots.

Not everyone shared Elsie's taste. While Natica lived most of the time with her mother, she, like Coudert, had a room of her own at her father's, too. Her personal tastes ran to less fussy, more modern elegance, and she banned Elsie from festooning her walls with either eighteenth-century wallpaper or antique mirrors. An

---

* For hundreds of years, thin paper cut into rectangular strips and glued together into panels formed the basis of wallpaper. This particular wallpaper was the original Chinoiserie, very valuable, and handmade.

† The wallpaper along with the furniture and other artifacts were sold off by the Sixth marquess of Anglesey, William Paget, as a direct result of the First World War. Baron William Paget obtained the estate in 1546 during the last year of the reign of Henry VIII.

artist in her own right, Natica knew how to stand her ground. Elsie was thwarted in their first skirmish—only to regroup and
mount a surprise attack for another. By chance Natica was in her
room when Elsie pounced—accompanied by two muscle-bound
deliverymen. They carried the treasured token of Elsie's taste, a
dressing table, painstakingly selected for Natica. Although Natica
appreciated that it was beautiful, the vanity was simply not practical. Natica explained that she wanted "something bigger with lots
of drawers and a triple mirror. That's really what I'd like. We could
have one made. It wouldn't cost very much; there's a place on Third
Avenue—"

Natica might as well have stabbed the decorator. "Third Avenue!" Elsie gasped. "That dressing table came out of Versailles and
it cost ten thousand dollars. If it was good enough for Marie Antoinette, it's good enough for you!" she shrieked, storming off.

"And do you know," Natica said, "it was a real fight to save
Daddy the money. In a way I think he resented it. He thought Elsie's taste was God and it was heresy to go against it."[4]

At 1040 Condé became quite the host. Guests at that first
housewarming dinner dance included a broad cross-section of café
society, including one of the future founders of the Academy of
Motion Picture Arts and Sciences, Richard Barthelmess; the concert violinist and composer Efrem Zimbalist; the actress Katha-
rine Cornell, dubbed "First Lady of the American Theater" by
Alexander Woollcott; the author, engineer, inventor, cartoonist,
and sculptor Rube Goldberg; the dancers Fred and Adele Astaire;
the composer George Gershwin; the songwriter and dramatist Arthur Hammerstein; the owner of the Algonquin Hotel and host to
the Round Tablers, Frank Case; the comic actress Ina Claire; and
Vogue and Vanity Fair in-housers, Edward Steichen, George Jean
Nathan, Edna St. Vincent Millay, and of course Edna, Carmel, and
Frank.[5] Some bright spark remarked that the only person not invited
was "Silent Cal," America's thirtieth president, Calvin Coolidge.

Frank Crowninshield had recently commissioned a lampoon by e. e. cummings called "When Calvin Coolidge Laughed"* that followed a cavalcade of disasters stemming from the president's unforeseen mirth. Perhaps Condé thought it would have been impolitic to invite Coolidge, who never joked and was noted for his inertia, to such a fast and fantastic party.

It was the first of Condé's bimonthly celebrations at 1040, and it was unforgettable. The guests were carefully selected from his A-, B-, and C-lists—A for society, B for people in the arts, C for other celebrities—and then broken down further into married couples and single men or women. But what really mattered to Condé were the people in the arts, not the smattering of *Social Register* types. Red Newsom, *Vanity Fair*'s "Well-Dressed Man" columnist, couldn't help noticing that *everyone* from the magazines was invited, "from the stockroom, the messengers, the typists, the editors and right on up," as were "a dozen or so of the most wanted call girls in New York."[6] Contrary to myth, there was no snobbery attached—just extreme attention to the guests' sensibilities. Questions needed answering before the invitations went out: Who was Cary Grant's latest lady? Can we invite his ex? Who had crossed over to the shortly-to-be-divorced list? Was Mr. Du Pont still married? Could Mrs. Vanderbilt sit next to George Gershwin? Or, more significantly, who, in fact, was sleeping with whom—and did society know—and should we turn a blind eye?

Nothing was ever left to chance for these big mise-en-scènes. Their postmortems were constructed with equal care: number of invitations, percentages of acceptances from each list, how many days' notice had been given, and the cost of each and every item. On the day of the party, when dressed for the occasion, Condé

---

* In *Vanity Fair*'s April 1925 issue, Coolidge was portrayed as an incorruptible man, which after Harding was both needed and refreshing. The only problem was that he made government policy of laissez-faire seem positively vibrant. According to Irving Stone: "By forcing government to lie supine, he paved the way for a world depression which led blocks of nations to demand a form of government which would control everything." (Source: *The Aspirin Age*, "Calvin Coolidge: A Study in Inertia," 1924, 140.)

made the rounds: checking on the caterers, the flower arrangements, and putting on any finishing touches required; ensuring
that each table in his Chinese Chippendale ballroom had full,
round cases of cigarettes; that the orchestra leader was primed to
begin playing just as the first guest arrived; and discussing the
drinks with the barman (and presumably, which bathtubs held the
chilling champagne and wines). Once this routine was accomplished Condé could relax for the evening ahead. To some, like
Edna, it might have seemed stage-managed, settling over time
into a predictable routine, but all Condé wanted was to provide
the most exceptional setting for his truly remarkable guests to perform their magic.

20. THE NEW AND RENEWED KIDS IN TOWN

*You have to look at the competition and say you're
going to do it differently.*
—CONDÉ NAST, AND LATER, STEVE JOBS

T he year 1925 was a momentous one for other reasons, too.
Normally the advent of a competing magazine on the market would be a good reason for Condé to worry. Frank was
pleased to put Condé's mind at rest when Harold Ross's *The New
Yorker* hit the newsstands on February 21, 1925. It was printed on
cheap paper and was a slim issue (some thirty-six pages), Frank
related in a brief memo. Too many words, too many cartoons, and
there was fiction—an apparent kiss of death. Only one page dedicated to profiles. Its theater section and "Talk of the Town" did
not rival *Vanity Fair*'s.[1] Frank said its logo, the iconic green-gloved
early nineteenth-century gentleman holding up his monocle to ex-
amine a butterfly fluttering before his eyes, exemplified the upper
crust of a bygone age but hardly spoke to the flappers, bohemians, and swells of their times. It was Corey Ford, formerly of *Vanity Fair*, who dubbed the iconic *New Yorker* dandy "Eustace Tilley"
in his series of comic articles that ran in the magazine's first year.
But the cover left itself open to other interpretations: Was the gentleman really the image of the discerning New York reader, or was
the reader being mocked as foppish for his attire and ridiculous
for his monocle-gazing at a butterfly? The playwright Ben Hecht
put it rather more succinctly. "How the hell could a man who
looked like a resident of the Ozarks and talked like a saloon

brawler"—Hecht wondered about Ross—"set himself up as pilot of a sophisticated, elegant periodical? It was bounderism of the worst sort."

But Ross was a man on a mission, and all he lacked was an angel. His Round Table friends thought he'd become a bore about it, schlepping around a dummy of his New York magazine for more than two years, looking in vain under any stone for an investor, the Round Tabler George S. Kaufman wrote. Ross, undeterred by Dorothy Parker's dismissal—or maybe it was in sheer desperation—turned to his friend Alexander Woollcott for an introduction to Condé. Woollcott refused.[2] By chance, after a party given by Raoul Fleischmann, the millionaire founder of the General Baking Company, Ross asked if he would invest. Fleischmann agreed to stump up $25,000, so long as Ross and his wife, Jane Grant, would put in a like amount themselves.[3] Hundreds of thousands of Fleischmann's dollars would follow before Ross got his format right. In the meantime Condé Nast Press in Greenwich picked up the contract to print *The New Yorker*.[4]

Condé was riding high. He was famous, rich, and a member of some of New York's most exclusive clubs: the Racquet and Tennis, Piping Rock, Tuxedo, Dutch Treat, Riding, Knickerbocker, National Links. He was a regular visitor to friends at Newport and Aiken, South Carolina, where the superrich and powerful, like his friend the financier Bernard Baruch, unwound in winter. He was a welcome figure in the Hamptons on Long Island for summer relaxation, and naturally in Paris and London.

Best of all, by May 1925 Condé knew he would soon be a free man. Clarisse had established French residency to make the stain of divorce remote from what remained a puritanical New York, in high-society terms. *The New York Times* reported in an article on May 29, 1925, "Mrs. Condé Nast Files Suit for Divorce in Paris": "Mrs. Condé Nast, formerly Miss Clarisse Coudert, has filed a petition for divorce in a Paris court against her husband, the New York publisher. . . . When their daughter, Miss Natica Nast, was introduced into society in January, 1923, entertainments were given by her parents separately. . . . It had been said that neither Mr. Nast nor his wife would consent to a divorce, as both have been brought up in the Catholic faith."[5]

Clarisse, accurately described in other newspapers as "prominent in society," had rejected the notion of divorce for years due to her Catholic sensibilities. Then, too, the idea of freeing Condé to marry again—perhaps even to start a second family—was torture to her. But she hadn't reckoned on falling in love again at this late stage in her life—this time with a dashing stockbroker with devastatingly dark Spanish good looks, José Victor Onativia III, ten years her junior.[6] He was so charismatically enchanting that when his daughter Dorothea (by his first marriage) was engaged in 1932, the newspapers only commented on how handsome he was.[7] In 1922, Onativia became a partner in the new brokerage firm of Dean & Onativia. His three partners had specialty commodities-exchange interests and manned the firm's Chicago office. Onativia ran the company's New York Stock Exchange headquarters.[8] So Clarisse married her stockbroker on April 10, 1926, at the Municipal Building in New York, almost shame-facedly, not announcing the wedding beforehand.[9]

At last Condé was free. Whether he realized that he should change how he lived as an eligible, very wealthy, middle-aged bachelor isn't clear. For the next few years he surrounded himself with some of the most stunning women in the world, without any hint that he might remarry. Back then, in the bygone days before prenuptial agreements and widespread charges of sexual harassment against powerful men, the worry was markedly different from today. Wealthy men feared gold diggers, and Condé simply wanted to enjoy his freedom. Besides, he was a renewed man in America's most vibrant city. *Vogue* described New York as a city that twinkled like diamonds, mentioning the "crowding of Fifth Avenue with motors flashing in the sun, the tumult of smart restaurants, the anguished haste of dressmakers and modistes, and the sandwiching of picture exhibitions and special matinees for the illuminati between luncheons at Marguery's and first nights of the luscious and glittering summer reviews."[10]

In the second half of the 1920s, *Vanity Fair* was busily making over the modern female image from helpless, languid nymphs wearing sinuous silk or clinging lamé in—of all things—an advertisement for the Condé Nast Education Bureau where the best schools and professional courses were listed, captioned "The Era's Changed": "But times have changed!" it shouted. "Women don't faint at the slightest provocation. Most girls, before they are twenty, become interested in the world in general and in some work in particular!"[11] This was no empty exclamation to young women everywhere, but rather a progressive statement of the time—time when cloche hats, short hair, and art deco were key indicators of chic. Of course this campaign for the modern woman was aimed at the sophisticated female readers of *Vogue*, and the multitude of women who accepted and even embraced a domestic life for decades to come.

Condé had made *Vogue* the first internationally published magazine ever. He was sure he had rectified the management issues in London. *Vogue Patterns* remained strong, and with Yoxall's eye on the pattern business in England, Condé believed the British title would show a profit in 1926. Equally, he was sure that the Vogels would turn the corner into profitability at French *Vogue*. Of course the publishing group's value relied heavily on American *Vogue*, whose circulation was approaching 130,000. *Vanity Fair*'s circulation was nearing its peak of 90,000, and while only marginally profitable, it remained a dear project, close to both Condé's and Frank's hearts. Condé Nast Press, from a standing start in 1921, had earnings well in excess of two million dollars, and was the runaway success story of the entire organization.[12]

Marriage was in the air, too, for Condé's friends and associates. On March 10, 1926, he attended Elsie de Wolfe's wedding to the British diplomat Sir Charles Ferdinand Mendl in Paris. Aged sixty-one, the bride wore a simple Chanel frock, gloves, and a high, flowered toque. Henceforth she would be known as Lady Mendl. Elsie was six years older than the groom, but that was the least of the oddities in the union. She maintained her residence at the Villa Trianon at Versailles, while Mendl, rumored to be homosexual, lived in his own apartment on the avenue Montaigne in the capital. Since Elsie had lived with Bessie Marbury, it was widely assumed that the marriage was for companionship—and the whitest of *mariages blancs*.[13]

In New York a tall man of few words with a penchant for outdoor pursuits came into Carmel's life. George Palen Snow, a lawyer by profession and a sportsman by inclination, had more than his fair share of rough edges. He lived a communal existence on his Rolling Hills Farm with his friend and fellow foxhunter, Chalmers Wood. Palen, as Carmel called him, adored the great outdoors. Although he was tall, sporty, and had a patrician air about him, Carmel seemed most attracted by the fact that he had never been married. She overlooked his dislike of city life, his debilitating stutter, his Episcopalian religion, and was charmed by the "boyishness about this big man in his forties that you couldn't resist." Carmel was no youthful chick herself, staring head-on at her fortieth birthday in just over a year.* Palen was genuinely fond of Carmel, too; and tried to teach her how to ride, play golf, and generally appreciate the outdoor life—of course without the slightest hope of success. Still, both pretended not to notice, each more than likely recognizing that this was their best—and final—chance at marital bliss.[14]

When Carmel told Palen that she would have to go to Paris for the fall collection, and would be sailing on the *Mauretania* that August, it forced him to make a decision. Sending her a cable, Palen simply wrote: "May I sail on the Mauretania with you? Reply paid." Deciphering this as his proposal of marriage, she responded: "Reply accepted."[15] Despite his drawbacks, Palen was no

---

* Carmel was born on August 27, 1887.

mean catch. From one of the old New York moneyed families, he had been brought up to be the epitome of the nineteenth-century gentleman. He graduated Harvard in the class of 1904, had a seat on the New York Stock Exchange, and was a member of the New York bar and a partner in his father's real estate and insurance firm of Snow & Snow, located on Park Avenue. Significantly, Palen understood that his bride wished to continue working after they were married. Work was her passion, just as country pursuits were his. He never asked her to give up her job. And so the happy couple departed for Paris where Carmel worked, and Palen did whatever Palen was likely to do in a city.

When they returned to New York, Carmel was a renewed woman. Although she still felt Edna's weight on her back, Carmel thrust forward to ensure *Vogue*'s future by attracting youthful readers. As she saw it, while persuading its established audience that "To Age Gracefully Is an Art"—one which *Vogue* readers would naturally want to learn—Carmel also wanted younger women from Next-Stop-Nowhere to aspire to the fashionable life in New York, London, Paris, or even the French Riviera; and that they should use *Vogue* to guide them. Carmel championed young artists like the American Carl Erickson, who signed his work simply "Eric"; and the Russian-born Baron George Hoyningen-Huene, who had become the chief photographer at French *Vogue* in 1925. In a world before the "youth market" in magazines, it was Carmel's job to marry the French adage that a woman never achieved her own chic until the age of forty with the younger woman's desire to hurry things along quite a bit.

It was shrewd business thinking to attract younger female readers if *Vogue* wanted to outlive its current audience. But Carmel's real aim was to expand the magazine's offerings to include fiction and the serialization of popular books. Yet, try as hard as she might, Carmel could not get either Edna or Condé to consider it. Carmel was paying attention to market forces, while Condé and Edna clung to the tried and tested Condé Nast formula. One of Carmel's friends, Anita Loos, had agreed to have her irreverent and bestselling book, *Gentlemen Prefer Blondes*, serialized in *Harper's*

Bazar. Sales of the magazine tripled after its serialization in 1925—
to say nothing of the book's ongoing sales. Men were tremendous
fans of Loos's book. As a result men's advertising was included for
the first time in a woman's magazine.

Carmel's frustration at their obstinacy was palpable. "I think I
determined from the moment I read the first installment [of Loos's
book] that if I were ever the editor of a magazine," Carmel remi-
nisced, "I would publish fiction, which *Vogue* refused to publish.
Though our business as a fashion magazine was to show fashion,
our business as journalists, it seemed to me, was to make an exciting book."[16]

In London, Harry Yoxall faced the ongoing challenge of making
British *Vogue* profitable. The greatest hurdle to overcome was that
he knew precious little about fashion. His specialty was foreign
advertising, and his classics studies at Oxford's Balliol College had
helped him only to think things through clearly. So he thought
long and hard. Yoxall knew that fashion had always percolated from
the top down, ever since the first court and its courtiers. When
silks, damasks, and furs were outlawed for the lower echelons of
society, they became the "must have" items of clothing for the very
people who were forbidden to wear them. Great clothes had always
been aspirational. Even Shakespeare had complained "that the
fashion wears out more apparel than the man" in one of the first
commentaries on ditching an outdated wardrobe. Yoxall felt that
the rapid changes in ladies' fashion came about through a combination of commercialism and an underlying sexual motivation—
to be better than the woman next door, and to attract and hold a
man.[17]

Nonetheless the London of Yoxall's 1920s had only the British
branches of Worth and Paquin to offer as high fashion for women.
Lucile and Reville, the only two home-based fashion couturiers,
had retired. That said, it was Lucile who first put into practice the
concept of specialist models to show her creations, rather than famous women from the stage or the British aristocracy. Once used,

it became an industry-wide gold standard. Paris remained the nexus of women's fashion design, with London maintaining its preeminence in sportswear for the countryside (Barbour, Aquascutum), men's tailoring (notably on Jermyn Street), and specialty luxury items (Aspinal's). For women who couldn't go to Paris twice yearly, the larger department stores had their workrooms, where derivative designs were chosen from the "gown departments" by the head buyers. These formidable and helpful arbiters of "just the right thing" had fought their way to the top of their profession on Regent Street or in Knightsbridge, and their word on fashion became an unshakable gospel.

In Britain fashion seemingly traveled by horse and buggy in the twenties. British *Vogue*'s pattern business sold well immediately in London; six months later sales would pick up in the so-called home counties* and provincial big cities; and finally in the deep provinces and small cities another six months after that, just as *Vogue* wanted to withdraw the pattern as outmoded.[18] Yoxall thought that to be more successful, British *Vogue* needed to become "mechanized" and travel faster. To accomplish that, management would need streamlining. Condé's solution to British *Vogue*'s management problems was the Yoxall-Schneider-Todd troika. Instead he produced three chefs spoiling the title's "broth"—or five, if Condé and Edna were counted.

Edna, whose strength was fashion, agreed with Condé that the Bloomsbury Set was simply too highbrow to attract the female audience the magazine served and deserved. Fashion chic did not always gel with the intelligentsia, and British *Vogue*'s losses in 1925 of £25,000† proved it. According to Yoxall, "Everybody realized that Dorothy Todd had to go." Circulation had fallen from more than sixteen thousand in 1916 to well under nine thousand.[19] It was just a question of when, how, and who could replace her. Yoxall decided that the quickest way out of the red was to promote the *Vogue*

---

* The home counties are those that surround London: Essex, Hertfordshire, Buckinghamshire, Berkshire, Surrey, Kent, and Sussex.

† The average exchange rate for sterling to dollars in 1925 was £1 = \$4.83.

Pattern Book, which attracted women who read the magazine's section on styles for a limited income. Yoxall was also concerned about the macroeconomic situation. His diaries are full of woeful tales about the fall of the French franc, the collapse in circulation and advertising, and how to publish with the minor strikes leading up to the great General Strike of 1926. Todd felt that these commercial matters were beneath her dignity.

In fact, however, during the 1926 General Strike, which lasted for nine days from May 3 until May 12, Yoxall prepared as if going into battle for what could have sounded the death knell of British *Vogue*. In doing so he emerged triumphant. No one knew at the outset *if* the General Strike—called in sympathy for 1.2 million locked-out coal miners—would last a day, a week, a month, or longer. Yoxall admitted that while it was an anxious time, it was "fun privately," because anyone who wasn't a union member just pitched in. Publishers were put on notice that they too would be affected when the "printers of the *Daily Mail* refused to produce an issue containing a leader that criticized" the TUC, the national federation of trade unions. Yoxall had:

> taken the precaution of having seven thousand copies [of British Vogue] delivered to the office, and the few members of the staff who then had cars went out selling them to the newsagents.... Then everyone would load up their car with as many parcels as it would carry, to be delivered round London and the Home Counties. Back in the afternoon to the office to chalk up sales. Finally one took one's neighbours home, and swapped experiences, over well-earned drinks, with more dashing friends who had been driving buses and even locomotives."[20]

The most memorable incident of the strike for Yoxall, however, remained his journey to the Penge station bookstall, some nine miles southeast of central London. The man in charge asked for a quire—twenty-six copies—of *Vogue*. As that seemed quite a lot to Yoxall, he asked if he was sure they could be sold. "Lor' bless you," the man replied, "they'll read anything now they haven't got the newspapers."[21]

Dorothy Todd was invisible in Yoxall's reminiscences. And it was her very invisibility that proved her undoing. Yoxall had written memo after memo to Condé in New York about Todd taking off just when she was most needed. Yet no reply came until Condé's cable of September 13, 1926, demanding that Todd be sacked along with her *maîtresse en titre*,* assistant editor Madge Garland. "Nast's fatal procrastination," Yoxall fumed, "when any unpleasant doing or thinking is required," left British *Vogue* in a precarious position. "We are left now with a fight, as she [Todd] tries to sour her old contributors, and the fashion and advertising world against us."[22] The incident also made Condé act out of character.

Todd consulted a lawyer, and according to Vita Sackville-West, writing from her garden only twelve days after Condé's cable, Todd was advised she could get "£5,000 damages on the strength of her contract. Nast, when threatened with an action retorted that he would defend himself by attacking Todd's morals. So poor Todd is silenced, since her morals are of the classic rather than the conventional order. . . . This affair has assumed in Bloomsbury the proportions of a political rupture."

Given the adversarial nature of the British legal system, Condé's uncharacteristic threat must have come with sound legal advice. Todd and Madge Garland had been living openly and flamboyantly as a lesbian couple in a country where male homosexuality remained illegal until 1967.† Virginia Woolf wrote that "the Todd ménage is incredibly louche: Todd in sponge bag trousers; Garland in pearls and silk; both rather raddled and on their beam ends."[23] (Meaning that Todd wore men's checked trousers in the pattern of a toiletries bag, and rather graphically, that both were intertwined

---

* "Official lover."

† The Labouchere Amendment in Section II of the Criminal Law Amendment Act of 1885 prohibited "gross indecency" between males. Contrary to popular belief, it was never illegal to be a lesbian in the United Kingdom.

in a lovers' embrace.) Woolf came out of the affair badly herself, accusing Todd of speaking with "a hostile & cautious greed" and "getting my money back," before going on to say that "she is going to bed with Garland and flirting with Osbert [Sitwell], I presume. She is tapir like, & the creatures nose snuffs pertinaciously after Bloomsbury."[24]

So much for friends and "whoring after Todd" in *Vogue*.

21. FIREFLIES IN THE GARDEN PARADISE

*Everything that is made beautiful and fair and lovely is
made for the eye of one who sees.*
—RUMI

I n Paris, the night of May 21, 1927, was punctuated by the
cries of news vendors: "The American has arrived!" The Montmartre nightclubs Zelli's and Chez Florence gave free champagne to its American clientele. Not to be outdone by the chic
palaces' largesse, cheap bars around the city gallantly offered a
glass of inferior brandy to their own Yankees. That evening millions of column inches rolled off the presses, echoing their adula-
tion around the world for Capt. Charles A. Lindbergh's solo flight
across the Atlantic in his plane, *Spirit of St. Louis*. Nowhere was
his hero-worship greater than in Paris. Even age-old restrictions
against the English language creeping into French were relaxed
when one of the more punctilious papers dubbed Lindbergh *le boy*
"seen giving *le shake-hand* to the President of the Republic with
whom he would *lunchera* that noon."[1] French *Vogue* covered all
the dizzying society events revolving around Lindbergh. On his return to the United States "Lucky Lindy," the press's darling, was
awarded the Distinguished Flying Cross by President Coolidge. On
June 13 New York gave Lindbergh the warmest of welcomes, greet-
ing him with thousands of cheering admirers and a near-blinding
storm of confetti as his cavalcade made its way along Broadway.
Lindbergh was simply "the most," as everyone said back then. He

even had a dance named after him—the greatest accolade of all—
the "Lindy Hop."

Of course Condé threw his fellow Midwesterner a party, and
Lindbergh came. Seeing "the sophisticated and educated guests
clawing at the hero and giggling hysterically when they touched
him," Edna's jaw dropped. Fortunately for Lindbergh, Natica
recognized his look of "dumb despair" and spirited him away to
Condé's bedroom. Only those who could be trusted to behave—
and bring down several bottles of champagne and glasses—were
allowed entry. Once ensconced, the select group barricaded the
door and partied on responsibly.[2] The melee in the ballroom embarrassed Condé, for whom good taste—which certainly did not
include mauling the guest of honor—was expected of anyone he
invited into his home. Of course Lindbergh had yet to speak out
as a staunch advocate of fascism.

Condé was aware of the two warring isms of the 1920s—
communism and fascism—as well as widespread racial intolerance. He hoped his magazines introduced a fresh aesthetic,
untarnished by all that was tawdry and hateful. The magazines
were born from his own extraordinary vision that was blind to
upper-crust prejudices about someone's upbringing, color, or
creed. He counted Jack Dempsey, boxing's world heavyweight
champion from 1926 to 1929—of Irish, Cherokee, and Jewish
stock—among his friends, and loved going to boxing matches
with Frank Crowninshield. Dempsey was invited also to write
about his sport for *Vanity Fair*. Since Frank and Condé had introduced Picasso to America—that died-in-the-Spanish-wool
Communist—why not invite the African American entertainer
who wowed French audiences, Josephine Baker, into his home
and magazines? Why not? Because it was not the "done thing."
To listen to popular jazz, which had its roots in African American music, you went to Harlem to imbibe the musical renaissance there—you didn't invite black entertainers into your home.
So naturally Condé threw a party for Josephine Baker in 1927,

too. And all New York came because they simply had to be there or be branded bigots. "Now *that* was historic," wrote Diana Vreeland, who was invited:

> We have a black *in the house. Her hair had been done by An-*
> *toine, the famous hairdresser of Paris, like a Greek boy's—these*
> *small, flat curls against her skull—and she was wearing a white*
> *Vionnet dress, cut on the bias with four points, like a handker-*
> *chief. It had no opening, no closing—you just put it over your*
> *head and it came to you and moved with the ease and fluidity*
> *of the body. And did Josephine move! These* long *black legs,*
> *these* long *black arms, this* long *black throat . . . and pressed*
> *into her flat black curls were white silk butterflies. She had the*
> *chic of Gay Paree. I was so thrilled to be asked. There was no*
> *living with me for days.*[3]

After the party *Vanity Fair* published an article about Baker's rise from the Plantation Club in Harlem to the toast of Paris, with a stylized illustration of Baker in her notoriously revealing banana costume. President Woodrow Wilson may have introduced segregation into the federal administration, but both Condé and Frank were color-blind. Before Alfred A. Knopf published the poems of Langston Hughes in 1926, four of Hughes's poems appeared in *Vanity Fair.*[*] Jews like Groucho and Harpo Marx were favorites at Condé's parties, and "The Education of Harpo Marx" by Alexander Woollcott was a feature article in the March 1926 issue of *Vanity Fair.* Race, color, sexual preferences, or religion never mattered to either Condé or Frank when it came to their friends, family, editors, or other employees.

The gifted Cecil Beaton entered the *Vogue* stage in London, both mindful of and thankful for its outward-looking tolerance. As a

---

[*] The September 1925 issue of *Vanity Fair* published Hughes's "Cabaret," "To Midnight Nan at Leroy's," "Fantasy in Purple," and "Suicide's Note."

man of many talents, at the time bisexual, and without many pennies to rub together, Beaton was in need of a champion. He made friends easily. He could write, illustrate, and make costumes and design for the stage. He was a master photographer with just the most basic tools of his trade. But his breakthrough came when he photographed the British poet and critic Edith Sitwell. Suddenly he was given a rush of photographic assignments—that is, when he wasn't designing costumes for fancy-dress balls, which he positively adored.

Beaton came to *Vogue* on the recommendation of British *Vogue*'s new editor, Alison Settle. He met Edna during her summer visit to London in 1927. Although Edna did not commission his photography initially, she did buy Beaton's clever spidery caricatures of well-known London society partygoers, actresses, and celebrities. For the next eleven years *Vogue* featured his pen-and-ink drawings depicting how Lady So-and-So wore her pearls and diamond tiara, and his stunning photographs. It was Beaton who would become the master photo retoucher— shedding several inches, not to mention pounds, from vain and overweight women like the cosmetics millionairess Helena Rubinstein.

Edna simply loved Beaton from the start. "I remember the day Cecil first came into my London office—tall, slender, swaying like a reed, blond and very young. The aura emanating from him was an odd combination of airiness and assurance," she wrote. "He used a small amateur kind of camera and had no studio. When he had been working for a few months I one day asked him who did his developing for him. "Oh, Mrs. Chase," he said. "Nannie does it for me at home in the bath tub."[4]

Beaton's first one-man show in London was in November 1927. The press reviews were excellent, calling for his work "to be ranked with the best which is done by perhaps the best half-dozen portrait photographers in London."[5] A year later Beaton came to New York, and with Condé's guidance, took America by storm.

Beaton epitomized an outrageous character in a Noël Coward play and found himself actually parodied in Coward's lyrics to his song "I've Been to a Marvellous Party" in the lines "Dear Cecil arrived wearing armour/Some shells and a black feather boa." Today Beaton is widely thought to have been the model for Nancy Mitford's Cedric Hampton in her 1949 novel *Love in a Cold Climate*, and one of the inspirations for Sebastian Flyte in Evelyn Waugh's 1945 *Brideshead Revisited*. Beaton's friend, Stephen Tennant*—the brightest star of England's Bright Young Things—referred to him as "The King of *Vogue*" as early as July 1927.[6]

In New York introductions to *Vogue*, which set "the pace in fashion, genteel living and entertaining," according to *The New York Times*, depended entirely on meeting Condé Nast. If you wanted to be part of his café society, the best way to manage it was by an introduction or by somehow bumping into him. That is precisely what the artist and model Elizabeth Miller did—albeit accidentally. She was wearing a Parisian dress when she inadvertently "stepped into the path of an oncoming car and was pulled back onto the sidewalk by a well-dressed stranger, into whose arms she collapsed." She ridiculously babbled on in French, evidently in a state of shock. Her bankerish savior, Condé Nast, examined her more closely. He quickly assessed that Elizabeth had "it"—that intangible quality of a quick mind combined with natural personal chic.

Condé knew that Edna was searching for a new look—one that would portray the modern woman with brio—and so, he invited Elizabeth to the office to think about working for *Vogue*. When Edna saw her, she immediately appreciated that Elizabeth was

---

* Tennant's friends, aside from Cecil Beaton, included British artist and illustrator Rex Whistler, the aristocratically outlandish Mitford sisters, the beautiful Lady Diana Manners (later Lady Diana Duff Cooper), and the Sitwells.

the ideal model of the modern woman with her short hair, long neck, and tall, slender body. Edna was thrilled. Elizabeth looked "smart." So Edna booked her to model for the French illustrator Georges Lepape, and Elizabeth's debut was published on the March 1927 cover of *Vogue*. Lepape rendered her against a backdrop of a Manhattan night skyline, looking straight ahead, a "determined figure in a helmet-like cloche." She seemed engaged with the world around her and was the kind of woman no one could move from her set course. Overnight Elizabeth became the archetype of the unflappable flapper, purposeful, androgynous, and yet possessing the insouciance and charm of youth.[7] Twenty-year-old Elizabeth would be known later as a surrealist, and as the war photographer Lee Miller.

All fashionable illustrations of the day showed girls with long necks, long arms, long fingers, and long, slender bodies. Sometimes they even showed the fashions they were meant to depict accurately, but mostly not. The challenge for women reading *Vogue* was that they could no longer see where the fastenings, folds, tucks, or seams were. While the artwork was a triumph of style over utility, it did little to serve—in Condé's own words— "those one hundred and more thousands of women who were so literally interested in fashion that they wanted to see the mode thoroughly and faithfully reported—rather than rendered as a form of decorative art."[8]

Although Elizabeth became the supermodel of her day, it was Edward Steichen who would truly transform her life. Steichen was an "intense Machine Age man" who understood that "nothing is as dead as yesterday's newspaper." He believed that photography was *the* modern art form—and the only appropriate response to the challenge set by the illustrators of *Vogue*.

As an art critic wrote in *The New York Times*: "The moving picture and the snapshot mark the tempo of our time." And Steichen repeated to his brother-in-law, the poet Carl Sandburg, that "art is the taking of the essence of an object or experience and giving it a new form so that it has an existence of its own."[9] Steichen's philosophy so moved Sandburg that he dedicated his book of poems *Smoke and Steel*:

To
COL. EDWARD J. STEICHEN
PAINTER OF NOCTURNES AND FACES, CAMERA ENGRAVER
OF GLINTS AND MOMENTS, LISTENER TO BLUE
EVENING WINDS AND NEW YELLOW ROSES
DREAMER AND FINDER, RIDER OF GREAT
MORNINGS IN GARDENS, VALLEYS,
BATTLES.[10]

So when the tall, rail-thin, rugged Steichen told Elizabeth during a shoot that he had abandoned the canvas to make art that was "of so much greater use than a canvas in a parlor" because "we are living in an age in which all things have to stand the test of usefulness," it struck home. After all, Elizabeth's father was an engineer and keen photographer, and she had frequently said that she had grown up in a darkroom. Long after she changed her first name to the androgynous Lee,* Elizabeth said, it was Steichen who "put the idea into my head of doing photography." He also told her about the inventive Paris-based photographer whose work reflected art's love affair with the machine, the New Yorker Man Ray. Soon enough Elizabeth would become Ray's muse, and he would teach her all he knew about photography.[11] But that was still in the future.

Models like Elizabeth Miller were also part of the scenery at Condé's parties, often dancing the Lindy or the latest craze, the Black Bottom. "We went to many parties at Condé Nast's," a *Vogue* model recalled. "He loved to mix the social, business, and theater communities, adding a few young things like Lee [Elizabeth] and

---

* She changed her first name to Lee in 1928. As Lee Miller she would be best remembered for her World War II coverage of the London Blitz, the liberation of Paris, and the Buchenwald and Dachau concentration camps for *Vogue*.

me." As for Elizabeth fearing advances from Condé, she affectionately called him "a harmless old goat."[12]

Times were good. The business was purring along, smooth as silk.
Thanks to Harry Yoxall's eye for detail and "assertive salesman-
ship" in London, the *Vogue Pattern Book* had taken off, limiting
British *Vogue*'s losses.[13] With Alison Settle as editor and Laurence
Schneider as advertising director, Condé had every right to feel the
title was firmly in the ascendant. Even the British aristocracy had
adopted *Vogue* as its own, with Lady Diana Cooper and fashion
icon Daisy Fellowes (married to a cousin of Winston Churchill)
often gracing its pages.

    Despite inflation in France and devaluation of the French
franc, Paris, too, was holding its own. French *Vogue* had a new
editor, the talented and charming Solange, duchesse d'Ayen. Although her aristocratic title no longer held sway, her husband,
Jean d'Ayen, was from the illustrious de Noailles family. They owned
the château built on the orders of Louis XIV for his mistress
Madame de Maintenon, but its upkeep impoverished the current
generation. With the addition of Solange as editor, Cosette and
her husband, Lucien, were free to concentrate again on their
own magazines. Michel de Brunhoff became Solange's managing editor.

With both European *Vogues* settling in nicely, it was no accident
that *Vogue*'s vice president, Lew Wurzburg, timed his own idea for
developing a German *Vogue* perfectly. Wurzburg's family came
from Germany, and he spoke the language. He waxed lyrical about
German *Kultur* to Condé and Frank. Didn't the Germans have the
most delightful classical music? And what about German expressionist art and the Bauhaus, that modern school that reunited
the applied arts and manufacturing? Surely they were far ahead
of American culture when it came to expressing modernism?
Condé discussed it with Edna, who put a damper on the notion

immediately—Germans, for her, had no taste, and expansion was out of the question.

The French occupation of Germany's industrial powerhouse of the Ruhr Valley in January 1923 and its ramifications seemed like ancient history to Condé. Frank was never especially interested in politics. That Lithuania had reconquered its territories from the Weimar Freikorps (freebooters, or paramilitaries) was surely an irrelevance to him. So was the NSDAP's attempted coup, or Beer Hall Putsch, in Munich, and German hyperinflation now that the new chairman of the Reichsbank, the pro-American Hjalmar Schacht, was in charge. The prison sentence of some upstart right-wing rebel called Adolf Hitler was more than likely just another press headline to them.[14] What mattered to Frank was precisely what Wurzburg had pointed out: Germany and Austria led the way in the expressionist and secessionist art movements, and had created groundbreaking cinematography as well, such as the 1920 expressionist film *The Cabinet of Dr. Caligari.*

Why shouldn't the hausfrau be exposed to the best fashions and standards of the beau monde? the men argued. "Even in Germany, Edna," Wurzburg said, "some smart women *must* exist." Though Condé kept his own counsel, he undertook market research, as he did with every business decision. Yet he ignored the bigger picture. Germany's Weimar Republic was crumbling under the will of the political right. As an arbiter of social and cultural trends, Condé saw only that Germany was pro-American. Its most acclaimed rendezvous in Berlin, Café Mignon, was the chic meeting place for those who loved all things American. Its patrons "drank dubious concoctions they thought were cocktails" and listened "to records of Whispering Jack Smith."[15]

And so German *Vogue* was born. It was the second title Edna had unsuccessfully vetoed. The Englishman Walter Maas of Paris's Dorland Advertising Agency notified the Berlin branch to be on the lookout for new *Vogue* offices in the capital. The *Geschäftsleiter* (managing director) selected, presumably through Dorland, was a Dr. H. L. Hammerbacher, who was whisked away to New York for a course in the fundamentals of American publishing methods and the Condé Nast formula. What Hammerbacher saw was an American opulence that most Germans could never have imagined. He smiled sagely and nodded, saying everything was *kolossal*.

Returning to Berlin several months later, Hammerbacher set up German *Vogue* in the style to which he felt he, and it, should become accustomed. Dr. Mehemed Fehmy Agha, Dorland Agency's studio chief, designed German *Vogue's* furniture, carpets, and curtains according to the luxury Hammerbacher had in mind. When Condé visited and gasped at the lavishness, he asked to see the balance sheet. Without his approval, German *Vogue* had been established "with a flourish" of his personal wallet. All Condé could hope was that German advertising would follow.

Soon enough, however, the New York headquarters ran up against the standard German plaint and response to virtually any business decision: This is not the German way of conducting business—implying, naturally, that whatever ran counter to German custom was the *wrong* way. Monthly accounts? This was not the German way. Semiannual accounts will do just fine. Translating French or English words common to both languages was *verboten*. "Couturier"? Don't be silly, Hammerbacher tutted. In German *Vogue* it will be *Schneidermeister*—"master tailor." And what about the magazine's name? *Vogue* was un-German. It must be translated, simply because everyone would believe that the intention was to call the publication *Woge*—one of the German words for "wave"—and of course this, too, would not be the German way.

Edna made her first visit to Berlin in early 1928 accompanied by George and Ira Gershwin and their wives, on a working vacation. That was how she discovered that the very name *Vogue* posed a near-insuperable problem. Dr. Agha had been sent "east" by Dorland to become Dr. Hammerbacher's permanent chief assistant. Fortunately Agha came to the rescue and explained to his boss that "to be 'in vogue' means to be on the crest of the wave of the times;

to be always at the summit of everything that is elegant, modern, beautiful, cultured. That is why the biggest, the noblest, the world-famous society and fashion magazine is called *Vogue*."[16] Hammerbacher was placated, and German *Vogue*'s first issue in April 1928 sold out in the first forty-eight hours.

If Dr. Agha hadn't come to New York's notice earlier, his saving the magazine's name now gave him mythical status. In Frank's eyes it was obvious that Agha was a genius. He was a chess addict, too, "a game which he plays extremely well, for a man without a beard." Naturally this made Agha Frank's hero.[17]

22. CASTING FOR PEARLS

There is a wisdom of the head, and a wisdom of the heart.
—CHARLES DICKENS

T he episode made Condé realize he was at a great disadvantage in not speaking any foreign languages. What he needed was someone he could utterly rely on to help as a sort of assistant-cum-troubleshooter. Someone who thought like him but could express himself well in several languages. As luck would have it, he met just such a man at dinner parties in Manhattan. Iva Sergei Voidato Patcévitch, called "Pat" by all, was a suave and debonair young investment banker who was looking to change his fortunes. Pat came from an aristocratic family that had served the Russian czars. Born in Tiflis, Georgia (now Tbilisi), he spent most of his childhood in Turkestan until he entered the Naval Academy at St. Petersburg. He remained there throughout the Great War and the Bolshevik Revolution, before finally escaping the Soviet Union aboard a British destroyer to Constantinople (now Istanbul).[1]

When Pat came to New York in 1923 with a friend, he already spoke seven languages fluently, including English. But they were greenhorns. When they disembarked, they couldn't believe how their Georgian friend Joseph had risen so quickly in New York's hierarchy. "Look at Joseph," Pat said, "He must already be an officer in the American Army!" Joseph was indeed wearing a uniform and beamed back at his friends. "It's nothing," he replied. "It's how we do things at Western Union."[2]

Pat began his employment as a runner on Wall Street for the firm of James H. Oliphant & Company at twelve dollars a week. Back then, Wall Street runners delivered securities between banks, and in carrying such valuable documents, Pat decided to wear an elegant striped suit and spats, along with a sporty ebony cane, to reflect the importance (in his eyes only) of his position. He then worked for Hemphill, Noyes & Company, grappling his way up from the bottom (earning the princely sum of fifteen dollars a week) to the executive offices by virtue of his passion for figures.[3] It helped too that Pat was glamorous, distinguished, a man of impeccable manners and breeding, a sublime dancer, and a bachelor. Soon he was on every New York hostess's A-list of single men for their parties. At one of the first dinner parties Pat attended, he met Millicent Rogers, a good friend of Natica Nast's.

Natica often suggested to her father that he should get to know Pat better. Of course, Condé had met the young man at the houses of their mutual friends, and soon enough included Pat on his own A-list of desirable bachelors for his get-togethers. When he finally acceded to Natica's requests and invited Pat to a small lunch with other business associates, Condé told his daughter afterward: "That seems an extraordinarily able young man. Why haven't you mentioned him before?"[4]

Pat told a different story about that fateful lunch. "I felt reasonably sure that Mr. Nast was going to offer me a job and I had made up my mind to ask a respectable salary, but there were other people at the luncheon and any business discussion was purely general. It was six weeks before I heard from him again. In those six weeks my asking price declined perceptibly."[5]

Condé was looking, too, to expand his Connecticut press operations. For a man whose preferred fragrance was printer's ink, it made sense to him to improve and modernize the Greenwich

printing plant—especially since Condé Nast Press was the most
profitable jewel in his growing empire. Toward the end of 1927,
Condé consulted with his bankers at Goldman Sachs. One of its
directors, a man he believed was a friend, Harrison Williams, persuaded Condé that borrowing money to pay for it was an ideal
solution.

Condé had no reason to question Williams—a noted expert
whose opinion and advice banks craved. He was an "insider" and
the next-door neighbor of J. P. Morgan in Glen Cove, Long Island.
Williams also had a fistful of directorships in dozens of other corporate pies. Then, too, he owned one of the largest power-generation
and utilities conglomerates in the United States, Williams Holdings, ever since power generation was thought of as "the next big
thing." A keen ocean explorer and yachtsman, he became friendly
with Condé during 1925, when Williams began dating Mona
Strader Bush, a society hostess featured regularly in *Vogue*. Williams married Mona in 1926, and Condé went to their wedding.
Since then Condé had relied heavily on Williams's investment
advice.[6]

And so Condé agreed to borrow the money to update and expand the printing plant's capacity to the tune of $2,044,000, to
be repaid over a four-year period from 1928 to 1932.[*] Even though
Condé was friendly with the political and economic gurus of the
day, like Bernard Baruch and the man Baruch had trained, Goldman Sachs's president, Waddill Catchings, it was his personal relationship with Williams that persuaded him to incur millions in
debt finance. What his experts failed to point out to Condé was
that house prices were falling, and the construction industry was
in a tailspin, even before he signed the loan agreement. If only
Condé had known that both Catchings and Williams were devis-
ing a corporate structure, at that very moment, to cash in personally on the overheated stock market.

---

[*] In 1923 Nast had already taken out a seven-hundred-thousand-dollar mortgage
bond covering the property of the parent company, Condé Nast Publications, Inc.,
which had yet to be repaid. (Source: CNA, MC005/Box 3)

Internationally there was a squeeze on credit in Europe, the gold standard was malfunctioning—thus creating balance-of-payments crises around the world due to gold outflows. A global downturn was already in the mix. Investors looking for other ways to make their money work for them turned invariably to the stock market.[7] Knowing the downturn was imminent, Catchings even supported Condé in April 1928 for the acquisition of the "white elephant"—the Grand Central Palace (and the adjoining Park-Lexington Building), which had nearly bankrupted its previous owners in huge tax assessments only a year earlier. Plans to improve the venue, known for hosting the automobile, boat, and flower shows, were already under way, with the lower floors dedicated to "themed" offices. A luxury hotel was also encouraged by zoning officials. With Condé's purchase, the building was revalued for taxation purposes at $9.6 million, nearly double earlier assessments. When Condé questioned why he should be buying the development, his experts reassured him that it was a wise move.[8] Just wait . . . he would thank them later.

Condé felt he was soaring in the clouds. What he lacked, however, was a millionaire's paradise on Long Island's North Shore. So he bought a Sands Point mansion for a vast sum and promptly began remodeling it. For a man of taste and pleasures who happily ignored what "society" thought, it was, again, an uncharacteristic move. He preferred the Automat to New York's fine French restaurants, chocolate ice cream from street vendors to crêpes Suzette, amusement arcades and the fights to the opera. He was often self-deprecating in a rather British way, calling himself a "glorified bookkeeper" and belittling his very real accomplishments in publishing. His charm and elegance beguiled high society and café society alike. So why the mansion on Long Island? Condé had fallen in love with the daughter of old friends, the George Volney Fosters, from Lake Forest, Illinois. He had known the girl since she was eight, and even bounced her on his knee. Her name was Leslie Foster.

Leslie had sandy-blond hair, an open blue-eyed gaze, delicate hands, straight white teeth, and a broad smile. She was five feet eight inches tall* with a shapely figure, and had a wonderful sense of humor. Leslie was pretty, patient, young, unspoiled, and intelligent, and like Condé, came from the Midwest. She was no high-maintenance highbrow gal with one eye on the stage, looking to use Condé as a convenient lever to catapult her career to stardom. She was unlike anyone else in his world, and he was immediately smitten. Their meeting was as natural as it was accidental. Leslie's parents had taken her to Nassau—a reward for completing a business and typing course in Chicago, evidently with a view to her becoming an executive secretary. They saw Condé at a nearby table in the dining room of their hotel and invited him to join them. After a polite interval Condé asked her, "Do you have a beau here?" Leslie laughed, shaking her head. Leslie was nineteen, Condé fifty-one.[9]

Leslie came to New York shortly after Nassau, and saw Condé as discreetly as was possible for such a well-known figure. What she hadn't told him was she had also taken a job at *Vogue*. An awkward eight months ensued, with Condé pretending there was no special relationship between them. That October he suddenly bought *American Golfer* magazine, without consulting Edna or Frank. Condé had become mad about golf as his own "fountain of youth" cure.[10] He wanted to be younger, not for vanity and not even for Leslie, who loved him as he was, but for himself.

Yet Condé gave the game away when he hesitantly asked Edna not to send Leslie's biographical information to the personnel department with the excuse, "I mean, why should they know how young she is?"[11] The only person he was fooling was himself. Leslie was the same age as Natica. His head told him that falling in love with a girl barely turned twenty was absurd, but they couldn't help themselves—they were in love. Besides, Leslie called off the affair repeatedly, whenever their age difference hit home. Then Condé persuaded her that they should continue seeing each

---

* 1.75 meters, the same as Condé.

other throughout the first half of 1928. When he left for Europe that summer, she sent a despairing letter—their age difference was too absurd. He cabled back asking her to marry him. She accepted immediately.

Their engagement came as a shock to the Fosters, but they put on a brave face. Edna, at her judgmental best, took Leslie out to dinner at the Cosmopolitan Club to try to talk some sense into her. Condé ignored Edna's disapproval, responding instead in a letter on his return to New York that September:

> DEAR EDNA,—Fact No. 1: I am a very rich man. Fact No. 2: Your devotion, industry, and very amazing intelligence have been a very great factor in accomplishing Fact No. 1. Fact No. 3: Having achieved great wealth at a time of great age, I find some difficulty in spending my money. Fact No. 4: I have found one expenditure that will give me supreme pleasure and that will compensate for my bald head and my trials and tribulations in accomplishing this wealth. Fact No. 5: I have set aside $100,000 which I want you to use for embroidery on the house you are about to build on Long Island.[12]

For his part, Frank maintained a dignified silence. Natica, who was living at 1040 Park Avenue with her father, had no idea that Condé was considering marriage, and had never been properly introduced to Leslie before the wedding. Fearing her reaction, Condé slipped a note of explanation under her door bearing the glad tidings, then left for the wedding in South Carolina. To both Natica's and Leslie's credit, after a rocky start they became fast friends, and would remain so.[13]

On December 7, 1928, the young lawyer and deputy attorney general of New York, Condé's son, Charles Coudert Nast, married Charlotte Babcock Brown at her parents' home. Condé's wedding gift was a co-op on East Seventy-second Street and five hundred dollars in cash to his new daughter-in-law. Cecil Beaton was invited and photographed the bridesmaids, but was "depressed at the way the bride had clearly dressed hurriedly and persisted in smoking a cigarette in her bridal gown."[14]

Twenty-one days later Condé Nast and Leslie Foster were married at the Aiken, South Carolina, home of Mr. and Mrs. George Foster. It was an intimate affair, with close family and friends attending. Only Frank was invited from the New York headquarters.[15] Their honeymoon would be at the same hotel where they had met in Nassau. There they met Mr. and Mrs. Coudert Nast, also on honeymoon. So that Natica would not feel left out, she was invited too. In January the honeymooners and Natica decamped for Palm Beach.

23. BOOM, CRASH, BANG, CLATTER

*The Jazz Age . . . was borrowed time . . . the whole upper
tenth of a nation living with the insouciance of grand ducs
and the casualness of chorus girls.*
—F. SCOTT FITZGERALD

Since Natica, her brother, Coudert, and his bride, Charlotte, were joining Condé and Leslie in Palm Beach at the tail end of their honeymoon, Natica suggested Patcévitch join them too. It was "just to be around," Pat recalled. "I took all my savings and went flat broke living high in Florida, but Condé and I came to know each other and in February 1929, I went to work on *Vogue*."[1] Both men saw numbers like the instruments of a symphony orchestra or the brushstrokes comprising a fine painting. Both also appreciated and analyzed what those numbers meant in raw dollars and cents. Pat would become Condé's trusted eyes and ears in the business's "hot spots," never embellishing the truth, always delivering hard messages—and, where needed, difficult solutions.

Early in 1929, some eighteen months after Williams and Goldman Sachs persuaded Condé to list his company on the New York Stock Exchange, Condé remained unaware that Waddill Catchings and Harrison Williams had already made their move. Of course they knew about the crashes in Germany and France, and especially what these meant for U.S. banks. Goldman Sachs was involved in the whole unseemly business. They also knew that the overheated U.S. stock market bubble was about to burst. How much debris would be left behind was the crucial question. They wanted to cash in personally on what would become known as the Crash of 1929, and to do that they had to prepare the groundwork swiftly and carefully. So that January, Catchings set up the Goldman Sachs Trading Corporation, an investment trust with $100 million of capital from Goldman Sachs. Shortly afterward he resigned his position with the investment bank to head up the trading company, creating what was euphemistically called a "Chinese wall"—meaning that he would not be privy to any inside information from the bank. Catchings knew that this was just window dressing, since he held the bank's good name, not to mention a vast fortune of the bank's money, at the trading corporation.

Catchings was also Condé's personal banker until he became the force behind Goldman Sachs Trading Corporation, alongside Harrison Williams. Nonetheless, Catchings continued to advise his "old friend," just as Condé's fellow Piping Rock clubman, Harrison Williams, did. Goldman Sachs remained Condé's investment banker. It chose not to educate Condé in the meaning of what was happening in Europe regarding its indebtedness to American banks, the instability of its political regimes, and how the bank was cashing in on their misery.

Since Catchings had set up his investment vehicle, it was time to go on the attack. That February *The New York Times* quoted Catchings saying: "There is no such thing as a saturation point in this nation's development." Soon after, he began to promote his investment trust, warning that "diversification of common stock holdings is necessary," but that no one should be unduly concerned. America could rely on "trust companies to overcome their lack of confidence in common stock,"[2] Catchings said. No wonder. He was running the largest investment trust in American history, and months before the crash came, Catchings also set up Blue Ridge Investment Trust, a subsidiary controlled by Goldman Sachs Trading Corporation and Shenandoah Corporation. By June 1929 Catchings merged Goldman Sachs Trading with Financial and Industrial Securities Corporation, thereby gaining control of the Manufacturers' Trust Bank and the coveted chairman's seat on its executive committee board.[3]

Conde's halcyon days continued unabated, however, for the present. Leslie brought new meaning to his life. She adored him, and he showered her with attention and gifts, calling her his precious "Yorkshire Pudding" in private letters.[4] Pygmalion-style, without wishing to change his adorable wife's demeanor or personality, Condé set about suggesting help with Leslie's "deportment, her hair, her clothes. . . . He liked lavishing his wealth on her." Leslie understood that much of Condé's life revolved around his business and that as his wife she had to behave in the style her husband needed. Within no time she became an accomplished and natural hostess, and a breath of fresh air in New York's café society. A quick learner, she also became her husband's trusted business confidante.

Nonetheless, it took Elsie, Lady Mendl, and Johnnie McMullin to set Leslie straight on how to act when Condé wasn't at her side. They visited her in Paris while she was staying in a modest hotel awaiting Condé's arrival from London. Elsie took the young bride in hand: "You are now the wife of a very wealthy man, Leslie. You must live accordingly. Move at once to the Ritz and get a maid. I have already picked out the pearls I feel Condé should give you."[5] And so she did. Leslie later smiled at the recollection. "It was just as well I never warmed to those grand ideas," she said. "We hadn't been married a year when the crash came."

After their Paris trip Condé continued on to Berlin, while Leslie returned to New York. He had the unpleasant task of dealing with German *Vogue*. Writing to her from the Eden Hotel in Berlin, Condé expressed his problems:

Dearest Darling Leslie:
Don't think I'm neglecting you. Altho I have written little I have thought of you much and missed you greatly. I have before me here in Berlin a distressing perplexing problem. We have lost to date $350,000 and are still losing at a rate of $10,000 a month! I am still struggling with the great house of

*Ulstein** the German publishers. The[y] dominate Germany
as no Amer publisher even Hearst approaches [as] a
dominator of [all things] American. They are shrewd and
I am told not too honest. They want badly Vogue patterns.
I am trying to match my wits against theirs for a combination
of interest in such a way that they cannot kill Vogue once it is
in their hands. I am each night dead with thinking and
planning and figuring.*[6]

Condé spoke to her not as a wounded man, but as the owner of
a business would do to his closest business confidante. Hearst was
his ever-present threat, an almost unspoken daily concern, who
with each passing year became an even greater danger. Then, too,
Condé was worried that Ullstein would cease publication of German *Vogue*. That said, for them to keep publishing the title according to its unprofitable Condé Nast formula was not an option. No
deal could be concluded regarding the German publication, and
so it folded. Spanish *Vogue*—seemingly another folie de grandeur—
had barely gotten off the drawing board before it, too, was shut
down. It was a mistake for Condé to believe that he could understand the German market from New York—despite his own and
Wurzburg's German ancestry, and Frank's deep sympathy with
German expressionism. None of them realized that Berlin itself
was often likened in the 1920s to a desirable woman: "racy, cold,
coquettish, arrogant, snobbish, parvenu, uncultivated and common—a woman every man wanted to own."[7] Pan-Germanism
too, the movement that lay at the heart of the kaiser's reasons for
firing the first shots in the Great War, was experiencing a resurgence with the rise in popularity of National Socialism and Adolf
Hitler.

After years of hyperinflation partially caused by the onerous
conditions the Treaty of Versailles imposed on Germany after the
war, many Germans saw National Socialism as an expression of
patriotism. The terms of the treaty had also weakened the cur-

* "Ullstein" is the correct spelling.

rency, and its repercussions caused civil unrest on both sides of the political spectrum. When the first German *Vogue* hit the newsstands in the spring of 1928, the poisonous economic atmosphere had trickled down to ordinary people. Germany's Reichsbank minister, Hjalmar Schacht, had stopped the hyperinflation that had led to people needing wheelbarrows to transport literally trillions of paper marks to the bakery for a mere loaf of bread, but the scars remained profound and multifaceted. American banks, including Goldman Sachs, were placing unrealistic demands on Germany's economy, promoting their short-term loans at high interest to German borrowers, who then invested their borrowed cash in the falsely buoyant stock market for purely speculative purposes.

Back in 1927, the saying everyone repeated in world stock markets was that they were in a "new era of hope," buoyed by margin purchases on borrowed money. Those who had money seemed oblivious to the simple reality that Germany was obliged to continue its crippling reparations payments—by and large with finance provided by American clearing and investment banks—digging itself into a deep chasm of debt that could never be repaid. On May 11, 1927—eleven months before the first German *Vogue* was published—the Reichsbank considered that the commercial banks' reserves were too low. Two days later Schacht suspended all Reichsbank credit, launching the first "Black Friday" in Germany, some seventeen months ahead of America's darkest days.[*8] It should have come as a clear warning shot to Condé, who understood the significance of the numbers better than most, to change his decision to proceed with German *Vogue*.

Edna's view of the German situation had always been unenthusiastic, and she was delighted to learn that Condé wanted to unwind the company's commitment there. In fact, between the "misbegotten German baby" and the development of both British and French *Vogues*, Edna found that she needed to spend much of her time in Europe nursing her growing brood. Nonetheless, and despite Condé's pleas, she refused to name anyone as the dedicated

---

* Low bank reserves were also one of the causes of the 2008 banking meltdown.

editor for American *Vogue*. Her stubbornness was galling and un-necessary. So at long last Condé decided for her. Edna merely wrote later that "after much deliberation and consultation . . . Condé as-signed the post to Carmel in the spring of 1929."[9]

Never known to lavish praise on her subordinates, particularly the capable ones, Edna must have felt a stab when Condé wrote to her from New York during her spring 1929 travels to Europe that "Carmel seems to be very much on the job." Edna's response typically damned Carmel with faint praise: "That's the wonderful thing about Carmel. She was so good when not distracted. She had native good taste, which had been cultivated and developed by her work. She had ability, poise, and an engaging wit, but there were lapses."[10]

Edna's world-weary attitude toward her editor worsened after Carmel's marriage to Palen Snow. She begrudged that Carmel's priorities had changed. "In a way we felt that we had all married Palen, as the life he wanted to lead, the holidays he wanted to take and the parties he wanted to go to became Carmel's primary in-terest and she sought to rearrange her *Vogue* schedule accordingly." Most maddening for Edna was that no matter how much Carmel socialized of an evening, she seemed to require precious little sleep, and "got to her desk in the morning . . . as alert and able as ever."[11] Carmel's ability to eat little, sleep less, and remain at the top of her game was irritating to her boss. It had already become part of Carmel's legend.

Then, too, Edna was unable to stomach that everyone seemed to love Carmel. People thought the Whites (and now the Snows) "were just firecrackers," while Edna had a reputation for being for-bidding. Carmel sailed through her first pregnancy working harder than ever and actively participating in the August 1928 fall collection frenzy in Paris while six months pregnant. She gave birth to little Carmel that November, receiving a gift of Lanvin baby clothes from the fashion editor of French *Vogue*, Main Bocher.

The other change in Carmel's life, which Condé watched with some trepidation, was the promotion of her favorite sibling, Tom White, to the position of manager of Hearst's magazines—with

Harper's Bazar featuring prominently among them. "Blood, he reasoned was thicker than printer's ink," Edna wrote. According to her, Condé had asked Carmel to sign a contract as a means of retaining her, but Carmel refused, promising him instead that she would never go to work for Hearst or *Bazar*. Edna never revealed if she urged Condé to put Carmel under contract. If she argued the point later with Condé, he more than likely would have replied that he trusted in Carmel's loyalty.

In the same 1929 letter to Edna, Condé wrote about his new art director, Dr. Agha, formerly of German *Vogue*, who was taking up his position in New York. Fortuitously Condé's long-standing art director, Heyworth Campbell, had retired in 1928, making room for Agha. Condé was thrilled with his new man, writing, "Agha continues to give impressive evidence of his intelligence. For the first time in the twenty-one years that I have been running this shop the work of the art department of the paper is being lifted from my shoulders. He takes responsibility the way Lew takes it."

By then Leslie was four and a half months pregnant, and the happy couple were redecorating both Sands Point and 1040 Park Avenue. At the same time, Condé also attempted to salvage some money from the German *Vogue* debacle. Condé wrote to Leslie that September from Berlin: "Call [Elsie] Lady Mendl as she is leaving Paris very soon. Don't talk about your room as you are not doing it thru her office. You can say you left before I made final decisions as to things I saw at various places."[12] As far as he was concerned, the millions he had borrowed to invest on credit, with Goldman Sachs's advice, were secure.

So when Black Thursday, October 24, hit, Condé was in shock. On October 29 Condé Nast Publications stock had slid rapidly from the high of ninety-three dollars a share earlier that month to forty-eight dollars. By mid-November their stock was quoted at two dollars a share. Frank had sold his few thousand shares in early September at the high—fearing that he had done wrong. Harry Yoxall only got out when they were valued at fourteen dollars.[13] In

September 1929, too, Edna had drawn the first twenty thousand of the promised one hundred thousand dollars Condé hoped to gift her in September 1928. She never saw the rest. Persuaded by Condé's buoyancy about the stock market, she had even bought shares on margin, and regretted it. She said with twenty-twenty hindsight, "It had never appealed to me."

In the immediate aftermath of the Wall Street debacle, all senior staff took a 33 percent cut in salary. Condé slashed his own by 50 percent. The greatest portion of Condé's wealth was on paper, invested in Wall Street on the advice of his banker friends Waddill Catchings and Harrison Williams. By September 1929 Williams had become a director of many of the investment trusts that Catchings had either created or swallowed up. Unlike Condé, Williams had an inside track to the prosperity that lay ahead. Lured by tales from his own barber, mail clerks, and elevator operators earning fortunes by investing in common stocks and topped with the extravagant proposals of Catchings, Williams, and other bankers, Condé could be forgiven for feeling that investing in stocks had only an upside. But Condé's "inside track" experts fed his desire for expansion, leading him to borrow two million dollars from the old Equitable Trust Company at the beginning of 1929, and *then* allowing the experts to persuade him to invest the entire sum—lock, stock, and two smoking barrels—into the soon-to-be-issued stock of the new Goldman Sachs Trading Corporation, headed by Catchings with several members of the Sachs family on its board. Was their intention to bring Condé in out of the cold? No. It was their way of reeling him into their trap on borrowed money.

The saddest thing is that by early September 1929, Condé had made back his investment, on paper, plus a million dollars' profit. Edna suggested he cash out. No one was ever called a sucker for taking the money and running. Condé told Edna, in his disarming way, "I don't really understand all this myself, but I'm getting expert advice, my dear, expert. Bankers *know* about these things."[14] Condé was not a greedy man. He believed unswervingly in the advice of experts, and his experts—Catchings and Williams—told him to hold on tight. So what if he had made a million dollars? Early September 1929 was not the time to bottle. His investment in Goldman Sachs Trading Corporation would more than double his wealth before long, they had said.

PART IV

SAVING THE
EMPIRE

━━━●■○●━━━

*Since the break [in the market] we appear to be
losing more heavily than other magazines.*
—CONDÉ NAST TO LESLIE NAST, JANUARY 1930

※

24. BEWARE OF FRENEMIES

*General business conditions are unquestionably
fundamentally sound.*
—WADDILL CATCHINGS, *THE NEW YORK TIMES*,
OCTOBER 31, 1929

L ate in the summer of 1929, another woman entered Condé's
life. He was introduced to her at a dinner party. She told
him she was recently divorced. Like so many other society
women, she asked if he might be able to find her a position at one
of his magazines. Condé had already decided that this society lady
was different. She was no dilettante. She was rudderless but somehow impressive, and serious about writing. She was also stunningly
beautiful. Her name was Clare Boothe Brokaw. Condé invited her
to come speak with Edna at *Vogue*.

Of course Condé knew that Clare had been married to George
Tuttle Brokaw, who was a well-known New York dandy and Princeton man, and lived with his mother at their Fifth Avenue and
Seventy-ninth Street mansion. Brokaw was held to be New York's
most eligible bachelor, a first-rate golfer, bon vivant, and clubman,
with his own two-million-dollar inheritance. He had also fallen in
love with the porcelain doll Clare at first sight.[1] So the always-
calculating Clare, in the relative blink of an eye, dumped her
English officer boyfriend, Capt. Julian Simpson, writing that he
was too "willful, high-minded, and poor" and she too "romantic
and self-indulgent."[2] With George's mother's approval, the pair
were married in July 1923, a scant two months after they met.

Clare's engagement ring was a seventeen-carat blue-white diamond from Cartier. Their daughter, Anne Clare, was born the following year. In May 1929 Clare was granted a Reno divorce on the ground of "extreme cruelty."[3]

And so Clare dutifully made an appointment to see Edna in Vogue's office on the nineteenth floor of the Graybar Building, adjacent to Grand Central Station. Vogue's editor in chief had seen her fair share of aspiring editors in the past, so she set Clare the task of writing the detailed captions for which the magazine was famous. Surprisingly, Edna thought that this woman could actually write, and asked Clare to return in a few days' time after she had a chance to discuss her candidacy with Condé. Clare obeyed, but she found that Edna—and indeed Condé—had decamped for Europe for six weeks.[4] So Clare set about rebuilding her new life by renting an apartment at the Stanhope Hotel, at 995 Fifth Avenue, instead.

Rather than wait for another appointment or indeed a rejection from Condé Nast Publications, shortly after Labor Day, Clare Brokaw donned a tailored gray dress with a white collar and cuffs and went to work at Vogue. She told the receptionist that she was a new employee and was shown an empty desk. Eventually some papers were placed on it, and so she started work. "I kind of oozed on," Brokaw recalled later. "Nobody knew anything about me, not even the accountant."[5] Clare also oozed confidence, so when Edna returned, she naturally presumed that Condé had hired her. Condé was equally hoodwinked, thinking Edna had discerned Clare's underlying promise.

In truth Edna thought that Clare was rather overly grand—spreading a white cloth across her desk at breakfast and taking her coffee from a silver pot. Mrs. Brokaw would need to be cut down to size, Edna decided, feeding her a strict diet of captions to prove her point. Clare's deadpan captions were reminiscent of Dorothy Parker's, only with less bite and more style. She was especially good at writing them, too. Spread over five pages, her first words at Vogue were titled "Chic for the Newly Arrived." Clare warned mothers that the twenty-two-inch christening robe edged with the finest Valenciennes lace worn over that delicate silk slip to protect baby's tender skin might cost "a great deal more than mother's latest from Chanel." Baby's toys, too, were not beneath Clare's lofty gaze, since she spoke with some authority as a young mother when suggesting that these should be edible as "babies have a passion for playing with their food and eating their playthings."[6] While Edna was impressed, she nonetheless ensured that the "Newly Arrived" Clare was not given her requested byline.

Clare was born to Anna Clara Schneider in 1903—the second of Anna's illegitimate children—in a second-floor apartment on West 124th Street in Manhattan. Her father was William Franklin Boothe, a "salesman," who was reputedly irresistible to women with his outgoing personality, abundant lustrous dark hair, sensuous mouth, and athletic build. His main fault lay in the simple fact that he could not reject any female advances. On her birth certificate Clare, like her older brother, David, was acknowledged and given her father's name. In a familiar, sad tale, William was already married to Laura Brauss, his second wife, whom he deserted for Anna in 1901.

Clare's mother was just shy of her twenty-first birthday, and in her William met his nemesis. Toward the end of his life, he wrote a letter to Clare confessing, "When I met your mother, I had a big, prosperous factory. She was the sole cause of my losing it . . . her ambition and twenty-five years difference in age tells the whole story." Anna, or Ann as she later became known, was an eighteen-year-old at the time, petite, with violet eyes, pearly teeth, and a mass of chestnut hair, and with expectations and fantasies that exceeded William's ability to meet them. She also lied, telling everyone that she had been born into impoverished "Austrian nobility."[7]

Clare's childhood was one of "little deceptions" and downright lies. When William's wife, Laura, sued for divorce in New York on the ground of adultery in 1906, he denied the accusation. Of course Clare and her brother David were living proof of the claim, and Laura was awarded her divorce. According to New York law, as the wronged party Laura could remarry, while William could not "until the said Laura O. B. Boothe shall be actually dead."[8]

So the family moved away from New York and the stain of not being married, and finally settled in Nashville, Tennessee. Despite William's tremendous fondness for music and his ability on the violin, he had to opt for jobs that brought in more money to satisfy Ann. He changed his name to "Murphy" and took a job as the manager of the local Celery Ade soft drink plant. Clare and David were enrolled in the local school under the name "Murphy." In his spare time William taught music and played as a freelance violinist.

But he always wanted to make it as a musician. Suddenly in 1911, the family upped stakes and moved to the South Side of Chicago—living cheek by jowl with the stench of the local slaughterhouses and glue factories. Though William was employed by Chicago's Grand Opera Orchestra during the 1911–12 season, the family lived in greatly reduced financial circumstances. When Ann's father fell ill in September 1912 in New Jersey, she took the children with her to nurse him, knowing she would never return. Ann donned the mantle of the "grieving widow," telling local friends and family that her husband had recently died. Soon enough the children began to believe the fiction too. Ann eventually returned to her familiar haunts in Manhattan, calling herself "Mrs. Ann Franklin." To earn her living, Ann became a call girl, while Clare became a child actor in Broadway plays. The children met a raft of "uncles"—that is, until her mother met Joel Jacobs in 1915, a forty-eight-year-old bachelor of German-Jewish origin with slicked-down hair parted on the side, a prominent nose, dark eyes, and "the shoulders of a man whose ancestors had known the ghetto."[9] By the time he met the family, he was every inch the tycoon.

Clare introduced Jacobs as her guardian and liked him well enough. Whether he legally held that role is doubtful, but Jacobs called her his "angel" and would change her life for the better, forever. He bankrolled Ann in the style to which she wanted to become accustomed and paid for the private education of both Clare and David. Still, Clare did not make friends easily, unsure of how to tell her life story until that point. Her only friend's mother described her as "the most startlingly poised child I ever knew." Her fellow students at St. Mary's School thought she was a "most conceited girl" who nursed a "rage for fame."[10] Despite her mother eventually marrying Dr. Albert Austin, a surgeon at Greenwich Hospital, that rage for fame remained her guiding force throughout her long and successful life.

Given Clare's background, it was natural that she should join the ranks of those who thought Edna forbidding. Clare resented Edna's sense of entitlement and seeming superiority. Equally natural was Clare's gravitation toward Carmel and *Vogue*'s well-loved society editor, Margaret Case.* At *Vogue* "Maggie," as everyone called her, influenced style on both sides of the Atlantic, taught Clare a great deal about how style "trickled down," and gave the newcomer advanced fashion tips to update her rather mousy wardrobe.

But *Vogue* was always a convenient stepping-stone for the ambitious Clare Brokaw. Though Frank Crowninshield had a reputation as "a stealer of talent" from Condé's flagship publication, Clare went like a willing lamb into his fold. *Vogue* was Condé's gift to fashion, while *Vanity Fair* was the haute monde, the pinnacle of sophistication for any young woman with a burning ambition to rise like cream to the top. Frank described Clare as "the usual Dresden-china society figure, a shepherdess with pretty teeth, large, round blue eyes, and blonde hair." She had a slender neck, ankles, and wrists that made her seem singularly fragile. In brief, Frank effused: "She was, altogether, a bibelot of the most enchanting order." When Beaton first met her, he described her as "drenchingly beautiful." One of her many influential lovers claimed she had "uproarious breasts."[11]

---

* Margaret Case should not be confused with Margaret Case Harriman—the daughter of Frank Case, owner of the Algonquin—who also wrote for Condé Nast Publications at *Vanity Fair*.

In those soon-to-be dark days of October 1929, Condé was unaware of Clare's ability to take whatever she desired. When the Crash came, she was firmly part of the *Vogue* team, even though she had an independent income of almost $500,000 in a divorce settlement. It remained nearly intact, too, dropping a mere $1,200 annually from her United Cigar Store stock. The remainder of her trust of $425,000 was safely invested.

Condé was on the brink of bankruptcy. Even the infallible *New York Times* was oblivious to the signs his bankers had read into the future, declaring on January 1, 1929: "If there is any way of judging the future by the past, this new year may well be one of felicitation and hopefulness."[12] Big business made its rosy forecasts, indifferent to the gloom that pervaded the hardest-hit. News reports tried to buck up the doom mongers with their statistics. The increase in national income in goods and services had risen in the nine years between 1910 and 1919 by 10 percent, where from 1920 to 1929 the increase was a staggering 93 percent. Output per man-hour had doubled since 1909, and real wages more than doubled since 1914.[13]

The first whiff of a crash on Thursday, October 24, struck panic into the market. U.S. Steel had gone from 261¾ down to 193½, and General Electric, which had sold for 400 at the beginning of the month, was down to 283. Around noon that day Charles E. Mitchell, head of the National City Bank, sneaked into the offices of J. P. Morgan & Co. So too did William Potter, head of the Guarantee Trust; Seward Prosser, head of the Bankers Trust; and Albert H. Wiggin of Chase National. Together with Thomas Lamont of J. P. Morgan and George F. Baker of First National Bank, they agreed to form a consortium to shore up the market. They chose Richard Whitney, vice president of the New York Stock Exchange, to act on their behalf. The consortium was doomed to failure from the start.

In 1930 Whitney would be made president of the New York Stock Exchange, a position he kept until 1935. In March 1938 he was charged with embezzlement, and he and his firm, Richard Whitney & Co., were declared bankrupt. He was indicted by a grand jury and pleaded guilty. Whitney was sentenced to a five-to-ten-year prison term. On April 12, 1938, more than six thousand people came to Grand Central Terminal to watch Whitney escorted onto the train taking him to Sing Sing. He served three years and four months in prison before he was paroled.

As October's leaves fell and blew on a wet November ground, commentary on the state of the stock market was reminiscent of a community prayer meeting held to bolster the faith of its congregants. President Hoover joined the choir, claiming: "Prosperity is just around the corner." Today we might call it "fake news" or, more charitably, "building business confidence." Whatever moniker was used, it led Condé, and tens of thousands of others, down a rabbit hole. Investors were carried along by the course of events as if riding the wind, unable or unwilling to diagnose the true cause of the market's malady: greed. What no economist had recognized was that when the shooting stopped in 1918, an economic war had begun, and American banks were determined to win it. They lavished dollars on allies and enemies alike, promoting tariffs to encourage "infant industries" back home. They took advantage of European hyperinflation and the fall of foreign currencies: The dollar would reign supreme.

The robber barons of the nineteenth century had settled down to respectable wealth, adopting humane business practices—becoming government representatives, like Andrew Mellon. They were done taking advantage of Americans. Instead they plundered foreign shores and became monopoly kings of steel, aluminum, and energy. They convinced Americans that panics were a thing of the past. During the 1928 election, candidate Herbert Hoover promised voters, "A chicken in every pot, a car in every garage"— and was believed.

When winter took hold, Condé still hoped the panic would be short-lived. What he didn't realize was that this time, Wall Street had hit Main Street. The newspapers tried to downplay what was going on—even though the bottomlessness was on everybody's tongues. It was unpatriotic to report on the sudden failure of small banking and investment houses because every butcher, baker, and elevator boy in the country had been persuaded to buy, buy, buy. On November 9, 1929, Condé wrote to his wife: "Leslie dearest—Things here are still nervous and hectic. I never seem able to catch up. I was on the point of doing so when the market broke and brought in its train financial conferences that have taken three or four hours each day."[14]

In fact Condé was working all the hours imaginable to try to stop the slump in sales at his publications, while looking to restructure his debts. The strain was tremendous, and a series of seemingly unrelated physical problems began to appear—a sore arm, trapped toes—and Condé feared he was getting old. Leslie suggested he should go to Florida, see a physical therapist, and perhaps look to improve his golf game, which she knew gave him great pleasure. Besides, she advised, he could speak privately to Harrison and Mona Williams, who always wintered in Palm Beach. Just maybe Condé could get a better idea on how to handle his personal situation. So Condé went to Boca Raton and stayed at its luxurious club. It was a long train ride to Florida, but an even longer ride down for the stock market. By the time he reached Boca Raton, Condé heard about the suicides—grown men in such despair they jumped from their offices that touched the skies.

When Condé wrote home, he tried to put it all out of his mind. To boot, he was struggling with his health but put on a brave face for Leslie. "Leslie darling: We have had two beautiful days. I hope you have not run into blizzard weather in N.Y. This masseur is a wizard. He is giving me electrical treatments followed by massage and my arm is improving. He is now concentrating on my arm—an hour's treatment. Of the hour's treatment fifteen minutes is excruciating pain but he says he will send me north with a normal arm."[15] By now Condé knew that millions of contracts for luxury goods had been canceled. Advertising agreements with both *Vogue* and *Vanity Fair* were among the first to go. Jewelers, couturiers, fur houses, and vacation and steamship advertisers soon withdrew theirs too, or went out of business entirely.

Then, at last, he sent her a message: "The W. family are here." W. was Condé's code name for the Harrison Williamses.[16] He had taken Leslie up on the idea of meeting with them. Mona Williams, as a popular society hostess, and the first American woman ever to top the international best-dressed list, featured prominently in Margaret Case's juicy *Vogue* society column. For many, Mona had the truest flair for living well.

Born Mona Strader in Fayette County, Kentucky, she learned young that poverty was no impediment to presenting herself well. Her first husband was a former horsetrainer-turned-businessman, Harry Schlesinger, with whom she had a son. Schlesinger was much older than she, so when she met and fell in love with James Bush of Chicago—a wonder boy of his generation, then working only when the whim struck for the Equitable Trust Company. Equitable Trust was the bank from which Condé borrowed millions to invest in Goldman Sachs Trading. Bush was abundantly endowed with good looks—so Mona divorced Schlesinger. Only later did she discover that Bush had little else to offer. Stepping things up a gear, Mona recognized that beauty in her man was all well and good, but the Midas touch of Harrison Williams would suit her better, even if he was rather long-faced, with beady eyes.[17] Williams had been a widower for some years, and so in marrying Mona he indulged her every whim—from tearing down the family home on Long Island and rebuilding a new one from the shell of the tennis house, to constructing a new winter home at Palm Beach. He even advised Condé about *Vogue*, in which his wife loved to appear. So by 1929 Condé knew that the way to Harrison's heart was through his wife. Mona was delighted to see Condé at her door but regretfully claimed she could not help.

Condé returned to New York for Christmas, but in early January 1930 he faced increasingly frantic calls for repayment of his debts. Naturally the bills for the hideously expensive renovation at Sands Point rolled in, too. He sent Leslie to Palm Beach to stay at the Breakers Hotel, so she wouldn't see how frazzled he was. A rather dejected Condé wrote to her: "I feel well enough but I am depressed and worried. The 1929 Circulation reports are not so good for either Vogue Vanity or H&G and the competitors up . . . [their] magazines are cutting down our lead in advertising. This has nothing to do with the break in the market. It started before. Moreover since the break we appear to be loosing [sic] more heavily than the other magazines."[18]

Condé was clearly enraged by his expert friends who had urged him to expand on borrowed money; Catchings and Williams had made a killing. Early in 1930, he tried halfheartedly to build up Edna's morale, writing: "Most of the wise men in Wall Street and in the business world seem to think that the depression will not be a bad one, considering the seriousness of the stock market debacle, nor a very long one. They look for an upturn in business before the end of six months. This may be true," Condé said before lashing out. "But I don't think anyone knows a damn' thing about what is going to happen. If they have the wisdom to point out the future business for this coming year, that same wisdom should have enabled them to forecast the crash, yet even such institutions as J. P. Morgan & Company did not know it was coming." Cursing himself, Condé concluded: "Certainly I did not know enough to form my own opinion and I have no respect for the wisdom of the wise men, but as I am generally optimistic, I think we should do fairly well."[19]

Condé was worried and disgruntled. But did he really believe that even the bankers had not known it was coming? Or was that what Catchings and Williams wanted him to think? Catchings, confident that the crash was a mere matter of time, had prepared for it in advance. He had set out to plunder undervalued securities on the stock market and persuaded Goldman Sachs to invest one hundred million dollars in his certainty. Condé's other "friend," Harrison Williams, also served on the board of the Goldman Sachs Trading Corporation and its affiliate trusts, the Blue Ridge and Shenandoah Corporations. Five days before Condé's November 1929 letter to Leslie, Goldman Sachs & Co. confirmed that it still owned ten million shares in its trading corporation and had recently bought more shares to bolster its ability to acquire even more securities—inexpensively. In the same statement Harrison Williams, the main investor in Shenandoah, retained all his shares in that company *and* Blue Ridge. On November 4, 1929, the directors issued a statement to jittery investors:

> The corporation owns in conjunction with one of the largest and most successful public utility groups [Williams Holdings Group] a large portion of the Shenandoah Corporation which was formed for the purpose of associating these two interests in public utility and industrial and commercial enterprises. Shenandoah Corporation has large investments in such companies, as well as a large investment in Blue Ridge Corporation, which has a great independent capital invested in a broad list of high grade securities, and these companies are in excellent financial condition.... The corporation has a large interest in New York real estate... [and] many substantial investments in the securities of numerous companies.[20]

With seats on the board of directors of the corporations were also Sidney J. Weinberg of Goldman Sachs & Co. and its lawyer, John Foster Dulles.* Their job, so they claimed, was to help business regain confidence by sweeping up shares in viable companies—like Condé Nast Publications—that had plummeted to new depths. Another way of considering their business model, however, would be to venture that they knew the market was overheated and that they had resolved to pick up securities on the cheap, gaining control of vast swaths of American industry within weeks. No other corporate group in America had the capital—some $127 million in cash—to mop up the mess.[21] Condé Nast Publications was a

---

* John Foster Dulles (1888—1959) later served as secretary of state under President Dwight D. Eisenhower. His brother Allen Dulles was the first civilian director of the Central Intelligence Agency. Their grandfather John W. Foster, and their uncle Robert Lansing, also served as secretary of state in the Benjamin Harrison and Woodrow Wilson governments respectively.

minnow among the companies they effectively controlled as
the largest creditor; giants like general Foods, General Electric,
Manufacturers' Trust, and even Warner Bros., fell victim to their
plan.

While the acquisition of vast chunks of securities was under way,
somewhat surprisingly, Waddill Catchings—now serving on the
board of Condé Nast Publications, Inc., along with Sidney J.
Weinberg—suddenly took up residence in Reno, Nevada. Rumors
circulated, even in *The New York Times*, that Catchings was divorcing his wife.[22] During his absence, Weinberg would handle
affairs on behalf of both Goldman Sachs and its investment trading corporation. Of course Condé remained chairman of Condé
Nast Publications, Inc., with Frank Crowninshield, Edna Chase,
Lew Wurzburg, Dick Wright, Max Rossett (of Condé Nast Press),
and Condé's lawyers, Macdonald DeWitt and C. Coudert Nast, as
his codirectors. While the representatives of each business unit
had a voice, they were all beholden to the might of Catchings and
Weinberg.[23]

By January 30, 1930, the Goldman Sachs Trading Corporation
held assets worth some $233 million valued at cost or market price,
whichever was lower. This meant that the investment trading corporation was trading at $40.94 per share, which included the Blue
Ridge and Shenandoah Corporations that held bonds and debt
from Condé Nast Publications to a strained tune exceeding $5 mil-
lion. Condé Nast's market price was just above $4.00 a share.
Profits for the trading corporation were declared at a staggering
$30,979,778 for the year ending December 31, 1929, of which
Goldman Sachs & Co. were entitled to a 20 percent share. And
Waddill Catchings was the largest shareholder in Goldman Sachs
& Co. In the year-end report an ebullient Catchings declared that
"the main purpose of the corporation was to acquire its major investments for their inherent worth and prospects of future growth
and enhancement in value."[24]

Yet how did Condé's competition fare—particularly Hearst's

Harper Bazaar,* which was nipping ever closer to *Vogue*'s heels? *Bazaar* had picked up some of *Vogue*'s luxury advertisers by under-cutting its advertising rates. But what few realized outside the immediate Hearst organization was that Hearst's fortune was tied up in art and real estate holdings. Although no one dared put it into print, Hearst was strapped for cash, too. Where Condé's debts were $5 million, Hearst's were over $120 million and mounting quickly.[25] Hearst's eye-watering indebtedness help to put into per-spective the fact that the holdings in Condé Nast Publications were a mere pimple on the face of the largest investment trading cor-poration in the world.

Condé's overriding concern was losing control of his company to rapacious financial investors, particularly while his business was suffering. Worst hit was French *Vogue*, so to swiftly remedy the situation, Condé sent his trusted multilingual eyes and ears, Iva Patcévitch, to head up the French operations. Pat found himself in charge of more than French *Vogue* in Paris. Les Éditions Condé Nast, based on the Champs-Élysées, also owned 74 percent of *Le Jardin des Modes*; all the outstanding capital stock in Condé Nast Publications, Ltd., for the publication of *Vogue* in the British Em-pire; and the associated real estate in both Great Britain and France.[26]

Catchings was rejoicing in the spring of 1930. As a Reno, Nevada, resident, he began plundering weaker banks and real estate in the West. The purpose of the Reno residency was not to be closer to his victims but to establish himself in Nevada to divorce his wife, Helen, and marry his mistress, Mae Francis, who was a Goldman Sachs stockbroker. The wedding was followed by one of the most elaborate feasts ever held in Reno, *The New York Times* reported.[27]

On March 25, 1930, the birth of Leslie Adrienne Nast allowed both Condé and his young wife the briefest of moments to smile and coo at their very good fortune. Leslie could see the worry

---

* *Harper's Bazaar* had acquired its third *a* in November 1929.

etched on her husband's face and tried to give him respite from his woes, both at 1040 Park Avenue and at their Sands Point home. Photos of them at the time show a careworn Condé and a young, fresh-faced, delighted first-time mother. Despite their mutual joy, however, more than age was beginning to separate them.

After her pregnancy, and her tireless efforts to help Condé cope with his grim financial circumstances, Condé wanted Leslie to have some gaiety in her life and escape the claustrophobia of New York. It was agreed that she should go to Paris, leaving the baby home with him and a nurse. In truth, he was still trying to renegotiate his mortgage bonds with the elusive Catchings, but without success. Condé foresaw even more trying times ahead. All he could do was turn his full attention to the business of staying in business. But his thoughts often turned to his young wife. Unsurprisingly, his letter to Leslie dated July 30, 1930, ends with the lament: "It's too bad any worries must be borne by you. You are too young."[28]

Condé felt he had to protect Leslie from his darkest thoughts. On the other hand, he needed her by his side. Part of him felt she shouldn't have gone—despite his insistence—while his unselfish side wanted her far away. Maintaining his equilibrium was increasingly difficult. "The heat wave continues altho the weather department says it has ended," he wrote of the weather, as one often does to bring a loved one closer to home. "The temperature is down a little but the humidity is soaring. [Little] Leslie seems to be immune against hot weather. She is fat and smiling. I told the nurse to move to your room as it is so much cooler." Filling her in on home news, he gives Leslie notice of the birth of another child to Carmel and Palen Snow, but also shares his worries about a car accident she and her baby had on their way to their Southampton home: "On the way down—it was a rainy skiddy day—they were run into. Carmel['s] wrist and arm were so badly cut that it took eighteen stitches to patch her up—miraculous to relate the baby was in her arms but was not hurt! They were taken to the hospital, both covered with blood. Both are ok according to reports but Carmel is suffering from a neuritis in the injured arm & [wrist]."

Carmel never took much in the way of maternity leave, and

Condé still had hopes that after she finished having babies, she would become the natural successor to Edna. He realized he was overburdening Leslie—who had, after all, been sent to Paris to recuperate and enjoy herself. But the selfish side of Condé couldn't help writing about the staff party held at Sands Point:

> Well the staff house party was a huge success. It was so terrifically hot.... Claire Brokaw was the life of the party. She is an extraordinary ... able and intelligent woman. She led us into all sorts of games and was indefatigable at ping pong backgammon and swimming. Donald [Freeman, managing editor of Vanity Fair] was at her heels, the whole time, just like a little puppy dog and Margaret Case entered into the mood of the party. She enjoyed it tremendously and every one seemed to like her very much. The pool at night was entrancing under the green lights. The water is as sparkling as a jewel and it was so sizzlingly hot that the water could not be too cold.[29]

It is little wonder that soon after receiving his letter, Leslie booked her passage home.

Since Clare Brokaw had gone to work at *Vogue* the previous September, she had been at her ambitious best. Not satisfied with writing captions for Edna—even when she was caught with her foot in her mouth over her description of see-through silky underwear as "toothsome"—she sought to ingratiate herself with Frank from the get-go. Her ambition demanded that her name become one of the all-stars of *Vanity Fair* alongside Colette, Noël Coward, F. Scott Fitzgerald, D. H. Lawrence, Walter Lippmann, Dorothy Parker, and Edna St. Vincent Millay. *Vanity Fair*, with its striking covers and gift for dazzling prose, was her natural home, even if no one at Condé Nast knew it yet. So she offered Frank a hundred article ideas. Frank's jaw dropped at her astonishing speed and facility, and he couldn't help the patronizing joke that she must keep "a clever young man" under her bed.[30]

Clare hadn't long to wait. On October 30, with most of the nation in a state of shock from the Crash, she received a telegram at her apartment at the Stanhope Hotel inviting her to meet with *Vanity Fair's* managing editor. Aged only twenty-five, Donald Freeman was a Columbia University graduate and had studied in Europe. He spoke French and German fluently, which explained to some extent his promotion of the works of French writers. He had been made a member of the Légion d'Honneur for promoting French culture. His obvious intellectual prowess was hidden in a rather unprepossessing body, crowned with a receding hairline and amplified by his gourmand tastes and excesses—especially for banana splits and sherry-laced soup.[31] Clare was never one to allow a lack of good looks to get in the way of her raging ambition. Equally, Donald had been infinitely aware of Clare's fine figure and candid manner since her arrival down the hall at *Vogue*. The interview was just a matter of form. Prying her loose from Edna was equally easy: Chase, like Condé, was preoccupied with fears about the business road ahead.

Within six weeks Freeman worked his magic as Pygmalion, and Clare was a junior editor with an annual salary of $1,820, working next door to the boss. Frank was delighted too, claiming a plot she "outlined for a blocked author to be 'worthy of de Maupassant or Turgenev.'"[32] Freeman's book-lined bachelor apartment on East Nineteenth Street in Manhattan, inevitably, was where he and Clare made love.

Shortly after the staff party at Sands Point, Clare's first article lampooning the upper crust of New York—"Talking Up—and Thinking Down," or "How to Be a Success in Society Without Saying a Single Word of Much Importance At Any Time"—appeared in *Vanity Fair*. It took a machete to New Yorkers by claiming that the art of conversation, refined until the "Nineteen Hundreds in the salons of France and England, received its death blow at the dinner tables of the modern capitals."[33] Another *Vanity Fair* star was born. No one but Condé could have kidded himself that Clare would be satisfied with a lowly management position.

25. IN THE DEATH THROES

I lost my shirt in Goldman Sachs.
—CONDÉ NAST TO HELEN BROWN NORDEN

C ondé had sleepwalked into a Faustian bargain courtesy of his friends at Goldman Sachs Trading Corporation and its parent company. Without ever intending to do so, he had allowed control of Condé Nast Publications to slip through his fingers into the icy grip of his banker buddies, led by the tall, slender, smooth-talking Tennessee "gentleman," Waddill Catchings, and the Mephistophelian majority shareholder of the Shenandoah Corporation, Harrison Williams. But that was in 1930. Worse was to come in 1931.

The new year opened cruelly. In February, Condé was diagnosed with prostate cancer and told he must have the gland removed urgently. Days later a mind-numbed Condé was admitted to New York's Presbyterian Hospital for a radical prostatectomy. This was several decades before any function-saving medications, therapies, or devices had been developed. It rang the death knell to his sex life as he had known it. Permanent erectile dysfunction was as much a certainty as sterility. Naturally the life-changing diagnosis made Condé despondent. Not only for himself, but especially for his wife. Leslie stoically tried to reassure him that it changed nothing between them, and that they would somehow manage—the money did not mean anything to her, but his good health did.[1]

Radiation treatment and a deep understanding of cancer in those days was haphazard, despite the best care. Condé periodically underwent radiation therapy in various forms even at the end of his life, and never uttered a word to a soul.[2] As far as Leslie was concerned, he was recovering admirably from the condition and they would readjust their horizons accordingly. But her husband still needed persuading. Condé buried himself in work and often sent Leslie and their baby daughter away to give them respite from the cruel hand they had been dealt.

As the months inched by, Sands Point quietly—almost silently—went on the market, as Condé approached his friends one by one to see if he could interest them in a private deal. Early that summer, around the same time as Catchings was made head of both Blue Ridge and Shenandoah, Condé wrote to Leslie, who was in England with the baby and Natica. Their friend, mentioned only as Charlie, had "turned down S.P. He was very nice but said he did not dare make any commitments in these times. Don't repeat this to anyone but Natica. Looks as if Charlie too had not guessed the market altogether correctly for this was a grand opportunity for him. I hope you saw Harrison Williams. I hope you and Natica are having a good time. I will feel very much better if I know you are. Onto all my love."[3]

Although Condé wanted to stem the tide of relentless bad news, Leslie remained his most trusted confidante and adviser. In July Condé dashed off another note to Leslie with the mixed news that he had rented Sands Point from August 1 to January 15, 1932, for six thousand dollars, lamenting, "No better terms could be had."[4] To Leslie's ear he seemed desperate. Granted he was also suffering from the unremitting heat and humidity of a New York summer without air-conditioning, he said. Then, in the next sentence, he wrote:

Blue Ridge, thru Catchings have driven me into a state of mental pulp over my own affairs. I feel a little better because

I have been started on the road of not caring. Their first offer
was a price of $200,000 for renewing the note. I wrote
Catchings a sharp note which . . . [between] the lines was
rather insulting, declining his suggestion. He has come back
with another proposition which, in effect, is even more hurtful
to my interests. They are damn fools for they are killing me and
my spirit and they will miss my inspiration and management
of their publications.[5]

By "their publications" Condé meant *Vogue*, *Vanity Fair*, and
House & Garden.

In truth Condé was most stung by the fact that he hadn't had
any letters from Leslie in a while. "Your [lack of] correspondence
is rather cruel," he wrote. "I should have thought particularly under
the ordeal of suffering that I am going through that you could, out
of each week's time put aside an hour of that week for a few lines
but apparently an hour a week is a lot of time."[6] These few lines
were uncharacteristically unkind, speaking loudly of the near-
intolerable pressure he felt, rather than any lack of feeling or devotion on Leslie's part.

But Leslie *did* write and tried to help. Evidently she had made no
progress with Williams or Mona, just as Condé had failed with Catchings. By August, once Williams had returned to New York, Condé
orchestrated a chance encounter. Afterward he wrote to Leslie:

When Harrison heard I was at the Piping Rock Club he
scolded me for not letting him know and ordered me over to
his place. I spent Saturday with him—36 holes [of golf]—just
he and I. I dined along with him alone. Sunday morning
lunched alone with him. During all of this time there was no
mention whatever of my affairs. Sunday afternoon he
proposed a tour of the [Long Island] sound in his boat. I then
got up my nerve and decided I would broach the subject. I
told him I was making no progress with Catchings. I
explained how desperate my situation was. I am completely
mystified at his attitude. All thru three hours even days of

close contact—he was charming, affable and as friendly as he
could be—(I forgot to say I spent Sunday night with him too
coming in on the boat with him) but in discussing any affairs
he spoke of Blue Ridge and Catchings as "they."... Just as if
Blue Ridge was not his and he had no pecuniary interest
whatever in the deal.

He even said [it] with enthusiasm[.] Evidently he has his
own way of doing things. When he told me I had the whip
hand his eyes gleamed and his voice worked up to an
enthusiasm that would have been appropriate had he been
telling me that I had the whip hand over a company owned
by a bitter enemy of his! Why my mind does not crack wide
open, why I am not carried off a raving maniac, I just don't
understand. I suppose when it's all over, successfully or
otherwise, I shall collapse.

Then, rowing back, recognizing that his words would alarm
Leslie and Natica, he added, "As it is physically I never felt better
and my mind never clicked better." He also claimed: "Golf has
saved me." But in reality the stress was too much to bear, and he
reverted to his dark feelings once again: "Golf . . . has saved me
from cracking up because away from work in contact with people
my plight bores into my brain and I just escape tears but golf takes
me out of myself and gives my tight nerves and wearied brain their
needed rest."

More than likely on rereading his letter, Condé resolved to write
something positive: "You have not written me a line about Leslie
except that she has lost the sunburn and is called the Duchess of
Sands Point," he continued. "Do you see . . . Lady Duff? Have you
met any of my friends—The Carstairs? Have you been to any parties? Have you seen Winston Churchill again? Am I never to get
to you and England?"

But then desperation engulfed him yet again:

God, what have I done to be so punished. Please destroy this
letter instantly and don't breathe to a single soul even a

suggestion of what I have written about H. If you see Mona
say that I had written that "I spent a delightful week end with
Harrison that he had been most kind and sympathetic," but
not that I was still so pressed and harassed with difficulties
that I could not yet get away but that I was praying that at
any moment the clouds would lift so I could jump on a boat
and come to you.

If you think well of it you might even write her as I have
just dictated, but don't criticize Catchings or go into details.[7]

Their lives were in turmoil. By the time Condé's letter reached his
wife in England, she had met a forty-two-year-old investment
banker called Reginald Benson, whom everyone called Rex. Like
Leslie, he had a natural talent for making friends, from the tea
lady to prime ministers. Rex, with his sky-blue eyes and wide smile,
infused a room with bonhomie the moment he entered. Educated
at Eton College, Rex left the University of Oxford's Balliol College
in 1909, eager to enter the military.

The following year he became a junior officer in the Ninth
Queen's Royal Lancers, and in 1913 served as an aide-de-camp to
Sir Charles Hardinge, viceroy of India. With the outbreak of war,
he rejoined his regiment, and at the Battle of Aisne, Rex said he
"had two horses shot, and had a pipe taken out of my mouth by a
shrapnel bullet."[8] In the First Battle of Ypres and later at Mes-
sines, under constant German fire, he and two others defended a
regimental first-aid post housing wounded soldiers, for which he
won the much-coveted Military Cross for bravery. Rex had been
gassed and wounded in the Second Battle of Ypres, sustaining a
devastating injury to the brachial artery and nerves in his right
arm, and undergoing numerous operations to regain its use. With
his arm still in a sling, he was covertly sent to Paris to head up
the British secret service (MIIC). Always with a nose for a trouble
spot, Rex was in Ireland during the Easter Rising of 1916, before
returning to France to work as liaison officer with Gen. Louis
Franchet d'Espèray, commanding the Groupe des Armées du nord,

and then with Marshal Philippe Pétain at the French headquarters at Compiègne.[9] His work in France won him the Croix de Guerre as well as membership in the Légion d'Honneur.

Rex's military career was an unending story of courage and dedication to duty. In 1922 he resigned his commission and was soon entrusted by Prime Minister David Lloyd George with an important secret mission to reopen trade with the Soviet Union. While Rex didn't speak a word of Russian, he was nonetheless tasked with trading a large cargo of tea, among other basic commodities. His Russian-speaking companion was hurled unceremoniously into prison, leaving Rex, disguised as a Russian, to travel across the country to Moscow. Undaunted, he sold ten thousand pounds' worth of goods, hiding the cash inside his boots.[10]

Dashing, intelligent, modest, and handsome, Rex was the sort of man, on paper at least, who might make any woman swoon. His escapades were also enough to cause any parent to be sick with worry. In 1924 his father said "enough," and Rex became a partner in the family investment banking firm of Robert Benson Ltd., joining his two brothers. With the Crash of 1929,[*] the bank had to deal with its exposure to U.S. securities, leaving the investment management side of the business shaky, and its traders literally playing tiddlywinks at their desks. Rex's main focus when he met Leslie was the revitalization of a dormant investment trust, the English and New York, which had formerly a capital of $750,000 that had shrunk to a value closer to zero.

While Rex threw himself with gusto into saving the investment trusts, the scars he suffered from the war remained. In early 1931 Rex visited the French battlefields, reliving memories of all the young friends he had lost. Even his old Etonian friend, Denys Finch-Hatton, who later gained posthumous worldwide fame as Karen Blixen's lover in her book *Out of Africa*, had died in an airplane crash in Kenya that May.[11]

---

[*] Rex's father, Robert Henry Benson (1850–1929), had died shortly before the October Crash.

Rex could hardly know that Leslie would be a welcome compli-cation. Asked by his friend and colleague Michael Colefax to ac-company an American woman to Paris as a favor, since he was heading to France himself for a bit of R&R, Rex wrote, "[I] found myself escorting Mrs Condé Nast to France. Have quickly, and hopefully temporarily, lost my heart to Leslie Nast who is the most charming American." After crossing the English Channel and spending a few days in Le Touquet together playing golf and whil-ing away moonlit evenings at the casino, he confided: "I am over-whelmed by her charm and sympathy which is rare in Americans for she has all this vitality and companionship as well." But the next entry was incongruous: Rex lent Leslie his driver, Kenny, and his Bentley to go on to Paris, while he returned to London.[12] Had he told her he loved her, and she refused him? And where were Natica and the baby? Had Leslie gone ahead without them? The absence of detail is tantalizing.

That Labor Day weekend Condé wrote again to his wife. The let-ter is simply dated "Friday midnight," and began: "My darling girl: I have just sent you my long telegram telling you of Harrison's si-lence. I thought I had experienced my worst 'zero' hour the night you sailed for Europe but this hour is hardest of all to bear. I had so looked forward to taking you into my arms after these long lone-some weary days and nights but it would seem that this respite and joy is to be denied me." After discussions with both Wurzburg and Frank it had been agreed that "it would be suicidal for me to leave [and] that I must remain here and go to one after another of the dozen or more important men that I know to see if I can get one or better to form a group among them who will help me out. For the next three weeks I shall not even go to the office but de-vote all my time to interviewing these men."

Condé had been waiting two seemingly interminable weeks to hear back from Harrison Williams. He had also been in touch with other powerful friends, including Bernard Baruch, hoping to set up a consortium to bail out his company, all to no avail. "Do not let a single word or expression escape from you to Mona or anyone else of my chagrin and amazement at Harrison's action," Condé continued. He was anxious to hide his despair:

> On the contrary if you see Mona tell her that I have written you that Harrison has been very kind and sympathetic but that my affairs are in such shape that I do not dare leave [for England]. Indeed you might go out of your way to see Mona so as to make this statement to her. <u>Please destroy all my letters to you</u> at least all that make any reference to Harrison. Mona may yet save the day, for H. told me he had helped a number of people because of her solicitation... though... he has not even telephoned to say that he can't do anything.[13]

Leslie agonized over the business, too, and remained deeply devoted to Condé in spite of her growing attraction to Rex. They had seen a lot of each other, apparently without either Natica or the baby in tow. Leslie saw how Rex's eyes sparkled whenever he saw her. His warmth and charm were exhilarating. What's more, Rex played piano beautifully, often singing songs by Cole Porter, who had become his friend in Paris toward the end of the war. He gave her a blissful escape from all her worries.

Leslie knew she should return to New York at once. But as luck would have it, "Little Leslie" came to the rescue with a case of the mumps. At the same time Rex had to undergo surgery, yet again, on his bad knee. During his ten days in the hospital, Leslie visited him regularly, and Rex wrote again in his diary, "I suppose I am hopelessly in love with her for I can see no fault."[14]

On October 2 Leslie told Rex that she was going to sail for New York on the seventh. Immediately he decided to accompany her, ostensibly to renew his contacts with the brokerage houses of Clarke Dodge, Kidder Peabody, and others.[15] Aboard ship Rex and Leslie spent time with H. G. Wells, who was traveling to the United

States for a book tour. Often Wells would take refuge with the pair to avoid the unwanted attentions of other passengers. "He leaves you feeling blue," Rex recorded in his diary, "but you cannot remember what he said that occasioned it."[16]

Condé was at the dock to meet the ship and was introduced to a "quaking" Rex. He needn't have feared. Condé seemed to take to him immediately, suggesting that Rex take Leslie out the following evening because he had the tedious task of attending an all-male dinner. Of course Rex was only too happy to comply. So, Leslie and Rex went to a play and dinner the following evening, and they saw each other again during the course of his three-week stay in New York. As he prepared to leave, Rex knew that she was miserable.[17]

Leslie did the only decent thing and confessed to her husband. Rather than shout and argue about how he felt betrayed, Condé saw their predicament as a perfect solution to their collective problems. As only someone who truly loves another can do, he set her free—with his heartfelt blessings. He had voiced his concerns so many times about how unfair life had become for Leslie, particularly since his prostate operation. His magnanimity seemed a cursed relief to them both.

No one knew in advance that the Nasts had agreed to divorce. It was only when Leslie married Rex Benson in November 1932 in London that a simple statement was made to those whom they felt should know. Leslie would live in England—or wherever Rex would make his home. "Little Leslie" would grow up during the school term in New York and live in her father's apartment at 1040 Park Avenue. In spite of it all, Condé and Leslie would remain devoted to each other for the rest of his life.

Understandably Condé was at his lowest point. More than likely, he hadn't seen the Associated Press story early that November that a Boston stenographer, Margie O'Brien, had brought a lawsuit against Goldman Sachs and its trading investment corporation for five hundred million dollars for negligence, fraud, and violation of the Sherman Anti-Trust Act. Goldman Sachs's shares, according

to the newswire, were once "as popular as orange drinks on Broadway" until October 24, 1929, when they traded at 121¼. O'Brien's
lawsuit was the biggest to date, and named Waddill Catchings,
Harrison Williams, Sidney J. Weinberg, and three members of the
Sachs family as those who had defrauded stockholders.[18]

26. THE STAIN OF DEFECTION

*I hope that the "price" was high enough to compensate
you for your loss of prestige and honor.*
—CONDÉ NAST TO CARMEL SNOW, DECEMBER 1932

C ondé never reproached Leslie for her choices. Their divorce was the most amicable possible. He had even urged her, "Marry him. He will make you happier than I can."[1] Their enduring devotion to each other throughout his life is a testament to both of them. Leslie's choice was not a betrayal, but a blessing.

While Condé and Leslie prepared for their separate futures, there was an incident at the office. Edna was approached by an unnamed smooth-talking "gentleman." In a private conversation he explained to her the company was run too extravagantly, and in the future, expenditure must be "pared to the bone." Indeed, Mr. Nast himself would most likely be asked to leave. "Of course . . . they realized that somebody who knew the ropes must be retained," Edna said. "They had made inquiries and, it seemed, had received a good report about my ability, and my 'sound business brain'. They were prepared to make a worthwhile deal with me." More than likely it was Catchings, who, aside from Sidney Weinberg, was the only banker on the Condé Nast board.

Edna was livid, calling the gentleman and his cronies "nothing but bankers." Winding up for the real punch, she thundered: "Your ignorance about anything that isn't the stock market is absolute and, judging from the messes you get yourselves into, most of you

are pretty ignorant about that. . . . Mr. Nast made a mistake in trying to play your game, yes, but as a publisher he is a great and
successful and knowledgeable man who can run rings around
you. . . . If Mr. Nast goes, I go."[2] Edna, too, felt that Goldman
Sachs was responsible for all their troubles.

What was Catchings trying to achieve? Hadn't his and Williams's stalling tactics already utterly destroyed Condé's business
confidence? Hadn't more and more of Condé's personal investments been pledged to underwrite and protect the original loans
made to buy shares in the sinking ship of Goldman Sachs Trading
Corporation? The fact was that Wall Street was beating its own
jungle drums regarding Catchings. Some said he had been engaged
in shady dealings to swindle stockholders of perfectly sound businesses. As far back as 1928 there had been talk surrounding the
merger of Warner Bros.—pioneers in talking pictures—with First
National Pictures and Vitaphone.[3] Then, too, there was the parlous financial situation of the Equitable Trust, from which Condé
borrowed, another of their target banks. It would take another
three years before the collusion with Catchings was uncovered by
stockholders, and the Warner brothers found themselves on the
wrong end of a lawsuit for giving away more than $6.5 million in
common stock to Catchings and Goldman Sachs.[4] Worse still,
Goldman Sachs was unhappy with the investments Catchings had
made with their money. At last, thick black smoke rose from Wall
Street's chimneys to reject Catchings as their uncrowned pope of
investment trusts. It would take years to undo the harm he had
done to his once-fervent followers—years that Condé felt he no
longer had the power to give.

So when he spoke to Edna, Catchings was actually trying to
save his own skin. Another man was about to hold all the cards.
Catchings and, to a lesser extent, Williams would get their come-
uppance in metered doses over the next five years. With the Goldman Sachs Trading Company's own shares languishing at an
enticingly low figure on the stock market, the savviest entrepreneur of them all saw the opportunity to pounce in January 1932.
Floyd B. Odlum, the president of Atlas Utilities Corporation, made

a dawn raid, ensnaring Catchings and Williams. Their investment trust had shrunk to less than a tenth of its original trading value and had booked losses in excess of $289 million.[5] Yet as far as Goldman Sachs was concerned, it was business as usual. Odlum's stake was significant, but not yet enough to require a public reporting. They tried to ignore Odlum, but his name alone made the undervalued stock shoot up from 1⅞ to 3⅝, or more than double its value, in a day. The reason? Where Goldman Sachs Trading Corporation, including Blue Ridge and Shenandoah, had sunk to less than a tenth of its listing price, Odlum's Atlas Utilities Corporation had—in the same period—quadrupled its value on the stock market.[6]

Fortunately the uncertainty surrounding the business did not seem to affect the employees at *Vogue*. That said, the issues of American and French *Vogue* through early 1934 were anemic shadows of the halcyon days of the Roaring Twenties. The titles had suffered from an enormous fall in advertising. Yet British *Vogue*, under the guiding hand of Harry Yoxall, had flourished. Notwithstanding any downturn in advertising, all *Vogues* and *Vanity Fair* remained world leaders with their innovative cover designs, whether it was Carl Erickson's first impressionist cover (signed "Eric") in November 1930 or the first-ever color photograph cover by Steichen in April 1932.

Cecil Beaton's contributions to *Vogue* and *Vanity Fair*, too, were a draw for many readers. Not only could Beaton sketch whimsical characters as a lighthearted accompaniment to articles, but his photographs rivaled Steichen's, and his writing was original and witty. Above all, Beaton had a knack for making friends with the great and the notable, making *Vogue*'s content exciting.

Not yet committed to homosexuality, Beaton had lost his virginity to the society woman Marjorie Oelrichs,* nicknamed

---

* Oelrichs was the daughter of the Four Hundred's Marjorie and Charles Oelrichs, whom Condé courted for *Vogue* in its early days. Known as Bubbles, she was the

"Bubbles," and described in *Vogue* as having "waxen skin and eye-brows like butterflies." Anita Loos called Bubbles a high-society Mae West. But soon enough Beaton's affections were overwhelmed by Adele Astaire, the dancing elder sister of Fred. He had met both women during his first trip to Palm Beach. And of course Beaton was taken in hand, and off to Hollywood, by none other than Anita Loos and her theatrical producer husband, John Emerson, as a sort of "finishing school about America."[7] In a few short years Beaton had penetrated the ethereal worlds that all America wanted to get to know, Hollywood and New York.

But there was always something of the bad boy in Beaton. An inkling of the disaster yet to come appeared in a diary entry shortly after he met Irving Berlin and his former *Vogue* editor wife, the Catholic heiress Ellin Mackay, aboard the train bound for Los Angeles. Beaton wrote that he was in thrall of the "lovely assortment of film people, Jew producers very flashily dressed, pale mauve collars, purple ties, custard blondes, with cream-coloured faces, scarlet lips and eyes swollen with make-up and curly headed young men all on their way to make good, to become stars."[8]

After weeks in Hollywood, Beaton was invited to San Simeon, William Randolph Hearst's fortress-mansion. Hearst "standing smiling at the top of one of the many flights of garden steps" greeted Beaton personally. Of course word reached a beleaguered Condé, who naturally thought Beaton was being groomed to jump from the sinking ship onto the life raft of *Harper's Bazaar*. Condé lost no time in firing off a genteel but forthright telegram to Hearst at his *Los Angeles Examiner*:

> SORRY TO BOTHER YOU WITH THIS DETAIL BUT TOM WHITE
> I AM TOLD IS ENROUTE BETWEEN CALIFORNIA AND NEW YORK
> SO I HAVE NO RECOURSE BUT TO YOU STOP BAZAAR EDITORS
> ARE MAKING CECIL BEATON AN OFFER VIOLATING OUR TWO

---

society woman who became famous for advertising Lucky Strike cigarettes, and married dance-band leader Eddy Duchin in 1935. She died six days after giving birth to their son, Peter.

OR THREE YEAR OLD AGREEMENT NOT TO MOLEST EACH
OTHERS STAFF STOP HAVE HAD NO WORD BAZAAR'S
WITHDRAWAL FROM OUR AGREEMENT SO HAVE SURMISED
THIS BEING DONE WITHOUT THE KNOWLEDGE OF
HEADQUARTERS STOP WITH BEST REGARDS AND APOLOGIES
FOR BOTHERING YOU STOP CONDE NAST.[9]

Wittingly or not, Beaton used Condé's paranoia about Hearst to extract a minimum guaranteed contract of three thousand dollars per year from *Vogue*.* Not only did Beaton remain with Condé Nast, but he positively prospered. In the first quarter of 1931, his earnings were $4,035—roughly $66,250 today—with the promise of much more. Edna had already commissioned eight London letters, dozens of illustrations, and photographs, including full-color double-page spreads. Beaton was earning nearly $200,000 in today's values, while still only twenty-seven years old. But Edna sounded a warning bell: "Of course, if you are flitting about too much, it may not be possible for you to do as much as we like."[10] The "flitting" was a problem—Beaton traveled with ease among London, Paris, the Riviera, New York, Los Angeles or anywhere else his mood or friends cared to take him.

The last thing Condé needed in those dire times was to lose key people to Hearst. He ran his company with great generosity on the basis of trust. Carmel Snow had become especially precious to Condé—particularly since the loss of her third child and only son shortly after the baby's birth. The birth in 1932 of her fourth child, a daughter, was bittersweet, all the more because of the ambulance accident while traveling with the baby to her Southampton home. In contrast, Edna's relationship with her spirited editor was a seesaw of emotions, though Edna referred to Carmel "as a favoured daughter and began to look upon her off-spring as *Vogue* descendants."

Carmel's perspective was at variance with Edna's. "My judgment on *Vogue* . . . continued to be disputed by Mrs. Chase, just

* Approximately $49,000 today.

as my brilliant managing editor's [Frances McFadden] was also disputed."[11] Carmel cited the time when McFadden wanted to publish a collection of photographs of Queen Mary, taken over decades, wearing the same style hat. The news clipping service *Vogue* used captioned it: "The toque that she made famous." McFadden added the witty "A Lady who is too Great to change her Fashion," which Carmel immediately approved. Edna overruled them. Despite Carmel's having been given overarching responsibility for *Vogue*, it was clear, in her own words, that her "wings as an editor were beginning to sprout, but at *Vogue* I would never be able to use them."[12]

Away from the hothouse relationship with Edna, Carmel had always refused to sign a contract with Condé—claiming she'd never work for Hearst even though her favorite brother did. On March 5, 1927, she wrote Condé a memo asking for two weeks' leave to go to see her mother-in-law in Aiken, South Carolina. Condé replied he was "a great deal surprised" at Carmel's request. "It seems to me," he continued, "that a little reflection would show you that if Mr. Wright, Mr. Freeman, [. . .] the Advertising Managers, and other important members of staff demanded two weeks' vacation every two or three months, and got them, that this business would soon be on the skids. . . . It always hurts me very much whenever I am unable to meet your wishes."[13] But Carmel would not be deterred.

She went to see Condé privately in his office. She gave her reasons for needing more vacation time—from wanting to socialize, to having a young family, to being a wife not always free to make her own choices. Condé wrote her a lengthy letter dated March 11. In the most courteous fashion, he still refused to budge: "I think you appreciate also how anxious I have always been to meet your wishes and make you happy in your work. I have taken all these things into consideration in the effort to bring myself around to your point of view. But my common sense and business judgment tell me that it would be a silly thing to attempt to run this business on a two months' vacation policy."[14] Condé acknowledged that the strain of being a fashion editor did take its toll, but that a two-week vacation in the summer remained the "optimal time" to go on holiday, and it would be ruinous to consider anything else. Within days Condé sent a third letter attempting to strike a compromise: Carmel could take one week's leave. She replied on company letterhead that it would be "not worth my time" to go to Aiken for one week, and therefore to consider the matter closed.[15]

But it wasn't. Carmel had decided to do as she pleased. That November, Condé wrote Carmel again: "I understand from Edna that you do not plan to return until December 24th. . . . I said to you repeatedly that under all the circumstances three weeks in Paris and two weeks on the ocean was all the time that I thought we could spare you." He went on to say that his recent interview with Carmel had been "a very distressing and painful one."[16] Clearly Condé's feelings were on show. Still, he finally gave in to Carmel's "request." No sooner was she back in the office, however, on January 17, 1928, than she reopened the subject of her vacations. Condé invited her to restate her reasons.

So when Condé went to visit Carmel in the hospital after the birth of her daughter in October 1932, he thought he had put any unhappiness she had once felt about her vacations behind her. The company had worked around her pregnancies and the death of her infant son, treating her as a permanent fixture. Condé was heading to Europe. He wanted to wish her and the baby well and kiss them good-bye. For the rest of Condé's life, he would quote Carmel saying that day: "If you were to fire me today I'd be back tomorrow, I love my work so much."[17] Later Carmel claimed she never said any such thing.

Within days, a man called Richard Berlin, head of the Hearst magazine division and a colleague of her brother Tom's, came to call. (Tom was conveniently out of town.) Berlin told Carmel if she took over as fashion editor of *Harper's Bazaar*, top management at the Hearst organization—meaning "the Chief" himself—believed that she could resuscitate its fortunes. "What Mr. Berlin offered me was an opportunity and *challenge*." Theoretically it was a demotion, since the editor in chief, Arthur Samuels, would remain, but her salary would be the same. The attraction of no Edna proved too alluring, and she accepted at once.[18]

"This is treason!" *Vogue* employees cried. Edna moved in to limit the damage and demanded "loyalty pledges" from other employees, neglecting for some unknown reason the talented Frances McFadden. Carmel claimed that the Hearst offer was her "Irish luck."[19] But there was no luck in it. Carmel made a calculated defection at a time when Condé was at his most vulnerable—and aboard ship heading to Europe. When he heard, Condé cabled Harry Yoxall to come to Paris to help him through the crisis. When Yoxall walked into his hotel room, Condé was drunk. Normally abstemious, it was the first time in his life he needed to blot out the world.[20]

When he returned from Europe, he undertook the onerous task of writing to Carmel, setting the record straight from his point of view:

> There does not often arise, in the management of a business, a tie of honor so binding as that which existed between you and me. Its binding character arose not only because your word was pledged, but because the circumstances under which that pledge was given were so unusual as to make the promise, for a person of character, an invisible one.... The first ... [circumstance] was the constant and long-repeated raids conducted over a period of fifteen years, upon the personnel of my organization, by Harper's Bazaar ... and no one was more outspoken as to its unfairness than you.
>
> The second ... was the appointment of your brother as manager of the very property in whose behalf those raids had been conducted ... you came to me and said that I could dismiss from my mind the danger involved in your brother's appointment as Manager of the Bazaar. You said that while blood was thicker than water, no combination of circumstances could persuade you to join the Bazaar staff; that no contract covering this situation was necessary

*because you were willing to give me your word of honor that
you would never desert the* Vogue *staff for the* Bazaar....
*When I was on the water in October this year, you admitted
to Edna and Leslie the existence of that pledge, but cast it
aside and said: "Well, Palen has lost so much money."*[21]

Something in Carmel's story stank of three-day-old fish. If Carmel had taken a demotion, but was earning the same money at *Bazaar*, how could the excuse, "Well, Palen has lost so much money" hold water?

Condé's outrage and frustration were tangible:

*Had you broken your word in financial circles as you did with
me, you would never again have been engaged by a reputable
institution in Wall Street.*

*. . . We had gone through ten years of association together,
during which time there had grown up between us, not merely
a close and confidential business relationship, but an
intimate, personal, almost family relationship as well.
Notwithstanding that, you lacked the courage or candor to
face me openly.... Then showing how completely
characterless your action had become, you assured Edna,
Leslie, and Steichen of your gratitude for everything I had
done for you and cabled me messages of good will, and
assured me of your intention to work for the* Bazaar *without
injury to* Vogue.

*. . . I hope that the "price" was high enough to compensate
you for your loss of prestige and honor. You have lost not only
my confidence and respect but the respect of your
collaborators in the Nast organization.... In answer to the
last paragraph of your cablegram sent to me in Paris, I must
say to you, "No, you cannot count on either my friendship or
my respect."*[22]

The following day, Condé wrote a short letter to Carmel's brother, Tom White, enclosing a copy of his last letter to Carmel.

Condé admitted "This has been one of the unhappiest experiences of my whole business career. I was genuinely fond of Carmel; I thought her a really great person—in every way a rarely fine character—and to suffer so complete a disillusionment and the breaking of what I regarded as a true friendship, has been a devastating experience." He went on to excuse White of any blame whatsoever, since he was away at the time the defection occurred, adding: "Had we both been here, Carmel could not have so completely deceived herself as to the nature of the action that she took."[23]

When Carmel wrote back to defend her actions against Condé's "bitterness," he replied that she was attempting to "befog" the issue and warned: "Your treacherous act will cling to you and your conscience today, tomorrow, and during the years to come."[24]

Condé neither forgave nor forgot Carmel's betrayal. To boot, she had taken Frances McFadden with her. Edna hastened to name the competent Jessica Daves as Carmel's replacement.

27. A VERY BRITISH SALVATION

As a consequence of this economic effrontery, the bankers were entrusted with world power for a decade and made a complete mess of it.

—JAY FRANKLIN, "THE TWILIGHT OF THE ECONOMIC GODS," *VANITY FAIR*, APRIL 1931

Condé had no time to wallow in the loss of either his wife or Carmel. Mercifully, aside from Carmel and Frances McFadden, stalwarts like Edna Chase, Frank Crowninshield, Edward Steichen, Cecil Beaton, and Jessica Daves, among a larger cast of employees, remained. Donald Freeman, managing editor at *Vanity Fair*, and Clare Brokaw, too, stayed loyal. Condé would have been especially concerned if Freeman had gone, since of all his publications, *Vanity Fair* had suffered most as the Depression deepened.

Its advertising had fallen by 20 percent. Neither Cartier jewelry nor $25,000 Mason & Hamlin pianos were to be seen in the publication for years. Guerlain and Chanel perfumes were out too. Tiffany & Co. ceded its inside front cover place to Listerine. With the final repeal of the Eighteenth Amendment voiding the Volstead Act in December 1933,* manufacturers of alcoholic drinks replaced the purveyors of luxury goods.

---

* Only with Utah's ratification of the Twenty-First Amendment on December 5, 1933, repealing the Eighteenth Amendment and voiding the Volstead Act, did control of the sale of alcohol revert to the individual states.

Clare Boothe Brokaw was at the height of her seductive powers. She had her eye on the top position at *Vanity Fair* and had already put her stamp on it, promoting the iconic "beer cover" of the magazine to celebrate the end of Prohibition. Back in May 1931, she had proposed to Condé that he should acquire the title *Life* and convert its defunct editorial formula to one more akin to a weekly version of the Parisian magazine *Vu* or one of the "Great Eight" illustrated publications in London*—in other words, a pictorial newsmagazine.[1] It was a grand, if not original, idea. But Condé was not in a financial or emotional position to dissipate his waning energies on a new publication. So he graciously declined Clare's rather forceful suggestion.

Clare's voracious sexual appetite and "rage for fame" were taking their toll at *Vanity Fair*, too. Freeman, a shadow of his former self, had become devoured by jealousy. The poor man was completely besotted by her, not recognizing that she had been using him as a leg up to his own job. Her ever-more-frequent arguments with him had become public property at the office; Freeman even believed the scurrilous rumor that Condé was divorcing Leslie so he could marry Clare. But Freeman didn't know his girlfriend. Understanding that one day her diaries would be useful for a future biographer to chronicle her rise, Clare made an entry in her June 1932 diary that both Condé and Leslie Nast had recently made passes at her—something that was blatantly untrue given Leslie's entanglement with Rex and Condé's continued love and respect for his wife.[2] Nor did Freeman know that Clare was sleeping with Bernard Baruch *and* the ever-so-handsome Bill Hale (also a *Vanity Fair* employee) while she warmed Freeman's bed. When Leslie telephoned Clare on Sunday, October 2, 1932, to say that Freeman had been in a car crash en route to his Rhinebeck, New

---

* The "Great Eight" were combined in 1928 under one ownership as the properties of Illustrated News Ltd., located at 1 Aldwych in London (now a luxury boutique hotel). The publications were *Illustrated London News, The Sketch, The Sphere, The Tatler, The Graphic, Illustrated Sporting and Dramatic News, The Bystander,* and *Eve.*

York, home, at least Clare rushed to his hospital bedside. The twenty-nine-year-old Freeman died later that day. Still, Clare's grief was short-lived. The next day she went to St. Thomas's Episcopal Church on Fifth Avenue in Manhattan, wept over his coffin, and after a solitary dinner, visited a male friend's new apartment, where they made love until four in the morning. Two days after Freeman's funeral she was in bed again with Bill Hale.[3]

Six days after Freeman's death, Condé formally offered Clare the job as managing editor of *Vanity Fair*. "I am the only one who can do it," she wrote in her diary. "They must give it to me."[4] She also claimed that Condé asked if she would "allow" Frank to be replaced as editor in chief. Though Frank's maxim was the title should "cover the things people talk about at parties," Frank, according to Clare, failed to recognize that "contemporary cocktail conversation had begun to concern itself with economic and social needs rather than fashionable gossip." Whether her antennae were attuned to some potential trap or she simply told "the truth according to Clare," Frank stayed, with her blessing.

And so Clare carried on regardless of the Condé Nast formula. She knew best, even though she'd had a mere three years' experience in publishing. She began cultivating politicos at the State Department, with John Franklin Carter (writing under the name "Jay Franklin") as her main source.[5] The regular feature "We Nominate for the Hall of Fame" was supplemented by Clare's satirical "We Nominate for Oblivion." Her sideswipe at a tabloid publisher, Bernarr Macfadden, for having "the raciest stable of cheap magazines" did no favors to Condé's Connecticut printing press. Macfadden canceled his fifty-thousand-dollar printing contract with Condé Nast Press immediately. It was the last thing Condé needed, and in his fury, he demanded to vet any future candidates for "Oblivion." According to Paul Gallico, the New York *Daily News*'s and *Vanity Fair*'s ace sportswriter—not to mention Clare's cowriter of a rather lousy three-act comedy called *The Sacred Cow*— "Oblivion" was "perhaps the most venomous and courageous feature ever published by a magazine."[6]

The incident could not have come at a worse time. Condé had

already approached Crocker-Burbank & Co. of Fitchburg, Massachusetts, his paper supplier, to buy as much of his debt as possible from Blue Ridge in early 1932. Any losses at Condé Nast Press would more than likely affect Crocker's business, too. Condé feared—rightly—as Floyd Odlum spread his legs under the table of the Goldman Sachs Investment Corporation and got *really* comfortable—that Condé Nast Publications, Inc.'s, notes, bonds, mortgages, and securities would be sold to the highest bidder. That July, Charles T. Crocker turned down Condé's pleas, giving him sound advice about how to retain control of his company through a voting trust to fend off unwanted suitors.[7] What Crocker hadn't understood, and Condé had, was that the empire could never be protected from a cash buyer. As Condé's first deadline of December 15 rapidly approached, his letters to Crocker became more and more pathetic. Again and again, he begged Crocker not only to extend favorable financing terms for the purchase of paper, which Crocker did, but also to take on a million-dollar note as an equity investment in Condé Nast Publications. Crocker refused. Condé's begging letters continued for nearly two years, always probing, forever hopeful and gentlemanly, and never successful.

Logically the cash buyer Condé feared the most was Hearst. Everyone knew that whatever Hearst wanted, he got, no matter the cost. The thought of losing out on art, buildings, newspapers, magazines, or people that Hearst wanted to work for him was pure anguish to the man. Often Hearst would not even see what he bought: It was the thrill of the chase, the act of possessing, that drove him. Price was always secondary to getting his own way. In fact there were two huge Hearst warehouses—five-story buildings at Southern Boulevard and 143rd Street in the Bronx—that served as repositories for his art. Thousands of articles, from the merely curious to the beautiful and rare, were housed there. Most, Hearst had never seen. What Condé did not know was that despite Hearst's obsessive and expensive tastes in acquisitions of all sorts (including his fifty-million-dollar art collection), he was "scratching around for pocket money."[8]

Nonetheless, Floyd B. Odlum was in no hurry. He had oodles of cash at his disposal. As president of Atlas Utilities Corporation, he was also no fool. He'd parlayed an original forty thousand dollars in cash in 1923 into one hundred million in the aftermath of the Crash of 1929. Still, Condé would not have taken heart at Odlum's rising successes. By 1932 Odlum was on the main board of Goldman Sachs & Co., and in January 1934 he said: "Changes . . . have been taking place with almost kaleidoscopic rapidity. It is not the function of an investment trust management as such to try to direct such forces, but it is most emphatically its function to try to foresee the general effect on securities prices . . . and to adjust the portfolio accordingly."[9] Essentially, if a company's trading improved significantly in 1933, Odlum would consider selling for cash, so long as he could make a handsome profit. Such was the case with Condé's publishing business. Since he demanded quarterly statements from all his publications, Condé was in a better position than most owners to determine just how vulnerable the company was in a sale to the highest bidder. The fact was, Condé knew his business was improving.

In Paris, Iva Patcévitch had done a wonderful job at French *Vogue*. He worked hand in glove with Harry Yoxall and their joint advertising manager, Lawrence Schneider, in London. French and British *Vogues* purred along like a well-oiled engine, sharing advertising placement where the client had both French and British interests, and even personnel as required. British *Vogue's* fashion editor, Nada Ruffer, whose fear of flying was only overcome by her love of Pat, became his wife in April 1933. Edna, clearly a dog lover, referred to them as a "brace of elegant greyhounds," slender and stylish.[10]

Alison Settle, Yoxall's managing editor of British *Vogue*, had not only maintained but grown the title's popularity with society and the arts. The acclaimed artist Augustus John had agreed to create a drawing for her—breathtakingly delivered at 11:55 P.M., five minutes before his deadline. Yoxall's management of the double issue with Settle had also doubled sales, and profitability had risen so much by 1932 that the publication raised its advertising rates without a murmur. The *Vogue Pattern Book* sold throughout the British Empire, in Europe, and in Egypt. Condé was thrilled.[11]

With Patcévitch at the helm in France, and keeping a watchful eye on the finances of the European magazines, Condé knew he needn't worry about their profitability. The two men were so like-minded that Pat was asked to hunt for a friendly buyer of the corporation's debt from Odlum as early as 1932. Condé also set Walter Maas of the French Dorland Agency onto the trail of the ownership of the Great Eight illustrated magazines in London. The three men gave a code name to the man they hoped would be inclined to "invest in" rather than rescue Condé Nast Publications. They called this British press magnate NERO. Maas wrote a brief memo to Condé, copying Pat, with the fruit of his investigation. "According to my information, the Great Eight is capitalised with $10 million (£2 million)," Maas declared. "The shares are held by the Inveresk Co. Ltd which in turn is controlled by certain banks. I was given to understand that these Banks had offered NERO the totality of the shares of the Illustrated Newspapers Ltd at a price of 6/8 for each £1 share, which is exactly 1/3 of their face value."[12]

So, who was NERO (aside from the mad Roman emperor known for fiddling while everyone else fled the Roman fire)? His name was William Ewert Berry, elevated to the peerage as Lord Camrose in 1929. Camrose had purchased the Amalgamated Press magazine empire from the executors of the estate of Lord Northcliffe, Condé's journalistic hero, right from under the nose of Northcliffe's younger brother, Lord Rothermere.* Of course Camrose and Rothermere became mortal enemies. Camrose's Amalgamated Press boasted more than seventy magazines, a highly

* Rothermere was Harold Sidney Harmsworth. Northcliffe was his elder brother Alfred Harmsworth.

profitable encyclopedia and book section, and in South London, three large printing works and paper mills. To consolidate what was intended as a wholly integrated publishing operation, Camrose's Allied Newspapers had acquired one of the largest paper mills in the world. When the eldest Berry brother, Lord Buckland, died in a riding accident in 1928, Camrose and his brother, Viscount Kelmsley, inherited Buckland's vast coal and steel holdings.[13]

Although Condé had a nodding acquaintance with everyone of importance in the publishing industry in Great Britain, discussing such a delicate matter as the investment in his company from across the Atlantic was impossible. Condé needed someone independent to plead his case, all without appearing to shake a begging bowl under the nose of this British Nero. The man Condé identified for the job was the investment banker Leo d'Erlanger. He probably first became friendly with d'Erlanger when the Englishman married a former *Vogue* model, Edwina Pru.

Edwina was a Texas beauty whom Condé had chosen as one of the models during Jean Patou's American collection promotion back in 1924. When Edwina later struggled as an actress, Condé kept in touch, sending hampers of food, before finally giving her a job at *Vogue*. Condé had dated Edwina back then and had even given her jewelry. When she heard of Condé's woes, she placed an overseas call to him. "She wanted to give me back a valuable pearl necklace I'd given her years ago," Condé later recalled. "Of course I refused, but wasn't it good of her to try to help me?"[14] Neither Edwina nor d'Erlanger could forget his many kindnesses.

D'Erlanger was a devout Catholic, a disciplined creature of habit, and a popular after-dinner raconteur with a wit to match Frank Crowninshield's. Above all, he was a man of immense courtesy and charm.[15] Beneath all his Etonian sophistication and polish, d'Erlanger had a reputation for honesty and foretelling the future, more than likely enhanced by the role he played in the lucrative financing of airplane manufacture in the 1930s. It took little to persuade d'Erlanger he could successfully broker a deal.

His task was made easier by the increase in profitability at British *Vogue* and its French sister. Both operations showed combined profits of $88,000 in 1934. In fact d'Erlanger knew Yoxall had lent the parent company $100,000 that year.[16] Still, d'Erlanger's chances of success rested on whether Camrose and Kelmsley, and their partner, Lord Iliffe, wanted to have greater American exposure in their portfolio of publications. The magazines they owned—including the Great Eight—were pale reflections of *Vogue* in terms of fashion. *Vanity Fair*, while barely profitable, was the love child of the American intelligentsia. *House & Garden* held a prominent position in the burgeoning American home-design market, and *American Golfer* appealed to Camrose's love of outdoor pursuits, although he was a keen yachtsman rather than a golfer.

From November 1932 and throughout all of 1933, Condé and d'Erlanger negotiated in London with Camrose for a comprehensive solution to Condé's financial problems. Patcévitch and Schneider foresaw multiple complications that would force the American company to book a loss of three hundred thousand dollars because of the convoluted relationship between Walter Maas, the Dorland Agency, and *Vogue*. It was the beginning of ill feeling between Maas, Schneider, and Pat that lasted until the beginning of World War II. Maas, it seemed, was trading on the name of *Vogue* on the one hand with advertisers, and, on the other, neglecting important British and French *Vogue* business to pursue new Dorland business in Italy.[17] Pat feared that a potential three-hundred-thousand-dollar book loss in the accounts of the American parent company would sink any deal with Camrose. To boot, Condé had informed several less discreet friends about his prolonged negotiations—including Johnnie McMullin, who "in turn whispered it secretly to George [Hoyningen] Huene," Pat wrote to Schneider with a clear rolling of the eyes. "When those two know something, all of Paris knows it within twenty-four hours . . . ," Pat continued, without finishing the obvious thought.

He needn't have worried. Not only had d'Erlanger facilitated the purchase of the 171,000 shares in, and the entire debt of, Condé Nast Publications, Inc., at an advantageous price from Odlum, but Condé was also given 40,000 shares. A future right to purchase a second tranche of 40,000 shares was also granted by

Camrose, at a price to be agreed. At last Condé had a mechanism to regain control of his company. A further three hundred thousand dollars in working capital was provided through d'Erlanger's investment bank to cover potential losses caused by the Dorland problem. A promissory note of $4.8 million was also purchased by Vogue Studios, Inc., which was owned in turn by Condé's three children, Coudert, Natica, and Leslie. Throughout the negotiations a more suitable code name than NERO was found, and Camrose became BARROW, and later "our friend." Camrose and his partners saw that the only sensible thing was to leave Condé in charge, without any interference, to mastermind the company's financial recovery. All this largesse was considered a gentleman's agreement, with no press announcements or public statements. For many years Camrose's acquisition of Condé Nast Publications remained the best-kept business secret in both London and New York.[18]

On February 1, 1934, Condé sent a rather expansive telegram (for him) to Grace Moore, care of Metro-Goldwyn-Mayer in Hollywood: DEAR GRACE I WANTED YOU TO BE AMONG THE FIRST TO KNOW THAT I AM OFF THE HOOK STOP NEGOTIATIONS WERE SUCCESSFULLY CONCLUDED YESTERDAY GIVING ME BACK CONTROL OF MY PROPERTIES BEST LOVE CONDE.[19] Since Moore's 1931 marriage to Valentín Parera, a self-effacing Spanish actor happy to be known as "Mr. Moore"—he looked like the silent-film star John Gilbert—Condé had stayed in touch with her as an old friend. His relief from the strain can still be felt, even across a timespan of more than eighty years. He had a silent publishing partner in Camrose who understood the business. Condé was delighted to write to Charles T. Crocker, too, that his worries were over: "I regard the arrangement as highly satisfactory, . . . and [it] will permit me to work out the company affairs with highly successful publishers who know the business, instead of with bankers who are ignorant of it."[20]

Less than a month later Camrose arrived in New York. It was his first visit to the United States in twelve years. He had been invited by Condé to come and see the operations he had just rescued.

Asked by *The New York Times* about the economic outlook in Great Britain, Camrose replied that "conditions were generally improving . , , and unemployment was steadily growing less." He voiced concerns about "what the dollar was going to do, but he was confident that the United States would pull through."[21] Camrose was no gambler and knew a win-win situation when he saw one. If Condé's business recovered, so much the better. When—for neither Camrose nor d'Erlanger had any doubts—the dollar rose against sterling, then he would also have made a treasure chest full of dollars to trade outside any currency restrictions existing in Europe at the time. Camrose returned to England reasonably happy with his investment. In the ensuing years he'd invite Yoxall to lunch to interpret the endless stream of figures and, less diplomatically, to bemoan the extravagance of American publications.[22]

As far as the world was concerned, Condé Nast remained New York's favorite publisher, owner of *Vogue* and *Vanity Fair*, host of the most sensational parties, and arbiter of American glamour. For all those who were critical of his many kindnesses, his generosity to friends and employees, it had gone unnoticed that it was because of who Condé was, and not what he appeared to have, that he had survived and would thrive.

28. BUT WHO'S TO SAVE *VANITY FAIR*?

*Jack the Ripper has always been . . . the most exciting, thrilling,
gruesome, spectacular, mysterious and blood-curdling of
murderers. Your version, however . . . seems to leave me
strangely disappointed.*

—CLARE BOOTHE BROKAW EDITING DREW PEARSON

C lare Brokaw thought she had a "nose for news" and a genius for making authors write.[1] Who would dare criticize
her? A talented chameleon, Clare knew how to play
people—women as well as men—but it was power she thirsted
after. The question was: Would being the managing editor at *Vanity Fair* quench her bloodlust? Condé and Frank had made *Vanity
Fair*, a fact that Clare conveniently forgot. When a popular magazine published an article titled "The Many Faces of Clare Boothe
Luce" after her marriage to the *Time* magazine publisher, Henry R.
Luce, the most frequently heard comment was: "I thought she had
only two."[2]

Vanity Fair was a fabulous stepping-stone for a woman in sti-
letto heels with a burning ambition that left her constantly fam-
ished for more backs to climb over. Anyone who was worth noting
in art, literature, music, politics, sports, the theater, or films, came
through the photographic studios at *Vanity Fair*, and Clare made
sure she met them all, from circus performers to singers, writers,
baseball stars, and even a fifteen-foot python from the Bronx Zoo.
Society women were featured, even if they did not abound as in
the pages of *Vogue*, with Mona Williams leading her very own in-
ner circle of chichi. Some said it was because she had the eyes of a
Bengal tiger (which she did) and had been named the Best Dressed

Woman in The World, but more likely it was due to Condé's suggestion, to try to get Mona to help him before he found salvation with Camrose.

Steichen was still the top banana of photography, but Beaton was closing in fast—whether it was to touch up Helena Rubinstein's jowls to order, write witty ditties, or doodle whimsical cartoons to accompany articles. The fact was that *Vanity Fair* had become the spiritual home for all photographers, known and unknown, even if Steichen remained "the Colonel" in charge of his troops. Among the clever caricaturists and artists from the world over who held on to the magazine's coattails were the Hungarian Marcel Vertès; America's own Bill Steig; France's Christian "Bébé" Bérard; the Italian Paolo Garretto; Eduardo Benito and Guillermo Bolín from Spain; the German refugee Georg Grosz; and the unknown artist discovered by Frank, the ever-so-talented Mexican, Miguel Covarrubias.[3] All contributed to making *Vanity Fair* the most visually exciting publication in the United States in the 1930s.

Freelance writers even took less money just to appear in *Vanity Fair*'s pages. Why? Panache. Flair. Readers who got what they had to say. *Vanity Fair*'s gallery of writers was as impressive as its artists and photographers from day one. Long gone were the trio of Parker, Benchley, and Sherwood, but that didn't stop Frank from occasionally having the men write articles. P. G. Wodehouse chipped in as well, when not writing books or playwriting for Broadway. Its contemporary stable of writers and editors had talent, too, from the Vassar dropout Helen Brown Norden, who began work in charge of book reviews and film, to the drama critic George Jean Nathan, and Clare's part-time lover William Harlan Hale. Continuing past "go" with sports editor Grantland Rice, who directed the *Daily News*'s Paul Gallico, and Red Newsom (later replaced by Lady Astor's nephew, Tommy Phipps), writing "The Well-Dressed Man" column, to the ever-witty Corey Ford (using the pen name John Riddell)—they were all deliciously wicked. Like Circe, Clare held all these men in thrall of her energy, intelligence, delicate charm, and delectable beauty.

Vanity Fair's offices were—kindly put—informal. More accurately, it was pretty much of a zoo. Even the general office workers wanted in on the act. One day a mail room clerk for all the magazines, Ruby Stevens from Brooklyn, took things too far. Edna fired Ruby for turning cartwheels in the corridor between the offices of *Vogue* and *Vanity Fair*. Ruby later appeared in *Vogue* once she'd become famous as Barbara Stanwyck.[4] If Ruby had turned her cartwheels inside *Vanity Fair*'s offices, she would have had a round of applause, and maybe a job, too, instead of the ax. Still, Hollywood would have been the poorer for it.

Articles appearing in the magazine in those days reflected the devil-may-care attitude of its talent. *Vanity Fair* called itself "The Kaleidoscopic Review of Modern Life." After an introduction from "THE EDITOR'S UNEASY CHAIR," works by artists and writers were found ranging from "From the World of Ideas," "In and About the Theatre," "Concerning the Cinema," "The World of Art," "Literary Hors d'Oeuvres," "Satirical Sketches," "Sports and Games," and everyone's favorite catchall, "Miscellaneous." Illustrated "Impossible Interviews," like those between Albert Einstein and America's first superstar astrologer, Evangeline Adams, or Greta Garbo and Calvin Coolidge, peppered its pages. There were pieces as varied as "Marseilles: Chicago of the Latin World," by Paul Morand, and "Not on Your Tin-Type," by Helen Brown Norden, with a caption "Five highly unlikely historical situations by one who is sick of the same old headlines," including "J. P. Morgan becomes a soapbox orator" and the one that nearly caused an international incident, Emperor Hirohito dragging a coolie cart and carrying a scroll, captioned "Japan's Emperor gets the Nobel Peace Prize—for invading Manchuria."[5] There was a slap on the wrist for that one. It was one thing to poke fun at American bankers, quite another to provoke a foreign power that was already seen as belligerent.

The question might well be asked: *How* did Clare Brokaw think she could improve on such a good thing? *Vanity Fair* was always the poor relation in terms of profitability. When Condé suggested looking at making it a weekly, like *The New Yorker,* she complained to her diary that while she favored such a challenge, "So near are we to going on the rocks" that it might sink the very boat they were trying to save.[6]

Having clawed her way to the position of managing editor that she had been after for two years, Clare was already moving on. She craved political power even more, and so politics rose to prominence, even on *Vanity Fair*'s covers. Since Frank was one for immediately turning away from the front pages of newspapers to the crosswords, bridge commentaries, or arts sections, it was an easy feat. It was made simpler, too, because Condé disliked President Roosevelt's New Deal. Lampooning FDR with her pet Washington insiders became a hallmark of Clare's tenure as the title's managing editor. From September 1932 until December 1933, eleven *Vanity Fair* covers were devoted to political cartoons about various aspects of the political failures of Roosevelt's first term in office. February 1934's cover had FDR riding a bucking bronco in the shape of the United States. The March issue showed him as an éminence grise masterminding the movers and shakers of the nation—depicted in neon green. Clare Brokaw was showing and voicing her strong anti-FDR bias through *Vanity Fair,* with Condé's tacit approval. Frank, meanwhile, collected more African masks.

Given that Roosevelt's popularity from his first term had increased to an election landslide in his second term—523 electoral votes to Alf Landon's 8—*Vanity Fair*'s politics was alienating a goodly portion of newsstand readers, and potentially some of its subscribers, too.* Articles that were sympathetic, encouraging, and even flattering to the new European dictatorships in Italy and Germany also appeared. The most overtly fascistic article appeared before Hitler seized power in January 1933. Written by John Franklin Carter in the June 1932 issue to coincide with the Democratic primary, it was called "Wanted: A Dictator!" He advocated a sus-

---

* The popular vote was 27.7 million for Roosevelt (Democrat) and 16.6 million for Landon (Republican). Only Vermont and Maine voted Republican.

pension of the 1932 elections, stating: "We must declare an immediate truce on party politics and create, legally or *illegally*, an emergency organization, if the executive power is to rescue the national finances and the national credit from the nerveless hands of a lobby-ridden Congress. The alternative is chaos."[7]

Vogue, while never commenting on anything political, nonetheless gave, in "*Vogue*'s Eye View of the Mode" in June 1933, a shameful commentary on Mussolini's New Rome: "a Rome resurrected by Mussolini from glorious ruins to glorious life; a city bathed in mysterious floods of light, where the policemen wear white piqué gloves and hats, where the Opera has all the pre-War Vienna glitter of jewels and uniforms . . . and where the noblewomen emanate the splendour and dignity of the palaces they inhabit."[8]

Worse still, there were alternative magazines both subscribers and newsstand readers could and *did* prefer, like Harold Ross's *The New Yorker*, printed at Condé's Greenwich printing press. Designed specifically to appeal to New Yorkers, it was stealing away readers who didn't want to focus on politics. Dorothy Parker was a frequent contributor with her biting satire, like her "Arrangement in Black and White." E. B. White—he of the beloved *Stuart Little* and *Charlotte's Web* wrote for *The New Yorker* for over fifty years—forcefully commented on the disgrace of a black boardinghouse.[*] Although Ross often used offensive and politically incorrect words to describe those from minority groups, Ross's cofounder, Raoul Fleischmann, was Jewish, and Ross had dozens of gay and lesbian friends and staff members, including his Paris correspondent "Genêt," Janet Flanner.[9] Those who wrote for *The New Yorker* were every bit as celebrated for their prose as writers for *Vanity Fair*. Some often wrote to varying audiences in both magazines. Yet Condé didn't see *The New Yorker* as a threat. He thought that because they had coexisted happily for nearly a decade, there was room in the market for both magazines.

---

[*] Elwyn Brooks White was also a world federalist, advocating a worldwide federal system under the principles of national subsidiarity, solidarity, and democracy.

What Condé hadn't bargained for was *Esquire*. The Chicago publisher David Smart and the editor Arnold Gingrich launched *Esquire* as primary competition to *Vanity Fair* in October 1933. It neatly captured most of *Vanity Fair*'s menswear advertisers. Then, too, it published stories by Ernest Hemingway, John Dos Passos, and Dashiell Hammett, with Bobby Jones on golf and Gene Tunney on boxing in its first issue. Overnight there was a bigger boy in town who hit hard at *Vanity Fair*'s core readers. *Esquire's* eight to twelve pages of menswear advertising per issue to *Vanity Fair*'s two was a body blow. Coupled with the defection of most of Frank's top men's fashion artists and its immediate circulation of 150,000, *Esquire* became the proverbial last straw that broke *Vanity Fair*'s back.

So where was Condé Nast during all this? Battered, beaten, down-trodden from years of trying to save his publications and company, he was nursing the emotional wounds from a devastating cancer that hit his manhood and cost him his marriage. Other men might have thrown in the towel—or worse, thrown themselves out a skyscraper window. But the deal with Camrose meant that Condé could appreciate his personal life once more. Soon enough a shining and unexpected new light, in the shapely figure and dark allure of Helen Brown Norden, came into focus. Helen was raised primarily by her grandmother in upstate New York. Highly intelligent, with a biting wit worthy of Dorothy Parker, Helen was "too smart for the room" and naturally dropped out from Vassar. Petite, slender, with a mysterious brown-eyed gaze and Roman profile, she resembled an Italian beauty with her long, dark brown hair parted in the middle and always pulled into a bun at the nape of her neck.

It was Clare Brokaw who "discovered" Helen through mutual friends—twice removed—in November 1931. After meeting with Condé and Frank, she began work on January 4, 1932. It wasn't until arrangements with Leslie had been finalized that Condé asked Helen out on a date that August—to New Jersey's Palisades

Park—where they drank beer, played pinball, and gorged on chocolate ice cream. Helen didn't fit the mold of ingenue or society lady or actress. She was an activist on the political Left, which, like the title of her memoir, made her feel a *Stranger at the Party*. Well, that and the fact that Condé disapproved of communism as much as he did the New Deal, fascism, and modern art. Until Helen, "Condé's girls were usually lovely blondes," she wrote, "and in comparison I felt like something out of *The Last of the Mohicans*."[10]

Helen's social conscience made her stand out from the crowd. Later she wrote that she was surprised that Harrison Williams was a frequent guest at Condé's sumptuous parties. Had Williams counted the bucket loads of gardenias perfuming the air at the legendary penthouse gatherings, wondering if Condé understood that he still owed him four million dollars, she asked? Did Condé ever actually *listen* to the inanities spoken by the women in their high, cold-as-ice voices commenting on the latest play, book, or film with their predictable "Absolutely foul, darling," or "Too blushmaking," or "Too, too divine," and think it passed as commentary? Helen wondered. And what about the poor *Vogue* editor who "found her husband in bed with the butler ('The butler! Oh, well, buggers can't be choosers.')"* Then, of course, they couldn't miss out on Mimsy Taylor, that socialite model with the most exotic Balinese face who had run off to Quito with the playwright and novelist Ben Hecht.† "Quito? But why Quito, of all places? My dear, her family must be wild. Why couldn't he have taken her to the Riviera?" Well, of course, it could all be explained by the mere fact that her aunt, Countess Dorothy di Frasso, had seduced Gary Cooper into going on safari with her to Africa . . . and so on, and on.[11]

Helen's assessment of Condé was heartwarming. She described

---

* Always erroneously attributed to Winston Churchill, this was first uttered by the British academic, literary critic, and Oxford don, Sir Cecil Maurice Bowra, warden of Wadham College, Oxford (1938–70). He used the quip to explain his engagement to "a plain girl." The character of Mr. Samgrass in *Brideshead Revisited* by Evelyn Waugh is thought to be modeled on him.

† Hecht later wrote the play *To Quito and Back*.

him as "a kind, gentle, tolerant man" devoid of any hubris, dishonest tricks, or vanity. He was not a snob and never lied or lost his temper—even though they disagreed politically and often editorially—with Condé preferring to employ the shopworn phrase, "Can't we have a meeting of minds?" to declare the peace.[12] She was proud that she had become Condé's mistress between the end of 1932 and 1936. Unusually, Helen has no place among the many memories of Condé's younger daughter. Granted, Leslie was quite young when their affair ended, but she was a perceptive child who often wondered at the same age why her parents had divorced. It was obvious they were still devoted to each other, she remembers vividly.[13]

It raises the very real question if Helen's description of her love life with Condé was all that she claimed. Most perplexing is Helen's graphic portrayal of their lovemaking.[14] Astonishingly, she gives away the fact that the only way Condé could continue an active sex life was to engage in oral sex. No doubt he had trusted her to keep his secret, but he was mistaken in his confidante. Where he was intensely private and discreet, Helen hung her sex life out on a laundry line for all to see, including her contracting syphilis at the age of nineteen and her treatment with Neosalvarsan and mercury.* He would have more than blushed at her "show-and-tell." Notwithstanding her highly visual depiction of herself as Condé's mistress, Helen does make one crucial statement: Condé was no "desk chaser." He was a man who never had nor never would trade on his fame, position, or power, and she boldly states, "He was no casting-couch seducer."[15] Although Helen portrayed herself as the last great love of Condé's life, he was not besotted by her as he had been by Leslie. Evidently, he did not introduce her to "Little Leslie" as a significant other, either. Helen was a pleasant diversion from the continuing problems at *Vanity Fair*: He was still having trouble fathoming why readership was falling off.

---

* Neosalvarsan (neoarsphenamine) was the primary treatment for syphilis before the development of antibiotics. It was available from 1912 but was a highly unstable compound. Sterility in women was one possible outcome from its use.

Although Condé had always considered *Vanity Fair* a men's magazine, there was a distinct hint of perfume wafting through its pages.
Its readership was predominantly male, but there were a great
many women who enjoyed its articles and especially its visual feasts
in illustrations, photographs, and original design layouts. Its "literary hors d'oeuvres" were delicious satirical sketches that tickled
the imagination. Most significantly, it reflected Frank Crowninshield's genius and tastes. But it was Condé's determination to create excellence and pioneer color printing that set the bar higher at
Vanity Fair than any other publications in its genre. It had always
been beloved by its readers. So why was it losing more and more
money?

First off, the magazine had bruising competition—not only for
readers but for advertisers—from *The New Yorker* and *Esquire*.
Then, too, there was a cuckoo in the nest in the form of Clare Brokaw. Bernard Baruch was still her lover, while she embarked on a
heartless affair with Paul Gallico—who wrote in a moment of pure
frustration that he would love to "shred" her. Clare was developing ideas for more plays and dabbling with her political ambitions.
When the fourth issue of *Vanity Fair* under her aegis was published
in March, anticipating the end of Prohibition, the title's advertising had also dropped to its lowest level since 1919—and *Esquire*
was only in the planning stages.[16] Condé saw that Clare had her
eye firmly off the ball. So he tried to reason with her.

Clare's management style and her irregular hours—always a
bugbear for Condé—did not go unnoticed: "I do not think you can
do your job effectively with such a combined absence and lateness
record as the sheets show for you during the past three months. . . .
I'm not asking you to observe the established nine o'clock arrival
hour, but an hour between quarter to ten and ten." While reasonably agreeing that she might conceive ideas more readily at home
than at an office with its constant interruptions, Condé saved his
most devastating criticism for the end: "For the past three or four
months, you have contributed no articles . . . with all your talent,

I don't think you can be an editor, write books, and become a play-wright all at one time. One or other of these will fail." There was also the fact that "on specific material and broad editorial policies" her judgment was not "entirely seasoned or dependable."[17]

When Condé criticized Carmel on the subject of her vacations, she quit. It took Clare another six months to advise Condé that she would be seeking "an independent career," resigning only once she realized that *Esquire* presented a clear danger to the survival of *Vanity Fair*. Her resignation took effect on February 15, 1934.* Condé and Frank agreed that, for the time being, Helen seemed the right person to replace Clare, despite her having even less ex-perience than their departing managing editor. Throughout all of 1934 and most of 1935, the financial situation did not improve.

With Camrose firmly in charge of the purse strings, Condé could no longer purr along with *Vanity Fair* as he had done previ-ously. He recognized that readership trailing off was less of a prob-lem than the loss of advertising. While he tried to resist the inevitable, ever since the Crash of 1929, advertising revenue from couturiers, department stores, interior designers, furniture man-ufacturers, and the building trade had taken a nosedive at both *Vogue* and *House & Garden* as well as his French publications. Many luxury-goods advertisers had gone to the wall in the inter-vening years of the Depression. The repeal of Prohibition had re-placed some of the lost advertising revenue, but it was a relative drop in the sea. Even *Vogue Patterns* was drowning in red ink in the United States, since the competition was able to produce cheaper designs. The only bright spot in the Nast empire was the *Hollywood Pattern Book*.[18]

Condé himself fell into the Hollywood trap in 1935, when he

---

* Clare was already dating Henry R. Luce by the time she quit to write her first stage play, *Abide with Me*. Her second play, *The Women*, became a smash hit in 1936, the same year she married Luce. Of course Condé threw the opening-night party. Hav-ing married "success," Clare was able to garner an international career in journalism and became a Republican congresswoman from Connecticut from 1943 to 1947. Later Clare would become the first woman ambassador. Her postings were Italy and later Brazil.

provided an uncredited consultancy to the movie *Wife vs. Secretary*, about a fashionable magazine publisher (Clark Gable) whose wife (Myrna Loy) believes he's having an affair with his secretary (Jean Harlow) while the magazines are under threat from a Hearst-like rival. Condé can be seen on film, walking into his apartment at 1040 Park Avenue.[19] Hollywood chic had replaced high society and haute couture in the minds of America, so what could he do to save *Vanity Fair*?

As Condé thought through the myriad changes to the economic, social, and cultural landscape to their logical conclusion, the sad reality struck: Crowninshield's dedication to affluence, humor, the upper crust, and leisure no longer resonated with advertisers and the nation. Nor could Condé change the format of *Vanity Fair*, since both he and Frank believed the magazine was a sacred institution. With newer magazines that spoke to the increasingly somber mood in the United States and Europe in the mid-1930s, Condé had to face the simple fact that the *Vanity Fair* formula no longer worked.

Sustaining six-figure losses and merely shrugging was a thing of the past, with Camrose as his silent partner. Something had to give. And so, in December 1935, in the saddest decision of his entire career, Condé told Frank that *Vanity Fair* would have to cease publication. Its final issue would be published in March 1936. Although Condé hoped to resurrect it at some future date, and decided to incorporate the title into *Vogue*, a bright light had gone out in both men's lives, from which neither would fully recover. Only 4 percent of *Vanity Fair*'s subscribers remained loyal to the new-look title. Men's clubs canceled their subscriptions to what had become a women's magazine. The staff was gutted, naturally. Helen continued seeing Condé after she left the combined magazine in December 1936. Condé gave her an evening bag that Christmas with a note: "With a hell of a lot of love for darling Helen." He even asked her to marry him—more than once, she wrote. But the political activist in her would not allow a marriage to a man who held opposing views. Besides, she didn't love him.[20]

The greatest tragedy was reserved for Condé's boon companion,

Frank Crowninshield. Although he remained a valued consultant to *Vogue*, overseeing articles on sports and the arts, he was heartbroken. In the immediate aftermath of the death of *Vanity Fair*, Frank went to Boca Grande, Florida, for an extended "vacation." He wrote Helen a wistful note: "I came here for a six weeks rest after 45 years of the publishing business. We had fun, didn't we, despite the worries and fears? Oh, why don't you write? You have a definite flair for it. Some day you will show the world what a witty, imaginative, shrewd writer you are. I shall always treasure your friendship. We must help each other, dear."[21]

She took his advice and before the year was out wrote the outrageous "Latins Make Lousy Lovers" for *Esquire*. Eventually Helen also married the only man she said she ever loved, Jack Lawrenson, a union organizer for the National Maritime Union. Helen, now Lawrenson, remained friendly with Frank and Condé for the rest of their lives.

29. "OF CABBAGES . . ."

"The time has come," the Walrus said,
"to talk of many things . . ."
—LEWIS CARROLL, *THROUGH THE LOOKING-GLASS*

When *Vanity Fair* finally folded in March 1936, Europe was halfway through its "Pink Decade" of the 1930s, when communism seemed the antidote to the poisonous fascism of Mussolini, Hitler, and the latest addition to the roll call of dictators, Francisco Franco.* The United States remained inward looking. With worry abounding for the economy, Americans saw the rise of smash-and-grab gangsters like Baby Face Nelson, John Dillinger, and Bonnie and Clyde, and the legit nightclub investments of mobsters and bootleggers in posh clubs like El Morocco and the Stork Club. Then, too, there was the first Dust Bowl of the "Dirty Thirties" and the proliferation of hoboes hopping the rails to nowhere. To escape the grim realities, the country became ever-increasingly mesmerized by the stardust of Hollywood. Henry Luce's *Time* magazine captured all that *Vanity Fair* had missed in world events. Meanwhile, Frank, in his new unexciting role as consultant to *Vogue*, mostly busied himself with divesting himself of his valuable art collection to the Museum of Modern Art and other collectors. Condé had no alternative than

---

* Franco narrowly lost the 1936 elections in Spain and tried to mount a coup d'état against the Popular Front. It failed, unleashing the bloody Spanish Civil War (1936–39).

to concentrate on rebuilding the fortunes of his remaining magazines, particularly in France. With Iva Patcévitch, he restructured
the management at his French publications, moving Michel de
Brunhoff to French *Vogue* and Lucien Vogel to *Jardin des Modes*.
France, like Spain, had turned communist in 1936, but somehow
business had to continue as usual.

In Britain its "humanistic" intelligentsia turned to earnest, even
breathy "pink prophesies" propagated in magazines like *The Week*[*]
or *Plan*, favored by Bertrand Russell, Rebecca West, and Bloomsbury's Leonard Woolf. *Vanity Fair* shut down just when Mussolini
bombed grass huts and gassed young spear-carrying warriors in
the medieval African kingdom of Abyssinia (now Ethiopia); the
Nuremberg Laws deprived Jews of civil rights in Germany; Hitler
retook the Rhineland without a whimper; and Franco was armed
by his fascist allies to fight the Spanish Civil War, eventually winning power. *Vanity Fair* was meant to pick up on matters discussed
at dinner parties and entertain its readership. But the sad fact was
that the times they lived in meant that "thinking" peoples' conver-
sations weren't remotely funny or entertaining. Both Condé, so
mired in his own problems, and Frank had missed a crucial trick.
But how could they be expected to see beyond their noses, given
that simultaneously Europe was again on the agonizing march
toward war?

According to British *Vogue*'s Harry Yoxall, no one could accuse
columnists writing for *Vogue* of being part of the intelligentsia or
indeed, focused on anything but fashion. While a harsh assessment, in the world of 1936 his remark was correct. *Vogue*'s photographers warred over copying one another's work, or always
attempting to better images that had gone before. They missed the
malady encroaching on civilized society, now that *Vanity Fair*'s
voice had been silenced altogether. *Vogue* couldn't *see* the Union
Jack planted firmly on everything from Cheddar cheeses to the lions in Trafalgar Square and signs in dress shop windows. Nor did

---

[*] Back in the thirties it was not a serious magazine. Today it has become a significant barometer of national and world news.

it notice that Europe bristled with emotion at the prospect of another war. Instead, Edna asked Yoxall if British *Vogue* was accurately reflecting the spirit of austerity felt throughout the world. Yoxall replied that their American society columnist, Johnnie McMullin, was hardest-hit when it came to self-denial, since he "had to let his valet go and makes up the bed in the wagon-lit himself as he travels from resort to resort.[1]

At French *Vogue* the perspective remained strictly attuned to problems of fashion. Who could control Chanel in her vituperative outbursts against Elsa Schiaparelli—and what about "le shocking" pink of the fashion world? Could Solange d'Ayen control their latest enfant terrible artist, Bébé Bérard, who required a constant supply of booze and opium? While Condé, Edna, and even Dr. Agha thought Bérard something of an aberration, Solange persuaded them that Bérard had a huge following on the Paris fashion scene. "I use every weapon I can think of," Solange told Edna. "Frankness, confidence, charm, jealousy, pride, even tears." Bérard was often ill, "and he gets into black moods and has a nervous breakdown whenever the external situation goes worse." Bettina Ballard, French *Vogue*'s fashion editor, would often have to hold dresses against herself to calm Bérard's nerves as he drew them. Hats were worn by French *Vogue* staffers, or at times by Bérard's dog. As he literally sweated onto the paper while he drew, he would deftly turn his tears of toil into amusing decorations—windows or butterflies or other flights of fancy—making his pictures even more admired.[2]

Cecil Beaton cherished the addition of Bérard to *Vogue*'s ranks. Together they would hang out with Cocteau and Boris Kochno, the former secretary of the impresario Serge Diaghilev.* When Huene stormed out of *Vogue* straight into Carmel's arms at *Harper's Bazaar*, thanks to Dr. Agha's blunt criticism, Bérard replaced him. Beaton was delighted with the increasingly difficult Agha for removing Huene, his greatest rival. "That gave me such stimulus

* Diaghilev had died in Venice in 1929.

to work well and not consider the magazine a rubbish heap," Beaton wrote in his diary.[3] Even when French *Vogue* hadn't liked any of his drawings executed one day, and Beaton upset a ladder in Mainbocher's studio the next, splashing India inks and paints over the couturier's new carpet, Beaton's spirits remained unusually buoyant.

Always easily influenced, Beaton's head was also turned by Cocteau's kind remark that he had "an elegance unforeseen." "Cocteau says . . . I have succeeded in spending my life in an unreality made up of fun," Beaton wrote in his diary, ". . . so much too much fun and my interests are limited to the joys of certain superficial forms of beauty, to sensual delights only to a certain blunt degree and with too many people, too many light quick sketches, quickfire articles and photographs galore."[4] Beaton was fascinated by Cocteau's charm and the unimaginable fact that he was so outré yet entirely accepted by the most conservative elements in French society. It was something Beaton himself aspired to be.

Despite the pull of Paris, the peripatetic Beaton longed for new adventures and soon sailed to New York—although not staying very long—before joining Mona Williams at her Palm Beach home. Beaton had become quite the darling of her chichi set, often meeting them on the French Riviera, or wherever Mona's desire took her. Homosexuality was still illegal in Britain*—and Beaton, who was desperate to become heterosexual, created quite an unhappy incident with Maureen Dufferin, an heiress to the Guinness fortune, who had married Basil Hamilton-Temple-Blackwood, fourth Marquess of Dufferin and Ava, in 1930.

While staying at the Harrison Williamses' in Palm Beach, Maureen was invited to a dinner party where she was seated next to Cecil Beaton. She was greatly relieved, since he was the only person she knew there. Beaton offered to see her home, since he longed to see her sitting room (described as "a mixture between a Turkish harem and a brothel"), some four minutes' walk from the dinner party. She gladly accepted. As they entered her suite of

---

* Homosexuality was only decriminalized by the Sexual Offences Act of 1967.

rooms, Beaton made a beeline for the bedroom, throwing Maureen onto her bed and beginning to make love to her. It was, to say the least, shocking, since she had always thought of Beaton as gay. What Maureen hadn't known was that he had resolved to give heterosexuality another go. Of course, she realized that no one, especially her husband, would ever believe that Beaton—of all people—had made such a ham-fisted lunge at her. She burst into uncontrollable fits of laughter, obviously wounding his fragile ego. He dashed out, deeply embarrassed. The following evening, at another dinner party, Beaton was seated yet again next to Maureen. In a shrill voice, Beaton announced to the assembled guests that he was sitting next to "the biggest bitch in London."[5]

At the time Beaton also felt undervalued by *Vogue*. The feeling was mutual. That summer Edna bluntly told Beaton that he should not return to New York in the autumn because another, fresher photographer had been employed. Horst Paul Albert Bohrmann, who styled himself simply Horst, was more than a fresher photographer: He was Beaton's rival for top dog now that Steichen had retired.* Edna and Condé felt Beaton's drawings and photography were too heavily influenced by Bérard and Cocteau. Condé expressed his real disappointment, grading Beaton's work with a B. Still, Beaton shouldn't have felt crestfallen; Condé gave an A only five times in the years 1934–35. Dr. Agha also chipped in, adding that Beaton's work should not appear in *Vanity Fair* since it "should publish only the work of people who are excellent art-photographers."

Both Condé and Edna agreed that Beaton's photographs had lost their edge. The surrealism of the twenties no longer represented the modern world of the thirties. Condé believed that *Vogue*'s covers for the decade needed to be sleeker, more contemporary. Beaton hadn't clicked that Steichen's 1932 *Vogue* color cover of a woman in a bathing suit holding a red beach ball had signaled a change in Condé's thinking. The power base of haute couture was under threat by increasingly well-made ready-to-wear.

---

* Horst's 1939 French *Vogue* photograph, "the Mainbocher corset," showed the couturier's wasp-waisted look, anticipating Dior's "New Look" of 1947.

Contemporary practical fashions were for active, industrious women, making the "intangible quality of chic" something that needed to be captured with modern color photographs. In 1930 Condé spent $101,000 on art and around $40,000 on photography. Two years later only $73,000 was spent on art, with photography climbing to $60,000. A thorough analysis of photographic versus art covers was made by Condé, and by the end of 1936 photo covers were declared the winner by a huge margin. By the end of the decade the amounts spent on photography would far outstrip those spent on art.[6]

Beaton went off in a huff to Russia.

Beaton hadn't known that Mona's fabulously wealthy husband, Harrison, and his investment trust partner, Waddill Catchings, were coming under ever-closer scrutiny by the relatively new Securities and Exchange Commission (SEC), set up in 1934 with Joseph P. Kennedy, Sr., as its chairman. A second case was filed against Catchings (and thirty-one other directors of the Foreman-State National Bank) in August 1936 for the illegal cancellation of a promissory note for $880,000.[7] By the time the SEC was finished with him, Catchings was charged with fraud in his dealings with twenty-four companies including ten banks, four insurance companies, two department stores (one of which was Bonwit Teller), and one public utility, Williams Holdings. His only punishment was a five-figure fine he had no trouble paying. In all, Catchings had controlled more than $1.695 billion in assets, including controlling shares in Chrysler Corporation, Warner Bros., and Manufacturers' Trust Bank.[8] He would be remembered as the man who nearly broke Goldman Sachs. Williams was heavily fined, but sailed on unscathed, with his trophy wife, Mona, until his death in 1953.

30. "... AND KINGS"

Cocteau says I'm Malice in Wonderland.
—CECIL BEATON'S DIARY, 1935

No one at *Vogue*—least of all its society editor, Johnnie McMullin—believed that within eight months of King George V and Queen Mary's Silver Jubilee in May 1935, the king would suddenly die. Still less believable were the king's final moments. He was given a lethal dose of two injections of morphine and cocaine to hasten his death, so *The Times* would be able to report it reliably. It seems, too, that his last words were, "God damn you!"[1] Whom could George V be cursing? More than likely it was his son and heir, Edward Albert Christian George Andrew Patrick David Windsor, "David" to his friends, and on his father's death, King Edward VIII. Why would the king be damning his own son and heir? In three words, Wallis Warfield Simpson.

On that chilly January 20 evening, McMullin was at a charity function for the League of Mercy,* sitting next to Wallis and Ernest Simpson. Afterward they went together to their friend Betty Lawson Johnson's home, where Wallis received a telephone call from the prince, who was at Sandringham with his dying father.

---

* The League of Mercy was a charity founded in 1899 by Royal Charter during Queen Victoria's reign to recruit large numbers of volunteers to help the sick and ailing at hospitals in the days prior to the National Health Service. It was reestablished in 1999 to honor hospital volunteers.

He reported that the king was sinking rapidly. "It was very impressive," McMullin wrote breathlessly to Edna, "we were sitting in
Betty's little room" when "the telephone rang and the <u>King</u>"—are
you keeping up?—". . . announced the news to us about twelve-
thirty." The time of George V's death was 11:05 P.M., conveniently
for *The Times*'s deadline.[2]

Edna immediately saw the journalistic benefits of such an inside track. But McMullin claimed that His Majesty seemed unaware precisely what was going on. "Dearie, dearie, the price one
pays for his friendship is high!" McMullin wrote. Little wonder.
In New York, and indeed throughout the United States, the prospect that Mrs. Simpson—Wallis from Baltimore—would become
queen of England had Americans clamoring for every detail. Edna
came up with the idea of devoting an entire coronation issue to
Edwardian England—its fashions, customs, and social life under
each and every King Edward since 1239, and ending with the affable Edward VII, grandfather of Edward VIII. Of course Edward
VIII, *Vogue*'s very own "king of chic," would feature as its finale,
but with so little of his reign behind him, *Vogue* would need to
speculate on his bright future.[3]

Another thread to Edna's plan led straight back to Beaton, who
had first met Wallis in the early thirties "in a box of American
bums at the Three Arts Club Ball," when he commented that Wallis was "a brawny great cow or bullock in Sapphic blue velvet."
And that was the nicest thing he had to say: "To hear her speak
was enough," Beaton wrote in his diary. "Her voice was raucous
and appalling. I thought her awful, common, vulgar, strident, a
second-rate American with no charm. Now she is all that is elegant. The whole of London flocks after her as the mistress and
possible wife of the King."[4]

The king's younger brother, "Bertie,"* the duke of York, and his
duchess, Elizabeth, who were next in line for the throne, privately
called Wallis "that woman." The court gossip that this American
from Baltimore might make Bertie and Elizabeth king and queen

---

* Albert Frederick Arthur George Windsor.

terrified them. Being monarchs would disrupt their idyllic private life and require even more work with a speech therapist to correct Bertie's stammer (a story so beautifully portrayed in the 2010 film *The King's Speech*). Privately, too, they might have repeated George V's last words.

Beaton had photographed Wallis Simpson during the Silver Jubilee celebrations of May 1935. By then his poor opinion of her had completely changed. "I found her bright and witty. She had become enormously improved in looks and chic." But Beaton rejoiced in being outrageous and wrote in British *Vogue*'s 21 August 1935 issue that: "Princess Marina's picture hats have put Mr Winston Churchill's in the shade and are seriously weighed in comparison with the Duchess of York's smile, and only a certain American hostess, whose head has been turned by rankers [those who value people by their rank in society], has not been impressed by the pomp and beauty of the court balls."[5]

In November 1936 Beaton was asked to photograph Wallis again. He asked her to pose "as though bowing"—known today as "the Diana Look"—and Wallis stared sharply at him. He sensed, rather than knew, that there was something haunting and sad about her. He even referred to her as "slightly shopsoiled and middle-aged and her breath smelt a bit." A few days later, when he went to sketch her, Beaton found talking to her easy: "I really found my hostess quite alluring. Her skin today was incredibly bright and smooth like the inside of a shell, her hair as sleek as only the Chinese women know how to make it. The dress was incredibly simple and the aura of gossip and the expensive flowers did the rest. She amused me a lot with staccato sentences and explosive bursts of laughter. I like her surprised eyebrows when she laughs and her face has great gaiety."[6]

It was only natural that such a curious creature as Beaton would ask if she planned to marry the king. She had forbidden him from repeating the question, but still replied that any rumors of marriage were "absolute rot." Undeterred, Beaton asked if she might fix it so that he could photograph the king. At that very moment Edward VIII walked in. "The King talked very quickly and darted around the room and rang bells, his hands very red and slightly horny, busily unravelling parcels. . . . Wallis's eyes sparkled. Her mouth turned down at the corners as she laughed and her eyebrows mocked pained surprise. . . . The King like a child during his play hour before dinner was told that we all must go." With a bundle of drawings under his arm, and the hope that the couple would somehow improve his prospects, Beaton took his leave with "so many secrets with which to regale the family."[7]

Edna was delighted with Beaton's two colorful sketches of Mrs. Simpson. She also bought a brief pen-portrait describing Wallis's drawing-room. "Her gaiety is contagious. Around her there are incessant squibs of laughter," Beaton declared.[8] At the same time McMullin wrote to Edna. "True, the Simpson situation is drawing-room gossip over here. *But* it has never been mentioned in the newspapers—in fact, her name is never mentioned at all. . . . If she becomes" a national figure "here, the feeling is very strong now, it may be the end of the monarchy." Indeed, "Gossip here is accompanied by shaking of heads and predictions of disaster," McMullin continued, "not the flutter of excitement that accompanies it in America—for here they feel they are sitting on a powder mine and the matter is no joke." McMullin then told Edna that "we have now decided not to mention her name even in a casual, social way in British *Vogue*."[9]

Neither Condé nor Edna fully understood what all the brouhaha was about. They had missed the fact that, at that time, no divorcée could be presented at court. The king was also the head of the Church of England, and as such, it was believed that he could not marry a woman who was twice divorced, particularly since she had been carrying on an adulterous affair with the king. Such a union went against the grain of public morality. The "abdication crisis" loomed large by the end of November 1936, shrouding the nation in an uncertain mourning. It would be impolitic for American *Vogue* to carry on with its plans regardless.

McMullin's hope for diplomacy was quickly dashed by Edna. No one—especially a subsidiary called British *Vogue*—would dictate terms to the publisher and his editor in chief as to what they could or could not publish. Before Yoxall responded, on December 11 the king famously broadcast to the world that, "I have found it impossible . . . to discharge my duties as King, as I would wish to do without the help and support of the woman I love." Whether Wallis liked it or not, whether she loved the king or not, she would have to marry him. "Make no mistake," McMullin warned, "we [Americans] are damned unpopular for the moment. . . . The present situation is entirely due to, and as a result of, American newspaper publicity."[10]

Edna was not amused. In fact she remained hell-bent on doing something for her ruined coronation issue. So she asked humorist and satirist Corey Ford to write a parody on the situation in the style of three or four well-known authors. McMullin was aghast: "If you come out with a skit on their future private lives, showing snappy illustrations depicting them playing double bagpipes, resetting Crown jewels or playing charades in royal robes, I shouldn't think I'd ever get very near them again."

Yoxall was apoplectic, beseeching Edna to abandon her ill-conceived brainchild. Even Michel de Brunhoff entered the fray: "The parody, with cartoon illustrations, seems to me from the brief description I have heard to be dynamite material—I mean from the international standpoint." Despite canceling the issue, Edna believed that it was all "a tempest in a teapot."[11]

What McMullin failed to report to Edna was that Wallis Simpson had been granted a decree nisi on October 27, 1936, in a nineteen-minute hearing at Ipswich Assizes in Suffolk, well away from the public glare of London. This meant that her divorce from Ernest Simpson would become "absolute," or final, six months from that date.[12] To McMullin's chagrin Wallis had hightailed it out of England for a safe berth with her old friend Katherine Rogers in Cannes. They had known each other since 1916 when they met in California, and Mrs. Rogers was the recently divorced Katherine Bigelow. Ten years later, they met again by chance in China, when Wallis was separated from her first husband, Earl Winfield Spencer. Katherine married Herman Rogers in the intervening period, and Wallis stayed with the couple in Peking (now Beijing). It was the following year, while staying at the Rogers villa, Lou Viei, in Cannes that Wallis determined to marry Ernest Simpson.[13]

No one at *Vogue* was aware that Wallis had fled England in Edward VIII's Rolls-Royce for the south of France in the company of a policeman known only as Inspector Evans of Scotland Yard. Nor were they aware that Inspector Evans had arranged with the French Sûreté to protect the household. Even fewer people knew that Herman and Katherine Rogers received more than five hundred letters in the first month alone addressed to "King Edward's Whore," or that the entire ménage had received death threats. Like any houseguest overstaying her welcome, Wallis had sunk to the status of an untouchable. But the situation was resolved when Katherine wrote to her friend of some fifteen years, Fern Bedaux. Fern and her husband, Charles, owned a large château in the Loire Valley near Tours called Candé, and Katherine suggested that it, with its secure, private park, "would be an ideal solution to an intolerable situation." Charles Bedaux said it was fine with him. And so Wallis went to Candé to await the arrival of Edward, no longer king but Duke of Windsor. While the move resolved the immediate security headache, it had an undesirable side effect. Charles Bedaux, who had dual French and American citizenship, had been cozying up to the Nazis to build a trans-Sahara pipeline. It was not the first—or the last—taint of sympathy for the Nazi cause to touch the royal couple.[14]

That Easter, McMullin and Elsie Lady Mendl lunched with Wallis at Candé. McMullin reported that Wallis wouldn't travel to Paris to have her trousseau made, but rather the dressmakers— most notably Mainbocher—would come to her. Even then Wallis claimed that she had no idea when the wedding would take place.[15]

Yet it was Beaton who bagged first prize in the abdication sweepstakes. Wallis summoned him to Château de Candé for the weekend to photograph her. Though he enjoyed himself among her friends, the Rogerses and the Bedaux, he lamented that "in Mrs. Simpson's entourage there is no smattering of culture, no appreciation in art of any form. . . . As a steady diet it would be impossible."[16] When left alone after midnight, Beaton and Wallis

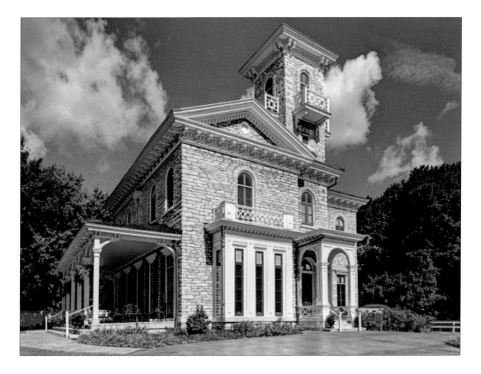

▴ Exterior of Louis Benoist's home. He was Condé Nast's maternal grandfather. The house is located on the outskirts of St. Louis and is now run by the Affton Historical Society. (*Courtesy of the Affton Historical Society*)

▴ Louis Benoist's bedroom. (*Courtesy of the Affton Historical Society*)

▸ Carmel Snow posing for Cecil Beaton in Condé's apartment, circa 1929. (*Courtesy of the Cecil Beaton Collection, Sotheby's*)

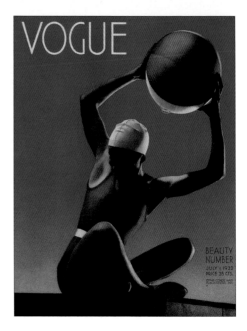

This *Vogue* cover by Benito from September 1, 1926, was one of the earliest to use a full palette and new electro-engraving techniques. (*Courtesy of Condé Nast Publications*)

The first color cover of American *Vogue* appeared on the July 1, 1932, cover, photographed by Edward Steichen. Many believed it spelled the death knell of graphic covers. (*Courtesy of Condé Nast Publications*)

Politicians standing on top of the globe with burning wick at the bottom, depicting the disarmament conference. One of many political commentaries on *Vanity Fair*'s covers. (*Courtesy of Condé Nast Publications*)

Mugs of beer and *Vanity Fair* spelled out with pretzels on red and white tablecloth to celebrate the end of Prohibition. (*Courtesy of Condé Nast Publications*)

The many faces of Clare Boothe Brokaw (later Luce) while managing editor at *Vanity Fair*. (*Courtesy of Condé Nast Publications*)

The *Vogue* magazine cover from July 15, 1916, is typical of the whimsical graphic designs of the period. *Vogue* would never have alluded to the Great War in Europe on its covers. (*Courtesy of Condé Nast Publications*)

Vanity Fair cover for March 1920, depicting the dance craze. (*Courtesy of Condé Nast Publications*)

The thirtieth anniversary *Vogue* magazine cover, January 1, 1923. (*Courtesy of Condé Nast Publications*)

The *Vogue* magazine cover from March 15, 1927, by Georges Lepape, depicting Elizabeth "Lee" Miller as the epitome of American style. Miller would go on to become an acclaimed World War II photographer for *Vogue*. (*Courtesy of Condé Nast Publications*)

Josephine Baker caricature published in *Vanity Fair*'s February 1936 issue. Condé believed in equality and promoted talent regardless of race, sexual orientation, color, or creed. (*Courtesy of Condé Nast Publications*)

The new Left Wing in

*T*HERE has long been, in the country at large, the greatest confusion, concerning New York society; a confusion principally due to the belief that society here—our solid, conservative, and responsible society—is, in its intent and *morale*, quite unlike that of other American cities.

That very common error has arisen, naturally enough, from the fact that New York's social arena is greater, its entertainments and places of amusement more varied, its ritual a little more regulated, and its visitors, whether from Europe or the West, more numerous.

But, actually, the great bulk of good society in New York is constituted (as it is in Boston, Philadelphia, Baltimore, Charleston, Chicago, Detroit, San Francisco, and a score or more cities) of sensible and decently bred people who live conventionally and put their families, work, private tastes, and public responsibilities before their pleasures and amusements.

But, in the past year or two, a new kind of confusion concerning our society has become general, due to the appearance of a newly formed, colourful, prodigal, and highly publicized social army, the ranks of which are largely made up of rich, carefree, emancipated, and, quite often, idle people. Furthermore, the morale of this new social battalion is in many respects at variance, not only with that animating the more conservative West and South, but also with that of older and more traditional society in New York itself.

This recent and widely discussed army of the Left, and the schism which it is supposed to have caused in the ranks of our good society, have called forth a remarkable volume of publicity. Indeed, half a dozen articles concerning it have appeared in national magazines, and a dozen in weeklies, dailies, and periodicals of fashion.

The February 1, 1938, issue of *Vogue* displayed the unredacted doodle by Cecil Beaton that caused him to be exiled from *Vogue* and the United States for many years. Condé withdrew all copies and reissued the magazine with the doodle redacted. (*Courtesy of Condé Nast Publications*)

New York Society

by FRANK CROWNINSHIELD

The burden of all this publicity has been to one effect; namely, that society here has become, not only democratized, but disintegrated; that all the old rituals have broken up, and the old barriers broken down; and that, to be more specific about it, three hundred or more fashionable people have become so intolerably fed up with what they thought the pomp, stuffiness, and retarded tempo of traditional society, that they seceded from it, *en masse*, and created an integrated and perfectly functioning social cosmos of their own. Into the maelstrom of this world, they have also managed to draw a goodly number of actresses, authors, editors, bankers, movie favourites, sportsmen, theatre managers, playwrights, and publishers of renown.

This colourful social group has now everywhere become known as Café Society, for the reason that so many of its activities—daily and nightly—take place in our better-known cafés and night-clubs.

Apparently, the votaries of the new cult prefer to go to bed at dawn and get up when they are rested; to dance—with the patient endurance of dervishes—at night-clubs; to dine well and drink late in cafés; to attend parties in which order must a little make way for fantasy; and to expose their furs and faces to the candid cameras which have now lent a new horror to our Broadway first nights. In short, it is the objective of these social gipsies, apparently without homes or families, to hunt down the flying figure of Pleasure, "pluck out his flying feather and find his mouth a rein."

In the country at large, where the true facts are not known, all these articles, and the avalanche of newspaper sequels which grew out of them, raised many doubts and increased many of the confusions concerning society in New York. People in the West, for example, have suspected that the group was symptomatic (Continued on page 165)

The original doodle contained anti-Semitic slurs, and was replaced by this apparently innocent version immediately. Condé was applauded for his handling of the unfortunate affair. (*Courtesy of Condé Nast Publications*)

• Mrs. Harrison Williams (aka Mona Williams, later Countess of Bismark), punching through paper. (*Courtesy of Condé Nast Publications*)

• Leslie Nast in a garden, wearing a ball gown. (*Courtesy of Condé Nast Publications*)

• Singer and actor Paul Robeson posing for *Vanity Fair* in a military jacket for *The Emperor Jones*. (*Courtesy of Condé Nast Publications*)

• From left to right: Edna Woolman Chase, Michel de Brunhoff, and Frank Crowninshield. (*Courtesy of Condé Nast Publications*)

talked until dawn. He thought she was a "strong force," possessing an intelligence that was subject, nonetheless, to "vast limitations." She was politically ignorant and had been "taken by surprise by the Abdication." Indeed, she had persuaded Edward VIII to delay all talk of marriage until after the Coronation and had even given the powers that be papers she had signed to stop her divorce from Ernest Simpson. According to Beaton, she confessed that she was "determined to love him, though I feel she is not in love with him. She has a great responsibility in looking after someone who, so essentially different, entirely relies upon her."[17]

Having the opportunity to get to know his subject better, Beaton created romantic pictures of Wallis in organdy dresses posed amid flowers in the shade of sunlit trees. Others showed Wallis seated peacefully in her bedroom, and standing by an antique credenza brimming over with blooms. Condé was thrilled with the photographs, and Edna devoted six pages to the shoot in American *Vogue*. It sold out the moment it hit the newsstands. Beaton was asked back to take the wedding photos on June 2, 1937, on the understanding that *Vogue* would be given first choice from the shoot.[18] With such access to the greatest social story of the day, he was now King Beaton.

But all roads to the top have potholes. There was a second photographer present: an "uninspired old hack" known only as Mr. Soper of Tilney Street, London. Edna waited to make her choice back at British *Vogue*'s offices, forbidding Beaton from selling any images to the general press first. Wallis was adamant, however, that some of his photographs should be available for general release. For "half a valuable hour" Edna and Beaton argued, giving Soper the crucial edge to sell his second-rate photographs to the press—first to the *Evening Standard* in London, then by radioing them to the United States. Edna fumed, believing the photographs were Beaton's and wrote: "I feel you have let us down badly . . . now we fear that anything we publish will be an aftermath." Beaton was quite understandably upset and demanded an apology for Edna's "disgusting letter." He told her if he had wanted to make a scoop, he would have sold his photographs in France. "I was inundated with fabulous offers," he wrote, "for my impressions and photographs," but had refused them all. "This row has wounded me so deeply that I have taken a great dislike to *Vogue* . . . if I were a brave and courageous person [I] would give it up entirely and start something else," Beaton confided to his diary.[19]

That September, Beaton sailed to New York for the winter. His disgruntlement with *Vogue* continued. "The weeks have flown . . . and all that results are a few pages more . . . in the inevitable *Vogue*. The weekly salary is a boon but the *Vogue* influence is now beyond a joke. It makes me limited more than ever." The frosty weather continued unabated between Beaton and Edna. Dr. Agha, who had always denied Beaton's genius, added a pinch of malice by spreading the word that Beaton wanted "to deny everything *Vogue* has worshipped for so many years . . . dowdiness for elegance, bad technique . . . for good technique."[20]

Unsurprisingly, as winter progressed Beaton tried to expand his network. He designed Tallulah Bankhead's costumes for *Antony and Cleopatra*—his first foray onto Broadway. Sadly for Beaton, the critics panned the play, one of them wittily commenting: "Tallulah Bankhead barged down the Nile last night as Cleopatra—and sank."[21] That said, Beaton had garnered a powerful fan. Orson Welles asked if Beaton might be interested in designing the costumes for his forthcoming productions of *Henry IV*, Parts I and II, and *Henry V* on Broadway. What a question! Beaton nearly bit Welles's hand off.

Diversifying even more, Beaton decorated a December party for Loelia, Duchess of Westminster, designing gigantic caricatures of famous and notable New Yorkers; he learned to dance the Big Apple, as one did in New York; gave Broadway opening-night parties; and for *Vogue*, photographed the star actress, Mrs. Patrick Campbell, with her Pekingese, Moonbeam, and "an old Polish frog . . . with a huge casket of jewels"—Helena Rubinstein.[22]

Beaton remained easily influenced. His latest friend, Pavel Tchelitchew, a Russian émigré surrealist painter and set and costume designer,* resented the power of Jews in Hollywood. With the Jewish producer, David O. Selznick, and his Jewish director, George Cukor, then making front-page news with their hunt to cast Scarlett O'Hara in *Gone With the Wind*, Tchelitchew spewed about Jewish control of Hollywood. Beaton listened . . . and began to repeat many of his friend's anti-Semitic "jokes."

Beaton was riding high in January 1938, until Monday, January 24, when his world collapsed. The telephone rang at 9:30 A.M., waking the sleeping king of photography. It was a reporter asking about Walter Winchell's nationally syndicated column that day. Winchell? What did Winchell have to do with him? Well, said the reporter, Winchell wrote:

> THE FEBRUARY ISSUE OF VOGUE, the mag, contains some hidden anti-Semitism!...A magnifying glass is necessary to detect it in Cecil Beaton's lettering for Frank Crowninshield's article on New York society page 73....As frixample: "Ball at the El Morocco brought out all the damned kikes in town."...Another is: "Why is Mrs. Selznick such a social wow? Why is Mrs. Goldwyn, etc. Why is Mrs. L. B. Mayer?' Another shows a telegram which reads: "Party darling. Love Kike." None of those remarks had anything to do with the Crowninshield text.[23]

In his diaries Beaton claimed he was ill, baffled, and not anti-Jewish. But before publication Margaret Case had spotted his offensive remarks and warned Beaton to remove them. He snapped: "Always the same story. Let them alter the whole beastly thing!" Flouncing off, he washed his hands of the matter and "forgot all about it." But that was rather disingenuous of Beaton. "So delighted was he with his little trick," Winchell (who was also Jewish) wrote, "that he spread the news among his intimates, gloating of how he had put one over. . . . Naturally, that is how we heard about it." Others suspected that it was Dr. Agha who was the whistle-blower,

---

* Tchelitchew collaborated with Serge Diaghilev and George Balanchine.

wishing to rid himself of this troublesome photographer, illustrator, and writer who had wormed his way into Condé's affections.[24]

If Beaton thought he was untouchable and would not suffer any consequences, he was wrong. Condé was personally affronted. His elder daughter, Natica, had married the virtuoso cellist Gerald Warburg, a Jew, and Condé was exceedingly proud of him. Frank felt violated that his article should be associated with such vitriol. Margaret Case was undeniably shocked. Fortunately Edna was on vacation in the Caribbean. Summoned to *Vogue*'s offices, Beaton noticed "the faces of various editors and the group of lawyers, advertising men and others clustered outside Condé's office." He resolved to explain himself clearly to Condé and claimed it would blow over. So the excuses flowed. Aside from the excuse of poor health, Beaton denied that he was anti-Jewish. It was true that he resented "the people that run Hollywood and pretend to make an art of what they know is an industry." Besides, Beaton argued, the "appalling catastrophe" was merely the fault of Condé's editors for not changing the wording, "for it was never meant to be seen or if seen at all only for submission to Dr. Agha in the art department."[25] A serious Condé accepted Beaton's apology.

Again, if Beaton thought that this was the end of the matter, he miscalculated. That night, having trudged through pouring rain to the opera, he found Condé's butler waiting for him with a typewritten note that said: "I would appreciate very much your coming to the house at ten o'clock—before if you can make it. Please be here by ten at any rate." Handwritten at the bottom, Condé added: "I am so terribly distressed over horrible mess—Forgive me for asking you to run away from the opera."

When Beaton arrived he was hurried into the dining room, which seemed "sinister, devoid of its usual gaiety." Condé wasted no time. "We're in a tough spot. . . . I could not mind more if I were losing my own son but I can see nothing else but to ask for your resignation," handing Beaton a statement he'd prepared for the press.

Still not understanding the gravity of his situation, Beaton wrote in his diary that Condé's statement was pompous: "I had a feeling of freedom—and I have never more felt as ambitious. I had complained so much about the restrictions of *Vogue* and now I was free in so far that I would not be able to appeal to the same public . . . in future."

Friends tried to persuade Condé to withdraw all 130,000 copies of the insulting *Vogue*. A redacted version was printed and distributed. However, Condé showed a personal solidarity with the self-important Beaton by bringing him to one of Mrs. Gloria Morgan Vanderbilt's lunches. Beaton found many new friends among fellow anti-Semites, while losing the valuable commissions from Orson Welles and George Cukor. Clare Boothe Luce claimed, "Henry [Luce] wouldn't now touch him with the end of a ten-foot barge-pole." Jokes abounded, some calling Beaton the "Heillustrator." Edna wrote from Nassau: "I am frantic. . . . I did not see anything but the names on the envelopes which I asked you [Beaton] to change." Everyone had an opinion. Even Beaton had new excuses for his behavior: "I would not have been Jew conscious . . . if it were not for Pavlik's [Tchelitchew's] hatred of them." Then he said that he thought the word "kike" implied "vulgar people"—as if that were any better!

Soon after, Beaton had a flaming row with Irene Selznick in a New York flower shop and was asked by the owner to leave and never to return. Condé suggested Beaton beat a retreat from New York, too. As he sailed that April, Beaton was still certain that it would all blow over and New York would welcome him again in a year. But a letter from Condé dated April 21, 1938, crystallized *Vogue*'s position: "Although I am ready to believe that you have no really anti-Semitic feelings and what you did had in your mind no more significance than a 'prank,' nevertheless you chose, most unfortunately for all of us, to play this prank in such a way that you plunged me, as a publisher into a political and racial situation completely out of character with *Vogue* and entirely at variance with, and distasteful to, my own feelings."

Beaton would not be able to carry out any further obligations under the terms of his contract, due to expire on March 31, 1939. Cannily he told Condé that he hadn't breached the terms of their agreement, and that Condé's dismissal statements were "highly damaging to his considerable reputation."[26] To settle matters quietly, Condé paid him $15,729 on December 5, 1938, and a second payment of the same sum on January 5, 1939.*

Beaton's American career was in tatters. He continued to defend his actions and his responses for the rest of his life. McMullin thought Beaton had been stupid rather than malicious. Others thought Beaton was an arriviste, a social climber, the king of snobs, who hadn't recognized the error of his ways. Many years later Irene Selznick said: "He paid heavily, very heavily. He was punished."[27]

For his handling of the unnecessary and damaging affair at *Vogue*, Condé received universal plaudits. It cost *Vogue* some $36,000. While Condé never repeated Cocteau's sobriquet of "Malice in Wonderland" referring to Beaton, it must have resonated with him as appropriate.

* The exchange rate was $4.94 to the pound sterling. (Source: www.telegraph.co.uk /money/special-reports/from-5-to-122-the-200-year-journey-of-the-pound-against -the-doll/.)

31. ANSWERING THE DISTANT CRY OF WAR

In England and here, everybody is making ready
to face a long war, and to face it, life must indispensably
resume its normal course.
—MICHEL DE BRUNHOFF TO CONDÉ NAST,
SEPTEMBER 15, 1939

D espite the near loss of it all, Condé still lived at 1040 Park Avenue. His nemesis, William Randolph Hearst, remained master of San Simeon, too. Their rivalry fizzed on, though Condé felt it was wrong of the press to poke fun at Hearst as "an old man," as it had begun to do.* President Roosevelt had raised the profile of "the forgotten man," who had been starving in shantytown "Hoovervilles." In August 1936 *Vogue's* breathless special feature admired Hitler's country retreat, Haus Wachenfeld in Berchtesgaden—soon to be renamed the Berghof—with its "gemütlich" coziness and lack of "agitated simplicity" so overwhelming in the Führer's Berlin home. Some readers shook their heads at *Vogue's* misstep in choosing to equate the Führer with chic and charm. Seven months later, the small Basque town of Guernica in Spain was leveled by Hitler's Luftwaffe and Mussolini's Avazione Legionaria.[1] Then there was the Beaton affair. By the time Hitler had annexed the Sudetenland from Czechoslovakia on October 1, 1938, war—and when it would come—was on all Europe's mind.

"Ever since the crisis there have been almost daily items in the

---

* Hearst was ten years older than Condé. He was eighty-eight when he died, in August 1951.

press warning the public that they must 'prepare for further sacrifices,'" British *Vogue*'s advertising manager, Bill Davenport, wrote to Condé in November 1938. "This has cast a chill over consumer buying, particularly in the luxury trades. . . . As to the general situation, England has weathered plenty of difficulties in the past."[2]

For two years, though, Condé had had his mind on the launch of a new magazine, rather than world affairs. War was a distant threat to Americans, and so the hydra-headed "Project Arden" was honed until its launch in February 1939. "Entertainment is Hollywood's business, but its byproduct and most powerful magnet is glamour," Condé wrote, introducing *Glamour of Hollywood*. He recognized "the demand of the thousands of women, the young in particular, who are eager to learn the fashion and beauty secrets of the Garbos, the Dietrichs, and the Crawfords. . . . *Glamour* is planned to do for Hollywood what *Vogue* has done so magnificently for Paris and New York."[3] Surely this was not a class publication like those Condé had promoted throughout his career? *Glamour* was a mass-market beast.

Condé disagreed. Henry Luce had proved with the raging successes of *Time* and *Life* that news was no longer the exclusive domain of daily newspapers. So, too, Condé believed, the subject of Hollywood and the glamour it promoted would be his personal sphere. "Each week, in the United States, 85,000,000 entrances are bought to the moving pictures.[*] Any power big enough to develop a concentration and universality of interest that will bring 85,000,000 people together weekly, evidently is an extraordinary power."[4] The critics were proved wrong. *Glamour*, Condé's final, and only start-up, magazine, would prove a tremendous success.

A month later Tommy Kernan, Condé's trusted man in Paris now that Patcévitch had returned to New York, wrote: "It is clear that the peace of Munich was a delusion." With great clarity he ex-

---

[*] In 2017 in North America alone, 1.24 billion tickets were sold to movie theaters—the lowest number since 1992. (Source: Statistica.com)

plained the real reason behind the annexing of the Sudetenland: "It was a terrific loss as France's only sure ally on the other side of Germany [Czechoslovakia] has been destroyed, giving over to Germany a fine fleet of war-planes, equipment for forty army divisions, and the Skoda ammunitions works, the second largest in Europe." Then, turning to local French matters, Kernan added: "At long last a distribution of gas masks is being made in Paris to the civilian population. . . . The present masks were manufactured in Czechoslovakia, so no one knows how far the distribution will get. . . . The atmosphere of Paris is heavy with this apprehension, and with its cargo of dead illusions. . . . In short, I will close up affairs here, and eventually find my way back to America."[5]

Then, in August 1939, Kernan told Condé he would do all in his power to protect "our copyright and titles," suggesting selling all their paper stock and safeguarding their accounting records in the cellar of the Champs-Élysées offices, as well as a second location. Kernan also traveled to Berlin to try to unblock the last of Condé's currency there, commenting: "The anti-Polish press campaign was already under way, full of lurid atrocity stories. . . . I found the world's daily newspaper[s] on sale in various places in Berlin, excepting the French communist papers . . . just as in America, an intelligent person can find out what the rest of the world is thinking or saying."[6]

At 11:15 A.M. on September 3, 1939, Britain's prime minister, Neville Chamberlain, spoke to the world on BBC Radio: "This morning the British Ambassador in Berlin handed the German government a final Note stating that unless we heard from them by 11 o'clock that they were prepared at once to withdraw their troops from Poland, a state of war would exist between us. . . . We and France are today, in fulfilment of our obligations, going to the aid of Poland who is so bravely resisting this wicked and unprovoked attack on her people."[7]

The following day Michel de Brunhoff wrote to Condé from Paris: "Already many of us are mobilized and of course, on account of the government's recommendations to send away from Paris as much people as possible, Thomas [Kernan] and I have retained very few collaborators to help put things in order in the Accounting Department and pay the last bills." Eleven days later, when there was no immediate bombardment of Paris, de Brunhoff wrote a calmer, longer letter to Condé, containing more news: "Paul Reynaud, our Treasury Minister, broadcasted a speech . . . in which he asked all non-mobilized people and the wives of the mobilized to do the impossible and reopen their shops or trades. He said it was the duty of all who could work and had not gone into the army, to help bring back money to France."

Touchingly de Brunhoff ended with: "I know, my dear Condé, that you have won many battles and I remember how, during the last great American crisis, your collaborators were compelled to admire you for your calm and your decision. I feel sure that you will do everything that is humanly possible to allow your French property to live."[8]

But not all French people shared de Brunhoff's or Reynaud's hopes. Coco Chanel notoriously resisted the call to return to work by closing her entire business in response to the declaration of war. Why, when others like the Italian couturier Schiaparelli and the Spaniard Balenciaga announced midseason collections? That summer Edna had seen Chanel at Solange d'Ayen's home. Edna thought Chanel looked nervous and depressed. Chanel admitted, "I'm afraid, madame, I'm afraid." What Edna hadn't known was *why* Chanel seemed so afraid. Since 1938, Chanel, a notorious anti-Semite, had been the lover of the Nazi spy Baron Hans von Dincklage.

Dincklage, an Abwehr (military intelligence) agent, had been resident in France since 1933 as part of Hitler's silent army of cultural spies working to influence France's right-wing intelligentsia. Chanel's pillow talk with Dincklage drifted from her Place Vendôme apartment straight to the Nazi foreign minister, Joachim von Ribbentrop, and then on to Hitler. Given Chanel's prior relationship with the Duke of Westminster, she was deemed a valuable asset to the Nazi cause.[9] She feared that the Allied forces might defeat Hitler. Then where would she be? At the very least ostracized, and her label worthless. At worst she could be tried for high treason and executed if found guilty. So against any patriotic feelings she undoubtedly had, Chanel hoped for Hitler's victory. Once the so-called phony war was over the following May,* Chanel moved into the Ritz—like all good collaborators—with her lover.

Condé felt powerless and nervous about the prospect of war. He wrote to de Brunhoff that "The normal burden of work . . . has increased ten-fold, as you can imagine, since the tragic news of September 3rd." Looking for a beacon on the horizon, Condé informed his French editor that "Congress has now repealed the Embargo Act and the United States will be free to supply France and England with war materials. I was delighted by this action as much as I dislike to see Congress passing any bills favored by Roosevelt!" Indeed, Condé believed that there was "ten times as much pro-Ally sentiment . . . as there was at the outset of the first World War. On the other hand, there is almost a unanimous determination not to be embroiled in the war."[10] Greatly heartened by Condé's obvious support, de Brunhoff and his team brought out the first "war version" of French *Vogue* that December—sporting a full thirty pages of patriotic advertisements when "we dared not hope for more than 7 or 8."

Then came the news Condé feared. "We held up the June *Frog* issue, which was ready to go to press three weeks ago, exactly on the day of the German invasion." The timing was appalling. Paper stocks were diminishing, and there was no promise of any replacements. The French government's undertaking to financially support the publication to the tune of 150,000 francs had not materialized, and Kernan thought he'd be unable to collect their advertising revenue. And de Brunhoff wrote: "All the efforts of the nation tend solely towards armament, the clothing of our soldiers,

---

* The Phony War to Americans, "the Twilight War" or even the "Bore War" to the British, "the Sitzkrieg" to Germans, or as the French called it, the "Drôle de Guerre," lasted from September 1939 to May 1940.

and the charity work that has become a gigantic task since the horrible exodus of the Belgium and the North of France populations."[11]

During the next month de Brunhoff and Kernan struggled to find ways to continue publication of Condé's French magazines, but the war overtook everything. Within six weeks of Nazi Germany launching its attack on Western Europe,* France surrendered. A month after Germany's rapid advances, Britain snatched a pyrrhic victory at Dunkirk with the rescue of more than 340,000 Allied soldiers aboard 861 vessels, most of which comprised a ragtag flotilla that joined the Royal Navy.[12] There were some 469,000 casualties, including the British Expeditionary Force in the Battle of France. Of these, there were 350,000 French casualties including 112,000 dead, 225,000 wounded, and 12,000 missing in action. By June 14 the swastika flag of the Third Reich was raised along the Champs-Élysées in Paris.

The capital and other northern cities, however, had become ghost towns. Millions of French citizens fled the onslaught, often with less than an hour to spare in their race to freedom. Those who could tossed some scant belongings onto carts or baby buggies, while others took to the roads as their own packhorses. So rapid was the invasion that uneaten meals were left on kitchen tables while cherished family photographs were scooped up, cumbersome frames and all.[13]

Vogue's Paris staff became part of the great exodus from the north to the southwest of the country, hoping to find themselves still in a "free" France. It was not to be. The financial situation of Condé's French publications was precarious, with some $20,000 in cash and $32,000 in receivables against some $46,000 in accounts payable. "From the letters received yesterday and the day before that, we learn that already, life seems to resume its normal course in Paris . . . many women asking for patterns, materials, and above

---

* Nazi Germany attacked Denmark and Norway on April 9, 1940. It launched its attack on the Netherlands, Belgium, France, and Luxembourg on May 10, 1940. France surrendered on June 22.

all, their magazine." De Brunhoff wondered if they might return to the capital and resume publication.[14]

Of course matters were not that clear-cut. With France divided between the occupied zone, where the rule of law was decidedly Nazi, and Vichy, where everyone pretended there existed every freedom of a democracy, most people stumbled about blindly amid the ruins of their former lives. Bordeaux, contrary to de Brunhoff's hopes, fell into German hands. Time and again Parisians were "encouraged" to return to the capital. This point was driven home to Condé personally by a telegram received from Sumner Welles, U.S. under secretary of state, who was able to intervene rather miraculously with a message from Kernan: RETURNED PARIS. REOPENING OFFICES. EVERYONE WELL. OTHERS RETURNING SHORTLY.[15]

America was not yet at war with Germany, and in the summer of 1940 had no intentions of becoming involved. That August, Kernan was in Paris to see if publication in any part of the country would be possible. Having secured a meeting with the German propaganda service (*Propagandastaffel*), which determined what could be published or disseminated, Kernan discovered that "not even a leaflet can be published without their permission, under penalty of death. . . . It is very important to continue publishing here, or otherwise we risk the seizure of our titles which would be handed over to any individuals who cared to exploit them." Nevertheless, Kernan's application to resume publication was met with "absolute hostility" until such time as he could submit a list of all "stockholders, directors and employees, and that we could not work again if there were any Jews among them or anyone else whom they did not like."[16] The interdiction also extended to private correspondence to America.

Kernan knew that Lucien Vogel, a member of the French Communist Party, who had written scathing articles about Hitler and Mussolini in his publication *Vu*, was safely ensconced in New York with his family, thanks to Condé's early intervention. Undoubtedly Condé's quick thinking saved Vogel's life. The only other member of the board and stockholder of French *Vogue* who was at risk was Walter Maas, an Englishman, whom Kernan suggested should resign immediately. Then there was French *Vogue*'s resident photographer, André Durst, who was part Jewish.

Unknown to Kernan, Maas had escaped to neutral Portugal's capital, Lisbon, "after days and nights on the road," and written to Condé for help. There was no problem for Maas to come to New York as a Nast employee, but Maas felt that his patriotic interests would be better served if he reached Canada—already at war with Nazi Germany. Condé wrote immediately to a Canadian senator friend of Maas's, Walter Edge, who was on a fishing holiday in Quebec. The wheels turned.[17] Within six weeks of writing his letter from Lisbon, Maas received his visa for Canada and cabled Condé with his thanks. Two days later Condé sent Kernan a radiogram with his preliminary agreement to proceed with the plan to reopen both French publications, even though he had a queasy feeling at the prospect.

Within two months Condé changed his mind. The thought that his staff were risking their lives weighed heavily on his conscience. He had "reluctantly reached the conclusion that, all things considered, it would be best to abandon the effort to resume publication until conditions will have returned to normal."[18] He then set out the provision to pay the employees as much of their salaries as possible for at least six months, or the forthcoming year if "we can afford it," in the event that they were unable to find other employment. "Many of our employees whom we have been obliged to dismiss may find themselves in serious distress this winter. Some provision should be made to furnish these deserving people with at least enough to buy food."[19] It was just as well that Condé had decided not to play ball with the Nazis, since the day after he sent the letter, he received a cable from Kernan that the propaganda service had "refused authorization for *Vogue* or *Jardin* to reappear." Kernan said it was due to anti-American feeling.

But that doesn't explain why *Harper's Bazaar* remained in print throughout the war. *Bazaar* also had an American owner. Yet Marie-Louise Bousquet, *Bazaar*'s French editor, attended Florence Gould's collaborationist salons throughout the war and was cozy with the head of censorship at the propaganda service, Gerhard

Heller, *and* Helmut Knochen, head of the Nazi secret police. That said, *Bazaar*'s position compared favorably to *Vogue*'s. Condé had asked Beaton for his resignation for insulting Jews, and worse still, Gerald Warburg was his Jewish son-in-law. Those facts alone were enough to forbid *Vogue*'s publication, even without a hint from Bousquet to the Nazis to eliminate her competition.

Harry Yoxall was in New York when Germany invaded Poland. He left for home the day after the declaration of war. Crossing the Atlantic on the neutral American ship *Washington*, he had his first encounter with a German submarine. The submarine commander had captured a Cuban vessel, the *Olive Grove*, which sent out an SOS in the hope of rescuing its cargo and mariners. Before blowing up the ship, the U-boat captain ordered the Cuban crew to man its lifeboats. Yoxall wrote in his diary: "There's at least one decent fellow in the German navy not contaminated by Hitlerism. Pity that he'll most probably, sooner or later, go to a sticky death."[20]

While Great Britain was deeply shaken by the war, the situation was inevitably different from that of occupied France. British *Vogue* urged its readers to "keep busy"—"learn to cook"—"sew or knit something, preferably not too complicated. This is not to put your dressmaker out of work but to give you something to do." For the former American model Elizabeth—redubbed Lee—Miller, London was where she chose to fight her war as a photographer. She approached Yoxall to wangle a work permit for her. Condé was thrilled and cabled his delight that her INTELLIGENCE FUNDAMENTAL GOOD TASTE SENSITIVENESS [AND] ART VALUES were again mobilized on behalf of *Vogue*. To have a woman he trusted standing by British *Vogue*'s studio head was a relief to the beleaguered publisher. As paper rationing went into effect in that coldest of winters on record, "relevance" rather than hemlines became the order of the day. Lee befriended Audrey Withers, British *Vogue*'s Oxford-educated socialist editor, who understood precisely the tone she should strike in wartime: "Women's first duty is to practice the arts of peace, so that, in happier times, they will not have fallen into disuse." In fact government officials sought Withers's support on many matters affecting civilian life. While still snapping society portraits and fashions, Lee would become an accredited U.S. army war correspondent for Condé Nast Publications in December 1942, later documenting atrocities in France and Germany.[21]

From September 1940 until May 1941, British cities were pounded by bombing raids. Although London bore the brunt of the attacks, later known as the Blitz, the Luftwaffe also bombed the main Atlantic ports of Liverpool and Southampton, and the North Sea port of Hull. Other cities hit included Bristol, Belfast, Birmingham, Cardiff, Coventry,* Glasgow, Manchester, Portsmouth, Plymouth, and Sheffield. Bombing was an inevitable fact of life, and Britain prepared for the worst with calm. Doing his bit, Yoxall "wrote sealed letters to every member of the London staff, telling them what to do in case of emergency." He had also had the foresight to set up a war issue of British *Vogue* long before he left London for New York.[22]

Bomb stories became the staple meal of the British press. Yoxall lamented that everyone had one. British *Vogue*'s New Bond Street offices were continually bombed, as was Yoxall's home in London's Borough of Richmond. One day Yoxall himself was just coming off Air Raid Precaution (ARP) duty at 6:30 A.M. when he received a call from the corporate secretary to tell him that the Condé Nast print building had been destroyed. Yoxall drove as near as he possibly could to Fleet Street, leaving his car on the Strand. A number of manhole covers "suddenly blew off . . . gyrating through the air like clay pigeons; the effect was comic—but not so comic for an auxiliary fireman who got in the way of one and had his thigh broken [. . .] I ducked down into Fetter Lane," Yoxall wrote. "The roof of our building and all the floors down to the ground had collapsed. The walls began to bulge, and I had to leave the scene of our disaster."

---

* Controversially Churchill and the War Office were alleged to have known of the Coventry attack in advance but chose not to warn the population for fear that the enemy would immediately understand that their Enigma code had been broken.

In a single night British *Vogue* lost 450,000 patterns and 400,000 magazines and books, not to mention (so Yoxall thought) the company cat, Ginger—whose job it was to discourage mice from eating the paper patterns. But cats are made of sterner stuff, and when Yoxall was allowed into the building after the fire had cooled, he dug Ginger out of the rubble, still alive. From then on Ginger would not leave his safe basement.[23] Fortunately Yoxall had managed to keep the master patterns, films of the cutting charts, and one of each of the pattern-cutting machines in his basement at home, enabling British *Vogue* to continue production, although on a much-reduced scale. It had been twenty years since Yoxall had "smelled a war"—the brick dust, explosives, flying earth—all of which vividly brought back to life the horrors of the earlier conflict.

The New York office took up a personal collection for London and sent more than six hundred pounds to be distributed to those who'd lost their belongings in the air raids. It was the first of many needed care packages gratefully received. Condé had set the tone for his entire company: Unless or until America entered the war, he would save his employees first, then his publications.

PART V

WITH THE EYE OF AN EAGLE

◄━━━◦■◦━━━►

England now in the third year of war has lived through most of the tomorrows which are about to face the United States.
—Memo from Condé Nast to
Edna Woolman Chase,
February 20, 1942

※

32. HOW TO WIN IN THE END

What a man does for others, not what they do for him,
gives him immortality.
—DANIEL WEBSTER, AMERICAN POLITICIAN

Though shopworn, the phrase "war changes everything" is nonetheless true. Who would have thought that American *Vogue* would carry such features as "WHAT PARIS WOMEN WEAR IN WAR TIME" or describe "turbans, berets—no silly hats; Schiaparelli's blue wool suit for nocturnal '*alertes*' and Madame Lanvin's black tweed case to carry a British gas mask"? Or that the fashion artist Eric's sketches of "In the Ritz shelter—'abri' outfits by Molyneux and Piguet" would become a talking point?[1]

There were times when Harry Yoxall felt Condé was insensitive to Britain's plight, but Yoxall was equally unsympathetic to the brutal fact that even American *Vogue* needed to embark on an austerity program. Condé, ever vigilant, tried to keep abreast of the British and French situations, reading about the possibilities of the United States becoming involved in the war. He was preoccupied as well with the simple reality that the company's stock price hovered at around the two-dollar mark. Condé had saved the lives of Lucien Vogel and Walter Maas. Finally he got Tommy Kernan out of Paris and repatriated to the United States in November 1940. Kernan had tried—unsuccessfully—to collect the company's outstanding debts before he was whisked back home. Then, too, Condé quietly saved Michel de Brunhoff and Solange d'Ayen in a different way, by insisting on paying their salaries and giving them money to buy food for other employees, even after his magazines ceased publication. These were gestures that no one had expected and all were touched to receive.

Yet there were odd inconsistencies in Condé's behavior. Seemingly he didn't mind being photographed with Vichy France's emissary to the United States, René de Chambrun, who was also the son-in-law of Pierre Laval, the Vichy prime minister. Soon enough Condé's new "war editor," Millicent Fenwick, who had been part of the American *Vogue* editorial team since 1938, explained the political inadvisability of becoming embroiled with Vichy, warning Condé that it was a mistake to allow such a photograph to appear in *Vogue*'s pages. That de Chambrun was also a distant cousin of President Roosevelt and a direct descendant of the French hero of the American Revolutionary War, the marquis de Lafayette, held no water for *Time* and *Life*'s Henry Luce. Though de Chambrun had been Luce's friend before the war, he did not hesitate to publish de Chambrun's name on *Time*'s "Black List" of Frenchmen condemned by the French Resistance for collaborating with the Germans.[2]

From 1940, however, Condé was battling a different personal war. Frank Crowninshield continued as *Vogue*'s rara avis, sprinkling his bonhomie and sage reflections like stardust against the prevailing gloom. Condé's daughter Leslie was particularly thrilled whenever "Uncle Frank" was around.[3] Where Frank never lost his unique sense of humor, Condé had been fighting to win back the company for so long that he forgot how to stop.

Every possible moment was spent at the office, calculating profit-and-loss statements, seeing where he could gain that edge in the market, and dashing off short memos to his staff. Soon the golf outings, visits to the boxing ring, or even baseball games with Frank dwindled to a trickle, and by the end of the summer of 1941 they had all but stopped. Instead, Condé's memos became longer, ever more critical of his editors. Even though circulation was showing a slight increase, he was worried about the future, Edna and Jessica Daves agreed privately. Harry Yoxall was peppered with curt telegrams asking for the latest rationing and financial information at British *Vogue*. Solange d'Ayen's touching updates from the French Riviera in Vichy France were read, but Condé failed to respond to any of her letters in a meaningful way. Everyone felt that Condé needed a break, but he wouldn't hear of it.

So instead, the long memos continued, and their tone hardened. The long—indeed, very long—interoffice memos had begun as early as January 31, 1940, on the subject of "Display Titles and Sub-Captions." In the twenty-two-page memo he advised his editors that they had produced in the December 15, 1939, edition of *Vogue* "one of the dullest issues I had looked at in a long time."[4] Why? he wondered. With the precision and understanding of his craft so long admired by staff and competitors alike, Condé set about comparing and contrasting that particular issue of *Vogue*— page by page—with its nemesis Hearst publication, *Harper's Bazaar*, explaining in considerable detail why *Vogue* risked losing its way for lack of clarity. Apparently ignored by his editors, he fired off a second memo dated March 3, 1940. Referring back to his earlier letter, which Condé explained should have been titled "Clarity vs. Obscurity" with an explanatory sub-caption: "In the editing and publishing of magazines, clarity is a cardinal virtue; obscurity, an unforgivable sin."[5]

Condé instructed his editors that the most successful publishers were Henry Luce of *Time, Life,* and *Fortune* magazines, and the great Alfred C. W. Harmsworth, Lord Northcliffe, who had founded Associated Newspapers* in London and the old Amalgamated Press, which published seventy-two magazines at the time of Northcliffe's death in 1922. Northcliffe held even more extreme views than Condé about the lack of clarity in newspapers and magazines. Often referred to as the "Napoleon of Journalism," Northcliffe displayed his courage, leadership, and a clearheaded attack on any subject. "He had a volcanic intolerance of slipshod

---

* At the time of Northcliffe's death, Associated Newspapers comprised the *Daily Mail*, the *Evening News*, the *Sunday Pictorial*, the *Overseas Mail*, and the *Daily Mirror*. Of his seventy-two magazines, only the *Woman's Weekly*, the *Sunday Circle*, the *Family Journal*, and the *Woman's Pictorial* were focused on women's interests.

work," Condé wrote. "However, his interest in people was so deep, that it made him the master of popular journalism, for he was a realist who knew the things that lie nearest to the human heart."[6]

Ah, the human heart! That organ without which no one can live, was, in fact, the real problem. Condé had survived cancer, but in 1941 he had to face the reality of a failing heart. Survivors of serious heart disease were a rarity back then. Radium treatments, too, were on the cards for Condé, suggesting that the cancer had returned.[7] Condé was wise enough to recognize his mortality, and to handle it with a silent, valiant stoicism. A battle raged inside him, however. That was the reason for the memos: He had to impart some of his personal wisdom to his editors, and precious little time remained for him to do so.

Though cursed with a weak heart physically, Condé was normally bighearted when it came to the excellence of his staff. But, in case they might forget, he wanted to ensure that they understood what excellence meant to him. Loving what they did was the key, he said, and if they didn't love it like family, then they shouldn't be editing, illustrating, or writing. Battling with all these emotions, Condé felt, rightly or wrongly, that he had been dying for an unconscionably long time. The years of unremitting stress in business had taken their toll. There were too few memos he could write to convey his thoughts and ethos. When despondency set in, he believed this latest war might ruin all he had fought for since 1909. A third of his staff was scattered to the winds. British *Vogue* remained a stalwart companion but was nonetheless threatened.

None of this "written wisdom" was understood, even by his closest friends. To them his memos "reflected an irascibility," Edna wrote, "an almost haughty reliance on his own judgment, which seemed not so much self-confidence as censure of others." Most unusually for Condé, she felt he ignored the opinions of those he trusted the most: Iva Patcévitch, Lew Wurzburg, Frank Crowninshield, and herself. "His own judgment, indeed, became a kind of obsession with him. Everyone else's was poor," Edna lamented. "The old wonderful confidence in each other, the frank disagreements, adjusted and easily forgotten, the feeling of oneness were gone."[8]

Of course none of them knew that Condé was hiding his dangerously high blood pressure from them. From May 1941, buried between scores of charitable donations to organizations like Bundles for Britain, the Navy Relief Fund, the American National Red Cross, and Sacred Heart Church, Condé's receipts also show nine house calls from his internist at the beginning of May alone, indicating things were not as they should be.[9] Only his assistant, the loyal Mary Campbell, knew, and she was sworn to secrecy.

Condé's greatest solace remained his daughter Leslie. After "Big" Leslie married Rex Benson, they had two sons, David and Robin, and had moved to Washington, D.C., in 1941. Rex had been promoted to the rank of colonel and took up the post of military attaché to the British Embassy, under Lord Halifax.[*] "Little Leslie" remained at her father's side and attended the Brearley School in New York, visiting the Bensons in Washington during her longer school vacations. Her father wouldn't have had it any other way.

Condé often asked Mary Campbell if she thought little trinkets or gifts would suit Leslie, and Mary happily helped out. His grandson Peter—his son Coudert's little boy—joined Condé and Leslie at 1040 Park during his boarding-school vacations, and the children got along well. They were born in the same year and celebrated their birthdays, which were only days apart, together. Leslie was a pure delight to Condé. In contrast Peter always seemed troubled. Condé thought his grandson was quite handsome, save for his

---

* Churchill's first weeks in office were punctuated by Halifax's repeated insistence on the policy of appeasement, beautifully portrayed in the film *Darkest Hour* (2017). Benson's appointment owed a great deal to his work in the British secret service in World War I and his high-level personal connections in the United States. Churchill believed he might be able to persuade the United States to enter the war on the Allied side.

buckteeth, and wrote to Coudert that he would like to handle and pay for the boy's orthodontia.[10]

Yet with each passing year Peter became an ever-greater worry. Coudert and Charlotte had gone their separate ways in 1933. Charlotte had remarried a British diplomat who was then serving in Mexico. Clarisse and José Victor Onativia had divorced, too, and she was eager to control how the schooling of their grandson was handled. Throughout their long, tortuous, and detailed correspondence, Condé never once lost his temper. He managed, despite Clarisse's overbearing nature, to help provide Peter with a good home, full of fun and love. In April 1940 Condé wrote jokingly to young Peter, then staying with his grandmother, "It takes so long to come from Bronxville to New York by motor, that I decided to get you an airplane. You will find this easy work, I am sure—at least I find that the propellers go round very easily if you give them a push. Let me know when you decide to fly down to the city because I would like to see you arrive."[11]

Despite his natural levity with both Leslie and Peter, Condé was often preoccupied with his health and the office. At times he needed prodding by his domestic staff too. Leslie's great confidant was George Bey, Condé's valet and chauffeur. Always prepared to jump in, George had a sixth sense for intervening when required. "Peter had a horrid German governess who used to put English mustard on his tongue," Leslie recalled with a shudder. She confided in George, and "to her horror and delight," the next morning the German governess was gone.[12] Condé wanted only harmony at home.

Yet nothing could stem Clarisse's constant haranguing. She was also unpleasant to Leslie. "It was typical of Clarisse," Leslie said, "when Peter stayed, and Clarisse wanted to take him out occasionally, it would be under the stipulation that I should be removed from the apartment. I was only six years old, and they (Condé and Clarisse) had been apart for years." As an observant child, Leslie noted, too, that her father was constantly being put down by Clarisse, who took credit at every opportunity for his meteoric rise.[13]

Coudert was under a great deal of stress, too. His second wife, Juliet, was in and out of mental sanatoriums. She could barely handle her own life, much less a troubled young stepson's and a husband's. Coudert was an absentee father, serving from December 1940 in the National Guard. Then, too, on at least one occasion, George Bey needed to chaperone Peter to meet with his mother. Condé and Leslie were the only sure and safe people with the power to protect Peter from his tumultuous family life. Of course Natica and her cellist husband, Gerald Warburg, were tremendous favorites with the children whenever they came to visit. "Gerry and his brothers were like the Marx brothers." Leslie smiled, recalling some long-lost joke. "Though Natica could be serious. We remained friends always."[14]

The Warburgs' daughter, Jeremy, has wonderful memories of her grandfather to this day: "Grandpa Condé was very playful! He knew lots of magic tricks, done with coins hidden between his fingers. He could cup his hands together, blow through them, and make a loud sound like a foghorn," she recalled. "Grandpa Condé introduced a four-and-a-half-foot white plush rabbit into the family. She wore a blue checked gingham dress, and a white eyelet-trimmed pinafore tied with a big bow. She had eyelet-trimmed bloomers underneath her dress, and had red felt sewn onto her feet and ankles for boots." Jeremy wrote:

> Somewhere from long ago there is a snapshot of him standing, holding the paw of the rabbit by one hand and holding the hand of his very young daughter, Leslie, by the other. The name of the rabbit was Mrs. Bean O'Wean, and she was an Easter Bunny.
>
> She has lived in various homes over the years but for the past few decades she has been living with me. Her white plush fur has been cleaned and her garments are mended and refreshed. She has her special spot in the dappled sun on the landing, and every Easter she has her pride of place.
>
> Heirlooms come in many forms.[15]

Condé had been battling for his company's financial stability for so long that many had lost sight of the fact that his family had given him the greatest gift of all—the unqualified love of his children, old and young. Yes, he was sixty-seven years old, and yes, he was tired, but he knew above all that he was loved by those whom he cherished. That is true immortality and the only way any of us win in the end.

33. THE KING IS DEAD

*I shall always bless you for telling me that he thought of me
during his last days, it has given me great happiness.*
—LESLIE BENSON TO MARY CAMPBELL

L eslie Nast began her school year in September 1941 in
Washington, D.C. Since her mother and father led peripatetic lives, she took this change in her stride. Of course she
knew her father was ill, "but it wasn't something one talked about.
I had seen the oxygen machine in the corner of his office and was
very scared," Leslie said.[1]

On December 7, 1941, the Japanese attacked Pearl Harbor.
Everyone felt shock, revulsion, and horror. Everyone, that is, except the British, who had been begging the United States to provide military support for the past two years. At last the United
States would join in the fight. And nowhere was British joy more
obvious than at the Bensons' Georgetown home. "December 7,
1941, was a day-long celebration," Leslie remembers. "People were
coming and going all day long and into the evening. There was a
tremendous air of jubilation." The next morning as Leslie put on
her coat to go to school, her mother said, "Now remember, you're
a little American girl, so no rejoicing outside the house."[2]

On December 1 Condé had his first, and seeming last, radium
treatment.[3] Four days later and two days before Pearl Harbor, he
was hospitalized. Condé may have hoped it was the radium treatment that caused his shortness of breath. The story fed to his editors was that going into the hospital was precautionary: He had a

touch of pneumonia, nothing serious. The doctors were exaggerating. Mary Campbell knew better. Paid bills to nurses and to Doctors Hospital told the true story. Condé had suffered a serious heart attack. He was admitted to the hospital on December 5, 1941, and released a week later.[4] Afterward he had 24/7 nursing care through Christmas.[5]

Condé reflected at home through New Year's Day, 1942. In February he wrote to Edna that, "England now in the third year of war has lived through most of the tomorrows which are about to face the United States. Common sense dictates that we take many leaves out of her book of experience." Memos flew regarding economizing, printing memos on both sides of the paper (this was never done), and any other means of supporting the war effort. The testy memos about poor cover design, bad backgrounds and photography, and the purity of editorial pages continued too.[6]

That spring Condé visited Edna and her husband, Dick Newton, at their newly built home in Oyster Bay. Condé admired the hedge around the terrace, asking what it was. "It's mostly laurel," Dick replied. "Next spring it will all be in bloom." Edna recalled that Condé looked beyond the hedge to the "treetops silhouetted against the evening sky before replying. 'Next spring. . . . Oh, yes. I don't imagine I'll see that.'" His hosts thought that the remark referred to Condé's usual early-spring trip to Europe.[7]

Condé was thinking of the end, perhaps of the oxygen tanks stowed at home and in his private office washroom behind a filing cabinet. He had told only Mary Campbell and George Bey the truth. She became his office nurse; he, Condé's nurse at home. Later Condé brought Iva Patcévitch into his confidence. Mary and George begged Condé to tell his family, too. Coudert was stationed in the Pacific, so what good would that do? Condé argued. And why should he bother Natica, who had her own young children to think about? Then, too, Leslie had just turned twelve, and he didn't want to burden her either. The last thing Condé wanted was to feel his enlarged family's pity—both at home and in the office. To be helped by willing hands was not an end he wanted.

Since Edna suspected nothing, her nerves became frayed by

Condé's increasingly distant manner. "When he was absent from the office they said he had a cold. When we said we wanted to see him, and weren't afraid of catching it, the cold developed into pneumonia; he had to go to the hospital." Of course there was no pneumonia, but rather another heart attack. He recovered. Then, while visiting Leslie at summer camp, Condé climbed a hill with her and had another heart attack, his third official one. He had to be taken home at once and never returned to the office. He was sixty-eight and refused to recognize his illness publicly. To the end, he was a proud man.

One day that September, Frank sidled into Edna's office and sat down next to her. "Edna, you know Condé is far from well, and he seems terribly upset because you have not answered that long letter he wrote you more than a week ago. He thinks you must be very angry." Laying his hand on top of Edna's, he repeated: "Don't be angry, Edna." Shortly afterward Condé's letter, which Condé had personally addressed, was returned to *Vogue*. It read: "Private—Mrs. Richard Newton, Long Island."[8]

Edna read the letter with tears streaming down her face. "You and I have earned more than respectable places in the magazine world of yesterday and today—you as one of its great editors—I as one of its successful publishers," it began. Then he apologized if he had upset her: "I have become aware of the fact that the memos issued by me from time to time during the past year have offended you. I didn't realize to what extent until you told me the other day that my recent memo on covers killed your interest in *Vogue*."

His final two paragraphs read:

Edna, we have been a great team. I believe I have been a wide-awake and an intelligent publisher, but I am the first to admit to myself, and to acknowledge to the world, that, without you I could never have built Vogue. *We have built this great property together. Let us, together see it through the present crisis or those that may come after.*

I am carrying a heavy burden. I seem to have no interest in life but seeing these properties through. Whether I am to

break under this ordeal I do not know. But I do know that I
ought to be free from any unnecessary or added burdens.
Your feeling—I think unjustified—is, for me, a crushing load. It
would certainly make life considerably happier for me if I felt
that you would, in no way, resent this letter. It is written, dear
Edna, in the hope that no more barriers will ever arise
between us.

Later that day Edna visited him at 1040 Park Avenue. Her heart
burst at finding him propped up in bed with a shawl she had given
him around his shoulders. She "laid her head beside him on the
pillow" and whispered: "Oh, Condé, we have been through such a
long life together. I can't bear it to be marred by bitterness and
unhappiness. Is there anything in the world you want that I can
do for you?" Condé let tears slide down his cheek, and he patted
her hand. "He didn't say anything; he didn't have to." That weekend, on September 19, she received a telephone call at her Oyster
Bay home that Condé Nast was dead.[9]

His funeral was held at the Church of St. Ignatius Loyola on Park
Avenue. While not a religious man, he had maintained his adher-
ence to the Catholic Church. More than eight hundred people—half
of whom were employees—attended, crammed in every corner.
Condé's last love, Helen Brown Norden, now Helen Lawrenson,
was there. So was the unforgiven Carmel Snow, on her knees, saying her rosary. Dick Wright; Frank Crowninshield; his lawyer,
Macdonald DeWitt; Iva Patcévitch; and the advertising department
head, Frank Soule, were his pallbearers. Bernard Baruch, Averell
Harriman, and Henry Luce were honorary pallbearers.[10]

Leslie Benson thanked Mary Campbell for her many kindnesses: "You will be glad to hear that Leslie has kept amazingly
well—she has only had one breakdown which did not last long. It
certainly has been a great blessing that school re-opened right away
and she was able to throw herself into a busy and active life. But

she will continue to miss her father for a very long time as we all shall."[11] Mary Campbell gave "Big Leslie" tremendous solace by telling her that Condé had thought of her in his final days. She returned the favor by telling Mary: "It must have been a great comfort to Mr. Nast to have had you there to help him through and in maintaining his courage to keep his secret."[12]

Mary was the point person for all of Condé's surviving family—his sister, Ethel, and his children. To Coudert she wrote a long, typewritten letter apologizing for the shock he must have had in "hearing it [the news] over the radio as I understand you did." She explained that:

> *It has been just terrible knowing that this heart condition hung over Mr. Nast's head and yet not being able to let you or anyone else know about it.... You will remember in May 1941 your father was quite sick at 1040 with an ear condition which threatened to develop into a case of mastoiditis. At the time he was in bed for weeks and took a great quantity of sulfanilamide.... Shortly thereafter, he noticed great difficulty in breathing, and consulted Dr. Poindexter, a heart specialist. For sometime prior to 1941, Mr. Nast had had some heart trouble—an "athletic heart" I believe—and he had had one or two slight attacks, but nothing of any importance—or so I was told at the time.... In December 1941 Mr. Nast had a severe attack (we said that it was near pneumonia, but it was really a heart attack) and was hospitalized as you know.... He had previously instructed us not to let anyone know of the condition, and in December he put this instruction in writing for our protection in the future. Your father dreaded more than anything else being considered an invalid.[13]*

While thousands of expressions of condolences were received, and *The New York Times* called Condé a "genius" in the field of publishing and "a lavish entertainer," no eulogy could better the one in Britain's *Scope* magazine of November 1942. It begins with the headline: "Many are the industries which owe a debt of which they are unaware to the man who more than any other has influenced the style and elegance of the last three decades." It goes on:

> The name of the publisher Condé Nast is one which British publishers cannot honour too highly. That they may never have heard of it ... in no way diminishes the debt they owe to the man whose obsession with the idea of elegance in daily life transformed dress, publishing, furniture, pottery, cosmetic, glass and luxury trades from narrow fin de siècle stodginess to the pleasing elegant lines of today.
>
> The power of the printed word could not be more aptly illustrated.... His recent death at 68 is a loss which Scope, representing all industry, would find irreplaceable if it were not for the fact that the inspiration and influence of his work are now too far-reaching to be uprooted.
>
> ... The standard set by Vogue was a challenge manufacturers could not ignore.... It is not an exaggeration to say that his influence directly extended to Woolworth. Nast made his life-work a work of art, and would have asked no higher tribute.[14]

Mary had been entrusted with a letter, dated May 9, 1942, to hand to Iva Patcévitch after Condé died. Its contents came as a surprise. "When Mary gives you this you will be acting President of the Company. I would have told you my plans but I couldn't." Pat read on:

> I am turning the management of the property [magazines] over into your hands. I suggest you appoint Mary your personal assistant. Unofficially she has served me in that capacity for the past year and has demonstrated her value.
>
> It is a hard and difficult road ahead. You have proven your loyalty, integrity and business ability. I am confident that you will ably continue the outstanding leadership of our periodicals and push them to even greater prestige and brilliance.

*Good luck and my deep gratitude to you, dear Pat, for the
many things you have done for me.*[15]

Lew Wurzburg was shattered. He thought he was Condé's heir.
Still, Condé knew that to make his publications survive, they would
need the panache of a younger man. Pat was only forty at the
time—and a man who spoke seven languages. Condé knew that
his choice was the right one.

34. A NEW LEAF

It is my feeling that Time ripens all things;
with Time all things are revealed.
—FRANÇOIS RABELAIS

Within a week of Condé's death Iva Patcévitch was elected the new president of the company. Its passive majority shareholder, Lord Camrose, had approved Condé's choice prior to his death. Pat was the future.[1] Wurzburg would have been the choice of past loyalties, and not the man to face the rough terrain ahead. For Edna, her relationship with Condé had been a platonic marriage of some thirty-three years, and she mourned his loss as she would a husband's.

Given that Condé and his family were substantial stockholders in the company, he was also trying to protect their futures. According to his will, Condé's 7,900 shares of common stock in Condé Nast Publications, Inc., were valued at a mere $17,775.00. His shares in Park-Lexington Corporation—some 1,066—were valued at a dollar each. He had five hundred U.S. savings bonds, at a value of $75 per one hundred. There was $3,000 in cash, making the total value of his assets around $21,600.[2] That did not include his thirty-room penthouse at 1040 Park Avenue and its magnificent furnishings, or the apartment on East Seventy-second Street given to Coudert when he married Charlotte, which was still in Condé's name.[3]

Parke-Bernet were appointed by the executors as auctioneers for the contents of the famous residence. The family was not allowed to take away anything that was precious to them. "Some weeks after Grandpa Condé's death, my mother brought home several Parke-Bernet catalogues that listed all of Grandpa Condé's possessions in a very formal way," Jeremy Warburg Russo recalls. "My mother explained about 'the Crash' and said that Grandpa Condé had run out of money because of it. A friend of his named Lord Camrose had quietly given him the money he needed to keep going, but now there was going to be a big auction of <u>all</u> his possessions in order to raise more money. The money needed to pay off all the debts he had had to leave behind." Natica opened the catalogs to show Jeremy the photographs and read about her father's much-loved pieces of furniture. Jeremy could see that her mother was sad:

> She explained that normally after a death, family members could just keep some of their favorite things for their own, even if there were other things to auction or give away. But in this case, <u>everything</u> had to be sold. That meant that if my mother wanted anything, large or small, she would have to go to the auction and bid on it with her own money along with all of the others there, and maybe she would be highest bidder on a few things, or not. She looked so very sad telling me this part, and all I could do was squeeze her hand very hard. She told me that "Big Leslie" was in the same position. They were going to go to the auction together and that at least would be comforting to them both.
>
> They would just try to do their best.[4]

Condé's apartment was the surviving symbol of his love of elegance. The January 1943 Parke-Bernet auction became a litmus test of the uncertain times. No one was in a mood to buy with the country at war. Treasures that Elsie, Lady Mendl, had sold to Condé from Versailles went for a song. "A magnificent eighteenth-century map of Venice . . . superbly framed in lacquer and gold leaf," having "appeared countless times in *Vogue*—a slightly out-of-focus background for fashion photographs," had an opening bid of a paltry seventy-five dollars. "I was horrified," Edna wrote. "Condé had paid ten times that for the frame alone. . . . The auctioneer was indignant himself, but after firing a few insults at the assembled philistines, he raised the gavel. I couldn't bear it. 'One hundred and fifty,' I cried, more to galvanize the pack of unwitting poltroons into action than with any thought of buying it."[5] To her eternal dismay and disgust, Edna became its next owner for $150. She couldn't bear to hang it in her own home and gave it to her daughter, Ilka. Six Hepplewhite carved mahogany chairs sold for a mere $630. A Ch'ien-lung black-and-gold screen made a ludicrous $410. The sum total of Condé's worldly possessions—fine furniture, paintings, silver, porcelain—fetched a derisory $101,362.[6] They were worth more than twenty times that amount.[*] Thanks to Natica, "Big Leslie" was given some of the furniture that Natica was able to procure at the auction. It remains to this day at the home of Condé's daughter Leslie.[7]

Sands Point was gone, so all that remained was the apartment itself. And yet it stayed empty. To think of its ballroom, with the French parquet floor fitted to order by French artisans, opening out onto its wide and long terrace; its lavish furniture; its famous Chinese wallpaper so adored by his daughter Leslie, standing empty for "quite a few years" beggars belief. And while it stood empty, Natica and her husband, Gerald, moved with their family to a much more "ordinary" apartment in the same building when Jeremy was about ten years old. Natica, who was a painter, "was always looking for a studio space to work in." Arranging "with the building manager to rent an ordinary empty bedroom in the penthouse," Natica "happily set up her easel and canvases there. Sometimes," Jeremy recalled, "she asked me to pose for her, to be her model, and I loved it when she did. And that was how I ended up spending time in the penthouse!"

Whenever Jeremy was given a break from posing, Natica encouraged her daughter to "go explore the apartment. She said I

---

[*] His debts—all told, including taxes—amounted to more than an eye-watering $5 million.

could go anywhere I wanted! So much wood panelling and mar-
quetry! So many chandeliers! So many sconces! And there was a
little side staircase with a beautiful glossy railing entwined with
ivy and little flower buds. I put my hand out to catch my balance
on the railing and found myself touching just the regular wall . . .
my first introduction to trompe l'oeil painting!"

Like Leslie, Jeremy's "favorite place of all" was the ballroom
with its Chinese wallpaper and French parquet floorboards. She
remembers, "I would take off my shoes and socks and dance all
around, practicing my ballet pirouettes and jetés, my arabesques,
and my curtsies, all with great abandon!"[8]

The breathtaking apartment with its magnificent ballroom,
home to so many splendid revels since 1925, remained empty for
years. Eventually it had to be subdivided into the three apartments
as originally designed, before it could be sold.

By 1943 the danger of a Nazi invasion of Great Britain had passed.
Rex Benson was slated to return to the United Kingdom. Of course
the danger of attack from German U-boats remained a real threat,
so Leslie's children, including "Little Leslie," embarked from the
United States on a British warship in a large convoy. "It was arranged for the boys really. Rex and Leslie were great 'arrangers' of
things," Leslie remembers with a smile.[9] In fact the Royal Navy
ships that had been repaired in the United States were returning
home with a skeleton crew and a number of "special" British passengers. Thirteen-year-old boys (girls didn't count) were coming
home under a scheme to return them to the United Kingdom for
their secondary education. Somehow, Rex magically had Leslie—
the only American and a girl to boot—included among all the boys.
From 1943 the United Kingdom would become her home.

Patcévitch had quite a challenge ahead. His marriage to Nada
was over, so he was free to devote all his energies to the business.
Edna was delighted with Condé's choice. She knew that, despite

Wurzburg's expectations, Pat was the only option. He "had played an increasingly vital role in the management of the publications. He was as conversant as Condé—in some cases more so—with finance, labour problems, taxation—the whole host of functions that are part and parcel of running an enterprise with more than two thousand employees and varied and complex properties."[10]

For his part, Pat remained somewhat stunned. "It was funny," he told Edna, "the metaphor, I mean that occurred to me. I saw myself as one of those metal hoops that hold together a barrel; the staves were the complex organization our company had grown to be."[11] Pat became the glue, projecting a younger, brighter future while retaining the accumulated wisdom of his mentor. While he was no party giver in the same vein that Condé had been, he was "so glamorous" and gregarious, with a natural instinct for fun in any social situation. As one of New York's most attractive and eligible bachelors, he was not only inundated with invitations but aimed his sights high—for a time focusing on Marlene Dietrich.[12]

Some significant changes had been made shortly before Condé's death. Dr. Agha, who had become rather cantankerous, was asked to seek employment elsewhere. His successor, Alexander Liberman, slid into the role of art director, helping to guide editorial policy as if he were the only hand to fit the glove. As with Pat and Jessica Daves, Liberman possessed that unquantifiable and significant daring so needed to be a trendsetter rather than a follower. Although Edna had some knock-down, drag-out fights with Liberman, she acknowledged that he was a force to be reckoned with, particularly when he selected models who were "not *Vogue* material." Liberman said that what women looked like had changed, and "as journalists we should show them as they are, not as we think they should be."[13]

Despite the war and their new leadership, the publications prospered. Mary Campbell, dutifully made Pat's executive assistant, ensured that Condé's Leslies—big and small—were not forgotten, sending parcels of meat ("especially meat," Leslie Benson wrote) and whatever other delicacies Mary could lay her hands on.[14]

Vogue's coverage of the war continued just as Condé Nast had set out for the July 1, 1941, cover, "Vogue Women in Defense," showing a fashionable woman wearing a flight suit climbing into a biplane.

With the liberation of Paris in August 1944 came access to the French couturiers. Those who stayed in business had done so by agreeing to the Nazi edicts. Chanel, while not making clothes for the Nazis, had been an archcollaborator, and hightailed it for Switzerland until the dust settled—which in her case would be 1954. Surprisingly—shockingly, even—Chanel's collaboration with the enemy didn't make the American headlines. Instead it was her violation of the General Limitation Order, L-85, by the use of "Voluminous sleeves, widely flaring skirts, the heavy use of elaborate trimmings." The U.S. War Production Board (WPB), uninterested in true collaboration, held Chanel up as an example of extravagance, not understanding that by cutting fabric on the bias, less fabric could make clothes seem fuller. The WPB suggested, "It would be invaluable to the American fashion manufacturers if some restraint could be put upon the magazines, leading newspapers and wire services to keep them from showing Paris fashions which are in flagrant violation of our imposed wartime silhouette."[15] Edna thought their suggestion was laughable.

Liberation also brought long-awaited news of friends. "My first thought in our relief goes to our poor dear Condé," Michel de Brunhoff wrote, "who I am sure, would have been one of the first to be in Paris, which he loved so deeply." Then came the news of Tommy Kernan's arrest after he'd returned to France working for the Red Cross in 1941 to distribute milk to children. He had been interned for more than a year at Baden-Baden.

Solange and Jean d'Ayen's Paris home had been requisitioned by the occupiers. One evening her husband simply did not return from work. She sensed, rather than knew, he'd been arrested by the Germans. For months she went from prison to prison, asking if the parcel of food and clothing she carried could please be given to him. "At the time it was the only way to locate a missing person," Solange wrote. The packages were always refused, and Jean's name was not on any prisoner list. Six months later, a scared German soldier appeared on the doorstep of Jean's father's home, where the couple had been staying. He carried Jean's watch and a note written by Solange's husband. He *was* alive and being held at the top of a house in the avenue Foch.

Then came Solange's arrest and incarceration at the notorious Fresnes prison. No reason needed to be given. She never knew that her husband had been moved to Fresnes too. Eventually Jean d'Ayen was removed to Bergen-Belsen concentration camp, where he died of dysentery the day before it was liberated by the Allies in April 1945.

Their son, Maurice d'Ayen, aged nineteen, died two days after he had been cited for bravery in battle. Pascal de Brunhoff, son of Michel and also nineteen, fought in the maquis and was captured and shot by the Gestapo in a forest on June 10, 1944, four days after the D-day landings.[16] Like so many who survived World War II, Solange and Michel soldiered on. Michel cajoled and begged Pat that the only way to win was to resume publication of French *Vogue* immediately. Eventually Pat could only agree.

Mercifully, others escaped without any harm. Elsie, Lady Mendl, and her husband, Sir Charles, sat out the war in Los Angeles with Johnnie McMullin at their beck and call. Elsa Schiaparelli escaped on foot across to Spain and went on to Lisbon. When she arrived in New York, a newspaperman asked her about the brooch she was wearing. "It is a phoenix. . . . It is the symbol of France," she replied.[17]

As the horror of war and their personal losses receded, Pat steered a steady course, more often than not making Hollywood his main port of call. He was frequently seen at the homes of the Gary Coopers and the Jimmy Stewarts, all while pursuing Marlene Dietrich. Yet even then there were photographs of Pat with the woman he would marry in 1963, Chesbrough Lewis, the café-society beauty made even more famous by the stunning photographs of her by Horst and later Richard Avedon.[18] Another sleek brace of greyhounds. . . .

In 1947 Edna went to Europe for the first time since the war had begun. The fashion scene had a new name—Christian Dior and his "New Look," which flattered any figure with its cinched waist and ultra-full skirt. It was Carmel Snow, thriving at *Harper's Bazaar*, who dubbed Dior's genius as *his* "New Look," at his February 1947 show. It had been so long since Carmel's defection that Edna, and *Vogue*, had learned to take seeing her at fashion shows in their stride.

In England, Edna visited Lord Camrose and his wife at Hackwood Park, their late-seventeenth-century 260-acre home near Basingstoke.* Since tourists were allowed to bring foodstuffs worth fifty dollars into England, Edna, armed with baskets of food like Little Red Riding Hood, was an extra welcome guest. The Camroses were fortunate in being able to provide game from their estate, fish from their own river, and fruit and vegetables from their own garden. When Edna received a thank-you note from Camrose for the crock of British Cheddar cheese in brandy that she had *re*-imported, she was delighted to learn that "Winston [Churchill] came down for the weekend, and we both enjoyed the cheese enormously and send you our mutual thanks."[19]

Edna had soldiered on. As had Frank. Still, by the end of 1947, Frank's health was deteriorating rapidly. The doctors had operated on him in the hope of staving off his cancer, but their efforts had been unsuccessful. Helen Lawrenson, unaware of Frank's ill health, wrote to ask about a print of a Henri Rousseau painting she wanted to buy her husband. Although her details were sketchy, Frank knew at once that the print she wanted was of a Rousseau that hung in the Louvre, and no commercial print was available. That November,

---

* Hackwood Park was completed in 1687 by the fifth Marquess of Winchester, later Duke of Bolton. It has twenty-four bedrooms and twenty bathrooms. Berry bought the estate in 1936, and his son, Seymour, lived there until his death in 1995. The house was on the market in 2016 for £65 million.

Frank sent her a framed reproduction of Rousseau's *Passion in the Desert* (or *Sleeping Gypsy*), of a dark girl in the desert being eyed by a lion. Ever witty, ever Frank, he enclosed a note:

> *Dear Madame:*
> *I thought this might be of interest to you as a Rousseau*
> *collector. I happen to be the editor who arranged the sitting,*
> *chose the moon, the model, the ukulele and the feminine*
> *accessories. The scene is the Ladies Rest Room in the Condé*
> *Nast Publications. The recumbent lady is Helen Brown*
> *Norden. The male lion figure is Francis W. Crowninshield, a*
> *great admirer of this amorous passion in the desert. The*
> *picture shows the predatory old editor enthralled and*
> *intoxicated by the sleeping siren. Always admiringly, Frank.*
> *P.S. The editor's interest is indicated by his waving tail.*[20]

Frank died on December 28, aged seventy-five. With his death, Edna felt that a final light had been extinguished on laughter and kindness. It was increasingly a world she no longer wanted to understand. However, dedicated to the end, she hung on until the beginning of 1952, retiring as editor in chief. Jessica Daves inherited the helm, while Edna, never one to fully retire (especially since the death of her husband, Richard Newton, in July 1950), remained chairman of the editorial board.

With all the changes, Lord Camrose felt he had to make a gesture to Pat to remain dedicated and focused. In October 1952, a sweet deal was agreed giving Pat fifteen thousand shares in Condé Nast over the next ten years. When Camrose died in June 1954, aged seventy-four, his son John Seymour Berry continued to honor their agreement.[21]

In a speech Pat delivered on January 11, 1956, he said: "Just as in cooking and baking, it's the quality of the ingredients, their proportions and their blending that determine the result."[22] Through Condé's wise choice of successor, his empire had survived ten treacherous years.

35. A NEW HOUSE, A NEW EMPIRE

The joke goes like this: "Mitzi Newhouse asked her
husband Sam to buy her Vogue *while he was out.*
So he bought her the company."
—ANONYMOUS

W hen Cecil Harmsworth King, a nephew of both Lords
Northcliffe and Rothermere, offered to buy Amalgamated Press from the Berry family in 1958, Pat was put
on notice about a possible sale. He flew to London immediately to
meet King. Probably the most accurate statement (in a restrained
British way) would be to say that their encounter was unsuccessful. King owned the Daily Mirror Group, a mass tabloid publication. Pat thought King would have difficulty understanding the
ethos at Condé Nast Publications.

Pat had his long journey back to New York to ruminate. With
a brain that calculated facts and figures as fast as the early com-
puters, he recalled an obscure clause that Condé had insisted on
putting into the original agreement with Camrose. In the event of
a sale of Condé Nast or Amalgamated Press to a third party, the
company would have a six-month grace period to seek another
buyer, so long as it could meet the price of the original third party.
So he went on the hunt for a new owner.

On March 24, 1959, the business press was all abuzz. Mr. and
Mrs. S. I. Newhouse were buying a majority stake in the shares of
Condé Nast for approximately five million dollars. Pat insisted that
the press release also say that Mr. and Mrs. Newhouse were merely
taking a stake in the company as private investors and would be

invited to take seats on the board. To scupper any harmful rumors, Pat also said that there would be no changes at Condé Nast.

It was the Newhouse family's first foray into magazine publishing. Eventually they would become the sole shareholder, delisting Condé Nast Publications from the New York Stock Exchange. At the time of the acquisition Condé Nast was showing losses in excess of $255,000 on approximately $20 million in sales. The Newhouses' company, Advance Publications, already owned fourteen newspapers and television and radio stations valued at something like $200 million. In case anyone wanted to know why the Newhouses were making such an unusual purchase, *The New York Times* added that Mitzi Newhouse was a graduate of Parsons School of Design in New York and had studied fashion, home furnishings, and design in Europe. Hence the joke about her husband, known as Sam, buying her the company rather than the latest issue of *Vogue*. But, it was no joke. It was already crystal clear that the Newhouses were expert at buying distressed properties and making them profitable.[1] They were, and are, a family rich in economic traditions. While he was at the helm, Sam ruled with a velvet fist.[2] And he bettered the predictions.

Since that time there have been three generations of Newhouses, including cousin Jonathan, at the enhanced Condé Nast, which comprises the titles *The New Yorker*, *Condé Nast Traveler*, *Tatler*, *Allure*, *Architectural Digest*, *Wired*, *Brides*, *Bon Appétit*, *Golf Digest*, *World of Interiors*, *Men's Vogue*, *Teen Vogue*, and the revived *Vanity Fair*. The company has grown, retrenched, and grown again. The printing plant, a monument to the man who gave it his name, closed in 1964. Its valuable land in Greenwich, Connecticut, was sold, and three hundred dedicated employees had to find other jobs. Patcévitch announced Jessica Daves's retirement at the end of 1962. And so began the outrageously fashionable and funky new era of *Vogue* under the irrepressible *jolie-laide** Diana Vreeland—

---

* *Jolie-laide* literally means "pretty-ugly."

theoretically poached from *Harper's Bazaar*. Actually, she left *Bazaar* when Carmel was forced out of her editor's chair and Diana was passed over to take her place. "Was my name mentioned?" she asked Carmel back then. No, came the reply. What Carmel didn't say was that she urged the men running Hearst magazines *not* to consider her. Diana lacked discipline, judgment, and a strong work ethic, and was always late for everything, Carmel said.[3]

That may be, but *boy*, she had a sense of humor! Who else would open her autobiography: "I loathe nostalgia. One night at dinner . . . at the Oscar de la Rentas, Swifty Lazar, the literary agent, turned to me and said, 'The problem with you dollface'—that's what he always called me—'is that your whole world is nostalgic.' 'Listen Swifty,' I said, 'we all have our own ways of making a living, so shut up!' Then I punched him in the nose."[4]

Diana, later let go by *Vogue*, would say that the company was never good at "letting people go." Much the same could be said of most large corporations. What had really changed was the atmosphere of "the family" at work, so cultivated by Condé Nast during his lifetime. Nowhere did this prove more poignant than with the aging Margaret Case. Apparently they tried to get rid of her nicely, but in the end "the moving men came in and moved the desk she'd sat at for forty or fifty years." Soon after, Margaret Case jumped from her sixteenth-floor apartment window, neatly dressed in a raincoat fastened, belt tied, a neat little handkerchief, and a pair of slacks—you don't want to jump from a tall building in a skirt, Diana said.[5]

Particularly demanding—who wouldn't be as editor in chief of *Vogue?*—and at times off the wall, Diana also remained true to her friends, notably the photographer Richard Avedon, who followed her when she defected from *Harper's Bazaar*. While Avedon also established his own studio, his work at *Vogue* outshone all others. Even under Diana's successor, Grace Mirabella, Avedon's work appeared as covers for *Vogue* more often than not from 1973 to 1988. (Diana had landed on her feet at the Metropolitan Museum of Art in its Costume Institute.) By then Sam Newhouse's son, Si, was breathing fresh air into the flagging fortunes at American *Vogue*.

In 1963 Pat married the former Chesbrough Lewis, becoming her fourth husband.* Her daughter, Chessy Rayner, famous for her exotic beauty and lion's mane of hair, was one of the most photographed women in 1960s New York. Both mother and daughter were stunning and stylish, repeatedly modeling for Horst and Avedon. Chessy was also *Vogue*'s fashion editor from 1956 until 1964, when "the bubble" came "off the champagne" according to her husband, William Rayner. Chessy was exasperated "under her dictatorial boss, Diana Vreeland" and went in search of "less ephemeral and more creative" work, settling on interior decoration. Chesbrough Patcévitch's son, Charles Minot Amory, also worked for Condé Nast while Pat was its chairman.[6]

Pat retired in 1971.[7] In January 1976, *Business Week* declared Advance Publications "America's Most Profitable Publisher," picturing Sam and his two sons on its cover. "Seat of the Pants Management that Works" was how their formula for success was described.[8] Alex Liberman—the same art director who replaced Dr. Agha in the final days of Condé's leadership—had become the Newhouses' trusted "Silver Fox" who interpreted for, educated, and was trusted by Si. Due to their special relationship, Liberman wielded a power akin to Pat's own during his tenure. Liberman, too, was a Russian émigré who had begun his publishing career under Lucien Vogel in 1933 at Vogel's Paris-based magazine, *Vu*. He escaped from occupied France in 1941 with his second wife, Tatiana Yacovleva du Plessix, who was Jewish, and began working for *Vogue* on Vogel's recommendation.

By the time Liberman became editorial director for all Condé Nast magazines in 1962, including *Vogue*, he was Si Newhouse's

---

* Pat died in 1993 at the age of ninety-two. Chesbrough Patcévitch also lived to ninety-two, dying in 2005; they were married for 30 years. Chessy Rayner died of lung cancer in 1998, aged only sixty-six.

mentor and friend.[9] Eventually Alex Liberman would become deputy editorial chairman for Condé Nast United States and Europe from 1994 until his death, aged eighty-seven, in 1999. "No man in the Western world held more power over the fashion images of men and women than Liberman," *The New York Times* said. More than likely it was Liberman who engineered Vreeland's departure and Grace Mirabella's takeover as editor of *Vogue* in 1971, since he was determined to replace Vreeland's hauteur with a freedom and informality more befitting America. That meant that there would be "No more Ophelias dancing through the Plaza at dawn."[10]

In 1979, the year Sam Newhouse died, Si and his younger brother, Donald, bought Random House. After making myriad adjustments and changes—which some criticized as caring only about the bottom line rather than publishing great books—the brothers sold it again in 1998 to Bertelsmann of Germany. When asked why by *Publishers Weekly*, Si Newhouse replied:

> We are a family business, privately owned. The most important strategic goal we set for ourselves is to remain as a private business with all the advantages and disadvantages that entails. We are now in a transition period. My father founded the company and he died in 1979, I am 70, my brother is close to that age, and we have a third generation coming along.... This was originally a newspaper company and at its heart, it remains one. The magazines are the second major area, with cable interests next. We have also added business journals as part of the newspaper business. We arrived at the decision over the course of 1997 to sell the book publishing company if the right opportunity came along.[11]

Long before the sale of Random House, Si had been busy building their magazine empire under the umbrella of Condé Nast Publications. The name carried more than goodwill: It carried class. Millions of dollars later, it was a stunning achievement, thanks in no small part to Alex Liberman. He knew how Condé Nast and Frank Crowninshield had lamented the passing of *Vanity Fair* in March 1936. Si recalled: "It started with a conversation between Alex and me. We had a standing Thursday lunch at the Four Seasons, and Alex or I mentioned that we had abandoned *Vanity Fair*." It was Liberman who said: "It had always been the dream of this company to start *Vanity Fair* again."[12]

So they began discussing the possibility of reviving the title— in some ways as an alternative read to *The New Yorker*. After all, Liberman knew Si idolized and coveted *The New Yorker*. Like any good businessman, Si might have thought a little competition for *The New Yorker* would be no bad thing . . . maybe his long-hoped-for prize could fall into his lap if sales started flagging? Maybe Si could own both *Vanity Fair* and *The New Yorker* one day.

In 1981 the *Vanity Fair* project was reborn amid a fanfare of publicity, with many nodding sagely, giving credit to Si for spotting this languishing jewel in Condé Nast's Aladdin's cave. Clare Boothe Luce was contacted for a statement: "I do wish the new magazine could be as wonderful as the old," she said, "but I don't see how it can." Advance peeps from *Newsweek* and *New York* magazine weighed in, criticizing the new *Vanity Fair*'s editorial focus and its "aggressively ugly" look.[13]

Richard Locke was its first editor—a forty-year-old who had previously been the deputy editor of *The New York Times Book Review*. Truman Capote was drafted as its gossip columnist, and advertisers eagerly followed. Its first issue had articles by Nora Ephron, Gore Vidal, and Gabriel Gárcia Márquez with art and photographs by Richard Avedon, Irving Penn, and Andy Warhol. Liberman answered the critics about his choice of an untested magazine editor by saying, "We take risks;" but Locke lasted only three issues.[14] His *Vanity Fair* saw once-keen advertisers racing for the exit. The magazine was too intellectual, everyone agreed.

Leo Lerman, an old-hand features editor at *Vogue*, replaced him. Cut from the same cloth as Frank Crowninshield, Lerman was the man whom Leonard Bernstein, Gloria Steinem, Norman Mailer, Bob Fosse, Carol Channing, Jacqueline Kennedy Onassis, Joseph Heller, and Henry Kissinger simply had to have on their dinner guest lists. But still, the oomph Newhouse and Liberman were looking for just wasn't there, even after two years. Nevertheless no one was more shocked than Tina Brown—at the time languishing at *Tatler* in London and looking for a change—when she received a phone call from Liberman to come talk turkey about her taking over from Lerman.[15]

The age of celebrity had already been born. *Rolling Stone* and *People* were cashing in, and others followed. Tina Brown had her work cut out for her. She first joined *Vanity Fair* as a consultant on Lerman's watch in 1983; on January 4, 1984, Si wrote a staff memo congratulating him on a stunning job. "And also, effective immediately," the memo continued, "I have appointed a remarkable young journalist, Tina Brown, as Editor-in-Chief at *Vanity Fair*."[16] Frankly Lerman was happy to be relieved of the burden. All critical eyes were on the revised publication, comparing it unfavorably to the original.

Tina knew how to handle older men like Liberman and Newhouse. After all, her husband, Harold Evans, the former editor of London's *Sunday Times*, was her senior by some twenty-five years. Somehow it was good karma that they had been married at the home of Frank Crowninshield's nephew Ben Bradlee, the famous executive editor of *The Washington Post* during the Watergate scandal.

Tina had a few early hiccups, including Si's complaint about the title leaching money. Despite her vocal critics, she turned *Vanity Fair* into one of the hottest, slickest, page-turning magazines on American newsstands. She hired the best writers, photographers—anyone whom she felt could make a difference—for top money, and managed to keep both Liberman and Newhouse at bay. The gamble paid off. "We were baffled, struggling to get the right combination of people. . . . *Vanity Fair* was waiting for the right editor," Newhouse said, "and from the time she came in, it was clear she was capable of taking the *Vanity Fair* idea and updating and restating it."[17]

At long last, in 1985, the pens of the publishing world fizzed when Advance Publications purchased *The New Yorker* outright, delisting the company. The magazine's common stock was bought for $200 a share, or $142 million. The acquisition came on the heels of Advance buying a 17 percent stake in *The New Yorker* for approximately $25 million on January 2 that same year.[18] When Advance took over, adding the title to the Condé Nast stable, the magazine's earnings were only $6 million. Naturally changes were made, and its long-serving and respected editor, William Shawn, who had replaced Harold Ross in 1951, lasted only until 1987. Robert Gottlieb, formerly a top editor at both Simon & Schuster and Alfred A. Knopf, took over. He brought in the likes of Salman Rushdie, Saul Bellow, Antonia Fraser, John Updike, John Cheever, and John le Carré.

The following year Brown's husband, Harold Evans, founded *Condé Nast Traveler*, dedicated to "truth in travel." Condé Nast Publications was expanding rapidly, but Brown's luck was about to change.

In 1992 Brown became editor in chief of *The New Yorker*,* some claiming that she'd been ousted by the sheer genius of the rising megastar, E. Graydon Carter, *Vanity Fair*'s new top dog. For the next twenty-five years, longer than Frank Crowninshield was at the helm, Carter led *Vanity Fair* from strength to strength—making its post-Oscars party the toast and envy of every A-lister in the world. Condé would have been proud.

It was rumored that Carter tried to buy *Vanity Fair* shortly before he resigned in 2017—not wanting to cut costs again and fire the team he had so painstakingly put together. While he didn't succeed in snaring the publication, he did acquire the International

---

* She resigned in 1998.

Best Dressed List from the Newhouse family. In June 2018 the *New York Post* printed the rumor that he would soon be starting up his own publishing company.[19]

During the expansion of Condé Nast Publications under the New-houses, Grace Mirabella did much to revive the *Vogue*'s fortunes by refocusing on women's concerns. Remarkably, after thirty-six years at *Vogue*, seventeen of which she was editor in chief, she learned about her firing on television. The gossip columnist Liz Smith's *Live at Five* broadcast on NBC broke the news on June 28, 1988, naming Anna Wintour, the British-born editor of *House & Garden* (who'd been in her position for a year), as *Vogue*'s new editor in chief. "I think you can't fault a company for wanting a change. That's natural," Mirabella later told the press, "but how it was done—for a stylish company—is kind of tacky."[20] Anna Wintour has become synonymous with fashion and *Vogue* around the world. She began her career at Condé Nast as the editor of British *Vogue*. In short order she was brought to New York only a year later to turn around *House & Garden*, whose sales were lagging behind *Architectural Digest*'s. Ten months later Mirabella was unceremoniously out, and today Wintour still leads *Vogue*. She renewed the magazine's focus on fashion, keeping it as the market leader above *Harper's Bazaar* and *Elle*. That said, like Edna Woolman Chase, any potential successors she might groom to replace her on retirement, are thin on the ground. She is the fashion industry's main power broker—just like Edna and Carmen in their day—and also a fashion icon, even for nonfashionistas. The best-selling novel and film *The Devil Wears Prada* is allegedly a "composite portrayal" of Wintour and other fashion editors. Wintour reportedly said she always enjoyed a good read, but wasn't sure she'd have time to read the book written by her former assistant, Lauren Weisberger.

In 2013 Wintour became artistic director of all Condé Nast magazines, and in 2017 she was created a Dame Commander of the British Empire at Buckingham Palace. Seemingly, twenty years into the job—like Edna Woolman Chase—retirement is not something for Wintour to contemplate. Or is it?

Si Newhouse died in 2017, shortly before Graydon Carter resigned as editor in chief of *Vanity Fair*. Times are changing again, but Advance remains devoted to the bottom line—even if that means restructuring and losing valued staff. At the beginning of 2018, Condé Nast Publications comprised some fourteen magazines and eight digital publications. *Vogue* is published in twenty-four different countries, celebrating their individual "drama of life," such as the time-capsule one-hundredth anniversary issue of British *Vogue* featuring the Duchess of Cambridge on its cover—her first magazine photo shoot. While it is hard to maintain the "close-knit family" relationship from Condé's days across such far-flung territories, *Vogue* triumphs as a worldwide iconic brand that absolutely everyone knows.

And yet, press article after press article continues to indicate financial woes at the publishing company, and that it is "rumored" to be for sale. The ax has fallen many times on so very many jobs to cut costs, as newsstand magazine sales everywhere flag. Editors have come and gone, but Condé Nast still remains. The third generation of the Newhouse family is firmly in place. The latest buyer of the publishing empire is said to be Apple. Rumor or truth? The times we live in perpetually change, and nowhere do they shift faster than the fashion industry. That said, *Vogue* remains . . . more than a hundred years at the top of its game.

And so Condé Nast rumbles on. From strength to strength, one would hope. More than eighty years ago Condé Nast, the man, sat on his terrace at 1040 Park Avenue talking to a friend, then sighed, lamenting his parlous financial position: "I used to own all this," he said.

Yes, he certainly did.

CODA

Much has been made of the Newhouse management style, and its editors' alleged off-camera battles and wars. Even in Condé Nast's time, when the company's future was certainly the bleakest, editors were critical, muscular, even pugnacious in their relationships. Naysayers believed Condé's magazines would die before the man. Indeed, the death of Condé Nast Publications has been predicted almost since its inception by adversaries or publishers like William Randolph Hearst, or disgruntled former employees, wishing its magazines all manner of dire fates. Life is unfair that way.

One journalist even wrote: "What the American people have to realize is that *Vogue* magazine, which only a few years ago was very real, is now only a temporary illusion. A year, two years, five years, ten. Absolutely certainly no more."

Vogue's editor gave a swift rebuttal. "I see that you have with one stroke of your pen, condemned *Vogue* to death along with the whole fashion industry which, in our country, ranks third in the billion-dollar classifications. Along with them"—she paused for breath—"you have also, apparently, cast into oblivion that large group of people who build beautiful houses, buy fine art, patronize the opera, theatres and concerts, contribute their time and money to numerous charities, and add greatly to the amenities and the preservation of the art of civilized living."

In addition: "There are, today, thousands of manufacturers, designers, and merchants who depend upon the knowledge, the taste, and the integrity of *Vogue* for correct information and guidance in businesses that are dependent upon the element of fashion." Predictions of the future are often wrong. The editor who rebuffed her critic was Edna Woolman Chase; the year, 1940.

Clare Boothe Luce, better known as Clare Brokaw when she worked for Condé Nast, went on to fulfill her dreams—marrying a very wealthy and powerful man in Henry Luce, becoming a political activist, a congresswoman from Connecticut, and America's first woman ambassador to Italy. Thanks to Condé's foresight in protecting the title of *Vanity Fair*, it lived to be resurrected in the Newhouse era.

Vogue was hurt, but only momentarily, by Beaton's anti-Semitic doodles. Even Beaton's career recovered by the 1950s and beyond (thanks in no small part to the Royal Family) on the pages of *Vogue*. He went on to win an Oscar for his costume designs for the film *My Fair Lady*, starring Audrey Hepburn as Eliza Doolittle. Carmel Snow, so unforgiven by Condé, became one of the most important women in the world of fashion—even if she had to contend with a more difficult man than Condé in William Randolph Hearst.

That *Vogue* and *House & Garden* survived Condé's death is remarkable. It was due to the unswerving belief of Lord Camrose in his investment and the dedication of Edna Woolman Chase, Iva Patcévitch, and their staffs internationally. The Newhouse era is another successful chapter. It's one that Alexandra Shulman, the former editor in chief of British *Vogue* for twenty-five years, feels Condé Nast would be personally proud to have seen. None of us has a crystal ball. Maybe Advance will sell Condé Nast Publications, or maybe not. Prophecies of success or failure are tricky things. But after more than one hundred years in print, my bet is always on *Vogue*.

AUTHOR'S NOTE AND ACKNOWLEDGMENTS

After writing two biographies about people of questionable moral-ity, Hildebrand Gurlitt (*Hitler's Art Thief*) and Florence Gould (*A Dangerous Woman*), I wanted to write about an unsung hero who helped to modernize America and bring an unrivaled elegance to the world in the first half of the twentieth century. The last biog-raphy of Condé Nast, *The Man Who Was Vogue* (1982), by Caro-line Seebohm—a lovely portrait of the man—is also the *only* biography of this influential publisher. Unlike Nast's nemesis and owner of *Harper's Bazaar*, William Randolph Hearst, who has in excess of eighteen biographies published about him, I felt (as did my editor and publisher) that it was time to write a second biogra-phy of Condé Montrose Nast. Sadly, no one has written a book about Hearst's magazines, which would perhaps have made my job in writing about the rivalry between Condé and Hearst more even-handed.

Condé began his career with little more than the shirt on his back. He nearly lost that shirt and his empire in the Crash of 1929, but despite the odds—and thanks to the dedication of staff in Brit-ain, France, and the United States (his French staffers were in exile at the time of his death, having ceased publication under the Nazi occupation) and a substantial cash injection from Lord Cam-rose, the British publishing giant—Condé Nast lived on. In one of the industry obituaries (in the British journal *Scope*) written shortly after Nast's death, the writer concluded, "Imperceptibly the studied elegance of his publications *Vogue, Vanity Fair* and *House & Garden* did for advertising, packaging, display, and merchandising what it had done for printing. . . . Before [Condé Nast] it was taken for granted that elegance and design were the privileges of a very small circle. It is not an exaggeration to say that his influence indirectly extended to Woolworth's." Who would have thought?

Edna Woolman Chase became Condé's self-appointed chronicler with her *Always in Vogue*. It was nonetheless written with the benefit of twenty-twenty hindsight and made her the hero of the story. She was undoubtedly crucial to Vogue's success, and while I rely heavily on her, I treat her as a chronicler—highly knowledgeable, but not 100 percent reliable. The Condé Nast Archives, which sadly hold no material prior to 1922, other archival material, books, family remembrances, and private letters tell a fuller story.

I owe a debt of thanks to a number of individuals and institutions for their assistance in researching this book. First and foremost, naturally, is Condé Nast Publications. Without the expertise of especially Marianne Brown, and also Samantha Vuignier and Gretchen Fenston of the Condé Nast Archives in New York, this book simply would not have been possible. To Condé Nast Publications' David Byars, Cynthia Cathcart, Chris Donnellan, Joe Libonati, Miranda Muscente, Mitchell Owens, Ivan Shaw, and Shelley Wenger, my most sincere thanks. At the Oakland House Museum, the former family home of Condé Nast's maternal grandfather, Louis A. Benoist, I thank Charlie Brown and Jean McDaniel. I am extremely grateful to members of Condé Nast's extended family: Lady Leslie Bonham Carter (Condé's younger daughter); Jane Bonham Carter (Condé's granddaughter and Lady Leslie Bonham Carter's daughter); David Benson; Matthew Benson; Robin Benson; Jeremy Warburg Russo (Condé's granddaughter and Natica and Gerald Warburg's daughter); Condée Nast Russo (Condé's great-granddaughter and Natica and Gerald Warburg's granddaughter); and Alexander William Warburg Russo (Condé's great-grandson and Natica and Gerald Warburg's grandson). Julia Amory kindly shared family memories and photographs of Iva Patcévitch. Others to whom I am indebted are former Condé Nast editors Tina Brown and Alexandra Shulman. I would like to thank Dr. Amanda Foreman, Cynthia Hochswender, and Adrian Tinniswood, too, for their help. To my agent, Alexander C. Hoyt, and my editor at St. Martin's Press, Charles Spicer, and his assistants, Sarah Grill and April Osborn, and my copyeditor, Sue Llewellyn, thank you. Others who were helpful to me were Alexander Balerdi, Marjorie Bliss, Kate Butterworth, Pamela Head, Guy and Lucie Hiscock, Charlotte and Steve Sass, Bruce Weiner, Natasha and Rich Weston, and Jan and Dr. Phil Zakowski. I especially appreciate the medical advice Dr. Zakowski provided from Johns Hopkins Hospital, concerning Condé's health issues.

Above all, I hope that you, the reader, enjoy the book and will be pleased to discover more about Condé Montrose Nast, his life, his associates, his empire, and his times. As always, any errors are my own.

Susan Ronald

DRAMATIS PERSONAE

(In alphabetical order, except for three main personalities below).

CONDÉ MONTROSE NAST (1873–1942)—Pioneering American magazine publisher of *Vogue, Vanity Fair, House & Garden, American Golfer,* and *Glamour.*

EDNA WOOLMAN CHASE (1877–1957)—American editor in chief of *Vogue* from 1914 to 1952.

FRANCIS WELCH CROWNINSHIELD (1872–1947), ALSO KNOWN AS "CROWNIE" AND FRANK—American editor in chief of *Vanity Fair* from 1914 to 1936.

FAMILY

LOUIS A. BENOIST—Condé's maternal grandfather, a founder of the St. Louis Philharmonic Society and owner of the first private bank in St. Louis.

LESLIE NAST BENSON, NÉE FOSTER—Second wife of Condé Nast. She was only twenty-one when they married in December 1928.

ALBERT JULIUS NAST—William's younger brother by six years, Condé's pious Methodist uncle.

CHARLES COUDERT NAST—Condé's and Clarisse's son. A lawyer by training, he became a general in the Forty-Second Division of the New York National Guard. He was also a partner in the law firm representing Condé Nast Publications.

ESTELLE JOSEPHINE NAST—Condé's older sister by two years.

ESTHER ARIADNE BENOIST NAST—Condé's indomitable mother, whom Condé adored.

ESTHER ETHEL NAST—called Ethel by the family. Condé's younger sister by three years.

FRANZESKA WILHELMINA "FANNY" NAST GAMBLE—Condé's aunt who married into the "soap" family of William A. Gamble, co-founder of Procter & Gamble.

JEANNE CLARISSE COUDERT NAST—society woman who had aspirations to become a famous soprano. She married Condé in 1902, and always claimed that her family name had elevated him into society. The couple separated in 1919 and were divorced in 1925.

JOSEPHINE PULTE NAST—younger sister by two years of William Nast. Aunt of Condé who was unhappily married to Dr. William Andrews.

LESLIE NAST—Condé's younger daughter, born in 1930. She lived with her father after the divorce until shortly before his death. Her first husband and father of her daughter, Laura, was Peter St. Just. She is the widow of Mark Bonham Carter, son of Sir Maurice and Lady Violet Bonham Carter, and the mother of four adult daughters.

LOUIS NAST—Condé's older brother by five years. He lived almost all his adult life in Paris and earned his living as a concert pianist.

MARGARET ELIZA MCDOWELL NAST—Condé's paternal grandmother. Condé's ne'er-do-well father was her favorite child.

MARGARITE NATICA NAST—Condé's daughter with Clarisse. She became an acclaimed artist and mother of daughter, Jeremy, and son, Jonathan.

PETER NAST—Coudert Nast's only child, Condé and Clarisse's grandson. He was the same age as Condé's youngest daughter, Leslie. In 1958, as First Lieutenant Nast serving in his father's Forty-Second Division of the New York National Guard, Peter died, aged twenty-eight, in a plane crash while on a routine training run. He had five children.

WILHELM NAST—Condé's paternal grandfather. He was deemed the Father of German-American Methodism.

WILLIAM FREDERICK NAST—Condé's father. He briefly served as American consul to Stuttgart, Germany, the birthplace of his father, Wilhelm, before he was forced to resign for improprieties.

GERALD WARBURG—Natica's husband. He was a famous cellist and patron of the arts. His father was Felix M. Warburg of the Warburg banking family, and his mother was Frieda Schiff, daughter of the railroad financier Jacob Schiff.

GEORGE BEY—Condé's chauffeur and valet who, like "Dicky" below, was more a member of the family than a household employee.

CORA JANE RICHARDS, "DICKY"—While not properly "family," was treated as such. She was originally employed by Condé as a nurse to help Clarisse, who suffered from a phantom instability similar to the one that had haunted her own mother.

VOGUE STAFF MENTIONED

DR. MEHEMED FEHMY AGHA—Originally art director at German *Vogue*, he became art director for all *Vogues* and *Vanity Fair* in 1929.

BARRETT ANDREWS—First advertising manager and stockholder at Condé's *Vogue*.

RICHARD AVEDON—Photographer for *Vogue* and *Vanity Fair* who followed Diana Vreeland from *Harper's Bazaar*.

BETTINA BALLARD—Fashion editor at *Vogue* and author of the book, *In My Fashion*.

CECIL BEATON—Innovative British illustrator, photographer, and writer for both *Vogue* and *Vanity Fair*.

HORST PAUL ALBERT BOHRMANN, "HORST"—Top *Vogue* photographer in the 1930s and lover of George Hoyningen Huene.

HEYWORTH CAMPBELL—First art director hired by Condé Nast.

MARY CAMPBELL—Former physical education teacher who went to work for Condé Nast Publications in the 1920s as Condé's secretary. She became his assistant in his later years, keeping the secret of his ill health at the end of his life.

ELSPETH CHAMPCOMMUNAL—First editor of British *Vogue*.

BILL DAVENPORT—British *Vogue*'s advertising manager until 1936.

JESSICA DAVES—Managing editor of *Vogue* from 1932 until 1952. She took over as editor in chief of the magazine on Edna Woolman Chase's retirement.

BARON ADOLPH DE MEYER—French photographer for *Vogue* since 1913. He defected to *Harper's Bazaar* in the 1920s, regretted it, but was not given his job back.

DR. H. L. HAMMERBACHER—Managing director of German *Vogue*.

MARIE HARRISON—Second editor of *Vogue* and sister of Arthur Turnure, its founder. After Turnure's death in 1906, it was she who sold the family interest in the title to Condé Nast, while remaining editor of the magazine.

BARON GEORGE HOYNINGEN-HUENE, KNOWN AS HUENE—Seminal fashion photographer for *Vogue* in the 1920s and 1930s.

ALBERT LEE—Condé's assistant at *Vogue* and *Vanity Fair* until 1919. Afterward he was employed as the administrative head of British *Vogue* until the arrival of Harry Yoxall in 1923.

ALEXANDER LIBERMAN—Art director, editorial director for all Condé Nast magazines in 1962; then deputy chairman of editorial in Europe and the United States from 1994 until his death in 1999. Known as the "Silver Fox" he was said to have great influence with Si Newhouse, chairman of Condé Nast Publications from 1975.

WALTER MAAS—British head of Dorland Agency in France, Condé Nast's advertising agency in Europe. Dorland overlapped significantly with Nast's in-house team, and Condé held a stake in Dorland. With the outbreak of World War II, Condé helped bring Maas to safety in Canada.

MAINBOCHER, NÉ MAIN BOCHER—Chicagoan and once-frustrated opera singer who turned to illustration and fashion editing. He was the fashion editor of French *Vogue* until 1929, when he left to become a fashion designer and combined his first and last names into one. His most noted clothes were Wallis Simpson's wedding dress and trousseau.

THERON MCCAMPBELL—Began work for Condé at the Home Pattern Company in 1905 as his manager. He was Condé's first trusted finance man, following him to *Vogue* as its treasurer when Condé acquired the title.

FRANCES MCFADDEN—Managing editor of *Vogue* under Carmel Snow. She left *Vogue* for *Harper's Bazaar* when Carmel did in 1932, and later became managing editor at *Harper's Bazaar*.

JOHNNIE MCMULLIN—Humorous *Vogue* and *Vanity Fair* columnist on social affairs. He left *Vogue* to live with his good friend Elsie, Lady Mendl, and her husband to look after Elsie in her dotage.

HARRY MCVICKAR—Great-grandson of the American artist Stephen Whitney, Arthur Turnure's partner and first art director and illustrator of *Vogue*. He helped procure 250 names from New York's *Social Register* to fund the title.

GRACE MIRABELLA—American editor in chief of *Vogue* between 1971 and 1988. She replaced Diana Vreeland and was succeeded by Anna Wintour.

PHILIPPE ORTIZ—Condé's main negotiator with France. Previously he had worked for the French publishers, Braun et Compagnie in New York.

IRVING PENN—Acclaimed American photographer who came to *Vogue* after Condé Nast's death.

CHESSY RAYNER—Great beauty and socialite, formerly with *Ladies' Home Journal*, then *Glamour*, before becoming fashion editor of *Vogue*. She was the stepdaughter of Iva Patcévitch.

JOSEPHINE REDDING—The first editor of *Vogue* under publisher Arthur Turnure. Remembered as the unstylish wearer of sensible shoes and large hats, as well as a great lover of animals, she is credited with coming up with the title name *Vogue*.

LAURENCE SCHNEIDER—International advertising manager for *Vogue*, based in London but handling both the British and French titles, initially alongside the Dorland Agency, prior to World War II.

ALISON SETTLE—British *Vogue* editor from 1926 to 1935. She was a highly respected fashion journalist whose career spanned five decades. From 1937 until her retirement in 1960, she was the fashion editor for London's *Observer*.

CARMEL SNOW, NÉE WHITE—Fashion editor, then managing editor of *Vogue* until she defected in 1932 to *Harper's Bazaar*.

EDWARD STEICHEN—Head photographer for *Vogue* and *Vanity Fair* who was groundbreaking in his approach. He believed that photography was the only true mirror of his times.

DOROTHY TODD—Second editor of British *Vogue*, who promoted the values and writings of the Bloomsbury Set throughout her tenure.

ARTHUR BALDWIN TURNURE—Founding publisher of *Vogue*. Prior titles he began were *Art Age*, followed by *Art Exchange*. He sold these and became art director at Harper & Brothers. There Turnure was responsible for the first richly illustrated edition of *Ben-Hur*.

COSETTE VOGEL—First editor of French *Vogue*. Her brother was a children's book author and creator of *Babar*.

LUCIEN VOGEL—Husband of Cosette, a magazine editor and publisher of *Gazette du Bon Ton* and *Vu* in France.

DIANA VREELAND—Noted fashion journalist and fashion editor at *Harper's Bazaar* before becoming editor in chief at *Vogue* from 1963 to 1971.

ANNA WINTOUR, DBE—British-American journalist and editor. She has been the editor in chief of *Vogue* since 1988, and the artistic director of Condé Nast Publications since 2013.

AUDREY WITHERS, OBE—From 1931 at British *Vogue*, promoted to editor in chief by Harry Yoxall in 1940.

WILLIAM WOOD—First marketing director at British *Vogue*.

FRANCIS "LEW" WURZBURG—American administrative chief and vice president of Condé Nast Publications.

HARRY W. YOXALL—British administrative head of British *Vogue* and author of *A Fashion of Life*.

VANITY FAIR STAFF MENTIONED

ROBERT BENCHLEY—Writer, actor, and managing editor of *Vanity Fair* between 1918 and 1920.

CLARE BROKAW (NÉE BOOTHE, LATER LUCE)—Author, playwright, and managing editor of *Vanity Fair* between 1932 and 1933.

HELEN BROWN NORDEN—American journalist and author, former editor of *Vanity Fair* and lover of Condé.

TINA BROWN, CBE—British author and journalist and former editor of *Vanity Fair* and *The New Yorker* for Advance Publications.

TRUMAN CAPOTE—First gossip columnist at the revived *Vanity Fair*.

GRAYDON CARTER—Canadian author and journalist, former editor of *Vanity Fair* for twenty-five years for Advance Publications.

COREY FORD (AKA JOHN RIDDELL)—American author, screenwriter, and staff humorist at *Vanity Fair*.

PAUL GALLICO—American syndicated sports columnist and staff sportswriter for *Vanity Fair*.

ALDOUS HUXLEY—British novelist, writer, and philosopher; on staff at *Vanity Fair*.

LEO LERMAN—Former features editor at *Vogue* who replaced Locke as *Vanity Fair*'s second editor. He was succeeded by Tina Brown.

RICHARD LOCKE—First editor of the revived *Vanity Fair* in February 1983. The forty-year-old had previously been deputy editor of *The New York Times Book Review*.

ELIZABETH "LEE" MILLER—American-born supermodel and war photographer for *Vogue*.

DOROTHY PARKER—American wit and writer. Staff drama critic for *Vanity Fair* from 1916 to 1920. High priestess of the Algonquin Round Table.

GEORGE JEAN NATHAN—Satirist, literary and drama critic for *The Smart Set*, becoming *Vanity Fair* drama critic after P. G. Wodehouse left.

ROBERT SHERWOOD—American playwright and writer. Editor at *Vanity Fair* from 1919 to 1920.

EDNA ST. VINCENT MILLAY (WRITING AS NANCY BOYD)—American Pulitzer Prize–winning poet who was also a staff writer at *Vanity Fair*.

P. G. "PLUM" WOODHOUSE—British wit, author, playwright, and drama critic at *Vanity Fair*.

HOUSE & GARDEN

RICHARDSON WRIGHT—Editor of the title. A former newspaper man serving in Siberia and Manchuria, he was hired on his return in June 1914 as editor. He was a decorated gardener and writer of more than forty books on gardening. Wright was also president of the Food and Wine Society and chairman of the Horticulture Society of New York. He also wrote more than twenty books on eating, drinking, and country pursuits.

SOME FASHION CONTRIBUTORS

GABRIELLE "COCO" CHANEL—French couturier who began her fashion career as a milliner and opened her first shop early in 1914, introducing simpler designs and fabrics that harked back to her childhood.

JACQUES DOUCET—French Belle Époque fashion designer and art collector.

LUCILE, LADY DUFF-GORDON—British designer who opened her first fashion house in 1893 at 24 Burlington Street in London, serving wealthy clientele, including royalty and theatrical stars.

ELIZABETH "BESSIE" MARBURY—American literary and theatrical agent who was the hub of New York theatrical life. For many years she lived with her lesbian companions, Elsie de Wolfe and Anne Morgan (youngest daughter of J. P. Morgan) at the Villa Trianon at Versailles.

ELSIE DE WOLFE, LATER LADY MENDL—American-born Ella Anderson de Wolfe (1865–1950), credited with inventing the interior decorating profession.

JEAN PATOU—French fashion designer and founder of the Jean Patou brand. He was active from about 1912 until his death in 1936.

PAUL POIRET—leading French fashion designer in the first twenty years of the twentieth century. On the brink of bankruptcy after the Great War, he held on until 1929. His fashion house closed, and the remaining garments were sold for "rags."

ILLUSTRATION CONTRIBUTORS MENTIONED

Georges Barbier, Eduardo Benito, Jean Besnard, Bernard Boutet de Monvel, Pierre Brissaud, Arthur B. Davies, Helen Dryden, Jacob Epstein, Carl Erickson, Anne Harriet Fish, Paul Gauguin, Charles Dana Gibson, Paul Iribe, Augustus John, Rockwell Kent, Marie Laurencin, Georges Lepape, A. E. Marty, Charles Martin, Henri Matisse, Francis Picabia, Pablo Picasso, Man Ray, Kees van Dongen, Vincent van Gogh.

WRITING CONTRIBUTORS MENTIONED

FRANKLIN PIERCE ADAMS, "F.P.A."—Witty newspaper columnist noted for his "Conning Tower," member of the Round Table.

JOSEPHINE BAKER—African American entertainer and dancer.

DJUNA BARNES—American expatriate writer.

HEYWOOD BROUN—American journalist and sportswriter, member of the Round Table.

VERNON AND IRENE CASTLE—Popular Anglo-American ballroom dancers.

CHARLIE CHAPLIN—Comic, director-producer.

JOSEPH H. CHOATE—American lawyer and diplomat.

JEAN COCTEAU—French writer and illustrator.

COLETTE—French writer.

JOAN CRAWFORD—Hollywood actress.

E. E. CUMMINGS—Innovative American poet.

CLARENCE DARROW—Prominent American lawyer.

JACK DEMPSEY—World heavyweight champion, 1919–26.

THEODORE DREISER—American novelist and journalist.

ISADORA DUNCAN—Internationally known American free-form dancer.

T. S. ELIOT—One of the twentieth century's greatest poets.

DOUGLAS FAIRBANKS, SR.—Hollywood actor, producer, and writer.

DOUGLAS FAIRBANKS, JR.—Hollywood actor.

F. SCOTT FITZGERALD—American novelist and screenwriter.

JANET FLANNER—American expatriate journalist and columnist "Genêt" for *The New Yorker.*

FORD MADOX FORD—British novelist, poet, and critic.

ELINOR GLYN—British romance novelist and screenwriter.

J. EDGAR HOOVER—First head of the FBI.

HARRY HOUDINI—Internationally famed American magician.

LANGSTON HUGHES—African American writer and poet.

JOHN MAYNARD KEYNES—British economist who changed macroeconomic theory.

RING LARDNER—American sports columnist and satirical writer.

STEPHEN LEACOCK—Canadian humorist writer.

GYPSY ROSE LEE—American burlesque entertainer famous for her striptease.

SINCLAIR LEWIS—American novelist and first American Nobel Prize winner for Literature (1930).

CHARLES A. LINDBERGH—American aviator, military officer, explorer, political activist. and inventor.

WALTER LIPPMANN—American writer and political commentator, remembered as one of the first to introduce the term "Cold War."

JOE LOUIS—World heavyweight champion, 1937–49.

MYRNA LOY—Hollywood actress.

COMPTON MACKENZIE—English-born Scottish writer.

THOMAS MANN—German writer and winner of Nobel Prize for Literature (1929).

A. A. MILNE—English author and playwright, most noted for his *Winnie-the-Pooh* books.

JESSE OWENS—African American Olympian who won four gold medals at the 1936 Olympics.

COLE PORTER—American composer and songwriter.

PAUL ROBESON—African American bass-baritone singer, actor, and political activist.

BILL "BOJANGLES" ROBINSON—African American tap dancer and actor.

CARL SANDBURG—American poet, brother-in-law of photographer Edward Steichen.

GERTRUDE STEIN—American expatriate writer.

DONALD OGDEN STEWART—American author and screenwriter, member of the Round Table.

BERTRAND RUSSELL—British Nobel laureate, philosopher, historian, and critic.

BABE RUTH—American major league baseball legend.

WILLIAM SAROYAN—Armenian American writer and Pulitzer Prize–winning playwright.

GLORIA SWANSON—Hollywood actress and producer.

DALTON TRUMBO—American screenwriter and novelist.

H. G. WELLS—British writer across many genres.

EDITH WHARTON—American expatriate writer, especially of the Gilded Age.

WALTER WINCHELL—American syndicated newspaper columnist and radio personality.

THOMAS WOLFE—American author and journalist.

ALEXANDER WOOLLCOTT—American journalist and commentator, member of the Round Table.

WILLIAM BUTLER YEATS—Irish poet, Nobel laureate (1923), and major international literary figure of the twentieth century.

COMPETITORS MENTIONED

EDWARD WILLIAM BOK—Editor of *Ladies' Home Journal*.

RAOUL FLEISCHMANN—Main investor in Ross's *The New Yorker*.

ARNOLD GINGRICH—Editor of *Esquire*. He frequently employed the "unemployable" Dorothy Parker.

WILLIAM RANDOLPH HEARST—Condé's nemesis. Hearst's vast newspaper empire made him one of the most powerful men in America. His purchase of *Harper's Bazaar* put him into direct competition with Condé.

H. L. MENCKEN—"The Sage of Baltimore"—Journalist, scholar, and literary critic. He was literary critic of *The Smart Set* and later editor of *The American Mercury*, published by Alfred A. Knopf.

FRANK A. MUNSEY—Highly successful founder of *Munsey's Magazine*, first publisher to use advertising to subsidize all titles in order for them to be profitable.

HAROLD ROSS—Founding publisher and editor in chief of *The New Yorker*.

FRIENDS MENTIONED

FRED AND ADELE ASTAIRE—Dancing and acting brother-and-sister team.

MRS. CAROLINE SCHERMERHORN ASTOR—New York society hostess whose ballroom gave the Gilded Age "Four Hundred" their name.

BERNARD BARUCH—American Jewish financier, statesman, and adviser to American presidents. He was also Clare Boothe Brokaw's lover.

REX BENSON—British investment banker who married Condé's second wife, Leslie.

WILLIAM E. BERRY, LORD CAMROSE—Welsh-born newspaper magnate who bailed out Condé; he began his newspaper career with an advertising magazine.

WINSTON CHURCHILL—British statesman, prime minister, politician, and writer; winner of Nobel Prize for Literature (1953).

ROBERT J. COLLIER—Condé's college friend and publisher of *Collier's Weekly*. His father, Peter Fenelon Collier, was the publisher of the Collier's Library.

LEO D'ERLANGER—British investment banker who brokered the rescue of Condé Nast Publications.

MACDONALD DEWITT—Conde's long-serving lawyer. He brought Coudert Nast into his law firm as a partner.

MRS. STUYVESANT FISH, "MAMIE"—American society hostess who backed the first-ever charity fashion show in New York with *Vogue*.

HENRY R. LUCE—Publisher of *Fortune*, *Time*, and *Life*.

MARX BROTHERS—American comic actors. Groucho and Harpo were frequent guests at Condé's parties.

GRACE MOORE—Popular American opera singer who also appeared in films. She was Condé's lover in the early 1920s.

Note: The names of the society women and men featured in the pages of *Vogue* and *Vanity Fair* are too numerous to list. It is safe to say that if they were "talked about" or deemed to be "of interest," they were featured in both publications.

SELECTED BIBLIOGRAPHY

ARCHIVES
Condé Nast Archives
—MC001/2, 3, 4, 5, 6, 7, 8, 9, 10, 12, 20, 21, 23 III, 26
—MC005/3
— MC002/14
—*Vanity Fair* bound copies

Bodleian Library—University of Oxford
Vogue online, *Vogue* (British and French)
The New Yorker online
Harper's Bazaar online
Vanity Fair

British Library

Metropolitan Museum of Art
Diana Vreeland

Museum of Modern Art
Archives of Edward Steichen, Frank Crowninshield

New York Public Library Digital Archive

New-York Historical Society

New York Times TimesMachine
New York Times Archives

Newspapers.com

Private Collections
Letters from Condé Nast to Leslie Nast (1929–31).
Sir Reginald Lindsay Benson's private diary.

INTERVIEWS AND EMAIL CONTACTS
Robin Benson
Lady Leslie Bonham Carter
Cynthia Hochswender
Mitchell Owens
Alexander Russo
Condée Nast Russo
Jeremy Warburg Russo
Alexandra Shulman

PRIMARY AND SECONDARY BOOKS, ONLINE RESOURCES
Adams, Samuel H. "The Great American Fraud: Articles on the Nostrum Evil and Quacks." *Collier's Weekly*. New York: P. F. Collier & Son, 1905–1907, jstor .org.
Altman, Billy. *Laughter's Gentle Soul: The Life of Robert Benchley*. New York: W. W. Norton & Company, 1997.
Amory, Cleveland, and Frederick Bradlee, eds. *Vanity Fair: Selections from America's Most Memorable Magazine: A Cavalcade of the 1920s and 1930s*. New York: Viking Press, 1960.
Balsan, Consuelo Vanderbilt. *The Glitter and the Gold: The American Duchess in her own words*. London, Hodder, 2012.
Berry, Baron Michael. (Lord Hartwell). *William Camrose: Giant of Fleet Street*. London: Weidenfeld & Nicholson, 1992.
Bok, Edward. *The Americanization of Edward Bok: The Autobiography of a Dutch Boy Fifty Years After*. New York: Charles Scribner's Sons, 1922.
Brown, Tina. *The Vanity Fair Diaries*. London: Weidenfeld & Nicolson, 2017.
Camrose, Viscount William. *British Newspapers and Their Controllers*. London: Cassell, 1947.

Carter, Graydon, ed. *The Great Hangover: 21 Tales of the New Recession from the Pages of Vanity Fair*. New York: Condé Nast Publications, Harper Perennial, 2010.

———. *Vanity Fair's Tales of Hollywood: Rebels, Reds, and Graduates and the Wild Stories Behind the Making of 13 Iconic Films*. New York: Penguin Books, 2008.

———. *Vanity Fair's Writers on Writers*. New York: Penguin Books, 2016.

Carter, Graydon, and David Friend, eds. *Bohemians, Bootlegers, Flappers, and Swells: The Best of Early Vanity Fair*. New York: Penguin Press, 2014.

Case, Margaret. *The Vicious Circle: The Story of the Algonquin Round Table*. New York: Rinehart & Co., 1951.

Chase, Edna Woolman, and Ilka Chase. *Always in Vogue*. London: Victor Gollancz Ltd., 1954.

Christy, Jim. *The Price of Power: A Biography of Charles Eugène Bedaux*. Toronto: Doubleday, 1984.

Cowley, Malcolm. *Exile's Return: A Literary Odyssey of the 1920s*. London: Bodley Head, 1961.

Crowninshield, Frank, Dorothy Parker, and George Sheppard Chappell. *High Society: Advice to Social Campaigning and Hints on the Management of Dowagers, Dinners, Debutantes, Dances and the Thousand and One Diversions of Persons of Quality. . . .* London: 1915. Reprint, Andesite Press, 2017.

Davis, Mary E. *Classic Chic: Music, Fashion, and Modernism*. Los Angeles: University of California Press, 2006.

Dolmetsch, Carl. *The Smart Set: A History and Anthology*. New York: Dial Press, 1966.

Douglas, George H. *The Smart Magazines: 50 Years of Literary Revelry and High Jinks at Vanity Fair, The New Yorker, Life, Esquire and The Smart Set*. New York: Archon Books, 1991.

Etherington-Smith, Meredith, and Jeremy Pilcher. *The 'It' Girls: Lucy, Lady Duff Gordon, the Couturière 'Lucile,' and Elinor Glyn, Romantic Novelist*. London: Hamish Hamilton, 1986.

Flanner, Janet. *Paris Was Yesterday, 1925–1939*. London: Virago, 2003.

———. *Paris Journal, 1944–1955* New York: Harcourt Brace Jovanovich, 1965.

———. *Paris Journal, 1965–1970*. New York: Harcourt Brace Jovanovich, 1971.

———. *Janet Flanner's World: Uncollected Writings, 1932–1975*, New York: Harcourt Brace Jovanovich, 1979.

Gingrich, Arnold. "The Letters Racket." *English Journal* 25, no. 2 (February 1936): 91–101, jstor.org.

Harriman, Margaret Case. *Blessed Are the Debonair.* New York: Rinehart & Co., 1956.

Hunt, Lynn, David W. Blight, Bonnie G. Smith, Natalie Zemon Davis, Ernest R. May, eds. *Women's Magazines 1940–1960: Gender Roles and the Popular Press.* Boston: Bedford/St. Martin's, 1998.

Knudsen, Dean D. "Socialization and Elitism: A Study of Debutantes." *Sociological Quarterly* 9, no. 3 (Summer 1968): 300–308, jstor.org.

Kunkel, Thomas. *Genius in Disguise: Harold Ross of The New Yorker.* New York: Random House, 1995.

———. *Letters from the Editor: The New Yorker's Harold Ross.* New York: Modern Library, 2000.

Lachmansingh, Sandhya Kimberley. *Fashions of the Mind: Modernism and British Vogue under the Editorship of Dorothy Todd.* MPhil. thesis, University of Birmingham, England, September 2010.

Lawrenson, Helen. *Stranger at the Party: A Memoir.* New York: Random House, 1975.

Leighton, Isabel, ed. *The Aspirin Age: 1919–1941.* London: Bodley Head, 1950.

Luckhurst, Nicola. *Bloomsbury in Vogue.* London: Cecil Woolf Publishers, 1998.

Maier, Thomas. *Newhouse: All the Glitter, Power, and Glory of America's Richest Media Empire and the Secretive Man Behind It.* New York: Thomas Dunne Books, 1994.

Miller, Nina. "Making Love Modern: Dorothy Parker and Her Public." *American Literature* 64, no. 4 (Dec. 1992): 763–784, jstor.org.

Moore, Grace. *You're Only Human Once.* London: Latimer House Ltd., 1947.

Morris, Sylvia Jukes. *Rage for Fame: The Ascent of Clare Boothe Luce.* New York: Random House, 2014.

———. *Price of Fame: The Honorable Clare Boothe Luce.* New York: Random House, 2015.

Mott, Frank Luther. *A History of American Magazines 1885–1905,* vols. 4, 5. Cambridge, MA: Harvard University Press, 1957.

Ohmann, Richard. *Selling Culture: Magazines, Markets and Class at the Turn of the Century.* London: Verso, 1996.

Peterson, Theodore. *Magazines in the Twentieth Century.* Urbana: University of Illinois Press, 1956.

Pizzitola, Louis. *Hearst Over Hollywood: Power, Passion, and Propaganda in the Movies.* New York: Columbia University Press, 2002.

Poiret, Paul. *The King of Fashion: The Autobiography of Paul Poiret*. London: V&A Publishing, 2009.

Proctor, Ben. *William Randolph Hearst: The Early Years, 1863–1910*. New York: Oxford University Press, 1998.

———. *William Randolph Hearst: Final Edition, 1911–1951*. New York, Oxford University Press, 2007.

Richardson, Angelique. *Women Who Did: Stories by Men and Women, 1890–1914*. London: Penguin Books, 2005.

Rowbotham, Sheila. *A Century of Women: The History of Women in Britain and the United States*. London: Penguin Books, 1999.

Rowlands, Penelope. *A Dash of Daring: Carmel Snow and Her Life in Fashion, Art, and Letters*. New York: Atria Books, 2005.

Sandburg, Carl, Alexander Liberman, Edward Steichen, René d'Harnoncourt. *Steichen the Photographer*. New York: Museum of Modern Art, 1961.

Seebohm, Caroline. *The Man Who Was Vogue: The Life and Times of Condé Nast*. New York: Viking Press, 1982.

Showalter Elaine, ed. *Daughters of Decadence: Stories by Women Writers of the Fin de Siecle*. London: Virago, 2016.

Swanberg, W. A. *Citizen Hearst: A Biography of William Randolph Hearst*. New York: Galahad Books, 1961.

———. *Luce and His Empire*. New York: Charles Scribner's Sons, 1972.

Trapp, Frank Anderson. "The 1913 Armory Show in Retrospect." *College Art Journal* 17, no. 3 (Spring 1958): 294–296, jstor.org.

Vickers, Hugo. *Cecil Beaton*. London: Weidenfeld & Nicolson, 1985.

Vreeland, Diana. *D.V.* New York: Alfred A. Knopf (Borzoi Books), 1984.

Weaver, Angela. "Such a Congenial Little Circle: Dorothy Parker and the Early Twentieth Century Magazine Market." *Women's Studies Quarterly* 38, nos. 3 & 4 (Fall/Winter, 2010): 25–41, jstor.org.

Wilson, Edmund. *The Twenties: From Notebooks and Diaries of the Period*. London: Macmillan Ltd, 1975.

Wittke, Carl. *William Nast: Patriarch of German Methodism*. Detroit: Wayne State University Press, 1960.

Yoxall, H. W. *A Fashion of Life*. London: Heinemann, 1966.

NOTES

ABBREVIATIONS

AIV—Edna Woolman Chase and Ilka Chase, *Always in Vogue* (London: Victor Gollancz Ltd., 1954).

CNA—Condé Nast Archives, New York

ODNB—*Oxford Dictionary of National Biography*, Oxford University Press, online edition.

NYT—*New York Times*

TMWWV—Caroline Seebohm, *The Man Who Was Vogue* (New York: Viking Press, 1982).

PROLOGUE: THE RINGMASTER—1919

1. This saying was part of the initial advertisement for the circus.
2. *AIV*, 115.
3. Marion Meade, *Dorothy Parker: What Fresh Hell Is This?* (London: Heinemann, 1954), 35.
4. Ibid., 44.
5. *AIV*, 81.
6. Meade, *Dorothy Parker*, 43.
7. John Keats, *You Might as Well Live: The Life and Times of Dorothy Parker* (New York: Simon & Schuster, 1970), 43.
8. Ibid., 56.
9. *AIV*, 118, and Meade, *Dorothy Parker*, 57.

1. Living Down Mr. Disappoint

1. CNA, MC001/Box 6, horoscope, 1.
2. Carl Wittke, *William Nast: Patriarch of German Methodism* (Detroit: Wayne State University Press, 1959), 192–194. Note for clarity's sake, I have used Wilhelm to differentiate Condé's grandfather from his father, William, in the text.
3. *TMWWV*, 15–16.
4. Ibid. Note that in her book, Seebohm refers to Wilhelm Nast's journal as *Der Christliche Apologete*, whereas Wittke refers to it as the *Der evangelische Apologete*. Another difference occurs where Seebohm states that the journal's first edition was in 1839, as compared to Wittke's date of 1837. Both authors later refer to the journal as the *Apologete* after the first reference. I have adopted the name and date provided by Wittke, since his book is specifically a biography of Wilhelm Nast's activities.
5. Wittke, *William Nast*, 195.
6. Ibid., 197–198.
7. Ibid., 203.
8. Ibid., 199.
9. Ibid., 199–200.
10. Ibid., 200.
11. Ibid., 201.
12. Ibid., 202–203.
13. *TMWWV*, 20–21; CNA, MC005/Box 1, Folder 3.
14. Ibid.
15. Wittke, *William Nast*, 204.
16. Ibid., 205.
17. Ibid.
18. Ibid., 206.
19. Ibid., 207.
20. www.newspapers.com/image/37033933/?terms=%22William+F.+Nast%22, *The Sandusky Register*, October 14, 1890, 1.

2. Fanny's "Even-handed" Justice

1. Wittke, *William Nast*, 94, 216–217.
2. Ibid., 217–218.
3. Ibid., 218–219.
4. *TMWWV*, 23.
5. www.newspapers.com/image/138107639/?terms=C.+M.+Nast, *St. Louis Post-Dispatch*, February 10, 1889.

6. Ibid.
7. *TMWWV*, 24.
8. Ibid., 24–25.

3. It's Not What You Know . . .

1. www.newspapers.com/image/146340519/?terms=C.+M.+Nast, *Evening Star*, October 10, 1892.
2. www.newspapers.com/image/78663560/?terms=C.+M.+Nast, *The Sun* (New York), July 12, 1894.
3. *TMWWV*, 27.
4. Ibid., 28.
5. www.ancestry.com/mediaui-viewer/tree/10965519/person/48574086290 /media/7814647f-3656-4e26-8b05-5f5d96e1b1f5?_phsrc=ddi1&_phstart =success.
6. www.newspapers.com/image/84711041/?terms=Robert+J.+Collier, *Washington Times*, June 20, 1894.
7. *TMWWV*, 28-29; www.newspapers.com/image/16180021/?terms=%22St .+Louis+Exhibition%22, *The News* (Frederick, MD), March 4, 1895.
8. *AIV*, 53
9. Mott, *A History of American Magazines* (Cambridge, MA: Harvard University Press, 1938), 453.
10. Ibid., 454.
11. Ibid.
12. Ibid.
13. Ibid., 455.
14. Ibid., 456.
15. Ibid., 22.
16. Ibid., 23.
17. CNA, MC001/Box 6, Folder 15, Condé Nast, "Class Publications," 3, 4; reprinted from *Merchants' and Manufacturers' Journal of Baltimore*, June 1915.

4. The Adman Before *Mad Men*

1. Mott, *A History of American Magazines*, 27.
2. CNA, MC001/Box 6, Folder 15, Condé Nast, "Class Publications," 10; reprinted from *The Merchants' and Manufacturers' Journal of Baltimore*, June 1915.
3. https://babel.hathitrust.org/cgi/pt?id=nyp.33433023188596;view=1up;seq =105. (Collection of advertising pages from: *American* magazine, *Century* magazine, *Collier's* magazine, *Current Opinion*, *Everybody's* magazine,

Ladies' Home Journal, Life, Literary Digest, McClure's magazine, Munsey's magazine, Outlook, Review of Reviews, Scribner's magazine, Vanity Fair, Vogue, Woman's Home Companion, World's Work.)

4. https://babel.hathitrust.org/cgi/pt?id=mdp.39015036655762;view=1up;seq=21, 15.
5. Ibid.
6. Mott, *A History of American Magazines*, 457.
7. Ibid., 456.
8. *TMWWV*, 30. While the author noted that this quotation came from CNA, I found no letters prior to the period 1922 at the archives. I have assumed it is likely, therefore, that the letter quoted came from personal correspondence made available by the family. The date of the "ad pitch" is estimated as being from the end of 1902 to early 1903.
9. Mott, *A History of American Magazine*, 457.
10. www.newspapers.com/image/84730702/?terms=Robert+J.+Collier, *The Washington Times*, July 27, 1902, 23.
11. Ibid.
12. Susan Ronald, *A Dangerous Woman: American Beauty, Noted Philanthropist, Nazi Collaborator—The Life of Florence Gould* (New York: St. Martin's Press, 2018), 33.
13. For more on the Goulds, see Ibid.

5. Battling the Fakirs, Swindlers, and Manufacturers of Bad Whiskeys

1. W. A. Swanberg, *Citizen Hearst* (New York: Galahad Books, 1961), 81.
2. Ibid., 390.
3. Mott, *A History of American Magazines*, 455.
4. Swanberg, *Citizen Hearst*, see *American Magazine*, November 1906, 34.
5. Ibid., 81.
6. Ibid., see James Creelman, *On the Great Highway*, 177–178.
7. Ibid., 141, see *New York Journal*, March 18, 1898.
8. Ibid., see *New York Post*, March 21, 1898.
9. Ibid., 756.
10. Ibid., 538–539.
11. Ibid., 544.
12. Ibid., 460.
13. Edward W. Bok, *A Man From Maine* (New York: Charles Scribner's Sons, 1923), 127.
14. *Collier's Weekly*, October 7, 1905, 1.

15. Ibid., 3.
16. Ibid., 4.
17. Ibid., July 14, 1906, 69.
18. Ibid., October 7, 1905, 7.
19. Mott, *A History of American Magazines*, 461.
20. *Town Topics*, vol. 52, October 20, 1904, 3.
21. Mott, *A History of American Magazines*, 459.
22. Ibid., 459–460.
23. *TMWWV*, 31–32, see also *AIV*, 54.

6. A Natural Talent to Sniff Out Life's Patterns

1. Angelique Richardson, *Women Who Did: Stories by Men and Women 1890–1914* (London: Penguin Classics, 2002), xxxiii—xxxiv, see also William Barry "The Strike of a Sex," *Quarterly Review* 179 (1894), 317.
2. Ibid., xxxiv, see Henry James, *The American Scene*, 1907; (reprint, Penguin, 1994), 255, 256.
3. Ibid., see H. E. M. Stutfield "The Psychology of Feminism," *Blackwood's Edinburgh Magazine* 161 (1897), 105 and Max O'Rell, "Petticoat Government," *North American Review* 163 (July 1896), 102.
4. Ibid., see Marie Corelli, Flora Annie Steel, Lady Jeune, and Susan, Countess of Malmesbury, *The Modern Marriage Market* (London: Hutchinson & Co., 1897), 70–71.
5. Mary E. Davis, *Classic Chic: Music, Fashion and Modernism* (Berkeley: University of California Press, 2008), 9–10.
6. www.nysun.com/arts/father-of-the-four-hundred/18321/, *New York Sun*, August 9, 2005.
7. Ibid.
8. https://blog.mcny.org/2013/12/17/festivities-of-the-gilded-age-season/.
9. https://blog.mcny.org/2013/08/06/vanderbilt-ball-how-a-costume-ball-changed-new-york-elite-society/.
10. *TMWWV*, 42.
11. https://blog.mcny.org/2013/12/17/festivities-of-the-gilded-age-season/.
12. www.newspapers.com/image/163851733/?terms=%22Charles+Coudert%22, *New York Sun*, July 15, 1897. Note that *TMWWV* says that Charles Coudert was sixty-seven when he died, but both ancestry.com and all of Coudert's obituaries state that he was sixty-three.
13. *TMWWV*, 53.
14. www.newspapers.com/image/20450543/?terms=%22Charles+Coudert%22, *NYT*, November 16, 1897.

15. Ibid.

16. Ibid., January 5, 1898.

17. www.ancestry.com/family-tree/person/tree/8800990/person /25576080055/facts?_phsrc=eqs1&_phstart=successsource; www.news papers.com/image/330930979/?terms=%22Charles+Coudert%22, Washington, D.C., *Evening Star*, December 8, 1910.

18. *TMWWV*, 54.

19. Author email correspondence with Jeremy Warburg Russo, July 13, 2018.

7. How to Build a New Woman's Railroad

1. *TMWWV*, 57.

2. Ronald, *A Dangerous Woman*, chap. 3, "La Parisienne," 27–36.

3. Ibid.

4. www.newspapers.com/image/279105906/?terms=%22Home+Pattern +Company%22, *Buffalo Commercial*, September 23, 1904; www.newspapers .com/image/20479427/?terms=%22Home+Pattern+Company%22, *NYT*, September 24, 1904.

5. www.newspapers.com/image/20581411/?terms=%22Home+Pattern +Company%22, *NYT*, March 9, 1907.

6. Ibid.

7. *AIV*, 54.

8. www.newspapers.com/image/87856068/?terms=%22Home+Pattern +Company%22, *San Francisco Call*, December 13, 1907.

9. *AIV*, 24.

10. www.newspapers.com/image/86110136/?terms=%22Home+Pattern+Co mpany%22+AND+%22graded+patterns%22, *Brainerd* (MN) *Daily Dispatch*, April 5, 1909.

11. www.newspapers.com/image/20631653/?terms=%22Arthur+Turnure%2 2+AND+%22VOGUE%22, *NYT*, April 14, 1906.

12. www.grolierclub.org.

13. www.newspapers.com/image/20623095/?terms=%22Grolier+Club%22, *NYT*, March 17, 1884.

14. *AIV*, 23.

15. Ibid., 27.

16. Ibid., 28.

17. Ibid., 26.

18. Ibid., 23–24.

19. Ibid., 24–25.

20. Ibid., 26–27.

21. Consuelo Vanderbilt Balsan, *The Glitter and the Gold: The American Duchess in her own* words (London: Hodder, 2012), 45.

22. Ibid.

23. www.newspapers.com/image/20631653/?terms=%22Arthur+Turnure%2 2+AND+%22VOGUE%22, *NYT*, April 14, 1906.

24. *TMWWV*, 46–47.

25. *AIV*, 56.

26. Theodore Peterson, *Magazines in the Twentieth Century* (Urbana: University of Illinois Press), 254.

27. *Vogue*, June 24, 1909, masthead.

28. *AIV*, 57.

8. The Genie Bean Counter and His Class Publication

1. *TMWWV*, 61.

2. *AIV*, 67.

3. www.newspapers.com/image/118887002/?terms=%22Mrs.+Oliver+Belmont%22, *The Tennessean*, March 16, 1909; www.newspapers.com/image /118653591/?terms=%22Mrs.+Oliver+Belmont%22, *Indianapolis Star*, August 29, 1909.

4. Sheila Rowbotham, *A Century of Women: The History of Women in Britain and the United States* (London: Penguin Books, 1999), 45.

5. Ibid.

6. Ibid., 260; *AIV*, 62.

7. *TMWWV*, 63.

8. *AIV*, 58.

9. Ibid., 59.

10. Ibid., 59.

11. CNA, Condé Nast, "The Class Publication," reprinted from *Merchants' and Manufacturers' Journal* (Baltimore, MD), 1913, 4.

12. Ibid., 3.

13. *AIV*, 55.

14. Ibid., 59.

15. Ibid., 59–60.

16. Ibid., 65.

17. Ibid., 66.

18. www.newspapers.com/image/65398910/?terms=%22Mrs.+Arthur +Turnure%22, *New York Sun*, December 14, 1913; www.newspapers .com/image/20384209/?terms=%22Mrs.+Arthur+Turnure%22, *NYT*, December 13, 1913; www.newspapers.com/image/78927660/?terms

=%22Mrs.+Arthur+Turnure%22, *New-York Tribune*, December 14, 1913.

19. CNA, MC001/Box 6, DeWitt folders.

20. *AIV*, 61.

9. WHAT WOMEN WANT

1. *Vogue*, March 15, 1911, masthead.

2. *TMWWV*, 76.

3. Ibid., 103.

4. http://wheneditorsweregods.typepad.com/when_editors_were_gods /2010/09/frank-crowninshield-vanity-fair-conde-nast-editor-magazine-.html.

5. *AIV*, 71.

6. Ibid.

7. Ibid., 72.

8. Paul Poiret, *King of Fashion: The Autobiography of Paul Poiret* (London: V&A Publications, 2009), 14.

9. Davis, *Classic Chic*, 29–30.

10. *AIV*, 72–75.

11. Ibid., 208, 158. Quote on p. 158; see Axel Madsen, *Chanel: A Woman of Her Own* (New York: Henry Holt, 1990), 69.

12. British *Vogue*, early January 1922, 42.

13. *AIV*, 70.

14. George H. Douglas, *The Smart Magazines: 50 Years of Revelry and High Jinks at Vanity Fair, The New Yorker, Life, Esquire and The Smart Set* (Hamden, CT: Archon Books, 1991), 56–69; see also Carl R. Dolmetsch, *The Smart Set: A Magazine of Cleverness*, October 1914, 43.

15. Dolmetsch, *The Smart Set*, October 1914, 44.

16. *AIV*, 80.

17. Theodore Peterson, *Magazines in the Twentieth Century* (Chicago: University of Illinois Press, 1957), 256.

18. *AIV*, 87.

19. http://wheneditorsweregods.typepad.com/when_editors_were_gods /2010/09/frank-crowninshield-vanity-fair-conde-nast-editor-magazine-.html; Douglas, *The Smart Magazines*, 95.

20. Ibid.

21. Douglas, *The Smart Magazines*, 95.

22. *Vanity Fair*, March 15, 1914, opening-page editorial.

23. Meade, *Dorothy Parker*, 36.

24. Peterson, *Magazines in the Twentieth Century*, 257; see Geoffrey T. Hellman, "That Was New York: Crowninshield," *The New Yorker* 23, February 14, 1948, 72.

10. COUTURIERS, CUTTHROATS, AND CONFLICT

1 www.newspapers.com/image/20539479/?terms=%22Barrett+Andrews%22, *NYT*, June 21, 1911.

2. *AIV*, 90–91.

3. www.newspapers.com/image/20539479/?terms=%22Barrett+Andrews%22, *NYT*, June 21, 1911.

4. *AIV*, 91.

5. Ibid., 93.

6. Davis, *Classic Chic*, 52; see Beaton, *The Glass of Fashion*, 108.

7. Sonia Rachline, *Paris Vogue Covers* (London: Thames & Hudson, 2011), 16; Harry W. Yoxall, *A Fashion of Life* (London: Heinemann, 1966), 86–88.

8. Davis, *Classic Chic*, 49.

9. Ibid.; see "Au lecteur," *La Gazette du Bon Ton*, n.p.

10. Etherington-Smith and Pilcher, *The 'It' Girls*, 158.

11. *Vogue*, June 15, 1914, 35.

12. Ibid., 37.

13. *AIV*, 96.

14. Poiret, *King of Fashion*, 90.

15. Davis, *Classic Chic*, 22; see *La Gazette du Bon Ton*, June 1913, 165.

16. *Vogue*, June 15, 1912, 29.

17. Davis, *Classic Chic*, 22–23.

18. *AIV*, 98–100.

19. Ronald, *A Dangerous Woman*, 59.

20. Ibid., 58.

11. THE SPIRITED MRS. CHASE LANDS HER BIG FISH

1. *AIV*, 100.

2. Rowbotham, *A Century of Women*, 94–95.

3. *AIV*, 101.

4. Ibid., 102.

5. Rowbotham, *A Century of Women*, 60–61.

6. Ibid., 58.

7. Ibid., 64; see Vera Brittain, *Testament of Youth* (London: Arrow Books, 1960), 153.

8. *AIV*, 103.

9. Ibid., 104.
10. Ibid., 104–105.
11. Ibid., 106.
12. www.newspapers.com/image/79067057/?terms=%22Fashion+Fête%22, *New-York Tribune*, November 8, 1914.
13. Swanberg, *Citizen Hearst*, 326.
14. *TMWWV*, 99.
15. *AIV*, 107–108.

12. ENTER STAGE RIGHT FRANK CROWNINSHIELD—AND BROGUE

1. Cleveland Amory and Frederick Bradlee, eds., *Vanity Fair: Selections from America's Most Memorable Magazine—A Cavalcade of the 1920s and 1930s* (New York: Viking Press, 1960), 7.
2. Graydon Carter and David Friend, eds., *Bohemians, Bootleggers, Flappers, and Swells: The Best of Early Vanity Fair*, (New York: Penguin Press, 2014), 45.
3. Ibid., 45–49.
4. Douglas, *The Smart Magazines*, 99.
5. *Vanity Fair*, March 1914 editorial.
6. Amory and Bradlee, *Vanity Fair*, 7.
7. Carter and Friend, *Bohemians, Bootleggers, Flappers, and Swells*, 1–2.
8. Douglas, *The Smart Magazines*, 100.
9. Amory and Bradlee, *Vanity Fair*, 26.
10. *TMWWV*, 118.
11. Carter and Friend, *Bohemians, Bootleggers, Flappers, and Swells*, 2–3.
12. eprints.worc.ac.uk, "*Vogue* in Britain: Authenticity and the Creation of Competitive Advantage in the UK Magazine Industry."
13. *TMWWV*, 123.
14. British *Vogue*, September 15, 1916. Advertisement for Selfridges & Co. appears on page 17.
15. Carter and Friend, *Bohemians, Bootleggers, Flappers, and Swells*, 103.
16. *TMWWV*, 112, 110.

13. FROM VANITY FAIR TO MAYHEM

1. Meade, *Dorothy Parker*, 44.
2. Ibid., 45.
3. Ibid.

4. Ibid.

5. Helen Lawrenson, *Stranger at the Party* (New York: Random House, 1972), 62.

6. Ibid., 61.

7. Grace Moore, *You're Only Human Once* (London: Latimer House, 1947), 67–69.

8. Harry Hansen, "The Forgotten Men of Versailles," in *The Aspirin Age*, ed. Isabel Leighton (London: Penguin, 1964), 13.

9. Meade, *Dorothy Parker*, 52–53.

10. Keats, *You Might as Well Live*, 40.

11. Meade, *Dorothy Parker*, 53.

12. Ibid., 54.

13. Ibid.

14. Ibid., 55.

15. Robert Benchley, "The Social Life of the Newt," in *Vanity Fair*, ed. Amory and Bradlee, 37–38.

16. Keats, *You Might as Well Live*, 43.

17. Meade, *Dorothy Parker*, 56.

18. Ibid., 57.

19. Ibid., 58.

20. Thomas Kunkel, *Genius in Disguise: Harold Ross of The New Yorker* (New York: Random House, 1995), 48–50.

21. Ibid., 51–53.

22. Ibid., 57–58.

23. Meade, *Dorothy Parker*, 61.

24. Ibid.

14. BACK TO THE BUSINESS OF "FRIED FISH AND STEWED EELS"

1. Peterson, *Magazines in the Twentieth Century*, 256.

2. Howard Cox and Simon Mowatt, *Revolutions from Grub Street: A History of Magazine Publishing in Britain* (Oxford: Oxford University Press, 2014), 31.

3. Ibid., 37, 54.

4. Ibid., 54. In 1919, the calculated values for the Harmsworths' businesses were: Associated Newspapers, £4.2 million; Amalgamated Press, £4.2 million; and the Pictorial Newspaper Co. (owners of the *Daily Mirror* and *Sunday Pictorial*), £1.9 million.

5. *TMWWV*, 124.

6. *AIV*, 139–140.

7. Rachline, *Paris Vogue Covers*, 12.

8. Davis, *Classic Chic*, 218. The Vogel artist André Marty drew an illustration, "A l'Oasis," for *Modes et manières d'aujourd'hui*.

9. Ibid., 219–220.

15. How to Keep a Park Bench Warm

1. Meade, *Dorothy Parker*, 63. Also: Billy Altman, *Laughter's Gentle Soul: The Life of Robert Benchley* (New York: W. W. Norton & Company, 1997), 148–149.

2. Altman, *Laughter's Gentle Soul*, 150–151.

3. Meade, *Dorothy Parker*, 64.

4. Altman, *Laughter's Gentle Soul*, 154.

5. Meade, *Dorothy Parker*, 64.

6. Ibid.

7. Ibid., 57; Keats, *You Might as Well Live*, 55–56.

8. Altman, *Laughter's Gentle Soul*, 148.

9. Ibid., 136.

10. Ibid., 144.

11. Margaret Case Harriman, *The Vicious Circle: The Story of the Algonquin Round Table* (New York: Rinehart & Co., 1951), 7.

12. Keats, *You Might as Well Live*, 53–54.

13. Meade, *Dorothy Parker*, 66.

14. Amory and Bradlee, *Vanity Fair*, 24.

15. Ibid., 24–25.

16. Ibid., 25.

17. Altman, *Laughter's Gentle Soul*, 154.

18. Ibid., 155.

19. Meade, *Dorothy Parker*, 67.

20. Moore, *You're Only Human Once*, 54–55.

21. Altman, *Laughter's Gentle Soul*, 156.

22. Ibid.

23. Ibid., 157.

24. Edmund Wilson, *The Twenties: From Notebooks and Diaries of the Period* (London: Macmillan Ltd., 1975), 61.

25. Douglas Waller, *Wild Bill Donovan: The Spymaster who Created the OSS and Modern American Espionage* (New York: Free Press, 2011), 72.

16. "Ain't We Got Fun?"

1. For a brief summary of the effects of early German hyperinflation on Europe and America see Susan Ronald, *Hitler's Art Thief: Hildebrand Gurlitt and the Looting of Europe's Treasures* (New York: St. Martin's Press, 2015), 93–95.
2. Wilson, *The Twenties*, 54.
3. Ibid., 55.
4. Ibid., 56; *TMWWV*, 148.
5. Ibid., 54.
6. Penelope Rowlands, *A Dash of Daring: Carmel Snow and Her Life in Fashion, Art, and Letters* (New York: Atria Books, 2005), 56.
7. *AIV*, 121.
8. Rowlands, *A Dash of Daring*, 61.
9. CNA, MC001/Box 8, Folder 4, letter to Betty Penrose, May 1942; CNA, MC001/Box 12, Folder 25, letter to Yoxall, February 15, 1939.
10. Lawrenson, *Stranger at the Party*, 60.
11. *AIV*, 122.
12. Ibid., 122–123.
13. www.centre-robert-schuman.org.
14. *AIV*, 140.
15. Ibid., 140–141.
16. Ibid., 123–124.
17. CNA, MC001/Box 14, Folder 20, brochure about the Condé Nast Press.
18. Ibid.

17. The High Priestess Meets Her Forces of Nature

1. Diana Vreeland, *D.V.* (New York, Alfred A. Knopf, 1984), 58.
2. F. Scott Fitzgerald, *The Great Gatsby*, quoted in *TMWWV*, 13.
3. *AIV*, 80.
4. Ibid., 80–81.
5. Rowbotham, *A Century of Women*, 150.
6. Ibid., 147; see Nancy Mitford, *Zelda Fitzgerald: A Biography* (London: Bodley Head, 1970), 81.
7. *TMWWV*, 148.
8. Rowlands, *A Dash of Daring*, 68. See Alexander Liberman's interview (future editorial director of magazines at Condé Nast Publications).
9. Ibid., 61, 68.
10. Ibid., 34, 8.
11. Ibid., 45.

12. Ibid., 50.

13. Ibid., 52–53.

14. Ibid., 54.

15. *AIV*, 146.

16. Samuel Hopkins Adams, "The Timely Death of President Harding" in *The Aspirin Age*, ed. Leighton, 99–104; Rowbotham, *A Century of Women*, 152–153.

17. Nicola Luckhurst, *Bloomsbury in Vogue* (London: Cecil Woolf, 1998), 3; see Peter Quennell, *The Marble Foot*, 149; also in Cecil Beaton, *Photobiography*, 34.

18. Luckhurst, *Bloomsbury in Vogue*, 3.

19. Ibid., 12.

20. Ibid., 5.

21. *Vogue* (Paris), December 15, 1920, 5; *Vogue* (New York), January 15, 1922, 50.

22. Davis, *Classic Chic*, 209.

23. *AIV*, 144.

24. Ibid., 143–144.

25. *Vogue* (New York), January 1, 1923, 47.

26. *AIV*, 148–149.

18. ALL THOSE FLAMING "BRIGHT YOUNG THINGS"

1. *Vogue* (Paris), June 15, 1921, 21, 22.

2. Moore, *You're Only Human Once*, 80.

3. *TMWWV*, 8–9.

4. Jean Cocteau, "The Public and the Artist" in *Bohemians, Bootleggers, Flappers, and Swells*, ed. Carter, 172.

5. Davis, *Classic Chic*, 220.

6. *Vogue* (Paris), December 1, 1923, 4–5.

7. Ibid., 4.

8. Ibid.

9. *Vogue* (New York), May 15, 1925, 162.

10. Yoxall, *A Fashion of Life*, 54.

11. *AIV*, 150, 154–155.

12. CNA, MC001/Box 1, Folder 1, July 5, 1929, letter to Lew Wurzburg and Edna Chase.

13. *AIV*, 158.

14. Ibid., 162.

15. Yoxall, *A Fashion of Life*, 60–61.

16. *AIV*, 163–164.
17. Rowlands, *A Dash of Daring*, 74.
18. Ibid., 72–75.
19. Carl Sandburg, Alexander Liberman, Edward Steichen, and René d'Harnoncourt, *Steichen the Photographer* (New York: Museum of Modern Art, 1961), 7, 12.
20. *AIV*, 151–158.
21. www.newspapers.com/image/64552697/?terms=%22Clarisse+Coudert%22, Associated Press, *Vancouver Daily World*, January 12, 1924, 19.
22. Ibid.
23. Ibid.
24. *AIV*, 131.
25. Luckhurst, *Bloomsbury in Vogue*, 6–7; letter from Virginia Woolf dated September 1, 1925; *Vogue* (London), early October 1925, 55.
26. Luckhurst, *Bloomsbury in Vogue*, 18–19; Harry Yoxall diaries, 14 June 1923. The diaries were made available to Nicola Luckhurst for the purposes of this publication by his daughter, Lindsey Pietrzak.
27. Email from Jeremy Warburg Russo, Natica's daughter, September 2018.
28. Luckhurst, *Bloomsbury in Vogue*, 20. Harry Yoxall's unpublished manuscript was again made available to Nicola Luckhurst for the purposes of her publication by Yoxall's daughter, Lindsey Pietrzak, but it is unknown if the manuscript had been prepared with an eye to publication or not.
29. Yoxall, *A Fashion of Life*, 3.

19. LET THE GOOD TIMES ROLL
1. *TMWWV*, 2; author interview with Leslie Bonham Carter.
2. Ibid., 2–3; author interview with Leslie Bonham Carter.
3. When my family moved to New York in the 1960s, my mother wanted to buy Moss Hart's apartment, so I had a chance to see it. Like Condé's, it was a duplex with a sweeping staircase. Of course we couldn't afford it.
4. *AIV*, 174–175.
5. *TMWWV*, 1.
6. Rowlands, *A Dash of Daring*, 67.

20. THE NEW AND RENEWED KIDS IN TOWN
1. CNA, MC001/Box 1, Folder 23; *The New Yorker*, February 21, 1925, http://archives.newyorker.com/?i=1925-02-21#.
2. Kunkel, *Genius in Disguise*, 89.

3. Ibid., 92.
4. CNA, MC001/Box 14, Folder 19, description of printing business.
5. www.newspapers.com/image/355154262/?terms=%22Clarisse+Coudert %22, *NYT*, May 30, 1925.
6. www.geni.com/people/Jose-Victor-Onativia-III/6000000040327528308.
7. www.newspapers.com/image/415122114/?terms=J.%2BVictor %2BOnativia.
8. www.newspapers.com/image/35061723/?terms=%22Dean%22 +AND+%22Onatavia%22.
9. www.nytimes.com/1926/04/12/archives/mrs-conde-nast-bride-of-jv -onativia-in-surprise-wedding-at.html.
10. *Vogue*, February 1, 1926.
11. *TMWWV*, 162.
12. CNA, MC001/Box 14, Folders 1–19.
13. *AIV*, 175.
14. Rowlands, *A Dash of Daring*, 93.
15. Ibid.
16. Ibid., 90–91.
17. Yoxall, *A Fashion of Life*, 28, 50, 52. William Shakespeare, *Much Ado About Nothing*, III.3.6.
18. Ibid., 65–67.
19. Luckhurst, *Bloomsbury in Vogue*, 18–19.
20. Yoxall, *A Fashion of Life*, 125.
21. Ibid.
22. Luckhurst, *Bloomsbury in Vogue*, 21.
23. Ibid. Woolf's letter, quoted in the manuscript as well, is dated September 24, 1926, and written to Harold Nicolson.
24. Ibid. Virginia Woolf's letter is dated February 18, 1928.

21. Fireflies in the Garden Paradise

1. Janet Flanner, *Paris was Yesterday* (London: Virago Press, 1973), 26–27.
2. *AIV*, 173.
3. Vreeland, *D.V.*, 48.
4. *AIV*, 186.
5. Hugo Vickers, *Cecil Beaton: A Biography* (Toronto: Little Brown and Company, 1985), 100–101.
6. Ibid., 99.
7. Carolyn Burke, *Lee Miller* (London: Bloomsbury, 2005), 57–58.
8. *TMWWV*, 178–179.

9. Sandburg, Liberman, Steichen, d'Harnoncourt, *Steichen the Photographer*, 15.

10. Ibid., 17.

11. Burke, *Lee Miller*, 59–60, 69.

12. Ibid., 61.

13. Yoxall, *A Fashion of Life*, 130.

14. *AIV*, 178; Ronald, *Hitler's Art Thief*, 91–114.

15. *AIV*, 178–179.

16. Ibid., 182.

17. Yoxall, *A Fashion of Life*, 117.

22. CASTING FOR PEARLS

1. *AIV*, 205.

2. Ibid., 206.

3. Ibid., 206.

4. Ibid., 208.

5. Ibid., 208.

6. www.newspapers.com/image/411082832/?terms=%22Harrison+Williams%22; https://www.newspapers.com/image/83365978/?terms=%22Harrison+Williams%22.

7. www.economist.com/blogs/freeexchange/2013/11/economic-history-0.

8. www.newspapers.com/image/204755197/?terms=%22Park+Lexington+Corporation%22; www.newspapers.com/image/59871762/?terms=%22Park+Lexington+Corporation%22; www.newspapers.com/image/57570806/?terms=%22Park+Lexington+Corporation%22; www.newspapers.com/image/28087648/?terms=%22Park+Lexington+Corporation%22; www.newspapers.com/image/58064165/?terms=%22Park+Lexington+Corporation%22; *NYT*, April 13, 1928.

9. *TMWWV*, 293.

10. *NYT*, October 16, 1928.

11. *TMWWV*, 294.

12. *AIV*, 198.

13. Author interview with Leslie Bonham Carter, January 2018.

14. Vickers, *Cecil Beaton*; 114; *NYT*, October 19, 1928.

15. www.newspapers.com/image/355083398/?terms=%22Charlotte+Babcock+Brown%22.

23. Boom, Crash, Bang, Clatter

1. *AIV*, 209.
2. *NYT*, February 15, 1929.
3. Ibid., June 21, 1929.
4. The author was given access to fourteen private letters from a private collection in three of which Nast referred to his bride as his "Yorkshire Pudding."
5. *TMWWV*, 296.
6. Condé to Leslie Nast on Hotel Eden Berlin letterhead, dated simply "Thursday a.m.," from a private collection.
7. Ronald, *Hitler's Art Thief*, 127.
8. Ibid., 134.
9. *AIV*, 194–195.
10. Ibid., 194.
11. Rowlands, *A Dash of Daring*, 100.
12. Condé to Leslie Nast on Hotel Eden Berlin letterhead, dated simply "Thursday a.m.," from a private collection.
13. Yoxall, *A Fashion of Life*, 84.
14. *AIV*, 211–212.

24. Beware of Frenemies

1. Sylvia Jukes Morris, *Rage for Fame: The Ascent of Clare Boothe Luce* (New York: Random House Paperbacks, 2014), 116–117.
2. Ibid., 118, from her letter to Julian Simpson dated June 18, 1923.
3. Ibid., 159.
4. Ibid., 161–162.
5. Ibid., 163.
6. Ibid.; *AIV*, 202.
7. Morris, *Rage for Fame*, 18–23.
8. Ibid., 25.
9. Ibid., 36–37, 43, 44, 52.
10. Ibid., 56.
11. Ibid., 163–164, 216.
12. Thurman Arnold, "The Crash and What It Meant," in *The Aspirin Age*, ed. Leighton, 225.
13. Ibid., 225–226.
14. November 9, 1929, letter from Condé to Leslie Nast. Private collection.
15. Undated letter marked "Tuesday" from Condé to Leslie Nast, presumed to be written around January 1930. Private collection.

16. Ibid.

17. *AIV*, 201.

18. Letter postmarked January 28, 1930, 7 a.m. Grand Central, from Condé to Leslie Nast. Private collection.

19. *AIV*, 213.

20. www.newspapers.com/image/59885354/?terms=%22Harrison+Williams%22.

21. www.newspapers.com/image/59900784/?terms=%22Harrison+Williams%22; https://www.newspapers.com/image/288980049/?terms=%22Harrison+Williams%22.

22. *NYT*, February 28, 1930.

23. CNA, MC001/Box 22, Folder 11.

24. *NYT*, January 24, 1930.

25. Swanberg, *Citizen Hearst*, 484.

26. CNA, MC005/Box 3.

27. *NYT*, April 30, 1930.

28. Letter dated only Tuesday, postmarked July 30, 1930, Grand Central from Condé to Leslie Nast. Private collection.

29. Ibid.

30. Morris, *Rage for Fame*, 166.

31. Ibid.

32. Ibid., 167.

33. Ibid., 168–169.

25. In the Death Throes

1. http://urology.jhu.edu/erectileDysfunction/erectile_dysfunctions_RP.php, author interview with Dr. P. Zakowski, Mount Sinai Medical Center, Los Angeles, California; *TMWWV*, 315; based on that author's interview with Lady Leslie Benson.

2. CNA, Box 21, Folder 4, Condé Nast medical receipts.

3. Undated letter from Condé to Leslie Nast, most likely early June 1931. Private collection. Also *NYT*, June 11, 1930.

4. Letter from Condé to Leslie Nast, dated July 30, 1931. Private collection.

5. Ibid.

6. Ibid.

7. Letter dated August 16, 1931, from Condé to Leslie Nast. Private collection.

8. *ODNB*, s.v. "Sir Reginald Lindsay [Rex] Benson."

9. Ibid.

10. Ibid.
11. Excerpt from Sir Reginald Lindsay Benson's private diary. Private collection.
12. Ibid.
13. Undated letter from Condé to Leslie Nast, most likely Labor Day weekend, September 1931. Private collection.
14. *ODNB*, s.v. "Sir Reginald Lindsay [Rex] Benson." Excerpt from Sir Reginald Lindsay Benson's private diary. Private collection.
15. Unpublished family manuscript on the life of Rex Benson. Private collection.
16. Excerpt from Sir Reginald Lindsay Benson's private diary. Private collection.
17. Unpublished family manuscript on the life of Rex Benson. Private collection.
18. www.newspapers.com/image/414114807/?terms=%22Harrison+Williams%22; *NYT*, November 7, 1931.

26. THE STAIN OF DEFECTION

1. *TMWWV*, 315, author's interview with Lady Benson.
2. *AIV*, 216.
3. *NYT*, October 28, 1928.
4. Ibid., November 13, 1935.
5. Ibid., January 1, 1968.
6. Ibid., January 1, 1932.
7. Vickers, *Cecil Beaton*, 122–124.
8. Ibid., 125.
9. Rowlands, *A Dash of Daring*, 129; see telegram dated March 28, 1931, William Randolph Hearst Archive, Bancroft Library, University of California, Berkeley; Vickers, *Cecil Beaton*, 126.
10. Vickers, *Cecil Beaton*, 154.
11. Rowlands, *A Dash of Daring*, 130.
12. Ibid.
13. CNA, MC001/Box 10, Folder 13, memo from Nast to Snow dated March 8, 1927.
14. Ibid., memo from Nast to Snow dated March 11, 1927.
15. Ibid., exchange of letters between March 11 and 18, 1927.
16. Ibid., undated letter, probably November 1927.
17. Rowlands, *A Dash of Daring*, 132.
18. Ibid., 133.

19. Ibid., 135.
20. Ibid., 136.
21. CNA, MC001/Box 10, Folder 13, letter from Nast to Snow dated December 20, 1932.
22. Ibid.
23. Ibid., letter from Nast to Tom White dated December 21, 1932.
24. Ibid., letter from Nast to Snow dated January 7, 1933.

27. A VERY BRITISH SALVATION

1. CNA, MC001/Box 1, Folder 11, Brokaw to Nast, letter dated May 9, 1931.
2. Morris, *Rage for Fame*, 203.
3. Ibid., 206–209, 211.
4. Ibid.; see Clare Boothe Luce's diary two days earlier, October 4–5, 1932.
5. Ibid., 170, 181–182.
6. Ibid., 171; *TMWWV*, 320; CNA, MC001/Box 3, memo dated October 11, 1933.
7. CNA, MC001/Box 22, Folder 4, Crocker to Nast, letter dated July 14, 1932.
8. Swanberg, *Citizen Hearst*, 467, 483, 484.
9. *NYT*, January 2, 1934.
10. *AIV*, 209.
11. Yoxall, *A Fashion of Life*, 130–131.
12. CNA, MC001/Box 6, Folder 21, Maas to Nast, memo dated December 15, 1932.
13. *ODNB*, s.v. "William Ewert Berry, Lord Camrose."
14. Lawrenson, *Stranger at the Party*, 60–61.
15. *ODNB*, s.v. "Leo Frederic Alfred d'Erlanger."
16. *TMWWV*, 316.
17. CNA, MC001/Box 6, Folder 23, February 1934 correspondence between Patcévitch and Schneider.
18. Ibid., Patcévitch letter to Schneider dated February 2, marked private; Yoxall, *A Fashion of Life*, 92–93.
19. Ibid./Box 5, Folder 7, telegram dated February 1, 1934.
20. *TMWWV*, 316–317.
21. *NYT*, March 22, 1934.
22. Yoxall, *A Fashion of Life*, 93.

28. But Who's to Save *Vanity Fair*?

1. Morris, *Rage for Fame*, 214–215, 219.
2. Lawrenson, *Stranger at the Party*, 98.
3. CNA, MC001/cold storage, *Vogue* unpublished photograph, reference 20786V.
4. Lawrenson, *Stranger at the Party*, 81.
5. Ibid., 82–83.
6. Morris, *Rage for Fame*, 212; see Clare Boothe Luce's diary September 26 and 28, and November 18, 1932.
7. *Vanity Fair*, June 1932.
8. *Vogue*, early June 1933.
9. Kunkel, *Genius in Disguise*, 269–273.
10. Lawrenson, *Stranger at the Party*, 64, 68.
11. Ibid., 53–54.
12. Ibid., 59–60, 67.
13. Conversation with Leslie Bonham Carter, July 9, 2018.
14. Ibid., 60.
15. Ibid. Interestingly, all correspondence with Ms. Brown Norden has been expunged from the CNA.
16. Morris, *Rage for Fame*, 226, 227.
17. Ibid.; see Nast letter to Clare dated March 27, 1933.
18. *TMWWV*, 331–332.
19. https://pro.imdb.com/title/tt0028505/details.
20. Lawrenson, *Stranger at the Party*, 76.
21. Ibid., 96.

29. "Of Cabbages . . ."

1. *AIV*, 222–223.
2. Ibid., 233.
3. Vickers, *Cecil Beaton*, 180; see Beaton's diary, February 1935.
4. Ibid., 181; see Beaton's diary, February 1935.
5. Ibid., 182; see Lady Dufferin to the author.
6. Ibid., 186; *TMWWV*, 184–185, 187.
7. *NYT*, August 15, 1936.
8. Ibid., June 4, 1937.

30. ". . . and Kings"

1. www.historytoday.com/francis-watson/death-george-v
2. *AIV*, 240.

3. Ibid., 241–242.
4. Vickers, *Cecil Beaton*, 193; see Beaton's diary, November 1936.
5. British *Vogue*, August 21, 1935, 27.
6. Vickers, *Cecil Beaton*, 194; see Beaton's diary, November 1936.
7. Ibid., 195; see Beaton's diary, November 1936.
8. *AIV*, 242.
9. Ibid., 243.
10. Ibid., 245–246.
11. Ibid., 247.
12. https://www.historytoday.com/stephen-cretney/edward-mrs-simpson-and
-divorce-law.
13. Jim Christy, *The Price of Power: A Biography of Charles Eugène Bedaux* (Toronto: Doubleday, 1984), 138.
14. Ibid., 140. There is some controversy surrounding just how Bedaux became involved with Wallis. Janet Flanner wrote in *The New Yorker* that he cabled Rogers offering Mrs. Simpson the use of Candé. Her error is repeated in several books thereafter. Bedaux finished his days in a Miami, Florida, prison, accused of trading with the enemy and treason. He took his own life rather than face trial.
15. *AIV*, 250.
16. Vickers, *Cecil Beaton*, 197; see Beaton's diary, spring 1937.
17. Ibid., 198; see Beaton's diary, spring 1937.
18. Ibid., 198–199; see Beaton's diary, spring 1937.
19. Ibid., 200; see exchange of letters between Edna Woolman Chase and Cecil Beaton dated June 4, 1937.
20. Ibid., 204–205; Dr. Agha quoted by Cecil to Edna Woolman Chase, January 12, 1937.
21. Ibid., 206; see Lee Israel, *Miss Tallulah Bankhead* (New York: Putnam, 1972), 179–180.
22. Ibid., 207.
23. www.newspapers.com/image/261092600/?terms=Winchell%2C%2BWal ter%2BBeaton%2C%2BCecil.
24. Vickers, *Cecil Beaton*, 208.
25. Ibid.
26. Ibid., 208–212.
27. Ibid., 213; see letter from Irene Selznick to Hugo Vickers dated May 26, 1981.

31. ANSWERING THE DISTANT CRY OF WAR

1. *TMWWV*, 341.
2. CNA, MC001/Box 2, Folder 8, letter from Bill Davenport to Condé Nast dated November 3, 1938.
3. *TMWWV*, 332.
4. *TMWWV*, 333.
5. CNA, MC001/Box 4, Folder 5, letter from Tom Kernan to Condé Nast dated March 24, 1939.
6. Ibid., letter from Tom Kernan to Condé Nast dated August 25, 1939.
7. www.bbc.co.uk/archive/ww2outbreak/7957.shtml?page=txt.
8. CNA, MC001/Box 2, Folder 23, letter from Michel de Brunhoff to Condé Nast dated September 4, 1939.
9. Ibid., letter from Michel de Brunhoff to Condé Nast dated September 15, 1939; Ronald, *A Dangerous Woman*, 200.
10. CNA, MC001/Box 2, Folder 23, letter from Michel de Brunhoff to Condé Nast dated September 15, 1939; letter from Condé Nast to Michel de Brunhoff dated November 14, 1939.
11. Ibid., letter from Michel de Brunhoff to Condé Nast dated September 15, 1939; letter from Michel de Brunhoff to Condé Nast dated May 31, 1940.
12. William L. Shirer, *The Rise and Fall of the Third Reich: A History of Nazi Germany* (New York: Simon & Schuster, 1959), 884.
13. Ronald, *A Dangerous Woman*, 205.
14. CNA, MC001/Box 2, Folder 23, letter from Michel de Brunhoff to Condé Nast dated July 21, 1940.
15. Ibid./Box 4, Folder 8, telegram from Sumner Welles to Condé Nast dated August 6, 1940.
16. Ibid., Folder 9, letter from Tom Kernan to Condé Nast dated August 6, 1940.
17. Ibid., Folder 27, letters from Walter Maas to Condé Nast and Nast to Edge dated from June–August 1940.
18. Ibid., Folder 9, letter from Condé Nast to Tom Kernan dated October 18, 1940.
19. Ibid.
20. Yoxall, *A Fashion of Life*, 180.
21. Burke, *Lee Miller*, 200–202.
22. *AIV*, 207.
23. Yoxall, *A Fashion of Life*, 182.

32. How to Win in the End

1. *TMWWV*, 352.
2. Charles Glass, *Americans in Paris: Life and Death under the Nazi Occupation* (London: HarperPress, 2009), 234.
3. Author interview with Leslie Bonham Carter, January 29, 2018.
4. CNA, MC001/Box 6, Folder 8, memo dated January 31, 1940.
5. Ibid., memo dated March 1, 1940.
6. Ibid.
7. Ibid./Box 20, Folder 4, various receipts from Chase National Bank.
8. *AIV*, 295.
9. CNA, MC001/Box 5, Folder 12, various correspondence.
10. Ibid.
11. Ibid., April 2, 1940, letter from Condé Nast to Peter Nast.
12. Author interview with Leslie Bonham Carter, January 29, 2018.
13. Ibid.
14. Ibid.
15. Vignette provided to the author by Jeremy Warburg Russo, 2018.

33. The King Is Dead

1. Author interview with Leslie Bonham Carter, January 29, 2018.
2. Ibid.
3. CNA, MC001/Box 20, Folder 7, bill from Dr. George Andrews.
4. Ibid., Folder 4, bill from Doctors Hospital, December 12, 1941.
5. Ibid., receipts for payments to nurses.
6. Ibid./Box 1, Folder 22, various correspondence.
7. *AIV*, 298.
8. Ibid.
9. Ibid., 299–300.
10. Ibid., 300–301; Lawrenson, *Stranger at the Party*, 78.
11. CNA, MC001/Box 5, Folder 12, October 2, 1942, letter from Leslie Benson to Mary Campbell.
12. Ibid.
13. Ibid., October 14, 1942, letter from Mary Campbell to Coudert Nast.
14. Ibid., folder 23, *Scope* magazine obituary; *NYT*, September 20, 1942.
15. *TMWWV*, 365; CNA, MC001/Box 20, Folder 1, inventory of assets.

34. A New Leaf

1. CNA, MC001/Box 12, various correspondence.
2. *TMWWV*, 366.
3. CNA, MC001/Box 20, Folder 1. The duplex apartment at 1040 Fifth Avenue and the apartment on East Seventy-second Street were owned by Condé Nast Publications and had a book value of $1,369,518.
4. Vignette provided to the author by Jeremy Warburg Russo, 2018.
5. *AIV*, 302.
6. *TMWWV*, 367.
7. Author interview with Leslie Bonham Carter, January 2018.
8. Vignette provided to the author by Jeremy Warburg Russo, 2018.
9. Author interview with Leslie Bonham Carter, July 2018.
10. *AIV*, 303.
11. Ibid., 303.
12. Author interview with Leslie Bonham Carter, January 2018, and discussions with Julia Amory, Patcévitch family member.
13. *AIV*, 305; CNA, MC001/Box 1, Folder 21, correspondence regarding Liberman.
14. CNA, MC001/Box 1, Box 5, Folder 12, October 27, 1943, letter from Leslie Benson to Mary Campbell.
15. *AIV*, 316.
16. Ibid., 306–310.
17. Ibid., 287.
18. Discussions with Julia Amory, Patcévitch family member.
19. *AIV*, 323–324.
20. Lawrenson, *Stranger at the Party*, 97.
21. CNA, MC005/Box 1, Folder 2.
22. Copy of the speech provided by Julia Amory, Patcévitch family member.

35. A New House, a New Empire.

1. *NYT*, March 24, 1959.
2. Thomas Maier, *Newhouse: All the Glitter, Power, and Glory of America's Richest Media Empire and the Secretive Man Behind It* (New York: St. Martin's Press, 1994), 7.
3. Rowlands, *A Dash of Daring*, 465.
4. Vreeland, *D.V.*, 1.
5. Ibid., 176.
6. *NYT*, February 28, 1998. Chessy Rayner obituary by Mitchell Owens.

7. Ibid., September 15, 1993. To the Newhouse family's shock and horror, it pictured Sam Newhouse.
8. CNA, MC005/Box 1, Folder 3.
9. Maier, *Newhouse*, 50.
10. *NYT*, November 20, 1999. Alexander Liberman obituary by Dierdre Carmody.
11. www.publishersweekly.com/pw/by-topic/industry-news/people/article/40606-pw-the-random-house-acquisition-an-interview-with-s-i-newhouse.html.
12. www.vanityfair.com/culture/2013/10/birth-modern-vanity-fair.
13. Ibid.
14. Ibid.
15. Tina Brown, *The Vanity Fair Diaries: 1983–1992* (London: Weidenfeld & Nicolson, 2017), 18–21.
16. https://www.vanityfair.com/culture/2013/10/birth-modern-vanity-fair.
17. Maier, *Newhouse*, 243–250.
18. http://articles.latimes.com/1985-03-08/news/mn-32295_1_parade-magazine.
19. https://nypost.com/2018/06/21/graydon-carter-is-launching-his-own-media-company/.
20. http://articles.latimes.com/1988-08-05/news/vw-8567_1_grace-mirabella; telephone interview with Alexandra Shulman, April 13, 2018.

INDEX

Les Six, 183
Lewis, Chesbrough, 352, 358
Lewis, Sinclair, 59, 382
Liberman, Alexander, 350, 358–61, 376
Life, 36n, 278
Lillie, Beatrice, 191
Lincoln, Abraham, 13–20
Lindbergh, Charles A., 211–12, 382
lingerie, 89
Lippmann, Walter, 118, 382
Liquozone, 43
literary criticism, 90
literary renaissance of the new century, 86, 141–42
The Little Review, 86
Lloyd George, David, 129
Locke, Richard, 360, 379
Loelia, Duchess of Westminster, 312
London, England, 50–51, 206
London, Jack, 36
Loos, Anita, 205–6, 270
Lopokova, Lydia, 113
Louis, Joe, 96, 119, 382
Louis XIV, 143
Louisiana Purchase, 16
Lowry, Vance, 183n
Loy, Myrna, 382
Luce, Clare Boothe. *See* Brokaw, Clare
Luce, Henry Robinson, 36n, 287, 296n, 315, 318, 332, 333, 342, 366, 384
Lucile (couturier), 206
Lydig, Mrs. Philip, 77, 78n

Maas, Walter, 219, 282, 284, 323–24, 376
Mab's Fashions, 140
Macfadden, Bernarr, 279
Mackenzie, Compton, 6, 119, 382
magazines
    advertising in, 32–35, 68–69
    broad-appeal vs. class-focused, 80–81
    subscription lists of, 86
    vertical integration in, 140
Mainbocher (Main Bocher), 184–85, 302, 376
Maine, USS, 41
Mann, Thomas, 119, 382
Mann, Col. William d'Alton, 46, 53n
Manners, Lady Diana, 170, 191
Manufacturers' Trust Bank, 230

Marbury, Elizabeth "Bessie", 66, 77, 204, 380
Martin, Charles, 381
Marty, A. E., 381
Marx, Eleanor, 50
Marx, Groucho, 213
Marx, Harpo, 213
Marx Brothers, 170, 384
The Masses, 90
Matisse, Henri, 4, 87, 381
McAllister, Ward, 52–53
McBride, Robert M., 86
McCampbell, Theron, 60–62, 70, 75, 377
McClure's Magazine, 43
McDowell, Margaret Eliza Nast, 12–14, 374
McFadden, Frances, 272, 274, 276, 377
McKenzie, Semple, 58n
McMullin, Johnnie, 189–90, 231, 284, 301, 305–6, 308–10, 316, 352, 377
McVickar, Harry, 42, 65, 67, 377
McWhiney, E. E., 60
Mellon, Andrew, 247
Mellon Institute, 155
Mencken, H. L., 90, 383
Mendl, Sir Charles Ferdinand, 204, 352
Men's Vogue, 356
Methodists, 21
Metropolitan Museum of Art, Costume Institute, 357
"Midnight Frolics", 82
Milholland, Inez, 107
military-inspired fashion, 106
military uniforms, 105
Millay, Edna St. Vincent, 7, 119, 379
Miller, Elizabeth "Lee," 215–18, 325–26, 379
Milne, A. A., 118, 382
Mirabella, Grace, 357, 363, 377
Mississippi College, 31
Mitchell, Billy, 188
models, 112
    American compared with French, 186
    of modern woman, 216–17
modernity, 93
Moore, Estelle, 167
Moore, Grace, 127–28, 153n, 181, 285, 385
Morgan, Anne, 66n, 77